SCOTT FITZGERALD

Andrew Turnbull was born and spent his early years in Baltimore. He graduated from Princeton in 1942 and earned his Ph.D. in European history from Harvard in 1954. During the Second World War he served as a lieutenant in the U.S. Navy. After the war he worked in Paris for several years and returned to America to enter the Harvard Graduate School. From 1954 to 1958 he was an instructor in the humanities at the Massachusetts Institute of Technology. He then turned his attention to writing, until his death in 1970.

Mr Turnbull had done his research on Fitzgerald in Paris and on the Riviera and had written several pieces on him for the *New Yorker*. He also edited *The Letters of Scott Fitzgerald* (published in Penguins) and wrote a life of Thomas Wolfe.

ANDREW TURNBULL

Scott Fitzgerald

PENGUIN BOOKS

Penguin Books Ltd, Harmondsworth, Middlesex, England
Penguin Books Australia Ltd, Ringwood, Victoria, Australia

—

First published in the U.S.A. 1962
Published in Great Britain by The Bodley Head 1962
Published in Pelican Books 1970

—

Copyright © Andrew Turnbull 1962

—

Made and printed in Great Britain by
Cox & Wyman Ltd., London, Reading and Fakenham
Set in Linotype Georgian

Portions of this book appeared originally in
The New Yorker, and in *Esquire*

FOR

JOANNE

Contents

Foreword

ONE evening in the spring of 1932 I was walking with a friend down the lane of my family's country place outside Baltimore. As we approached La Paix, the old house on our property that had just been rented again, we noticed a man sitting motionless on the high front steps. Alone and pensive, he had been communing with the fireflies that twinkled across the lawn, but now he turned his attention to us and we felt ourselves being scrutinized. In the manner of eleven-year-olds we scrutinized him back, while pretending to be busy with our own affairs.

No word passed between us in the dusk. That moment, however, was the beginning of this book, for the stranger was the new tenant my parents had been talking about; he was Scott Fitzgerald.

Though an artist in prose fiction – with facets of the dramatist, the essayist and the social historian – Fitzgerald was fundamentally a poet. He said himself that his talent was in large part the poetic kind that matures early, and he had the poet's temperament as Wordsworth has defined it: '. . . a man speaking to men; a man, it is true, endowed with more lively sensibility, more enthusiasm and tenderness, who has a greater knowledge of human nature, and a more comprehensive soul, than are supposed to be common among mankind; a man pleased with his own passions and volitions, and who rejoices more than other men in the spirit of life that is in him; delighting to contemplate similar volitions and passions as manifested in the goings-on of the Universe, and habitually impelled to create them where he does not find them.'[1]

The picture of Fitzgerald on the cover of this book dates from 1933 when Fitzgerald was completing *Tender Is the*

1. Indicates a note at the back of the book.

Night. It is one of a group of photographs which his wife, Zelda, thought the best ever taken of him, and I prefer it to any other because it shows more of the man. The dissipation is there but also the fineness, the fire, the almost speaking sensitivity. It is Fitzgerald as I remember him and have tried to recapture him in some of these pages.

This book could not have been written without the gracious help of a great many people, a number of whom I have listed further on. At the outset, however, I would like to acknowledge a few major debts. First of all, to Fitzgerald's daughter, Mrs Samuel J. Lanahan, who patiently suffered my intrusions and lent me all the material I asked for. Harold Ober, Fitzgerald's literary executor, encouraged my project from the start and aided me unstintingly during the two and a half years before his death. Judge John Biggs, Jr, Fitzgerald's legal executor, was also of great service. No one brought me nearer the Fitzgerald spirit than Gerald and Sara Murphy, whose point of view combined deep affection with critical discernment and whose memories I checked and rechecked in the course of several visits. I am grateful to Fitzgerald's sister, Mrs Clifton Sprague, and to Zelda's sister, Mrs Newman Smith, for their friendly cooperation. Fitzgerald had kept typed copies of all Ginevra King's letters which were returned to her on his death and which she kindly let me see. I am grateful to Henry Dan Piper for lending me his biographical materials on Fitzgerald. I am grateful to Sheilah Graham for steady assistance in filling in the details of Fitzgerald's last years in Hollywood. Glenway Wescott, Matthew Josephson, Malcolm Cowley, John Kuehl and Katharine Fessenden were good enough to read and criticize my manuscript.

My greatest debt, beyond describing, is to my mother, Margaret Carroll Turnbull.

[1]

WE begin with the McQuillans, for they are the source of energy in this story.

In 1843, a lad of nine named Philip Francis McQuillan emigrated to this country from County Fermanagh, Ireland, and settled with his parents in Galena, Illinois. The parents drop out of sight, but Philip Francis, or 'P.F.' as he came to be known, appears in the Galena directories of 1854-6 as a clerk in a clothing store. In 1857, aged twenty-three, he moved to St Paul – a raw boom town and capital of the newly organized Minnesota Territory, well on its way to becoming the biggest wholesale distributing centre of the Northwest. McQuillan would ride this prosperity and see St Paul take on the lineaments of a small city. When he arrived, however, the streets were unpaved, Indians were much in view, and the air was redolent of the hides that hung in the shop windows.

McQuillan went to work as bookkeeper in a grocery concern, and at the end of two years started a grocery store of his own in a small, one-storey frame building. In 1860 he married his Galena sweetheart, Louisa Allen. Business prospered, and he moved to larger quarters in 1862, becoming a wholesale dealer exclusively. He moved again in 1869 and again in 1872 – this time to a four-storey warehouse of his own construction, one of the largest buildings in the city. By now his health had begun to fail. He suffered from Bright's disease and died in 1877 at the age of forty-three, leaving a personal fortune of $266,289.49 and a business with annual sales in the millions.

So ended a career which the obituaries called 'a living romance, for in the brief period of twenty years [McQuillan] passed, by his own unaided exertions, from the humblest beginnings to a place among the merchant princes of the country'. Thirty-nine wholesale houses shut their doors the day of his funeral. Among the mourners were St Paul's 'leading business men, professional men, educators, and men and women in all walks of life', as well as the boys and girls of the Catholic Orphans' Home, 'an institution that had no more generous friend than [McQuillan]'. Large numbers were turned away from the Church and a procession of a hundred carriages followed the coffin to the cemetery, 'making one of the most imposing demonstrations of the kind ever seen in the city'.

The success of his Grandfather McQuillan was the great social and economic fact in Scott Fitzgerald's background. It was the base he had to work from. For a boy growing up in the Midwest there was more substance in it than in the patents of nobility – the descent from old Maryland families – which came down to him on his father's side. From Grandfather McQuillan, he inherited his self-reliance and his honourable ambition. There was little of the idler and nothing of the sponge or the chiseller in Fitzgerald, who reserved his deepest respect for the self-made man.

A few years before his death 'P.F.' had built his family a residence in 'Lower Town', the old (now the business) section of St Paul. Like many houses of the period it had a cupola, but unlike them it was approached by a seashell walk bordered with conches – a detail which intrigued Fitzgerald who used to tell his daughter about it. Here, amid comfort rather than luxury, 'P.F.'s widow raised her five children of whom the eldest – Fitzgerald's mother – was born in 1860 and the youngest in 1877 after the father's death. Louisa McQuillan, Fitzgerald's grandmother, is remembered as a quiet homebody, always impeccably neat in the black silk ladies wore in those days. After her family, the Church was her chief concern. Every few years she took her brood to Europe (Fitzgerald's mother had been four times before her marriage), and it was said she went primarily to pay her respects to the Pope. Her children profited from their travels, for those were the days when going abroad meant staying awhile. You settled in the country of your choice and learned the language and brought home *objets d'art,* like the copy of the Sistine Madonna which hung in the McQuillan parlour.

In St Paul of the 1880s the McQuillans cut the figure of good, respected Catholics with what might snobbishly be called 'a very nice position'. 'P.F.' had been in wholesale rather than trade and that was considered 'all right'. The oldest boy, Allen – educated at Stonyhurst – danced well and belonged to the exclusive Cotillion Club. Annabelle, the second girl, was maid of honour in the wedding of Clara Hill, daughter of J. J. Hill, the railroad tycoon. But on the whole the McQuillans weren't fashionable, and the children inherited a strain of shyness from their mother who made no effort to launch them.

Fitzgerald's mother, Mollie, was romantically inclined though not romantic to look at. There were twists of amusement at the corners of her wide, comical mouth which someone likened to an old-fashioned syrup pitcher. Her face was a round moon, the features flattish. Her green-grey eyes, strikingly pale beneath dark, heavy brows, were the eyes of her son – beautiful in his face though in hers a little eerie. She read a great deal: current novels, biography, anything that came to hand, without stopping to evaluate. Not as shy as her sisters, she was eager to marry but men were less attracted to her than she to them. There was something about an army officer which came to naught, and then – approaching thirty with no other prospects – she decided to marry Edward Fitzgerald, a suitor of several years' standing.

Fitzgerald had been born in 1853 on Glenmary Farm near Rockville in Montgomery County, Maryland. Little is known of his father, Michael Fitzgerald, who died when Edward was two. Edward's mother, Cecilia Ashton Scott, was descended from Maryland families that had figured prominently in the colonial legislatures and on the governors' councils. Edward Fitzgerald's great, great grandfather was the brother of Francis Scott Key's grandfather, and Edward's first cousin was the son-in-law of Mrs Suratt, hung for complicity in the assassination of Lincoln. After Scott Fitzgerald

13

reached fame, his parents wanted him to write a book exonerating Mrs Suratt, but he said she was either guilty or a fool and in neither case was he interested.[2]

Rockville, though behind the Northern lines during most of the Civil War, was Southern in its sympathies. When Edward Fitzgerald was nine, he had rowed Confederate spies across the river, and all one morning he sat on a fence watching Early's battalions stream towards Washington in the last Confederate thrust. The Civil War was the drama of his youth and indeed of his entire life. In the early seventies, after completing the equivalent of third-year high at Georgetown 'University', he went to seek his fortune with less happy results than 'P.F.' McQuillan before him. He worked in Chicago for a while before coming out to St Paul where, in the late eighties, he was running the American Rattan & Willow Works, a small wicker furniture business.

That Edward Fitzgerald had been cut out for failure was not altogether apparent at the time of his marriage. There was an air of distinction about this small, dapper man with the Vandyke, the rich, well-cut clothes, the erect carriage, the leisurely gait, the manner courteous yet not without a twinkle. His looks were fine, almost too fine – like a pencil sharpened to the breaking point. One would never believe that this well-moulded head and delicate, sensitive profile could be a mask for dullness or stupidity. And yet – what sometimes amounts to the same thing – Edward Fitzgerald lacked vitality. As his son said, he came from 'tired, old stock'. In him there lingered a Southern indolence or gentleness or possibly just fatigue that made him unadaptable to the hustling Midwest.

After their wedding in February, 1890, Edward and Mollie went to Europe for their honeymoon. From Nice Edward wrote home, 'I have drawn a prize in a wife, one has to know her well to fully appreciate her.' And Mollie in her romantic vein:

It was beautiful tonight when we had our walk. Nice is right on the Mediterranean Sea you know. The color of the water is so blue and the moon was shining so bright and altogether it was a

14

perfect night for people in our situation. John [Edward's brother], if you ever get married and want a good time, in fact a perfect one, come here to Europe and spend a week at Nice. Ted and I have had a lovely time here and whatever happens in the future this one time in our lives will be without a flaw to look back upon.

Back in St Paul, their misfortunes began. Their first two children, both girls, died in epidemics shortly before Scott was born. 'I wonder sometimes if I will ever have any interest in life again,' Edward wrote his mother, 'perhaps so but certainly the keen zest of enjoyment is gone forever.' Mollie buried her grief. She never spoke of the dead children in after years, but Scott felt the repercussions and linked them with his career. 'Three months before I was born,' he wrote, 'my mother lost her other two children and I think that came first of all though I don't know how it worked exactly. I think I started then to be a writer.'

It was understandable that Mollie should spoil her beautiful boy who came in the wake of so much suffering.

Francis Scott Key Fitzgerald was born at 3.30 in the afternoon on 24 September 1896, at 481 Laurel Avenue. He was a strapping baby of ten pounds six ounces. The first recorded event of his life is found in his mother's Baby Book for 6 October 1896: 'Mrs Knowlton [the nurse] carried little "Scott" out for a few minutes. He went over to "Lambert's" Store and into "Kanes", the most important places around.' It is further recorded that he spoke his first word, 'Up', on 6 July 1897. Among his early bright sayings was, 'Mother, when I get to be a big boy can I have all the things I oughtn't to have?'

When Scott was a year-and-a-half, his father's business failed, and the Fitzgeralds went east to Buffalo where Edward Fitzgerald worked as a salesman for Procter & Gamble. In 1901 they moved to Syracuse and in 1903 back to Buffalo. The events of these early years were later pieced together by Scott in his 'Ledger', which contains a diary of his life by months. Here, in his own words and with his own unorthodox spelling, are some of the things that happened to him between his first and seventh birthdays:[3]

1897 Dec. Bronchitis. A specialist was summoned but as his advice was not followed the child pulled through.

1898 Apr. Tiring of St Paul he went east to Buffalo, New York, where with his parents he installed himself at the Lennox.

1899 Jan. He put on bloomers and went to Washington to spend the winter at the Cairo Hotel.

Apr. He returned to Buffalo and moved into a flat at Summer Street and Elmwood Ave.

June A persistent cough drove him to Orchard Park, New York. His mother feared consumption for him.

Aug. He returned to St Paul, visiting his grandmother McQuillan in her house on Summit Avenue near Dale Street. [Grandmother McQuillan had moved to upper, residential St Paul, the railroad yards have appropriated the site of her former house in Lower Town.]

1900 Jan. His mother presented him with a sister who lived only an hour.

Feb. He celebrated the new century by swallowing a penny and catching the measles. He got rid of both of them.

Mar. His parents sent him to school but he wept and wailed so they took him out again after one morning.

Sept. He had a party to celebrate his birthday. He wore a sailor suit about this time & told enormous lies to older people about being really the owner of a real yatch.

1901 Jan. He now went to Sarycuse where he took Mrs Peck's appartment on East Genesee Street.

July His sister Annabel was born. His first certain memory is the sight of her howling on a bed.

Aug. Again he went to Atlantic City – where some Freudean

complex refused to let him display his *feet*, so he refused to swim, concealing the real reason. They thought he feared the water. In reality he craved it. Also he attended the Buffalo exposition, the Pan American.

1902 Jan. He now moved from East Genesee Street to the 'Kassou' on James Street. He remembers Jack Butler who had two or three fascinating books about the civil war and he remembers hitting a delivery boy with a stone and cutting his head.

May He went to Randolph to his Aunt Eliza Delihant's place in Montgomery County, Maryland, where he made friends with a coloured boy, name forgotten – name Ambrose.

Sept. He entered Miss Goodyear's school and he and another little girl, name unknown, worked out the phonetic spelling of C-A-T, thus becoming the stars of the primary class.

1903 Jan. Naturally he moved again – this time to a flat on East Willow Street. He begins to remember many things, a filthy vacant lot, the haunt of dead cats, a hair-raising buckboard, the little girl whose father was in prison for telling lies, a Rabelasian incident with Jack Butler, a blow with a baseball bat from the same boy – son of an army officer – which left a scar that will always shine in the middle of his forehead, a history of the United States which father brought me; he became a child of the American Revolution [A member of the National Society of Children of the American Revolution]. Also he boxed with Edgar Miller the grocery man's son, egged on by his father. [Long afterwards this same Edgar Miller wrote him a fan letter which said, 'My Dad ran a store and market at the corner of Catherine and E. Willow Sts and you lived across the road and a hobby of yours at that time was to ride in the rear of the delivery rig and recite Friends, Romans, and Countrymen etc. at the top of your voice.'] His nurse pierced her ear for rings and he howled.

Apr. He went south to Randolph again where he was a ribbon holder with Jack Garland at his Cousin Cecilia's wedding. After the wedding he turned on his two black friends Roscoe and Forrest and with the help of a bigger boy tried to tie them up with ropes. He remembers crying one day in fury over the irrevocability of a decision – he had decided once too often that he did *not* want to go down town. He found his father's soap boxes and apricots quite diverting. He went on a trip with his father.

July He wandered off on the Fourth of July & was spanked in consequence, so he sat on the porch with his breeches down and watched the fire-works. [Fitzgerald elaborated this incident elsewhere: 'I ran away when I was [six] on the fourth of July – I spent the day with a friend in a pear orchard and the police were informed that I was missing and on my return my father thrashed me according to the custom of the nineties – on the bottom – and then let me come out and watch the night fire works from my balcony with my pants still down and my behind smarting and knowing in my heart that he was absolutely right. Afterwards, seeing in his face his regret that it had to happen, I asked him to tell me a story. I knew what it would be – he had only a few, the story of the spy, the one about the man hung by his thumbs, the one about Early's march.'] On Sunday mornings he walked down town in his long trousers with his little cane and had his shoes shined with his father. There was also a boy named Arnold who went barefooted in his yard and peeled plums. Scott's freudian shame about his feet kept him from joining in.

Sept. He had a birthday party to which no one came. [The children stayed home because it rained. 'Then,' says Fitzgerald in another account, 'I went sorrowfully in and thoughtfully consumed one complete birthday cake, including several candles (for I was a great tallow eater until I was well over fourteen.)'] He moved to Buffalo, New York, possibly in consequence where he had a dog named 'Beautiful Joe', a black cocker spaniel, and also a bycycle – a girl's bycycle. He was sent to school at the Holy Angel's convent under the arrangement that he need only go half a day and was allowed to choose which half. He lived at 29 Irving Place. ... He remembers 'Nana', Annabel's nurse. ... He remembers the attic where he had a red sash with which he acted Paul Revere. ... He fell under the spell of a Catholic preacher, Father Fallon, of the Church of the Holy Angels ...

Irving Place, where Fitzgerald spent the next two years, was a single tree-lined block – a lovely, sheltered spot for a poet to grow up in. Children played ball in the dappled shade or raced their buckboards down the sloping street, one of the first where asphalt had replaced the universal cobbles. Next door to the Fitzgeralds lived a boy named Ted Keating, and when spring came and the days weren't long enough to exhaust their young blood, Ted and Scott went to bed each with a string around his big toe, and the first one up in the morning ran over to the other's window and yanked the string.

But Scott's best friend, because of their mutual interest in the stage, was Hamilton Wende. Hamilton's family knew the Farnums; Dustin Farnum, later a star of the Westerns, and his brother William were acting in Buffalo summer stock. Each Saturday Hamilton got two complimentary tickets to the matinee at the Teck Theatre and always gave one to Scott. Chin cupped in hands, elbows on knees, Scott seldom spoke or took his eyes off the stage during the performance, and afterwards he and Hamilton rushed home to re-enact what they had seen. Scott's memory was prodigious; he could repeat long sections of the dialogue almost by heart. He was also a good prop man who, with a pillow case and a scarf of his mother's, could transform himself into a Turk or a pirate or a cavalier. Hamilton's contribution to their wardrobe was a tin sword and a couple of Teddy Roosevelt 'Rough Rider' hats, and with costumes thus improvised and a sheet on a string for a curtain, they gave performances for the neighbourhood children and charged admission.

Wende found Fitzgerald a generous, gay, appreciative, good-natured companion. Their only disagreements were over sports. After a day at school Wende would want to play football or baseball while Fitzgerald wanted Wende to accompany him to the Public Library. An indoor child who had spent most of his life in apartments and hotels, Fitzgerald shied away from athletics. 'Sissy', however, was too strong a word for him. 'It must have been about this time,' says his Ledger, 'that he gave a boy a bloody nose and ran home [from school] in consequence with a made up story. He and Jack Butler being the youngest boys in the neighbourhood, were the most frequently chased. He hit John Wylie with a stick and ended their friendship.'

Mollie seldom intruded on her son's occupations, but she was ambitious for him. If he and Hamilton were going to a party, she would tell Scott not to stay with Hamilton all the time but to get around and meet the other children. On several occasions she took Hamilton aside to explain that Scott was related to Francis Scott Key and second to none in honour of birth. About her son's clothes she was as fastidious as she was neglectful of her own. Other parents considered the local branch of Browning King's quite good enough, but Scott's Eton suits had an extra elegance, as if they had come by mail order from De Pinna's in New York. And when the other boys were wearing four-in-hands, Scott had a set of silk bow ties, each of a different hue, to go with Eton collars.

In September 1915, when Scott was nine, the Fitzgeralds moved to 71 Highland Avenue. Eternally restless, Mollie could always think of a reason why some house a few blocks away, or even in the next block, was superior to the one they had. In this case they were moving to a more prosperous neighbourhood where Scott quickly made friends, but not his parents who never got their roots down in Buffalo. To the other residents of Highland there was something secretive and forbidding about the Fitzgerald's life in the clapboard house with the single turret that resembled a witch's hat, and Scott was more apt to be playing at neighbours' houses than his own.

He frequented the Powells' across the street where there was usually a crowd of youngsters on the porch. Some of the girls were starting to have beaux, and Scott questioned these older ones, surprising them with his large vocabulary and his ability to size people up. In contrast to his playmates, so uncertain of their futures, he had definite ideas about his own. He knew, for example, that he was going to Princeton – his *partie pris* being based on a Princeton Glee Club Concert, during which he had been convulsed by a song about Mrs Winslow's Soothing Syrup.

He was, at this stage, a small-boned, pretty child with blond hair parted in the middle and large, luminous eyes – variously grey or green or blue. He was a tease but took it well if you teased him back, and there were signs of a precocious freshness. One day he got spanked because he thought it was funny to bow to everyone. Another time, at Miss Nardin's Academy, the Catholic School to which he had progressed from the Holy Angel Convent, he insisted that Mexico City was *not* the capital of Central America, with results which he later dramatized in a short story:

' "So the capital of America is Washington," said Miss Cole, "and the capital of Canada is Ottawa – and the capital of Central America – "

" – is Mexico City," someone guessed.

"Hasn't any," said Terence absently.

"Oh, it must have a capital," said Miss Cole looking at her map.

"Well, it doesn't happen to have one."

"That'll do, Terence. Put down Mexico City for the capital of Central America. Now that leaves South America."

Terence sighed.

"There's no use teaching us wrong," he suggested.

Ten minutes later, somewhat frightened, he reported to the principal's office where all the forces of injustice were confusingly arrayed against him.'

Though Fitzgerald was a rebellious student, he liked to read on his own. 'First there was a book,' he remembered, 'that was I think one of the big sensations of my life. It was nothing but a nursery book, but it filled me with the saddest and most yearning emotion. I have never been able to trace it since. It was about a fight the large animals, like the elephant, had with the small animals, like the fox. The small animals won the first battle; but the elephants and lions and tigers finally overcame them. The author was prejudiced in favour of the large animals, but my sentiment was all with the small ones. I wonder if even then I had a sense of the wearing-down power of big, respectable people. I can almost weep now when I think of that poor fox, the leader – the fox has somehow typified innocence to me ever since.'

From such beginnings Fitzgerald's taste evolved through *Scottish Chiefs, Ivanhoe,* and the Henry series to 'the thrill of the "Washington in the West" & "Raiding with Morgan" series in their crisp tissue wrappers.' Literary snobbism had set in; he scorned *The Youth's Companion* in favour of the *St Nicholas.* He wrote a history of the United States which got no further than the Battle of Bunker Hill; also a detective story about a necklace hidden in a trap door under the carpet, and an imitation of *Ivanhoe* called 'Elavo' and 'a celebrated essay on George Washington & St Ignatius'. His father read him Poe's 'The Raven' and 'The Bells' and Byron's 'Prisoner of Chillon'. Their mystery echoed in his soul, and on a trip to Niagara he heard 'enchanting voices in the dark'.

There were other trips – to Chautauqua, the Catskills, and Lake Placid. He went to Camp Chatham in Orillia, Ontario, 'where he swam and fished and cleaned and ate fish and canoed and rowed and caught behind the bat and was desperately unpopular and went in paper chases and running contests and was always edged out by Tom Penny. He remembers boys named Whitehouse, Alden, Penny, Block, Blair and one awful baby. He remembers "Pa" Upham singing "The Cat Came Back", and a sawdust road and a camera and making blueprints and the camp library and "Blow ye winds heigh-ho" and tournaments with padded spears in canoes and Pa Upham's Cornell stroke.'

Back home Fitzgerald began to take more interest in

sports. At a basketball game 'he fell madly into admiration for a dark-haired boy who played with melancholy defiance'. On the Highland Corner football team known as the Young American he was 'guard or tackle and usually scared silly'. His parents gave him a pair of ball-bearing roller skates that were too fancy to be any good. He was growing more manly by degrees, but there remained a chaste, delicate part of his nature which shunned life's coarseness and sweat. A play-mate remembers Scott's father, a soft-spoken gentleman if there ever was one, saying he would give five dollars to hear Scott swear. Scott's idea of a reproach was more subtle. Once, when an older boy took advantage of him in a game of quoits, Scott went into the house and came back bandying a phrase which no one understood; it was Latin for 'king of the quoit cheaters'.

Girls had entered his life. He was one of the stars of Mr Van Arnum's dancing class where manners were taught as well as the intricacies of the waltz and the Newport, where bows and curtsies had to be just so, and where the boys danced with handkerchiefs in their right hands so as not to soil the backs of the girls' dresses. Scott wore a black suit because his father had ruled that blue ones were 'common', and he was the only boy with evening pumps.

His romance with Kitty Williams began when he chose her as his partner to lead the Grand March. 'Next day,' wrote Fitzgerald in the Thoughtbook he kept locked up under his bed, 'she told Marie Lautz and Marie repeated it to Dorothy Knox who in turn passed it on to Earl, that I was third in her affections. I don't remember who was first but I know that Earl was second and as I was already quite overcome by her charms I then and there resolved that I would gain first place.' The climax occurred at 'Robin's party' where 'we played post office, pillow, clapp in clapp out, and other fool-ish but interesting games. It was impossible to count the number of times I kissed Kitty that afternoon. At any rate when we went home I had secured the coveted 1st place. I held this until dancing school stopped in the spring and then relinquished it to Johnny Gowns, a rival. . . . That Christmas

I bought a five pound box of candy and took it around to her house. What was my surprise when Kitty opened the door, I nearly fell down with embarresment but I finally stammered "Give it to Kitty" and ran home.'

Edward Fitzgerald, all this time, had been receding into the background. As a salesman he walked the streets and came home too tired to take much part in family life. His dismissal by Procter & Gamble in March 1908, was the trauma of Scott's childhood.

'One afternoon,' he recalled long afterwards,

the phone rang and my mother answered it. I didn't understand what she said but I felt that disaster had come to us. My mother, a little while before, had given me a quarter to go swimming. I gave the money back to her. I knew something terrible had happened and I thought she could not spare the money now.

Then I began to pray, 'Dear God,' I prayed, 'please don't let us go to the poorhouse; please don't let us go to the poorhouse.' A little while later my father came home. I had been right. He had lost his job.

That morning he had gone out a comparatively young man, a man full of strength, full of confidence. He came home that evening an old man, a completely broken man. He had lost his essential drive, his immaculateness of purpose. He was a failure the rest of his days.

Oh, I remember something else. I remember that when my father came home mother said to me, 'Scott, say something to your father.'

'I didn't know what to say. I went up and asked, 'Father, who do you think will be the next President?' He looked out the window. He didn't move a muscle. Then he said, 'I think Taft will.'

The blow was both a sorrow and a stimulus. Fitzgerald loved his father and always cherished such meagre camaraderie as they had known. He admired his father's style and breeding, and the beautiful manners which were more than breeding – which sprang, Fitzgerald knew, from a gracious heart. But Fitzgerald was ambitious, and it strengthened his ambition to feel that in a sense *he* was the man in the family and that great things were expected of him.

That summer the Fitzgeralds moved back to St Paul where the family resources were.

$\lceil 2 \rceil$

In the moment of crisis Scott had prayed his family wouldn't go to the poorhouse, but thanks to the McQuillan inheritance there was no danger. The Fitzgeralds had enough to get along on, to keep a servant and send their children to private schools, and after Grandmother McQuillan's death in 1913 their principal rose to $125,000 – a tidy sum for those years before the First World War. The McQuillan money was their sole support. Edward Fitzgerald made practically nothing as a broker in wholesale groceries. He kept his samples of rice and dried apricots and coffee in a roll-top desk in his brother-in-law's real estate office, but his wife was so clearly the source of all revenue that he was known to charge postage stamps at the corner store.[4]

'If it wasn't for your Grandfather McQuillan, where would we be now?' Mollie would say to Scott, who never knew hardship but rather the shabby gentility that has spurred so many of the great strivers and adventurers in history.

The first year after their return to St Paul the Fitzgeralds lived with Grandmother McQuillan, who had sold her house on Summit and moved to lesser quarters on nearby Laurel. Thus Scott was propelled into the Summit Avenue community which, at the time, meant fashionable, residential St Paul. Summit Avenue, a spacious wooded boulevard, sat picturesquely on a bluff that overlooked commercial Lower Town and the encircling Mississippi. The community, extending to the four parallel streets on either side, covered an area almost a mile square.

In this larger, more complex arena than he had previously known, Fitzgerald's personality quickly asserted itself. The other children were curious about the sprightly, keen-featured youth whose mother still dressed him in Eton caps and collars. He had an awareness, a pseudo-sophistication they hadn't met before though in other respects he seemed like one of them. He hid in the barns and chased about the alleys and threw stones at the 'Micks' from Lower Town and invaded trunks of old clothes to put on masquerades. He starred in 'Truth and Consequences'; when he had been in St Paul only a month, five girls confessed that he was their favourite boy.

His favourite girl was Violet Stockton, a summer visitor from Atlanta. Showing the future novelist's eye for detail, he wrote in his Thoughtbook,

She was very pretty with dark brown hair and eyes big and soft. She spoke with a soft southern accent leaving out the r's. She was a year older than I but together with most of the other boys [I] liked her very much.

She had some sort of a book called flirting by signs and Jack and I got it away from Violet and showed it to all the boys. Violet got very mad and went into the house. I got very mad and therefore I went home. Immediately Violet repented and called me up on the phone to see if I was mad. However I did not want to make up just then and so I slammed down the receiver. The next morning I went down to Jack's to find that Violet had said that she was not coming out that day. It was now my turn to repent and I did so and she came out that evening. Before, however, I had heard several things and as I found out afterwards so had Violet that I wanted to have justified. Violet and I sat on the hill back of Schultze's a little way from the others.

'Violet,' I began, 'did you call me a brat?'

'No.'

'Did you say that you wanted your ring and your pictures and your hair back?'

'No.'

'Did you say you hated me?'

'Of course not, is that what you went home for?'

'No, but Archie Mudge told me those things yesterday evening.'

'He's a little scamp,' said Violet indignantly. At this juncture Elenor Michell almost went into histerics because Jack was teasing her, and Violet had to go home with her. That afternoon I spanked Archie Mudge and finished making up with Violet.

In September, Fitzgerald entered the St Paul Academy

where he came under the tutelage of 'Pa' Fiske and C. N. B. Wheeler. Fiske, dispenser of Latin, Greek, and mathematics, was almost a caricature of the old-fashioned pedagogue. His locks were all in a tangle behind, and his pince-nez slid down towards the end of his nose as he sat in his chair twirling a pencil which he occasionally dropped. One day when Fitzgerald, along with several others, was kept after school, he asked Fiske if he knew any Latin jokes. Fiske thought a moment and came up with a Latin pun which amused no one, but showed Fitzgerald's disposition to create entertainment from the most unlikely materials.

Wheeler was more Fitzgerald's type. A small, wiry man with a goatee, he taught English and history and coached athletics. In later years he would remember Fitzgerald as 'a sunny light-haired boy full of enthusiasm who fully foresaw his course in life even in his schoolboy days. . . . I helped him by encouraging his urge to write adventures. It was also his best work, he did not shine in his other subjects. He was inventive in all playlets we had and marked his course by his pieces for delivery before the school. . . . He wasn't popular with his schoolmates. He saw through them too much and wrote about it. . . . I imagined he would become an actor of the variety type, but he didn't. . . . It was his pride in his literary work that put him in his real bent.'

Soon the school magazine was announcing that 'young Scottie is always bubbling over with suppressed knowledge,' and asked whether someone would poison him or find a means to shut his mouth. In class his mind wandered as he scribbled away at 'sketches' behind a propped-up geography book. This eccentric activity, which no one paid much attention to, was coupled with an attitude more difficult to ignore – a vague cockiness and aggressiveness as if to say, 'I'm not much now, but wait and see.'

Already Fitzgerald was living an inner life apart, yet he did not scorn the more mundane pursuits of his fellows. On the contrary, he had a healthy urge to compete, especially in athletics where his talents were mediocre. Though fast and fairly strong, he was small and not too well coordinated. But

28

he tried hard and could force himself to be brave, as if he had a conception of what a hero should do and was determined to do it.

Once, in a football game, he lay on the field after a scrimmage with the breath apparently knocked out of him. A moment later he was up, eager to resume play, but the coach made him quit because his chest was hurting (it was later found that he had a broken rib). As he limped off the field, he said, 'Well, boys, I've given my all – now let's see what you can do.' Another time he dropped a pass that lost the game and realizing the enormity of his act, he burst into tears – evoking a response from his teammates of 'Oh, hell, Scott, forget it – it's not *that* vital.' Perhaps his most memorable feat was performed against a much heavier team from Central High. As Central's captain, the biggest player on the field, bolted back with the kick-off, the St Paul team parted like the Red Sea until finally Fitzgerald made the tackle. But again he was hurt and had to leave the game. A friend who called on him next day found him strapped up and lying in bed, clearly relishing the role of the wounded veteran.

The truth was he didn't much care for sports though a sense of showmanship made him realize their importance. He approached them as would an actor who sees himself in the starring rôle, and if he couldn't be pitcher, or captain and quarter-back, he might refuse to play. Once, in a relay race, he insisted on being anchor man to reap the utmost glory. When his opponent overtook him at the last moment, rather than lose the race outright Fitzgerald intentionally slipped and fell. Afterwards he explained what he had done to a friend as if it were perfectly natural.

Deeply ingrained in him was a streak of exhibitionism which his mother encouraged. She would get him to sing for company (he sensed this was a mistake, he didn't have much of a voice), and when they called on the nuns at the Visitation Convent, he stood on the front steps for a quarter of an hour declaiming something he had written. To the nuns he seemed beautiful and animated, so intent was he, so brimming over with his subject. When it came to words – their colour, shape, and sound – Fitzgerald would always shine, though finding ideas to fit them was sometimes an occasion for bluffing. Thus he would memorize the titles in book-stores and speak confidently of what was in the books without having taken them off the shelves.

Life at his grandmother's was mildly depressing for someone as convivial as he. Each morning his two spinster aunts, all in black, went to mass with prayerbooks under their arms, and later in the day Mollie, also in black, set off with her bag of books to be exchanged at the Public Library. Behind the dim, row house was a narrow cinder-gritty yard. The stables across the alley went with the houses on the other side, and Fitzgerald liked to watch the coachmen in rubber aprons and boots wash down the carriages of these more prosperous and privileged mortals.

Mollie was determined that her children shouldn't be dragged down by their father's failure. She had the proper entrées, and in December 1909, Fitzgerald entered the dancing class that became his 'crowd' for the rest of his life in St Paul. The class met at Ramaley Hall, an oblong salon with pink walls and white stucco trimmings like the frosting on a cake. The dancing master, Professor Baker, was a round little man, white-moustached and bald on top, sometimes smelling of rum but always nimbly manoeuvrable when demonstrating the mazurka or the two-step. At times he would shout and develop apoplectic symptoms unbecoming the dignity and grandeur of Ramaley's, for his rule was incomplete. 'One day a week ago,' wrote Fitzgerald in his Thoughtbook,

some of the boys including Arthur Foley, Cecil Reade, Donald Bigelow & Laurence Boardman refused to do the Grand March. They went out in the hall and began to put on their [street] shoes. Mr Baker almost had a fit but his efforts to make them march were unavailing. Those of us that were in the march mushed it up every which way and now the grand march is abolished and we have three other dances in its place.

The wealthiest children came to Ramaley's in black

limousines with monograms and coats-of-arms on the doors and liveried chauffeurs in attendance. Those less wealthy drove with their mothers in the family electric, and those not wealthy at all rode the streetcar or trudged through the snow, swinging their patent leather shoes in a slipper bag. The girls wore frilly dresses of white lawn or dotted swiss with bright sashes, their hair done in pompadours and falling to shoulder length behind. The boys wore blue serge knickerbocker suits, and once a year there would be a cotillion with favours spread out on tables for the girls.

Dancing class epitomized the youthful struggle for popularity which went on in other forms all over the countryside, children in those days spending more time outdoors than they do now. They hiked in the woods, they bicycled and roller-skated along Summit, and far into the scented twilights they played hiding and running games in the big yards around the houses. The long winters, which gave Fitzgerald his images of tinkling sleighs and frosty breath, were the season of bob-sled and toboggan parties.

'These sleighrides,' Fitzgerald remembered:

Nowhere but in Minnesota had they such sleighrides. It would be three when we set out in thick coats and sweaters, the girls flushed and consciously athletic; the boys slightly embarrassed but rakish in jumping off and on with complete abandon, to a chorus of little shrieks of simulated anxiety. At a dusky five o'clock we'd reach our destination; usually a club, and have hot chocolate and chicken sandwiches and a dance or two by the graphophone. Then the dark and the crisp frost would come down outside and Mrs Hollis, or Mrs Campbell or Mrs Wharton would take the boy who had frozen his cheeks on the way out, home in her limousine, while the rest of us loitered on to the verandah and waited for the sleighs under the pale January moon. On the way out the girls always sat together, but going back things were different. Then there were mixed groups of four and six, and more than occasionally, of two; and the only unmeltable elements were at the front of the sleigh where the cross-eyed girl talked with painful concentration to the chaperon and in the back where the half dozen shy boys lurked and whispered and pushed each other off.

Girls, as a rule, liked Fitzgerald. He had conversational flair, and if they weren't susceptible to his refined good looks, they had to admit he was neat and presentable. His knickers were always the whitest and crispest at a party, his Norfolk jacket (pleats in front, belt all around) the best cut, and his high, chafing Belmont collar the most snugly joined over a diminutive knot. With boys his status was more ambiguous. He was a mixer, yet he seemed to withhold a part of himself in some secret, perhaps untrustworthy niche of his being. Too unorthodox to be a leader in the broad sense, he came up with so many ideas and was so deft in their execution that he would have to be called a catalyst. He was prime mover in a succession of boys' clubs that had brief, strife-torn existences. The Fitzgerald touch is noted in the initiation rites to one of them. 'The first member was Cecil, and Paul and I subjected him to a most terrible initiation which consisted of having him eat raw eggs and of operating on him with saw, cold ice, and needle accompanied by a basin.'

In Fitzgerald's presence boredom was unknown. Imagine that you and he were confined to the house of a rainy afternoon and the question arose to how to amuse yourselves. Fitzgerald has been leafing through the classified section of the phone book, and pausing at 'Artificial Limbs', he picks up the receiver. Without the trace of a smile he calls the Minnesota Limb & Brace Co. to order a wooden leg. They ask him to come in for a fitting. He says he can't walk with only one leg. They ask to visit him, but he raises objections. Then he questions them about their product in excruciating detail. Does it squeak? (By now you are laughing so hard that he has to flag you to be quiet.) If it squeaks, what brand of oil should you use? Can it be equipped with a rubber heel? If you kick another person, will it break? His curiosity satisfied, he repeats the performance with St Paul Artificial Limbs, United Limb & Brace, and the J. A. McConnell Co., which boasts 'the latest suspension techniques for above the knee amputations'. Tiring of the sport at last, he has not only made an hour go by in several minutes but has gathered considerable lore about artificial limbs which he files away for future reference.

His St Paul theatre companion was Sam Sturgis, son of an army officer. Every Saturday they went to the vaudeville matinee at the Orpheum, and at parties they re-enacted what they had seen. Fitzgerald made such a plausible drunk that some of the girls told their mothers that he had been drinking, but far from minding this adverse publicity, he revelled in his reputation of a thirteen-year-old roué.

Sometimes he staged his drinking act on the streetcar, and when the conductor tried to help him, Fitzgerald spurned his aid. There was also the father and son act, with Fitzgerald playing the father and Sturgis the son, though they appeared to be the same age and size. Asked for his fare, Fitzgerald would go through all his pockets before producing a wallet which opened into a sort of miniature accordion. Each of the thirty or forty compartments had to be searched for the non-existent change. When the conductor, bent on doing his duty, turned to Sturgis, Fitzgerald pointed to the sign which said that children six and under paid no fare. The conductor now lost patience and Sturgis burst into tears. Fitzgerald deplored the injustice of it, provoking the laughter of the other passengers. A further object of the game was to keep it going till the car reached the top of the hill on Selby Avenue when it was an easy walk home.

Bright, gentlemanly, attractive, Fitzgerald had no trouble making his way in St Paul. He was asked everywhere, but his parents didn't circulate among the parents of his friends, for Edward and Mollie Fitzgerald were on the fringes of society as it was then constituted.

Before the Civil War St Paul had had an aristocracy of blood. An occasional pioneering immigrant bought into the upper crust, but for the most part society was made up of old, established Eastern families, the young men having gone west for their health or for adventure. They were by and large a professional group that looked down on business. During the boom of the sixties and seventies, however, a number of merchant and banking families had come to the fore. Some of the old aristocrats moved back east, while others moved away from Summit Avenue, repelled by the influx of *nouveaux riches*. When Fitzgerald was growing up, there was still a sprinkling of Eastern aristocrats at the top, but their importance was dwindling before the sons and grandsons of business magnates who had made their fortunes in groceries, plumbing, or shoes. Aristocracy had become synonymous with wealth, though because of its Eastern ties there remained more of a sense of hierarchy in St Paul than in other Midwestern cities. St Paul was a 'three-generation town'; Minneapolis, Kansas City, Milwaukee could boast of only two.[5]

St Paul, however, was typically Midwestern in that for a man to be important he must *do* something, he must have a solid, remunerative calling, and Edward Fitzgerald – a well-bred enigma – did nothing that anyone could see. Mollie might still have established herself, for the McQuillans were 'good old settlers' and families of less note had forged to the top in a generation or two. But by worldly standards Mollie was not attractive; she was thought a little 'goofy' and her appearance was odd. Her sallow skin had grown surprisingly wrinkled, there were dark discolorations beneath her pale eyes, and her fringing, cascading hair was a byword; daughters told their mothers, 'For heaven's sake, comb up your hair or you'll look like Mrs Fitzgerald.' She dressed, as someone said, 'like the ark'. Everything sagged. The plumes of her antique bonnets drooped as if perpetually rained on, and in an era when skirts were excessively long and full hers were longer, fuller, and more apt to be trailing in the dust than anyone else's. Somewhat broad for her height, she walked with a slight lurch, and she spoke in a droll manner, dragging and drawling her words. If she hadn't seen you for a while, she might greet you with, 'Oh, how you've changed!' – accompanied by a dire look which implied that the change was not for the best. Or, if you merited such attentions, she would criticize your hat and ask to go with you the next time you bought one.

But she was kind and people were cruel about her. They called her a witch and made fun of her high buttoned shoes, which she wore with the top buttons unbuttoned because she suffered from swollen ankles and this type of footgear gave her relief. Her great hope was her son, whom she loved extravagantly as a woman will when her husband has in some ways disappointed her. Fitzgerald, however, was embarrassed by his mother – by her *faux pas* as well as by her complete lack of style. (As the model for the mother in his first novel he chose a *grande dame* who was also eccentric, but whose eccentricity ran to white leather furniture, tigerskin rugs, Pekingeses, and toucan birds that ate only bananas.) Fitzgerald resented the way his mother coddled him – her urging him to lie down or soak in a hot bath – and her sentimentality made him wince. She hung texts in his room on the order of 'The world will judge largely of Mother by you'.

He was less critical of his father who had the elegance and decorum his mother lacked. Edward Fitzgerald carried a cane, and wore a cutaway and grey gloves on Sunday, and was very proud of his son who wanted desperately to admire him. But life had not been kind to Edward Fitzgerald. His failure gnawed at him, and much of the time he seemed old and depressed. He soothed his discouragement by drinking more than he should, though in this regard he wasn't offensive.

Thus Fitzgerald loved his father but could not respect him, and though he grudgingly respected his mother for running the family and keeping it solvent, he found her difficult to love. Because both parents fell short of his ideal, Fitzgerald, a fierce perfectionist, liked to imagine himself a foundling. In *The Romantic Egotist*, an early draft of *This Side of Paradise*, the hero tells neighbours that he was discovered on the doorstep with a label designating him the descendant of Stuart kings. In the story 'Absolution', the little boy believes he is not his parents' child, and Jay Gatsby, Fitzgerald's alter ego, springs from 'his Platonic conception of himself'. In a late autobiographical piece, 'Author's

House', Fitzgerald recalled 'my first childish love of myself, my belief that I would never die like other people, and that I wasn't the son of my parents but a son of a king, a king who ruled the whole world.'[6]

The fall of 1909, his second year at the St Paul Academy, Fitzgerald began publishing in the school magazine. His first contribution, 'The Mystery of the Raymond Mortgage', bespoke the influence of Gaston Leroux and Anna Katherine Green, whose detective fiction he had been devouring and analysing. Later he recalled the exaltation of his literary debut.

Never will I forget the Monday morning the numbers came out. The previous Saturday I had loitered desperately around the printers down-town and driven the man to indignation by persisting in trying to get a copy when the covers had not been bound on – finally, I had gone away and almost in tears. Nothing interested me until Monday, and when at recess, a big pile of the copies were brought in and delivered to the business manager I was so excited that I bounced in my seat and mumbled to myself, 'They're here! They're here!' until the whole school looked at me in amazement. I read my story through at least six times, and all that day I loitered in the corridors and counted the number of men who were reading it, and tried to ask people casually, 'If they had read it?'

Fitzgerald published three more stories in the next two years. 'Reade, Substitute Right Half' tells of a 'light-haired strippling' who enters the game when his team is losing and single-handedly turns the tide. In 'A Debt of Honor' a Confederate who has fallen asleep on sentry duty is pardoned by General Lee and redeems himself at Chancellorsville by a heroic act which costs him his life. 'The Room with the Green Blinds' mixes history and fantasy. Fitzgerald imagines that John Wilkes Booth has escaped after the assassination of Lincoln and for years has been hiding in a ruined Southern mansion. The story tells of his being captured and killed.

The spring of 1911 a new intoxication entered Fitzgerald's life. The headquarters for his group was the Ames's yard at 501 Grand Avenue. 'It had a child's quality,' he remembered. ' . . . There were deep shadows there all day long and ever something vague in bloom, and patient dogs around, and brown spots worn bare by countless circling wheels and dragging feet.' Here the children played games called 'Run Sheep Run' and 'Beckons Wanted', told secrets in the treehouse, and showed off on the rings and horizontal bars. Sometimes the boys snatched the girls' hair ribbons and darted off with them, returning them for a kiss which meant a brush on the cheek. Here it was that Fitzgerald experienced his 'first faint sex attraction', recaptured long afterwards in one of the stories about Basil Duke Lee, who is a portrait of the artist as adolescent.

Basil rode over to Imogene Bissel and balanced idly on his wheel before her. Something in his face then must have attracted her, for she looked up at him, looked at him really, and slowly smiled. She was to be a beauty and belle of many proms in a few years. Now her large brown eyes and large beautifully shaped mouth and the high flush over her thin cheekbones made her face gnome-like and offended those who wanted a child to look like a child. For a moment Basil was granted an insight into the future, and the spell of her vitality crept over him suddenly. For the first time in his life he realized a girl completely as something opposite and complementary to him, and he was subject to a warm chill of mingled pleasure and pain. It was a definite experience and he was immediately conscious of it. The summer afternoon became lost in her suddenly – the soft air, the shadowy hedges and banks of flowers, the orange sunlight, the laughter and voices, the tinkle of a piano over the way – the odor left all these things and went into Imogene's face as she sat there looking up at him with a smile.

In real life Imogene Bissel was Marie Hersey. Hubert Blair, who takes her away from Basil in the story, was Reuben Warner. A year younger than Fitzgerald, Warner had an animal magnetism, a purely masculine appeal which the more sensitive and cerebral Fitzgerald felt unable to compete with. Warner was the self-assured man of action Fitzgerald longed to be; Warner tap-danced, played the drums, excelled in a number of sports, and did stunts and parlour tricks which made him the centre of all eyes. Like Basil, Fitzgerald came to realize a little sadly 'that though boys and girls would always listen to him while he talked, their mouths literally moving in response to his, they would never look at him as they had looked at Hubert.'

Remembering that impassioned spring, his last at the St Paul Academy, Fitzgerald wrote,

My imagination ran riot through the breezy morning with the window open at [school] and the long cool evenings when [Bobby Schurmeier] and I would walk down town to the stock-company and see the week's offering and wander home by the ever romantic lamp-light. The [Ames's] yard grew stale and we longed for bigger fields, so we romanced by night as we loitered in the dim streets and built air-castles that stretched to Mont Martre where we were to have dinner together when we were twenty-one, and to the glorious international intrigues to be managed in an atmosphere of cafes and dark women and secret messages.

During the summer Fitzgerald began to smoke and acquired his first long trousers in anticipation of the fall when he was going East to boarding school, for his parents had decided he needed disciplining. Shortly before he left, a song by the young composer Irving Berlin cast its spell over him. It was called 'Alexander's Ragtime Band', and it had in it the lift and beat of the new century.[7]

[3]

THE lure of the East. The glamour of the seaboard states for
the sensitive soul born and nurtured in the Midwest. In one
of the Basil stories Fitzgerald described the anticipation that
filled him as he left for boarding school. 'Beyond the dreary
railroad stations of Chicago and the night fires of Pitts-
burgh, back in the old states, something went on that made
his heart beat fast with excitement. He was attuned to the
vast, breathless bustle of New York, to the metropolitan
days and nights that were tense as singing wires. Nothing
needed to be imagined there, for it was all the very stuff of
romance – life was as vivid and satisfactory as in books and
dreams.'

A forty-minute ride from New York via the Jersey tubes,
on the outskirts of Hackensack, was the Newman School,
which drew its sixty pupils from wealthy Catholic families
all over the country. Known as a 'lay Catholic school', or one
that prepared its students for secular universities, Newman
included a sprinkling of Protestants and no one was obliged
to attend Mass save on holy days. For a school of its size
Newman was well equipped: a large, ivy-grown main building, several adjoining cottages, an up-to-date gymnasium,
two football fields, a baseball diamond, tennis courts, and an
outdoor hockey rink on the edge of the Hackensack marshes.
The boys ate in a common dining hall and lodged the usual
complaints against the food, though from the vantage point
of college Newman fare was remembered as quite palatable.

And yet the gap between the ideal and the reality, which
lends pathos and humour to all human enterprises, was particularly evident at Newman. The school flourished in an
atmosphere of hilarious chaos and Irish individualism which
would have horrified the renowned Cardinal for whom it was

named. Dr Jesse Albert Locke, Newman's founder and head-master, was a Catholic convert of 'proper Bostonian' outlook. He had conceived of the school as a small-scale Catholic Eton, but since the boys were constantly breaking the rules and just escaping being caught, what he achieved was a sort of academic hare and hounds.

The spring before Fitzgerald's arrival, when Halley's comet was due and unaccountably late, some of the students trooped out to the highway at midnight under pretext of scientific observation and repaired to a roadhouse to drink beer. One lazy afternoon a sit-down strike was staged: the boys adjourned *en masse* to the baseball field, returning for dinner to find the beaten masters sitting gloomily at table, for it wouldn't do to expel the whole school. During study hall strange chants would erupt, as for example, 'Fly open Polly! – Fly open Polly! – Fly open Polly!', meaning that an absent-minded master, nicknamed 'Polly' for his parrot-like beak, had forgotten to complete his dressing arrangements that morning. In spring there was snake season, when every boy had a pet garter snake. Some went in for large, black gopher snakes that made a thudding sound as they coursed down the corridor during the exercise period before 'lights out'. The Newman of this period has been compared to Clongowes Wood, the famed Jesuit school outside Dublin, where the students showed a like talent for writing, acting, leading and rebelling. Many Newmanites came from the same stock that produced James Joyce and Oliver St John Gogarty and the lesser known young men, who found their way into the Abbey Theatre and the flying columns of Michael Collins.

Fitzgerald approached this organized tumult with the im-aginative will-to-conquer which he lavished on all new ex-perience. From boys' books he had learned the steps whereby one became the hero of one's school. In the back of his mind there was perhaps a regret that he wasn't going to a more prominent academy, to Hotchkiss, say, or Andover. When a girl in St Paul claimed never to have heard of Newman, Fitz-gerald answered, a shade defensively, 'It's a good school – you see, it's a *Catholic* school.' He wouldn't have chosen it for himself, yet he rose to its challenge.

Here is his self-appraisal as he was about to enter Newman.

I had a definite philosophy which was a sort of aristocratic egotism. I considered that I was a fortunate youth capable of expansion to any extent for good or evil. I based this, not on latent strength, but upon facility and superior mentality. I thought there was nothing I could not do, except, perhaps, become a mechanical genius; still I traced special lines in which I considered [I] must excell, even in the eyes of others. *First:* Physically – I marked myself handsome; of great athletic *possibilities*, and an extremely good dancer. Here I gave myself about eighty per cent. *Second:* Socially – In this respect, my condition was, perhaps, most dangerous, for I was convinced that I had personality, charm, magnetism, poise, and the ability to dominate others. Also I was sure that I exercised a subtle fascination over women. *Third:* Mentally – Here I was sure that I had a clear field in the world. I was vain of having so much, of being so talented, ingenuous [ingenious] and quick to learn.

To balance this I had several things on the other side. *First:* Morally – I thought I was rather worse than most boys, due to latent unscrupulousness and the desire to influence people in some way, even for evil. I knew I was rather cold; capable of being cruel; lacked a sense of honour, and was mordantly selfish. *Second:* Psychologically – Much as I influenced others, I was by no means the 'Captain of my Fate'. I had a curious cross section of weakness running through my character. I was liable to be swept off my poise into a timid stupidity. I knew I was 'fresh' and not popular with older boys. I knew I was completely the slave of my own moods, and often dropped into a surly sensitiveness most unprepossessing to others. *Third:* Generally – I knew that at bottom I lacked the essentials. At the last crisis, I knew I had no real courage, perseverance or self-respect.

So you see I looked at myself in two ways. There seemed to have been a conspiracy to spoil me and all my inordinate vanity was absorbed from that. All this was on the surface, however, and liable to be toppled over at one blow by an unpleasant remark or a missed tackle; and underneath it, came my own sense of lack of courage and stability. If I may push it farther still, I should say that, underneath the whole thing lay a sense of infinite possibilities that was always with me whether vanity or shame was my mood.

A sense of infinite possibilities . . .

Fitzgerald tells us elsewhere that at fifteen a Puritan conscience made him consider himself a great deal worse than other boys, but with the temperament outlined above one might have foreseen that he was heading into trouble at Newman. At dinner the first evening, since everyone else was shy and silent, he felt very much at home by comparison and asked rather too many questions about the football team and its prospects. It had been suggested that because of his age he repeat Fourth Form, but he struck such an air of dignified astonishment that he was put probationally in Fifth. Reporting for third-team football practice, he took to telling the others what to do; then suspecting his lack of diplomacy, he tried to smooth it over with, 'Excuse me for bossing everyone around, but I'm used to being captain of the teams in St Paul.' Meanwhile he paraded his store of general information. In class his hand waggled convulsively at all questions.

Athletics, he knew, would provide the crucial test. They were taken seriously at Newman, which fielded good teams although its ranks were thin. In due course Fitzgerald was promoted to quarterback on the second string where he ran afoul of O'Flaherty, the coach, who, in his other capacity of history teacher, was already tiring of Fitzgerald's freshness. As one of the lightest men on the seconds Fitzgerald feared the pounding he had to take from the varsity, and soon O'Flaherty was accusing him of cowardice. The varsity captain joined in the reproof. The younger boys took up the cry and before long Fitzgerald was a pariah. He was underdog in several fist fights, one of which he provoked in sheer desperation. He began to walk in the least-used corridors and spent most of his time in his room. His marks suffered. He was called exclusively by his last name. Something about his bitter sulkiness goaded the masters into punishing him for every petty offence, and losing their sense of justice, they piled on the demerits.

A few shafts of light penetrated the gloom. Once, after he had been taken out of a football game for being yellow – only this time he knew he hadn't been – he wrote a Kiplingesque poem which was published in the *Newman News*. Thus he learned, as he afterwards wrote, 'that if you weren't able to function in action you might at least be able to tell about it, because you felt the same intensity – it was a back-door way out of facing reality.' Another memorable experience was the Princeton–Harvard game when Sam White, the Princeton end, raced ninety-five yards with a blocked field goal for the winning touchdown. 'Sam White decides me for Princeton,' Fitzgerald wrote beside the ticket stub in his scrapbook. On trips to New York he was getting his first taste of big-time musical comedy – George M. Cohan's *The Little Millionaire*, and Ina Claire in *The Quaker Girl*.

Christmas was a long time coming, but finally the holidays were upon him, bringing a welcome respite in St Paul. The Fitzgeralds had left Grandmother McQuillan's house the fall of 1909, and after a year at 514 Holly Avenue and another at 509, they had come to rest at 499. In October Aunt Clara had died of tuberculosis. She was the prettiest of the three McQuillan sisters, the one most nearly resembling Scott in her fine blondeness. He stood in awe of his other aunt – Annabel – who deplored his parents' loose rein on him, his being allowed to read trash and attend vaudeville. Because Aunt Annabel did not spoil him, Fitzgerald respected her and called her 'the real matriarch of my family, a dried up old maid, but with character and culture'.

Fitzgerald went back to Newman determined to make good. The great bath of unpopularity had cleansed him of some of his conceit as he began the long climb out of the abyss. Poor marks put him on bounds at midyears. As soon as he got off, he went to New York and saw a musical, *Over the River*, which started him writing librettos of his own. About this time he befriended Sap (for *homo sapiens*) Donahoe – a classmate and one of the most popular and re-spected boys in the school. A quiet, modest, decent sort, who excelled in both studies and athletics, Donahoe was the rock to which the more volatile Fitzgerald instinctively gravitated. At the same time Donahoe appreciated Fitzgerald's originality, realizing he had something to learn from the other's wide-ranging interest in books and people. A further bond was the fact that both were Westerners in a predominantly Eastern school. Donahoe came from Seattle, and their friendship ripened on the long trips across the continent.

During spring vacation Fitzgerald went to Norfolk to visit a first cousin on his father's side, Cecilia Taylor. She was sixteen years older than Scott who as a child had been a 'ribbon holder' in her wedding. Now she was an impoverished widow with four little girls whom Fitzgerald treated with avuncular kindness, herding them into drugstores for sundaes and sodas. Cousin 'Ceci' was Fitzgerald's favourite relative; she would be the model for the charming widow, Clara, in *This Side of Paradise*.

The Southern trip was memorable for a visit to Ceci's brother – Thomas Delihant – then attending a Jesuit Seminary in Woodstock, Maryland. This visit gave Fitzgerald the setting for his story 'Benediction' – an embodiment of the religious sensibility which never left him, even after he strayed from the Church. Fitzgerald came from a religious background; the McQuillans were devout Catholics and his father was at least an observing one. From time to time Scott would fall under the spell of some magnetic priest and try to convert his Protestant friends, yet he could be impishly irreverent. During a service in St Paul, when he noticed that the candle held by one acolyte was dangerously close to igniting the lace on the back of another, he got the boy he was with laughing so hard that they were asked to leave the church.

His spring term was climaxed by a small athletic triumph. He won the junior field meet. His marks improved and his 'A' in ancient history delighted him because of the astonishment of O'Flaherty, the history-teaching football coach. Home for the summer, he basked in sudden popularity. The girls were attracted by his air of sadness and consideration, the result of his discovery at boarding school that others had wills as strong as his own and more power. But as usual he went rotten under praise, and the boys soon had enough of him. Periodically they ignored him, and he would go off by himself and write until he came up with some new scheme for the general entertainment.

Meanwhile Owen Johnson's *Stover at Yale* had become a sort of handbook, and in his desire to be a football hero he set up a tackling dummy in his yard. According to his Ledger, fifth form had been 'a year of real unhappiness', while of sixth form he wrote: 'Reward in fall for work of previous summer. A better year but not happy.' It had its moments though, such as the Kingsley game, said to be the most exciting ever played on Newman Field. Fitzgerald rose to brilliant heights that day, and one write-up attributed Newman's victory largely to his 'snap and bang runs'. Now five feet six and a hundred and thirty pounds, he was neatly well-built save for somewhat stubby legs. As substitute for the captain who was frequently injured, Fitzgerald saw action in six of the seven contests.

He played with fanatical intensity, his speed making him most effective around end, though being a bit clumsy on his feet he often seemed on the verge of falling. A younger boy who watched him from the sidelines recalled that Fitzgerald had 'a desperate, bent-forward, short-legged, scuttling way of running with the ball, but somehow it conveyed emotion, and when he was good, it was thrilling and when he was bad (as he often was) you had to look away from his visible shame.' Fitzgerald was an erratic, impetuous, self-willed player, not a natural like Sap Donahoe, who, though smaller than Fitzgerald and handicapped by poor eyes, quarterbacked the team with cool finesse. If Fitzgerald sparkled at times, at others he sank to ignominy. In one game he avoided an open field tackle, and several team mates who saw it rode him about it afterwards. Caring too much as he invariably did, he took the lapse harder than it deserved to be taken.

The great event of his autumn, though he couldn't know it at the time, was not the Kingsley game, but his meeting with Father Sigourney Webster Fay, a trustee of the school who would presently become headmaster. A Catholic convert from an old Philadelphia family, Fay had an infectious charm which made one forget his rather odd exterior. He was almost pure albino with thin flaxen hair, white eyebrows and lashes, and pink watery eyes that jiggled behind thick lenses. His soft bulk, his round face with a button nose surmounting several rolls of chin – anyone could see that Fay liked to eat. He also liked to sing and play the piano and gossip and tell stories which he punctuated with high-pitched giggles. He had a supply of Church jokes and pitied the Protestants for being unable to laugh at themselves. One of his whims was to say Mass in Greek or Celtic. Yet with it all went the ardour of the convert who had found in the Catholic Church the romance of his life. Fay's sophistication did not preclude a childlike faith which prompted him, on occasion, to bless the house he was visiting from attic to cellar.

Between Fay and Fitzgerald there sprang up an immediate *rapport* such as that between Father Darcy and Amory Blaine in *This Side of Paradise*. No doubt Fay's very accents are preserved in Father Darcy's 'Have a cigarette – I'm sure you smoke. Well, if you're like me, you loathe all science and mathematics.' Hitherto Fitzgerald had thought of the priesthood in terms of crude unlettered Irishmen, but here was a priest (Irish on his mother's side) who was also an intellectual, a man of the world, a familiar of Cardinal Gibbons and Henry Adams. Father Fay had a Continental air as did his assistant, Father Hemmick, with his silver-buckled pumps and cassocks tailored in Paris.

Fitzgerald was now living in the relative freedom of the Sixth Form Annex. His private life being less harassed, he was able to devote more energy to his writing and three of his stories were published in the *Newman News*. 'A Luckless Santa Claus' told of a man trying to give away twenty-five dollars on Christmas Eve and being beaten up for his pains.

In its colloquial realism and ironic bite, the story brings to mind some of Stephen Crane's hard luck pieces though Fitzgerald hadn't been reading Crane at the time. 'Pain and the Scientist' satirized Christian Science, while 'The Trail of the Duke' was a foray into the lives of the Fifth Avenue rich.

Fitzgerald, sure of his talent, was playing around with it as might a boy with a hot-rod, trying to see what he could make it do. He wasn't a hellion in the Newman tradition – by Newman standards he was even a bit subdued – but he resented all encroachments on his freedom. Often late to class, he wrote surreptitiously when he got there or involved the teacher in discussions which had nothing to do with the assignment, smiling superciliously when he disagreed.

The other students still had reservations about him. They found him a bit too fond of smoothing his blond, wavy hair and eyeing himself approvingly in the mirror. An unspoken bravado, some cocky assurance about his destiny, stood between him and his fellows, most of whom had no idea where they were going. But they handled him gingerly now. He was no longer their butt. They had grown to respect his quick intelligence, not to mention his skill in satirizing them in verse or epigram. Among the younger boys there was even a sort of informal 'pro-Fitz' society, for in contrast to the other fifth and sixth formers, who had a harmless but oafish way of knocking the small fry about, Fitzgerald always responded to their chorused greetings with a slight smile and spoke to each by name as he went about his business. He did not play up to them – indeed he gave them little of his time – but the relative maturity of his conduct won their approval. Likewise, when introduced to someone's parents in the corridor, Fitzgerald never failed to charm them with his gracious, spontaneous interest. He had an ease and courtesy that were well beyond his years, having skipped the stage most boys go through of being clumsy puppies.

In March the Newman Comedy Club presented *The Taming of the Shrew* (during rehearsals Fitzgerald had suggested how certain of Shakespeare's lines might be improved upon). The high point of the evening, however, was a curtain-raiser

47

written by one of the masters – *The Power of Music*. This period piece, set in the Graustarkian kingdom of Schwartzenbaum-Altminster, concerned the ambition of the Chancellor's eleven-year-old son to be a concert violinist. In his disgust, the Chancellor sequesters the son's violin, but the son steals it back to enter a royal competition for prodigies. At the play's end the Chancellor is preparing to horsewhip his son when trumpets sound without. Fitzgerald as King of Schwartzenbaum-Altminster – all resplendent in a white and gold hussar's uniform that had belonged to the musical comedy star, Donald Brian – enters with his arm protectively around the Chancellor's son. He explains that the son has won the competition and berates the Chancellor. To the second former who acted the son, it seemed at that moment that Fitzgerald *was* the king of some imaginary kingdom, and that he, the second former, could play the violin like Fritz Kreisler. Fitzgerald had cast his spell of belief, and the audience was unforgettably moved.

That spring, with graduation just ahead, Fitzgerald's mood expanded to the euphoria described in *This Side of Paradise*.

He moved his bed so that the sun would wake him at dawn that he might dress and go out to the archaic swing that hung from an apple tree near the sixth-form house. Seating himself in this he would pump higher and higher until he got the effect of swinging into the wide air, into a fairy-land of piping satyrs and nymphs with the faces of fair-haired girls he passed in the streets of Eastchester. As the swing reached its highest point, Arcady really lay just over the brow of a certain hill, where the brown road dwindled out of sight in a golden dot.

He was reading indiscriminately – Kipling, Tennyson, Chesterton, Robert W. Chambers, David Graham Phillips, E. Phillips Oppenheim. As a schoolmate said with unconscious irony, Fitzgerald got poor grades because he read so many books. But he skimped his classwork and later recalled that 'only "l'Allegro" and some quality of rigid clarity in solid geometry [had] stirred his languid interest'. Lying on the edge of the baseball diamond, or late at night with cigarettes glowing in the dark, he and Sap analysed the school. Fitzgerald liked to dissect people and put them in categories and prophesy how they were going to turn out.

He was definitely going to Princeton, attributing his preference to the fact that Princeton always just lost the football championship. 'Yale always seemed to nose them out in the last quarter by superior "stamina" as the newspapers called it. It was to me a repetition of the story of the foxes and the big animals in the child's book. I imagined the Princeton men as slender and keen and romantic, and the Yale men as brawny and brutal and powerful.'

Taking his entrance exams at the New York YMCA, he managed a little judicious cheating which he regretted ever after.

Summer sped by with only his Civil War drama, *The Coward*, to take his mind off the coming autumn. It was staged by the Elizabethan Dramatic Club, so-named for its 'directress', Elizabeth Magoffin. Fitzgerald did most of the directing, but Miss Magoffin – a large, plump, enthusiastic girl in her mid-twenties kept order at rehearsals with an attitude of 'the least we can do is learn our lines'. Her belief in Fitzgerald quickened his sense of dawning power. She gave him her photograph inscribed 'To Scott "He had that spark – Magnetic mark" – with the best love of the one who thinks so.'

The theme of *The Coward* was Fitzgerald's favourite of redemption through bravery; a Southerner, after refusing to bear arms, enlists and becomes a hero. The performance before a sell-out crowd at the YWCA auditorium netted $150 for the Baby Welfare Association, or more than twice the take from *The Captured Shadow*, Fitzgerald's play of the summer before. By request *The Coward* was performed a second time at the White Bear Yacht Club, where Fitzgerald had recently become a member.

As mainspring of the Elizabethan Dramatic Club, he had begun to show the qualities of a real impresario. He knew how to soothe the girl who had only been able to rent one costume for a play whose action extended over several years. (Her mother had suggested her saying, 'Here I am in the same old dress I was wearing when Sumter fell!') Then there was the girl who blushed at the line, 'Father, remember your liver!' and the girl who wouldn't say the business about cleaning her nails because it was undignified. All this had to be worked out. When it came to rewriting, Fitzgerald was indefatigable, retiring to a corner and tossing off new lines with his ever-facile pen. As an ad-libber he was equally skilled. During the performance at White Bear everyone was waiting for the cue *A shot without*, but no shot came. The boy in charge of firing had discovered at the last minute that his pistol contained a live cartridge instead of a blank. In his alarm he ran down three flights of stairs and out to the end of a pier, where he blasted away into the night. Fitzgerald, on stage at the time, filled the gap quite plausibly by rummaging for a box of cigars. His ingenuity was again tested when one of the actors said, 'Here comes Father now,' gesturing to the left. Whereupon the old man in his wheelchair hurtled in from the *right* – jet propelled, it would seem, for the stage was a raised platform, and it had taken considerable pushing to get the wheelchair up the ramp.

In August Fitzgerald began studying for make-up exams, as Princeton would not accept him on the basis of his marks in the spring.

'Are you really going to Yale [read Princeton] this fall?' a friend asks Basil Duke Lee in 'Forging Ahead'.

'Yes.'

'Everyone says you're foolish to go at sixteen.'

'I'll be seventeen in September. So long.'

[4]

THE re-exams in September did not yield Fitzgerald the necessary credits, but fortunately there was a board of appeals. Aspirants who were near the mark could go before the Admissions Committee and talk or 'bicker' their way into Princeton. Fitzgerald's live presence proved more persuasive than his blue books; among other arguments he mentioned the fact that it was his seventeenth birthday and it would be uncharitable to turn him down. For whatever reasons, the Committee approved him. On 24 September Fitzgerald wired his mother, ADMITTED SEND FOOTBALL PADS AND SHOES IMMEDIATELY PLEASE WAIT TRUNK.

The football pads and shoes might have been spared the journey. Though college players were an inch or two shorter and proportionately lighter than they are now, five feet seven and a hundred and thirty-eight pounds was still puny unless one had far more ability than Fitzgerald. A classmate remembers him catching punts in his black Newman jersey with the white-ringed sleeves – an eager, striving youth with lots of blond hair flying about. Somewhere Fitzgerald has written of 'the shoulder pads worn for one day on the Princeton freshman football field', but he told the present writer that he stuck it out for three days and withdrew semi-honourably with an ankle injury. (In *This Side of Paradise* the hero wrenches his knee badly enough to put him out for the season.) In any case football glory was now behind him, to his infinite regret. He would have to find some other way of catching the public eye.

Meanwhile he responded to the beauty of a Princeton that was smaller and sleepier than it is today. The railroad tracks came to the foot of Blair steps and Nassau Street was unpaved. Palmer Stadium was under construction but would not be used till the following autumn. Almost at once there

51

was born in Fitzgerald a reverence for this campus 'where Witherspoon brooded like a dark mother over Whig and Clio, her Attic children, where the black Gothic snake of Little curled down to Cuyler and Patton, these in turn flinging the mystery out over the placid slope rolling to the lake' and where 'topping all, climbing with clear blue aspiration, [were] the great dreaming spires of Holder and Cleveland towers.'

One evening in September, sitting on the steps of his rooming house, Fitzgerald witnessed the parade of upperclassmen which he afterwards described in *This Side of Paradise*. White-shirted and white-trousered, arms linked and heads aloft, they marched up University Place singing the all-stirring 'Going Back to Nassau Hall', written three years before. 'The song soared so high that all dropped out except the tenors, who bore the melody triumphantly past the danger-point and relinquished it to the fantastic chorus.' At the head of the column strode the football captain, 'slim and defiant, as if aware that this year the hopes of the college rested on him, that his hundred-and-sixty pounds were expected to dodge to victory through the heavy blue and crimson lines'.

Hobart A. H. Baker, the blond Adonis of a halfback who was Princeton's captain, weighed in at a hundred and sixty-seven. Among Fitzgerald's contemporaries there was more hero worship than there is now. Varsity football players were looked upon as demi-gods, and 'Hobey' Baker, captain of football and star of hockey – someone like Baker loomed so high in the heavens that he was scarcely visible. But Baker had the common touch. Now and then he came down from Olympus to fraternize with the freshmen, and Fitzgerald actually spoke to him one day in October.

A network of traditions kept the freshmen of yore severely in their places. After the nine-o'clock curfew they were expected to be in their rooms. They couldn't walk on the grass or smoke pipes around the campus, and they had to wear cuffless trousers, stiff collars, black ties, shoes *and* garters – everyone wore garters then – and black skullcaps known as 'dinks' or 'beanies'. For ten days they underwent the mild indignities of 'horsing', a bloodless form of hazing. The sophomores made them dance with their pant legs rolled or march to Commons lockstep express. A freshman sporting his best suit of a diamond pattern might be told to take off the jacket and play checkers on it with his companion. Freshman-sophomore hostilities reached their climax in the 'rushes' when the freshmen as a body stormed the sophomores defending the gym. Though supervised by upperclassmen, the rushes were bruising affairs; they had to be abolished Fitzgerald's junior year when a freshman was trampled to death under his own phalanx. By then horsing was extinct and the rules of dress were being eased.

And yet these college customs, criticized as pointless and childish, made for a drama and an *esprit de corps* which delighted Fitzgerald. His zest and curiosity were boundless as he expanded into his new environment after the compression of boarding school. He wanted to see, to know, to be, to experience, to explore. He wanted to do everything and have everything with an enthusiasm which made him very attractive. He was rushing out to meet life and to embrace it, unable to wait for life to come to him.

In those days the contrasts between East and West, between city and country, between prep school and high school were more marked than they are now, and correspondingly the nuances of dress and manners were more noticeable. Fitzgerald quickly grasped the prevailing code and adapted himself to it. In Commons, where the undergraduates ate during their first two years, he spied out the leaders and men of quality as opposed to the 'scuts' or 'birds', as the lower orders were then called. Though respectful to those he considered his superiors, he wasn't boot-licking; he would not, for example, take the empty seat next to the class president, but he noticed the man who did. He noticed everything, including such refiements as how a classmate treated his parents when they came to call. So-and-so put his arm around his mother as they strolled across the campus yet hardly spoke to his father. Such an observation would be pregnant with overtones for Fitzgerald.

At 15 University Place, known to its inmates as 'The Morgue', Fitzgerald was living with nine freshmen, including Sap Donahoe and several others from Newman. After they had fixed their rooms and bought all manner of pennants, posters, pillows, and class pipes, they took to lounging in a first-floor window seat and watching their classmates troop to Commons. It made a convenient lookout for the embryo novelist who never tired of analysing his fellows, of pigeon-holing them and imaginatively probing their tenets and values. What was so-and-so's ambition? Would he make it? What sort of background had he come from? If you took away this or that quality, what would become of him?

'That's Tom Hilliard,' Fitzgerald would exclaim, as a group from St Paul's School passed the window. 'Hilliard's going Ivy.'

Fitzgerald had a precocious knowledge of the upperclass eating clubs which students were invited to join the spring of sophomore year. Until then, the less said about them the better, but Fitzgerald kept a class list on which he wrote the club each individual seemed destined for.

Life at the Morgue consisted of the usual freshman shenanigans. There were wrestling matches, pillow fights, and interminable games of red-dog and poker. There were bicker sessions during which the problems of the universe were settled to everyone's satisfaction. When it was discovered that the gas could be extinguished all over the house by blowing in the upstairs jet, Fitzgerald, who lived on the top floor, staged blackouts at strategic moments. He had another trick of barging into people's rooms at two or three a.m. and parading back and forth before the mirror as he talked.

What he saw in the mirror was cause for hope. Handsome, pert, fresh, blond, he looked – as someone said at the time – like a jonquil. He parted his hair in the middle (at Newman he had parted it on one side), and though he slicked it down for formal occasions, it was usually a little windblown from his energetic life. His pale, clear skin was the kind that grows rosy with cold or with exertion, though at this stage its radiance was somewhat dimmed by adolescent pimples. Fitzgerald favoured Brooks Brothers suits; freshman year he had a greenish-grey tweed, on the order of an Irish frieze, that was very becoming. As was the fashion, he arched the wings of his button-down collars so that they pulled away from the buttons, and his dark, conservative ties bulged out in front at the approved angle.

Occasionally he and his companions went to Trenton to take in the bars and burlesque shows. Fitzgerald had tasted his first glass of whiskey the previous spring, and on a trip to New York he shocked Sap Donahoe by tossing down several Bronxes in quick succession. In the resulting mood of silliness he took Sap's arm on the way to the theatre and addressed him as his son for the amusement of passers-by. Fitzgerald was notoriously poor at holding his liquor, but he drank moderately as an undergraduate. It was still the era when parents promised their sons gold watches if they abstained till they were twenty-one. Alcohol in any form was forbidden on campus, and conspicuous drunks were frowned upon, so Fitzgerald, like most of his contemporaries, confined himself to beer in the saloons along Nassau Street.

His ambition had come to rest on *The Tiger*, a humour sheet, and the Triangle, purveyor of musical comedies. Having gotten an unsigned bit in the first issue of *The Tiger*, Fitzgerald bombarded that magazine with poems of the moon-croon-June-spoon variety, he-and-she jokes, and pseudo-comic sketches. He lay in wait for the editor outside his classes and slipped manuscripts into his hand on Nassau Street. As the editor was about to retire, he gave in from sheer weariness and printed a second squib by Fitzgerald.

The Triangle was harder to crash. The sheaf of lyrics which Fitzgerald submitted at tryouts were all turned down in favour of songs by well-known upperclassmen. Undaunted, Fitzgerald showed his interest by working on lights in the old Casino where Triangle rehearsals were held. Meanwhile he wrote blindly, incessantly, sometimes waking up in the small hours and strewing the floor with scribbled sheets which he threw in the wastebasket next day without examining their contents.

His studies were his least concern. He took forty-nine cuts freshman year, the maximum permitted without penalty. Dozing through classes, he evaded the professor's half-heard question with, 'It all depends how you look at it, sir – there's a subjective and an objective point of view.' Fitzgerald was no scholar though in other respects college excited him. He liked the big-time competition for power and status, certain that his talents would win their deserts. He thrilled to the poetry of Princeton – to the colourful crowds at the football games, to the snatches of song drifting across the campus, to the mellow lamplight back of Nassau Hall, to the whisperings in the pass at night in front of Witherspoon.

Going home for Christmas, Fitzgerald felt that oneness with the continent which he was to describe so hauntingly in *The Great Gatsby* – in a passage near the end which rises like a great wave out of the ocean, purging the brackishness and sordidness in what has gone before.

One of my most vivid memories is coming back West from prep school and later from college at Christmas time. Those who went farther than Chicago would gather in the old dim Union Street Station at six o'clock of a December evening, with a few Chicago friends, already caught up into their own holiday gayeties, to bid them a hasty good-by. I remember the fur coats of the girls returning from Miss This-or-That's and the chatter of frozen breath and the hands waving overhead as we caught sight of old acquaintances, and the matchings of invitations: 'Are you going to the Ordways'? The Herseys'? The Schultzes'?' and the long green tickets clasped tight in our gloved hands. And last the murky yellow cars of the Chicago, Milwaukee & St Paul railroad looking cheerful as Christmas itself on the tracks beside the gate.

When we pulled out into the winter night and the real snow, our snow, began to stretch out beside us and twinkle against the windows, and the dim lights of small Wisconsin stations moved by, a sharp, wild brace came suddenly into the air. We drew in deep breaths of it as we walked back from dinner through the cold vestibules, unutterably aware of our identity with this country for one strange hour, before we melted indistinguishably into it again.

That's my Middle West – not the wheat or the prairies or the lost Swede towns, but the thrilling returning trains of my youth, and the street lamps and the sleigh bells in the frosty dark and the shadows of holly wreaths thrown by lighted windows on the snow.

It was fun being home with his old companions, and yet to Fitzgerald's widening gaze, St Paul began to seem dull and provincial. He felt a need to startle these people out of their complacency. 'I think I'll put you in a story,' he would tell the girl beside him at a dinner party, implying that any moment he would be bursting into print, ' – what sort of a heroine would you like to be?' 'Are you really the richest girl in your boarding school?' he would ask the out-of-town visitor, while for Catholic maidens he reserved the question, 'Do you believe in God?'

The holidays over, he went back to the retribution of midyears. Failing three of them and passing four with low marks, he managed to stay in college by a narrow margin. In March he began a script for next year's Triangle, urged on by the club's new president, Walker Ellis. A wealthy, brilliant, cosmopolitan junior from New Orleans, Ellis was Fitzgerald's *beau idéal*.

By the end of April the Triangle competition had narrowed to two scripts – Fitzgerald's and that of a sophomore named Lawton Campbell. As Fitzgerald and Campbell had never met, Ellis did his best to keep them apart and play one off against the other. On 15 May Campbell submitted his final draft. He was discussing it with Ellis in the latter's suite when Fitzgerald came in, out of breath from his hurried climb up several flights of stairs. His hair was rumpled and his eyes were ablaze; those eyes that combined so many emotions – suspicion, eagerness, curiosity, good humour, compassion, irony. In his hand was a manuscript.

'Is Campbell's in yet?' he asked.

'Campbell's play is here and so is Campbell,' said Ellis, and the rivals were introduced.

They became friends, and during the next few weeks Fitzgerald often dropped in on Campbell for clues of how the competition was going. Fitzgerald had taken no chances; to improve his techniques he had steeped himself in the lyrics of Gilbert and Sullivan and the dialogue of Oscar Wilde. In the end his script was chosen, largely on the strength of the lyrics, which were said to be the most original ever submitted for a Triangle production. Ellis rewrote the book and signed his name to it, but in his copy of the programme Fitzgerald corrected the credits to read: 'Book and lyrics by F. Scott Fitzgerald, 1917. Revision by Walker Ellis, 1915'.

Freshman year, though Fitzgerald's best efforts went into the Triangle, the deeper side of him also found an outlet. By coincidence he had early become acquainted with a classmate of rare gifts. Let John Peale Bishop describe their first encounter.

[Fitzgerald] had, like myself, only arrived in Princeton; the Commons for Freshmen was not yet open; we sat side by side at a large round table in a corner of the Peacock Inn. It was the first time I had gone out alone, for in those opening days we stuck very close to the boys who had come down from school with us. It was by chance that I sat next to this youth, so quick to conversation; we stayed on when the others had gone. In the leafy street outside the September twilight faded; the lights came on against the paper walls, where tiny peacocks strode and trailed their tails among the gayer foliations. I learned that Fitzgerald had written a play which had been performed at school. Places were cleared; other students sat down at the tables around us. We talked of books: those I had read, which were not many; those Fitzgerald had read, which were even less; those he said he had read, which were many, many more.

In *This Side of Paradise* Bishop is Thomas Parke d'Invilliers with his 'cracked, kindly voice', his scholarly mien, his comparative innocence of social realities. Part of the Princeton code was not to appear to take one's studies too seriously, and Bishop had an unmistakable aura of bookishness. Worse, he wrote poetry about wreathed fauns and dying maidens for the highbrow *Nassau Lit*, and acted in the recherché productions of the English Dramatic Association. Some thought him a trifle British and affected – the way he said 'gyahden' instead of 'garden', and 'plahstah' instead of 'plaster'.

But Fitzgerald found Bishop a warm, generous, stimulating companion with a surprising streak of ribaldry and coarseness. Bishop had a wonderful belly laugh and on occasion would throw back his head and roar. He was imposing rather than handsome. 'Even as a freshman,' one of his teachers recalled, 'John had a self possession and self mastery which gave him the pose and bearing of a young English lord.' Because of a boyhood illness, he was twenty-one when he entered Princeton and seemed more mature than his classmates – almost like a young professor. With his superior grounding in literature, poetry especially, he was able to exert considerable influence on Fitzgerald's reading.

What Bishop gave Fitzgerald is plain to see. What Fitzgerald gave Bishop is harder to define though suggested in Bishop's beautiful requiem for Fitzgerald, 'The Hours'.

> No promise such as yours when like the spring
> You came, colors of jonquils in your hair,
> Inspired as the wind, when woods are bare
> And every silence is about to sing.

The summer of 1914 was still the summer of the Western world. In the last flush of Victorian tranquillity, war seemed remote and exciting, and when hostilities broke out in Europe Fitzgerald took a sporting interest in the German dash for Paris. Then he ceased to give it much thought, although like Amory in *This Side of Paradise*, 'if it had not continued he would have felt like an irate ticket-holder at a prize-fight where the principals refused to mix it up'.

Of more concern was his third play for the Elizabethan Dramatic Club. Despite the prevalence of such lines as 'No doubt you get my drift, or shall I snow again?', the newspapers called *Assorted Spirits* 'a roaring farce, clever throughout'. Again Fitzgerald packed the YWCA Auditorium. During a repeat performance at the White Bear Yacht Club a fuse burned out with a loud explosion and plunged the house into darkness at the very moment when a ghost was walking in the first act. Women shrieked, there were signs of panic, but Fitzgerald leapt to the stage and kept the audience at bay with an improvised monologue until the lights were repaired.

In September he returned to Princeton to find himself ineligible for the Triangle. Though his marks had improved slightly the spring of freshman year and though he had passed off enough conditions to become 'a sophomore in good standing', he would not be allowed to act in the show or go on its tour of distant cities. At rehearsals, he took a hand in the staging and direction. He also polished and rewrote his lyrics as they were set to music.

He was living by himself in 107 Patton, a tower room that overlooked the woods and fields sloping off towards Carnegie Lake. The Triangle took up most of his time, but he kept an eye on his classmates and their activities, knowing more about them than they would ever have suspected. On the whole his appraisal of others was objective and charitable, although with a few deadly strokes he could annihilate someone he didn't like. His classwork continued to lag behind his other interests. In chemistry he ignored the formulas and wrote collaborative verse with the boy beside him. An English teacher named 'Rip' Van Winkle made some slight impression on him, and he attended the aesthetic gatherings in Van Winkle's apartment, where Keats and Shelley were read aloud while the students sipped tea with rum in it.

In December the Triangle went on tour minus Fitzgerald, who nevertheless shared the glory of *Fie! Fie! Fi-Fi!* 'This delicious little vehicle,' said the *Brooklyn Citizen*, 'was announced as a musical comedy and the name can only be disputed to the extent that it is also given to innumerable Broadway productions that possess less vivacity, less sparkling humor and less genuine music.' 'Much of the success of the entertainment,' said the *Baltimore Sun*, 'was due to the clever lyrics of F. S. Fitzgerald, who has written some really excellent "patter songs."' And the *Louisville Post*: 'The lyrics of the songs were written by F. S. Fitzgerald, who could take his place right now with the brightest writers of witty lyrics in America.'

Strong wine of praise, and Fitzgerald's head was easily turned. 'The Triangle success,' he later told a classmate, 'was the worst thing that could have happened to me. As long as I'm unknown I'm a pretty nice fellow, but give me a little notoriety and I swell up like a poison toad.'

Once asked how he always managed to corner the most attractive girl at a party, Fitzgerald replied, 'I'm only interested in the best.' It was therefore natural that during the Christmas holidays in St Paul he should make a play for Marie Hersey's house guest, Ginevra King from Chicago. Ginevra was a startling brunette beauty, with the vivid colouring so valuable in a day when only actresses wore make-up. Just sixteen and a junior at Westover, she was already getting quantities of mail from Yale, Harvard, and Princeton. Like Isabelle in *This Side of Paradise*, she had a reputation for being a 'speed' and was capable of 'very strong if very transient emotions'. Fitzgerald did not meet her until the day before his departure for Princeton, but he monopolized her during the remaining breathless hours, and the Amory–Isabelle sequence in *This Side of Paradise* is a record of their colliding egotisms. Momentarily Fitzgerald stood out from the army of Ginevra's admirers. He was thought to be a difficult catch and philosophized about 'Life' in a way other boys did not. On Fitzgerald's side the attraction went deeper; for the first time he found himself irrevocably hooked.

En route to Princeton he wrote a telegram which he never sent: 'Dearest Ginevra – Pardon me if my hand is shakey but I write a very shaky hand. I have just had a quart of sauterne and 3 Bronxes in celebration of meeting Mr Donahoe a classmate of mine on the train.' Back in college he launched a voluminous correspondence. Ginevra promised to send him one of her 'homely pictures' and asked for his in return, as she had but a faint recollection of yellow hair, big blue eyes, and a brown corduroy vest that was very good-looking. Already Fitzgerald had occasion to be jealous. He heard that after his departure from St Paul Ginevra had gotten attention from his old nemesis, Reuben Warner, whose glamour was now enhanced by the possession of a Stutz Bearcat. When Fitzgerald wrote Warner for details, he wasn't reassured by the reply:

Scott, you are talking foolish when you say that I always beat you out, because I know damn well she likes you better than I, and god-damn it you always beat me out, but nevertheless we are friendly rivals. That's one consolation . . .

Wednesday morning Marie called me up and asked me if I would go to a pair of sixes with them – I said yes – and G.K. & I and J. Johnston & Marie went down with Mrs Hersey & some other hen as chaperone – Well when I saw those two I said, 'Reuben, no fun for you this after-noon,' But!! nevertheless I started to think of a plan how I would – (without the old ladies seeing me). I guess G.K. was thinking the same thing.

After I had been thinking for about ten minutes Ginevra suddenly picked up her muff and put it on her lap with her hands in it!! – I like a *damn* fool, just sat there – you know how you hate to start anything, *Then!!!* she nudged me with her sweet elbow and I looked at her and she looked down at her muff. Well! I just slid my massive paw in there and enjoyed the rest of the show. When I would squeeze, she'd squeeze back – hmn! Swell! Now listen Scott, I know you won't say anything about this to any one – Will you? Because you & I want to have a hell of a time next summer if she should come out to St Paul.

Rumours of other beaux trickled in to disquiet Fitzgerald, but Ginevra assured him he was first and her lengthy letters seemed to confirm it. She asked if he would like to visit her at Westover; she would 'worship' having him. Of course the circumstances of their meeting would be less than ideal. While they were together, they would have to sit in a glass parlour under the eye of a chaperone.

Fitzgerald went one day in February. Long afterwards, in his story 'Basil and Cleopatra', he recalled his first glimpse of Ginevra that afternoon. 'Radiant and glowing, more mysteriously desirable than ever, wearing her very sins like stars, she came down to him in her plain white uniform dress, and his heart turned over at the kindness of her eyes.'

Ginevra thought the visit a great success, and in her next letter she suggested they write each other daily, but Fitzgerald, who as usual had over-dreamed the occasion, was in despair. He wrote Ginevra that when she grew tired of his letters they would drift. He asked her impossible questions ('Describe your last affair') and talked of becoming a priest. He moralized: girls who were flirts, he said, would never get their share of life later on. When Ginevra went home for spring vacation, her reports of the good time she was having put him on the rack. 'Even now,' he began a letter, 'you may be having a tête-à-tête with some "unknown Chicagoan" with crisp dark hair and glittering smile.'

In March, groups of juniors and seniors began visiting the sophomores preparatory to inviting them to join the clubs. Evenings, Fitzgerald sat in a room with Sap Donahoe and several others, nervously awaiting the steps in the hall, the shuffling outside the door, the final appeasing knock. With the representatives of the clubs he was interested in he played the nice ingenuous boy, very much at ease and totally unaware of the object of the call, while the unwelcome delegations he took pleasure in shocking. Already known to upperclassmen for his work on the Triangle, Fitzgerald had his eye on Cottage, one of the four 'big' clubs whose president was Walker Ellis. He might have preferred Ivy – 'detached and breathlessly aristocratic', as he called it in *This Side of Paradise* – but he looked on Cottage as a respectable alternative. In the end, after weighing bids from Cap and Gown, Quadrangle and Cannon, he went Cottage with Sap Donahoe and passed out at the celebration.

His section in Cottage was polyglot and disjointed. As he afterwards wrote, he might have been more comfortable in Quadrangle, one of the nice smaller clubs where John Peale

Bishop and the littérateurs of the class were concentrated, yet he never regretted his choice. At Princeton the big clubs attracted most of the leaders and policy makers, and here as always he was shooting for the top.

By now Ginevra had returned to the comparative seclusion of Westover, and Fitzgerald, safely entrenched in Cottage, felt the moment had come to invite her to the sophomore prom. Ginevra expressed joy at the thought but wasn't sure her mother would be able to chaperon her. There was hope, however. ... When she wrote a few weeks later that her mother couldn't make it, Fitzgerald took it gracefully, though his true feelings were voiced in a quatrain of Browning's which he copied into his scrapbook:

> Each life unfulfilled you see
> It hangs still, patchy and scrappy
> We have not sighed deep, laughed free
> Starved, feasted, despaired – been happy.

By way of compensation, Ginevra invited him to go to the theatre with her after school let out. Nevertheless, their relations grew stormier. It seemed to Fitzgerald that Ginevra was looking beyond him while all his desires were centred on her. In a mood of revulsion he wrote her that he was tired of her, that she had no character, that he idealized her in the beginning but had soon realized his mistake. When Ginevra answered that it wasn't her fault she had been idealized, Fitzgerald relented.

Except for the troubles with Ginevra it was a happy spring, and perhaps the troubles had something to do with the more serious turn of his literary interests. Sap Donahoe remembered Fitzgerald bursting into the room with Francis Thompson's 'Hound of Heaven', which Bishop had gotten him to read. At such moments Fitzgerald was incandescent with enthusiasm. Literature was a form of intoxication, and many nights he read and wrote in his tower room till the cigarette butts littered the ash trays – then wandered up to Nassau Street through the darkened campus for string potatoes and milk at Joe's.

His name had begun to appear in the *Nassau Lit*. In the April issue he had a one-act play, *Shadow Laurels*, which tells of a Frenchman seeking news of his long-dead father in a Paris wineshop. The father had been a drunken roisterer but a lovely spirit – a sort of unsung François Villon. 'The Ordeal', Fitzgerald's story in the June issue, described the temptations of a novice about to take monastic vows. The clash of spiritual good and earthly evil was powerfully dramatized, suggesting some of the religious uncertainty in Fitzgerald himself.

Through his work on the *Lit* he had gotten to know its capable editor, Edmund 'Bunny' Wilson. College classes in those days were more separate than they are now, and not only was Wilson a year ahead of Fitzgerald, he was someone you met on his own terms; he wasn't going to seek you out unless he was sure it would be worth his while. A recluse, a burner of midnight oil, he had come to Princeton from the Hill School already possessed of a cool, objective intelligence and high critical standards. His erudition made him popular with the faculty; he was used to talking to older men about their subjects without being treated as a boy. To the bulk of the undergraduates, however, he was a withdrawn, literary figure, a well-dressed 'poler' or grind, a smug, conceited little fellow who wouldn't talk to you because he considered himself the brightest person around – which he may well have been.

Intellectually mature, he was socially somewhat backward and oblivious. He would start expounding in a casual group and go right on, unaware that the others were uninterested or laughing at him. In some ways he had found Princeton antipathetic. He recoiled from its provincialism, the emphasis on sports and clubs, the relative indifference to art and ideas (his twin passions), and he wasn't afraid to make his opinions known in the *Lit* editorials.

While he and Fitzgerald quickly recognized each other's ability, they stood opposed in a number of ways. Wilson was a born intellectual whose love of books and culture had led him to explore the surrounding life. Fitzgerald wasn't really an intellectual at all; his talents were of a different order. He had begun with a quick, instinctive love of life and, working in the opposite direction from Wilson, had found his way back to books. From this fundamental antithesis sprang other differences. Wilson had a rational, judicial cast inherited from his lawyer father who greatly influenced his style of thought. Fitzgerald lived in his imagination; he seethed with poetic invention and no one could match him for creative fire. Compared to Fitzgerald, so breezy and impetuous, Wilson seemed self-conscious, pedantic, a bit of a priss (he was the only child of a deaf mother to whom it was necessary that he speak very precisely). Wilson's world was the *Lit*, where he had become a focus for the more serious writers among the undergraduates. They deferred to his taste and judgement, for Wilson could tell you when a thing was literature and when it was not. On the whole, he scorned *The Tiger* and the Triangle, though he would show his versatility by writing the book for the Triangle's next production. Fitzgerald, with inverse snobbery, had begun by looking down on the *Lit* which he ridiculed as 'half a dozen men who, as the price of appearing in print, agree to listen to each other's manuscripts'. But you could tease Fitzgerald about *The Tiger* and the Triangle and he would enter into the spirit of it, while Wilson, haughty and aloof, brooked no jest about his enterprises.

Wilson, in a word, was less fun than Fitzgerald, though Wilson had enough wit of the satiric sort to be quite amusing when he chose. A pale, fine-featured youth, he was short-legged – not fat, but yet a little stocky in his clothes. He wore orange ties to go with his red-orange hair and rode an English bike, then a rarity on campus. His manner was quiet and composed, though among his confreres he had plenty to say in his high-pitched voice, and when the discussion grew heated he would bat his eyes and stammer with excitement.

In June Fitzgerald had the longed-for tryst with Ginevra in New York. They went to *Nobody Home* and then to the

Ritz Roof, and on his way to St Paul he called on her in Chicago. He continued to think of her as his girl although, as she pointed out, they had seen each other a total of only fifteen hours.

He spent July and August at Sap Donahoe's ranch in Wyoming. He didn't especially like the outdoor life, but not wanting to appear a sissy he went along with the cowhands and opened gates for them. He got drunk and won fifty dollars in poker. The ranch manager, who was carrying on a secret love affair, hated Fitzgerald for finding out.

Occasionally he heard from Ginevra summering in Maine, though hers were not the long soul-searching letters of the winter before.

[5]

As usual Fitzgerald went back to college early to wrestle with academic deficiencies. During the first weeks of September he was tutored in coordinate geometry by that small, brisk dispeller of darkness, 'Johnny' Hun.

'And now do you see it, Mr Fitzgerald?' Hun would ask, having explained the problem for the third time.

'No, Mr Hun,' Fitzgerald would reply with a gentle finality that cast no aspersions on Hun, himself, or coordinate.

Somehow he passed the make-up exam, but enough conditions remained in his other subjects to keep him ineligible for the Triangle, which, nevertheless, consumed a large part of his autumn. As secretary of that organization he carried much of the responsibility because the president was out for football. Fitzgerald wrote all the lyrics for *The Evil Eye*, book by Edmund Wilson. The previous summer Wilson had sent Fitzgerald the script, saying, 'I am sick of it myself; perhaps you can infuse into it some of the fresh effervescence of youth for which you are so justly celebrated. The spontaneity of the libretto has suffered somewhat from the increasing bitterness and cynicism of my middle-age.'

Though not allowed to act in the show, Fitzgerald had himself photographed as a chorus girl – his dress drooping off one alabaster shoulder, his features melting in a come-hither smile. The photograph was published in *The New York Times* and brought a flurry of fan mail. A girl wrote Fitzgerald that his impersonation of a woman was wonderfully charming and his impersonation of a man must be even more so. Charles Bornhaupt, impresario, offered to find him a booking on Broadway.

That fall Fitzgerald attended the meetings of the Coffee Club, a group of undergraduates that met periodically to discuss literature. John Peale Bishop was the presiding spirit and pretty much held the floor, though Fitzgerald added a welcome note of lightness and enthusiasm. If his background was spottier than Bishop's, he fell in love with the things he read and wanted to foist them on others in a breathless way. Coming into the room like an explorer, he would say, 'I've just finished *Cousin Pons,* one of the great experiences of my life. What a book! What a writer, Balzac!'

Meanwhile he was taking his prose and verse to Alfred Noyes for criticism (Noyes taught at Princeton from 1914 to 1923). Fitzgerald told Noyes he thought it in his power to write either books that would sell or books of permanent value, and wasn't sure which he should do. Noyes said he believed Fitzgerald would get more satisfaction in the long run from writing books of permanent value. Fitzgerald looked dubious, later divulging that he had 'decided to take the cash and let the credit go'. He wasn't overly impressed with Noyes. When John Peale Bishop's mother announced that she had just had tea with Alfred Noyes, the poet, Fitzgerald looked at her blankly and said, 'Oh – is he a poet?'[8]

The fall of junior year Fitzgerald could glance around him and feel he had reached a plateau. A Midwesterner from a small preparatory school, he had made the club he wanted, and his work for the Triangle – and to a lesser extent for *The Tiger* and the *Lit* – had brought him popular acclaim. He looked forward to being the Triangle's next president and even had hopes of being elected to that sacrosanct body, the Senior Council.

He realized, of course, that a story for the *Lit* or a song for the Triangle was nothing compared to a touchdown run in the stadium on Saturday afternoon. Athletics remained the highroad to undergraduate prestige – athletics being primarily football in which the Big Three dominated the national scene. It was the 'set teeth and clenched fist' era of the game when players wore small battered helmets perched on top of their heads, and in some cases no helmets at all. Tactics were mostly confined to orthodox running plays, though there was much talk of 'the open game', meaning passes and deception. While Fitzgerald wasn't the enthusiast he had been when a player himself, his blood still rose at the derring-do of a Hobey Baker or a 'Buzz' Law – he of the indolent loping walk whom Fitzgerald would never forget kicking from behind his own goal with a bandaged head. Fitzgerald liked to romanticize such individuals as Law, endowing them with a background and superlative qualities which others knew perfectly well they didn't possess.

Once more Fitzgerald was rooming by himself, though he had moved from distant Patton to 32 Little near the centre of the campus. Remarkably outgoing and gregarious for someone so sensitive, he was usually with people – teasing them, cajoling them, searching them out. For friends and acquaintances he always had a pleasant greeting, and if he spotted you across the campus, he would come over on the run to impart some latest anecdote, speculation, or rumour.

Among his favourite haunts was the 'Nass', that great leveller and democratizer of pre-Prohibition Princeton. Connie, the Negro bartender, brought pitchers of beer to the initial-carved tables where undergraduates from all the different clubs and activities gathered pell-mell. As a rule Fitzgerald would be talking intently to one person; he was a button-holer who preferred a *tête-à-tête* to general debate. He wanted to get to the bottom of things, and if he stopped by a friend's room to discuss campus politics, he was likely to remain several hours. Following closely with his expressive glance, he really listened while the other person talked, and his answers were whimsical and incisive, with a seriousness back of his fleeting smile. Contemptuous of dullness or hypocrisy, he admired excellence in any field and liked to analyse those who had made their mark. How, he would want to know, had this man become editor of the paper or that man captain of the football team?

He was constantly pumping people, but in an ingratiating way, for he knew, as he afterwards wrote, that 'you can stroke people with words'. He drew you to him by his courtesy and consideration and by the penetration of his pale, friendly eyes which seemed to implant something of himself in you – though the same eyes could flash diabolically when, having made a fool of you, he went into his dry noiseless laugh. Some thought him juvenile. He would come back from the Nass where he had been discussing the fine points of why a certain sophomore belonged in a certain club and then complain because he had to sit up all night doing an assignment. One moment he would dazzle you with a brilliant insight, and the next he would be mooning about his desire to be a football hero like a boy of twelve. He couldn't hold his liquor and liked to appear more drunk than he was. After one beer, he would allow his knees to sag and go into the drunken act that had amused the streetcar passengers in St Paul. He exaggerated his misdemeanours. Thus he might say he had spent the night in the gutter, when actually he had spent it curled up in a quiet corner of the campus.

Some wrote him off as a lightweight. They linked him with the Triangle, and while conceding him a mild sort of cleverness, they expected real talent to be of knottier grain. But Fitzgerald wasn't shallow in the obvious sense; he was too romantic for that. He saw the beauty of life and wanted to celebrate it and make others see it. There was something soaring and idealistic in his nature which constantly reached out for the experiences he hadn't had.

In November he went to the infirmary with malaria, then endemic around Princeton. Charles Arrott, in the class behind him, shared his sickroom and later recalled their conversation which went on desultorily over five or six days. When Fitzgerald began by talking about football, Arrott, a scrub on the varsity, thought it was a gesture to put him at ease. He soon realized, however, that Fitzgerald actually wanted to talk football for as long as Arrott would cooperate. Arrott had been reading Tolstoy's essays, and when he quoted the Russian as saying that the purpose of a work of art was to convey a moral, Fitzgerald disagreed violently. If

71

such were the case, he argued, then the greatest works of art would be nothing but 'damn good sermons'. He thought the artist's purpose should be to express emotions he had lived through in some palatable disguise.

Fitzgerald told Arrott that the Dean's office was hounding him about his grades. When Arrott said it took only a little time each day to do passing work, Fitzgerald agreed but said he couldn't find the time. It seemed likely he would flunk out at midyears, and using his sickness as a pretext he withdrew from college in December, intending to come back the second term and make up the courses he had missed.

When he went to Princeton in February, however, he was told he would have to repeat junior year. Running into Arrott on the campus, he said, 'Charlie, they've just flunked the brightest man in 1917 back into your class.' Fitzgerald managed to extract a statement from Dean McClenahan to the effect that 'Mr F. Scott Fitzgerald withdrew from Princeton voluntarily on January third, nineteen hundred and sixteen, because of ill health and he was fully at liberty, at that time, to go on with his class, if his health had permitted'.

The Dean's covering note said, 'This is for your sensitive feelings. I hope you will find it soothing.'

Fitzgerald went home to await the autumn, home being 593 Summit Avenue to which his family had moved in September 1914. Summit was St Paul's most elegant street, but the Fitzgeralds were living at the less elegant end in a three-storey row house with a brownstone front. It was narrow, deep, and dark, the more so because of Mollie's fondness for keeping the blinds drawn. Scott, as if forced upwards for light and air, occupied the top floor, his bedroom opening on a balcony that overlooked the street.

The years at Newman and Princeton had made him increasingly critical of his mother whose gaucheries were legendary in St Paul. For example, a gentleman of her acquaintance was ill, and there had been a conspiracy to keep the seriousness of it from his wife. One day Mollie and the wife were riding on the streetcar. When the wife asked Mollie what she was thinking, she replied, 'I'm trying to decide how you'll look in mourning.' Another time Mollie lent a book to a friend and later sent a note asking that the book be returned. The friend, under the impression that she had already sent it back, searched her house from top to bottom. She was about to notify Mollie that the book was lost when she turned over Mollie's note and saw on the back of it, 'I've just found the book, but since the messenger is here, I am sending this along anyway to wish you well.'

Up till now Fitzgerald hadn't had much to do with his sister Annabel, who was five years younger than he. She was quiet and pretty, and he was proud of her and anxious that she make the most of her possibilities. To this end he wrote her lengthy instructions from which these excerpts are taken:

You are as you know, not a good conversationalist and you might very naturally ask 'What do boys like to talk about?' Boys like to talk about themselves – much more than girls. Here are some leading questions for a girl to use. ... (a) You dance so much better than you did last year. (b) How about giving me that sporty necktie when you're thru with it? (c) You've got the longest eyelashes! (This will embarrass him, but he likes it.) (d) I hear you've got a 'line'! (e) Well who's your latest crush? *Avoid* (a) When do you go back to school? (b) How long have you been home? (c) It's warm or the the orchestra's good or the floor's good ...

As you get a little older you'll find that boys like to talk about such things as smoking and drinking. Always be very liberal – boys hate a pry – tell them you don't object to a girl smoking but don't like cigarettes yourself. Tell them you smoke only cigars – Kid them! ... Never try to give a boy the affect that you're popular – Ginevra always starts by saying she's a poor unpopular woman without any beaux. Always pay close attention to the man. Look at him in his eyes if possible. Never effect boredom. Its terribly hard to do it gracefully. Learn to be worldly. Remember in all society nine out of ten girl's marry for money and nine men out of ten are fools ...

Expression, that is facial expression, is one of your weakest points. A girl of your good looks and at your age ought to have almost perfect control of her face. It ought to be almost like a mask. . . . (a) A good smile and one that could be assumed at will, is an absolute necesity. You smile on one side which is *absolutely wrong*. Get before a mirror and practice a smile and get a good one, a 'radiant smile' ought to be in the facial vocabulary of every girl. Practice it – on girls, on the family. Practice doing it when you don't feel happy and when you're bored. When you're embarrassed, when you're at a disadvantage. That's when you'll have to use it in society and when you've practiced a thing in calm, then only are you sure of it as a good weapon in tight places. (b) A laugh isn't as important but it's well to have a good one on ice. Your natural one is very good, but your artificial one is bum. Next time you laugh naturally remember it and practice so you can do it any time you want. *Practice anywhere*. (c) A pathetic appealing look is one every girl ought to have. Sandra and Ginevra are specialists at this: so is Ardita, its best done by opening the eyes wide and drooping the mouth open a little, looking inward (hanging the head a little) directly into the eyes of the man you're talking to. Ginevra and Sandra use this when getting off their 'I'm so unpopular' speeches and indeed they use it about half the time. Practice this. (d) Don't bite or twist your lips – it's sure death for any expression. (e) The two expressions *you* have control over now are no good. One is the side smile and the other is the thoughtful look with the eyes half closed. I'm telling you this because mother and I have absolutely no control over our facial expressions and we miss it. Mother's worse than I am – you know how people take advantage of whatever mood her face is in and kid the life out of her. Well you're young enough to get over it – tho you're worse than I am now . . .

With such splendid eyebrows as yours you should brush them or wet them and train them every morning and night as I advised you to do long ago. They oughtn't to have a hair out of place. . . . I noticed last Saturday that your gestures are awkward and so unnatural as to seem affected. Notice the way graceful girls hold their hands and feet. How they stoop, wave, run and then try because you can't practice these things when men are around. It's too late then. They ought to be incentive then . . .

You see if you get anywhere and feel you look alright then there's one worry over and one bolt shot for self-confidence – and the person you're with, man, boy, woman, whether it's Aunt

74

Millie or Jack Allen or myself likes to feel that the person they're sponsoring is at least externally a credit.

Fitzgerald had continued to lose ground with Ginevra. In the fall he had taken her to a football game and after spending the evening with her had ended up 'with a pronounced case of melancholy'. In St Paul he played the field, his situation improved by his parents' acquisition of a second-hand Chalmers. It was no Stutz Bearcat, but if he were willing to endure its 'unaristocratic groanings and vibrations', he could 'torture it up to fifty miles an hour'. To say he knew how to drive was only a manner of speaking. When he wasn't woolgathering he was likely to be crouching at the wheel in imitation of Barney Oldfield, the first great dirt-track auto racer. A friend driving home with him from a dance remembered kicking the car out of gear periodically to hold Fitzgerald to a reasonable speed.

A dancing craze, symbolized by Vernon and Irene Castle, was sweeping the country, and Fitzgerald had begun to realize that enthusiasm was no substitute for expertise. He spent hours before the mirror practising the Maxixe, the Turkey Trot, and the Aeroplane Glide. It wasn't that he cared about dancing *per se*, but he wanted to be admired as he swept around the floor with the prettiest girl. When a road company visited St Paul, he sent the leading lady a note, asking if he might see her after the show. She accepted, and he and a friend took her and another actress dancing. Next day the four of them lunched at the University Club, creating a good deal of talk though it was all perfectly innocent.

At Princeton Fitzgerald knew boys who picked up girls at Bustanoby's and spent the night with them, but he would have none of it, for he was romantic and uncynical in his view of the opposite sex. One evening at White Bear Lake 'while the moon beat out golden scales on the water', he had overheard an ex-Princeton athlete propose to the debutante of the year, and he was so intoxicated that he 'was all for becoming engaged to almost any one immediately'. Mere carnality, however, had less appeal for him. He was clean-

75

spoken, and referring to Frank Harris's pornographic memoirs, he told a woman in later years, 'It's disgusting. It's the kind of filth your sex is often subjected to, the kind of lavatory conversation men indulge in. It bores me – you don't know how disgusting men can be!' There was no priggishness in it, only honest revulsion, and he added, 'Priests on the subject of sex I can't stand.'[9]

His aversion to promiscuity comes through in *This Side of Paradise*, in the scene where Amory and a friend visit the apartment of two girls they have picked up in a night club. 'There was a minute while temptation crept over [Amory] like a warm wind, and his imagination turned to fire, and he took the glass from Phoebe's hand.' Then he saw a man sitting on a sofa across the room, the same man who had been watching them in the night club earlier in the evening. The man's face had

a sort of virile pallor [as of someone] who'd worked in a mine or done night shifts in a damp climate. . . . His mouth was the kind that is called frank, and he had steady gray eyes that moved slowly from one to the other of their group, with just the shade of a questioning expresion. Amory noticed his hands; they weren't fine at all, but they had versatility and a tenuous strength . . . they were nervous hands that sat lightly along the cushions and moved constantly in little jerky openings and closings. Then, suddenly, Amory perceived the feet, and with a rush of blood to his head he realized he was afraid. The feet were all wrong . . .

Recognizing the Devil, Amory bolts the apartment.

At an age when the male sex drive is most powerful and disrupting, some shy fastidiousness was holding Fitzgerald back, and as he later described it, despair more than lust now drove him into a woman's arms. It had been 'a year of terrible disappointments & the end of all college dreams', and 'it seemed on one March afternoon that I had lost every single thing I wanted – and that night was the first time I hunted down the spectre of womanhood that, for a little while, makes everything else seem unimportant'. Out of the same despair he wrote a story about his failure at Princeton which he looked back on as his first mature writing, for in 'The Spire and the Gargoyle', published by the *Nassau Lit* the following winter, the themes and cadences of *This Side of Paradise* begin to emerge.

Returning to Princeton in the fall, he roomed with Paul Dickey who wrote music for the Triangle. Not only was Fitzgerald ineligible for the third successive year, but by dropping out of college he had lost the Triangle presidency and wasn't even an officer. Nevertheless he wrote all the lyrics for *Safety First*, as no one could touch him in this department.

Repeating the courses he had begun the year before, he felt he knew the material and didn't need to exert himself. An English major, he was irritated by the academic approach to literature and the Edwardian flavour of the Princeton English Department. He liked John Duncan Spaeth, who divided his time between coaching the crew and lecturing on the Romantic Poets, but he characterized his other instructors as 'mildly poetic gentlemen [who] resented any warmth of discussion and called the prominent men of the class by their first names'. In the back of his copy of Sidney's *Defence of Poesie* he wrote:

Gee this man — is terrible. I sit here bored to death and hear him pick English poetry to pieces. Small man, small mind. Snotty, disagreeable. Damn him. 'Neat' is his favourite word. Imagine Shakespeare being neat. Yesterday I counted and found that he used the expression 'Isn't that so' fifty-four times. Oh what a disagreeable silly ass he is. He's going to get married. God help his wife. Poor girl. She's in for a bad time.

Later Fitzgerald said it was John Peale Bishop who 'made me see, in the course of a couple of months, the difference between poetry and non-poetry. After that, one of my first discoveries was that some of the professors who were teaching poetry really hated it and didn't know what it was about.'

A notable exception to these strictures was Christian Gauss, then a professor of Romance languages and later

Dean of the College. Son of a German immigrant, Gauss had worked his way through the University of Michigan in three years and had come to Princeton in 1905 as one of Woodrow Wilson's 'fifty preceptor guys'. A benign little man, with a few strands of blond hair brushed across a balding forehead, Gauss had an underlying seriousness and bite; one felt it in the mild-fierce glint of his eyes behind pince-nez. In preceptorial one quickly discovered that he had been a reporter in Paris at the turn of the century, that he had met Oscar Wilde and had somehow been connected with the Dreyfus Case. His talk ranged far beyond the daily assignment and students found themselves lingering after the hour to continue the debate.

Gauss was Socratic. He suggested trains of thought the student could follow up on his own, calling it his business 'to start hares, not to catch them'. Full of dry quotations, he would tell a late arrival, 'You are welcome to Elsinore'; or, when a student was making a mess of it, he might interpose, 'Dear friend, for Jesus' sake forbear' – adding under his breath, 'Let him not blast in ignorance.' Gauss really liked undergraduates. By believing in them he called forth the best they had to give, and later, as Dean, he won a reputation for salvaging the wayward student and the maverick. He could be stern, yet he was almost sentimental about troublesome boys as if he thought they had more potential than the obedient ones. This may have been a factor in his liking Fitzgerald, who reciprocated the esteem. Gauss became Fitzgerald's hero in American education and one of the beacons by which he steered his erratic course.

The romance with Ginevra was drawing to a close. The previous summer, when Fitzgerald had been with her at a house party in Lake Forest, someone had remarked that 'poor boys shouldn't think of marrying rich girls'. In November Ginevra accepted his invitation to the Princeton–Yale game, but immediately afterwards she said good-bye to him at the station and walked around the corner to meet another boy. She stopped writing, and in January Fitzgerald gave up the chase.

Ginevra had been the princess for whom he sought fame and honours at Princeton in the spirit of a knight errant. She belonged to the moneyed aristocracy of Chicago and as such was beyond his grasp. To her he seemed a weak reed to lean upon, and the realization that he was not what she had in mind hurt him profoundly and coloured his whole outlook. Who can say how much of his longing for Ginevra went into Gatsby's timeless and untouchable love for Daisy Fay?

But Fitzgerald, the ironist, saw another side to it. What if he had won Ginevra? He now wrote a story for the *Nassau Lit*, 'The Pierian Spring and the Last Straw', in which an author wins his lost love and the fulfillment destroys his desire to write. He spends the rest of his days playing mediocre golf and being comfortably bored.

'Slowly and inevitably, yet with a sudden surge at the last, while Amory talked and dreamed, war rolled up the beach and washed the sands where Princeton played. Every night the gymnasium echoed as platoon after platoon swept over the floor and shuffled out the basketball markings.' It was the spring of America's entry into the conflict. Fitzgerald began to have thoughts of being in it himself, though for the moment he was engrossed in a battle on the campus.

Periodically there had been talk of abolishing the clubs, which were not only wasteful but snobbish in their exclusion of some fifteen per cent of each class. When Woodrow Wilson had been President of Princeton, he had tried to do away with them, and now they were under attack by the students themselves. Three sophomore leaders had refused to join. With support from the *Daily Princetonian* they led a crusade which reduced the usual number of sophomores entering the clubs by twenty-five per cent. The revolt was intelligently handled and might have wrecked the system, had not the war come along to disrupt college life.

Fitzgerald's position was that of a fascinated yet detached observer. Viewing the anti-club movement as drama and entertainment, he was chief architect of an issue of *The Tiger* which burlesqued the clubs and the reformers alike. He considered the clubs part of the established order and was bent on enjoying them, the more so because he had made a good one. At the same time he admired the reformers who were sacrificing social success to ideals of brotherhood and equality gleaned from Whitman, Tolstoy, and Thoreau. It was a time for idealism, and one of the sophomore ringleaders, Henry Strater, became the model for Burne Holiday, the rebel and pacifist in *This Side of Paradise*.

Fitzgerald would look back on this chaotic year as the foundation of his literary life. He had come to Princeton seeking a purchase for his talents and had tapped one avenue of advance after another, beginning with *The Tiger* and the Triangle. By degrees his centre of gravity had shifted towards the *Lit*, for he had made up his mind to be a great writer, if not in a class with Shakespeare then in the class just below – with Keats, say, or Marlowe. Even friends and well-wishers found his assurance somewhat irritating.

He got a foretaste of the life he anticipated when he visited Edmund Wilson, now a cub reporter in New York. Catching sight of Wilson from his taxi before they met, Fitzgerald formed a new impression of him.

I saw him walking briskly through the crowd wearing a tan raincoat over his inevitable brown get-up; I noted with a shock that he was carrying a light cane. . . . He was no longer the shy little scholar of Holder Court – he walked with confidence, wrapped in his thoughts and looking straight ahead, and it was obvious that his new background was entirely sufficient to him. I knew that he had an apartment where he lived with three other men, released now from all undergraduate taboos, but there was something else that was nourishing him and I got my first impression of that new thing – the Metropolitan Spirit . . .

That night, in Bunny's apartment, life was mellow and safe, a finer distillation of all that I had come to live at Princeton. The gentle playing of the oboe mingled with the city noises from the street outside, which penetrated into the room with difficulty through great barricades of books.

Such delights were far in the future. For the moment Fitzgerald assuaged his fevers by writing for the *Lit*. 'My head ringing with the metres of Swinburne and the matters of Rupert Brooke,' he remembered, 'I spent the spring doing sonnets, ballads and roundels into the small hours. I had read somewhere that every great poet had written great poetry before he was twenty-one. I had only a year and, besides, war was impending. I must publish a book of startling verse before I was engulfed.'

Poetry was his passion, yet his masterpiece, it seemed to him, was a story later reprinted in *Smart Set* with only minor changes – a story which in a way foreshadowed his whole career. 'Tarquin of Cheepside' – the reviewer in the *Princetonian* was sure he might be forgiven for spelling it 'Cheapside' – begins with a chase:[10]

Running footsteps. – Light, soft-soled shoes, made of queer leathery cloth brought from Ceylon, setting the pace; thick flowing boots, two pairs, dark blue and gilt, reflecting the moonlight in blunt gleams and flashes, following, a hundred yards behind. Soft Shoes cleaves the moonlight for a haggard second, then darts into a blind labyrinth of alleys and becomes merely an unsteady scuffling in the darkness ahead. In go Flowing Boots with swords lurching and with clumsy stumbling, cursing the black lanes of London.

The scene shifts to the lodgings of Peter Caxter, a friend of the pursued, who bursts in asking for asylum. Peter poles open a trap door in the ceiling, the friend jumps up with the agility of a tumbler, struggles for a moment on the edge of the aperture, and hoists himself into the attic. Moments later the pursuers arrive. As they search the rooms they tell Peter that a lady has been raped, and when they have gone, the friend comes down and asks for pen and paper. Peter rebukes him for his crime but the friend says, 'Peter, are you trying to interfere – what right have you? I am responsible only to myself for what I do.' Peter goes to sleep, and hours later the friend wakes him to show what he has written – a poem entitled *The Rape of Lucrece*. The friend is young William Shakespeare.

81

From the outset, Fitzgerald adhered to the Renaissance and Romantic conception of the writer as a man of action who experiences his material at first hand – not from lack of imagination, but so he can write about it more intensely. It is a perilous doctrine, even for the strong, and Fitzgerald would not always be as fortunate as the Shakespeare of his yarn.

The spring flowed by with long evenings on the club verandah while the gramophone played 'Poor Butterfly', a wistful ditty that was one of Fitzgerald's favourites. It seemed like the springs of other years except for the drilling every afternoon, but there was also a sense of finality. One evening Bishop and Fitzgerald roamed the campus, poetizing and philosophizing as 'a last burst of singing flooded up Blair Arch – broken voices for some long parting'. There used to be a song in the air at Princeton that has vanished since.

Though Fitzgerald would be back in the autumn to begin his senior year, he entered into the emotions of the class now graduating – *his* class – and tried to sum them up in a poem which he called 'Princeton – the Last Day'.

> The last light wanes and drifts across the land,
> The low, long land, the sunny land of spires.
> The ghosts of evening tune again their lyres
> And wander singing, in a plaintive band
> Down the long corridors of trees. Pale fires
> Echo the night from tower top to tower.
> Oh sleep that dreams and dream that never tires,
> Press from the petals of the lotus-flower
> Something of this to keep, the essence of an hour!
>
> No more to wait the twilight of the moon
> In this sequestrated vale of star and spire;
> For one, eternal morning of desire
> Passes to time and earthy afternoon.
> Here, Heraclitus, did you build your fire
> And changing stuffs your prophecy far hurled

Down the dead years; this midnight I aspire
To see, mirrored among the embers, curled
In flame, the splendor and the sadness of the world.

[6]

'HE was not even a Catholic, yet that was the only ghost of a code that he had,' says Fitzgerald of the hero in *This Side of Paradise*.

Religion is a predisposition quite separate from the intellect, which may reinforce or undermine it, and Fitzgerald had that sense of the infinite, of life's mystery which we associate with the religious temper. He was capable of awe. His sister remembered him as a devout boy who lost his influences at Princeton, where he came under such pagan influences as Wilde, Swinburne, Wells, and the early Huysmans. John Peale Bishop and Edmund Wilson had a similar effect on him; Wilson, especially, was a belligerent sceptic, as if on guard against the Protestant divines in his ancestry.[11]

With sights set on world acclaim, Fitzgerald had been drifting from the Church though not without a struggle. For a while he would go religiously to mass and make a point of not eating meat on Friday, then sink back into hedonism. The make-weight on the side of his religion was Father Fay whom he had been seeing off and on – at Princeton, at Newman where Fay was now headmaster, at Deal Beach where Fay's mother had a home. Fay yearned and brooded over his disciple, who reminded him in certain ways of his own youth. 'There are deep things in us,' Fay wrote Fitzgerald, 'and you know what they are as well as I do. We have great faith, and we have a terrible honesty at the bottom of us, that all our sophistry cannot destroy, and a kind of childlike simplicity that is the only thing that saves us from being downright wicked.'

Fay told Shane Leslie, a young Irish author visiting this country, that Fitzgerald thought it very clever and literary to leave the Church, but that he was rebelling against his upbringing and they must do their best to keep him in. Leslie had influence with Fitzgerald; he was handsome and well connected and had been at Cambridge with Rupert Brooke. In Fitzgerald's presence he and Fay would discuss the grandeurs of Catholicism, its saints, statesmen, and intellectuals, its Augustines, Richelieus, and Newmans. Fitzgerald drank it all in, later remarking that Fay and Leslie made the Church seem 'a dazzling, golden thing, dispelling its oppressive mugginess and giving the succession of days upon grey days, passing under its plaintive ritual, the romantic glamour of an adolescent dream'.

Fay had been chosen to head a Red Cross mission to Russia where, as a trusted friend of Cardinal Gibbons, he saw himself playing a rôle in the restoration of Catholic unity, now that the Revolution had cut the Greek Orthodox Church from its Tsarist moorings. He wanted Fitzgerald to accompany him as an aide, with the rank of Red Cross Lieutenant. 'Whether you look at it from the spiritual or temporal point of view,' wrote Fay, 'it is an immense opportunity and will be a help to you all the rest of your life.'

Fitzgerald was persuaded – by the adventure and secrecy of it, if not by the ideals involved. While waiting for the trip to materialize, he spent July at the home of John Peale Bishop in Charles Town, West Virginia, where he wrote 'a terrific lot of poetry mostly under the Masefield-Brooke influence'. (One of the poems, which *Poet Lore* bought but never published, was his first sale.) He went to Confession and talked a great deal of becoming a priest. Mrs Bishop feared he might convert her son, but Bishop laughed it off, saying that so weak a character as Fitzgerald would never convert anyone.

In September the Russian venture fell through because of the Bolshevik triumph, and Fitzgerald went back to Princeton to begin his senior year though his one idea was to get into uniform. During the summer he had taken exams for a provisional appointment to Second Lieutenant in the regular army, which meant he was likely to see combat sooner than if he were in the reserves. He wrote Edmund Wilson to find out 'what effect the war at close quarters has on a person of your temperament'. Wilson replied that so far as he had got no nearer the front than the Detroit State Fairgrounds, 'where I am associated in the errand of mercy [Wilson was in the Hospital Corps] with the sorriest company of yokels that ever qualified as skilful plumbers, or, an even less considerable eminence, received A.B. degrees from the University of Michigan'.

Awaiting his commission, Fitzgerald roomed in Campbell Hall with John Biggs – later a distinguished judge – who as an undergraduate seemed to share Fitzgerald's view that writing for the Triangle, *The Tiger*, and the *Lit* was of more consequence than one's academic work. When *The Tiger* was late to press, Biggs and Fitzgerald were capable of turning out an entire number between darkness and dawn. As a room mate, Fitzgerald had drawbacks. If Biggs's bed were made and the sheets looked cleaner than his own, Fitzgerald would climb in and go to sleep. He likewise availed himself of Biggs's books and clothes, though Biggs never saw any evidence that Fitzgerald was financially pressed.

Fitzgerald's commission came through the end of October, and in November he reported to Fort Leavenworth, Kansas, for three months' officers' training. He felt that his youth – and for that matter, the youth of his whole generation – was now officially over. 'If we ever get back [from the war],' he wrote his Cousin Ceci, 'and I don't particularly care, we'll be rather aged – in the worst way. After all life hasn't much to offer except youth and I suppose for older people the love of youth in others.'

In a letter to his mother he laid aside such world-weary posturing and told her bluntly,

about the army please let's not have either tragedy or Heroics because they are equally distastful to me. I went into this perfectly cold bloodedly and don't sympathize with the

'Give my son to country ect

ect

ect

or

'Hero stuff'

86

because *I just went* and purely for *social reasons*. If you want to pray, pray for my soul and not that I wont get killed – the last doesn't seem to matter particularly and if you are a good Catholic the first ought to.

To a profound pessimist about life, being in danger is not depressing. I have never been more cheerful. Please be nice and respect my wishes.

After Princeton, an army post on the plains of Kansas was like going to prison. The winter was exceptionally severe, and the trainees slept fifteen to a room with their belongings in trunks at the foot of their beds. The captain in charge of Fitzgerald's platoon was a blue-eyed West Pointer with a crumpled grin named Ike Eisenhower.

While envisioning himself a hero in the field, Fitzgerald could not conceal his boredom with the preliminary steps. He wrote or slept through lectures on 'Trench Behaviour', 'Sniping and Being Sniped', and 'The Lewis Gun'. In close-order drill he was the only man in his squad of eight who wasn't made acting corporal for a week (someone had to be corporal twice rather than entrust the squad to the vagaries of Fitzgerald). On a hike he put a piece of stove pipe in his knapsack to lighten it while making it appear he was carrying the prescribed load. He was apprehended and penalized, but he did not reform. In subtle ways he continued to ridicule the process of becoming an officer, and though he found a few congenial spirits among the graduates of Eastern colleges, most of his fellows looked down on him as soft, spoiled, and immature.

The truth was that he resented the army for taking up his time when he wanted to get on with the real business of becoming an author. Weekends, there were dances in Kansas City, but Fitzgerald spent his free hours in a corner of the officers' club at Fort Leavenworth where, amid smoke, conversation, and rattling newspapers he was turning out a novel. In October he had showed a manuscript to Father Fay, who declared it 'first-rate stuff'. He showed it to Gauss also, hoping the professor would recommend it to his publisher, but Gauss felt it wasn't good enough, even when Fitzgerald brought it back with every paragraph changed. Now, at Leavenworth, he was redrafting and expanding the whole thing, inspired by the belief that he was soon going off to be killed. On the successive weekends of three months he wrote a hundred and twenty thousand words, sending each chapter to a typist in Princeton as he completed it. Meanwhile he lived in the 'smeary pencil pages. The drills, marches and Small Problems for Infantry were a shadowy dream. My whole heart was concentrated upon my book.'

He had been corresponding with John Peale Bishop, an infantry officer likewise stifled by camp routine. 'Oh Scott,' wrote Bishop,

> I am hungry, hungry for beauty, for poetry, for talk, for kindly mirth, for subtle wit, for quiet hours and peace, for nights and late risings, for tweed knickerbockers, and *café au lait*, for all things I have not, for the sight of you and T. M. and Alex and Bunny, for a mistress, for love, for religion, for shirred eggs, for my copy of [Rupert Brooke], for all things severally and collected which the military profession has rudely banished from life.

Bishop had recently published a book of verse, and Fitzgerald sent him instalments of the novel, which Bishop found lacking in particularity. 'Stephen does the things every boy does,' he said. 'Well and good, I suppose you want the universal appeal. But the way to get it is to have the usual thing done in an individual way.' Bishop also complained that the book wasn't subjective enough. 'That's where the immense superiority of Youth's Encounter [by Compton Mackenzie] comes in. You give the *acts* of the boy. Mackenzie the *mind* and *soul,* moving through the action.' In subsequent drafts Fitzgerald would take these criticisms to heart.

In March he sent the completed manuscript of *The Romantic Egotist* to Shane Leslie, who proofread it and submitted it to Scribners, asking them to keep it no matter what they thought of it, for Leslie wanted Fitzgerald to go overseas feeling that he was at least a potential Rupert Brooke.

'You may depart in peace,' wrote Leslie, 'and possibly find yourself part of the Autumn reading banned by the YMCA – for use among troops.'

But Fitzgerald didn't go overseas. On 15 March he joined the Forty-fifth Infantry Regiment at Camp Taylor near Louisville, Kentucky. He was put in command of a company, and one day when the regiment was marching back from town through a blizzard, the general chanced by on horse-back. Fitzgerald had his arm up against the snow, and the general, tapping him on the shoulder, asked who he was. Fitzgerald gave his name without taking his arm down. Un-aware of the august presence, he failed to salute and call his company to attention. When they got back to camp, there was an order from the general for the whole regiment to march to town again.

In mid-April the Forty-fifth Infantry moved to Camp Gordon, Georgia, and two months later to Camp Sheridan, Alabama, where Fitzgerald was transferred to the Sixty-seventh, then forming from a nucleus of the Forty-fifth. The two regiments were brigaded as part of the newly-organized Ninth Division and brought up to combat strength preparatory to going overseas. Fitzgerald, now a first lieutenant, was assigned to a headquarters company, which entitled him to wear boots and spurs. He blossomed out in a pair of yellowish boots, the only ones in the division, which he persisted in wearing despite constant ribbing.

Camp Sheridan was near Montgomery, where Jefferson Davis had been inaugurated and where the first Confederate banner had floated from the capitol dome. A town of about 40,000, it was dominated by a clique of Confederate sons and daughters proud of their rural backwardness. Each morning Negro drovers herded cattle down the main residential street, and in September when the cotton had been baled, a procession of mule-drawn drays took it through the town to the warehouse. Negro women in calico dresses and bright bandanas sat on the bales plucking banjos or laughing with the children, while the men in straw hats and overalls roused their dust-caked beasts with a crack of the whip or a loud 'Geet-opp!'

Among the townspeople there lingered resentment against the Yankees, though a final accord between North and South was being reached at the Country Club dances, to which the officers of Camp Sheridan had a standing invitation. Fitzgerald was there every Saturday night, a trim figure in his Brooks Brothers uniform with the high, snug collars of the period. There was a dash about him, a greyhound leanness and elegance. His pallor accentuated the cameo incisiveness of his profile, and full face his long-lashed, dreamy eyes conquered with their fragile beauty of expression. You sensed his conceit of ambition, yet a kind of modesty made him responsive to and admiring of the qualities of others. Back of it all was the play of his catchy mind, forever weaving stories from the life around him. If such and such a person found himself in these unique circumstances, what would happen? Fitzgerald would take you aside and tell you all about it.

With his novel off his hands he succumbed to a vague restlessness, which may have had something to do with Ginevra King's impending marriage. He wrote his cousin,

Do you know, Sally, I believe that for the first time in my life I'm rather loansome down here – not lonesome for family and friends or anyone in particular but lonesome for the old atmospheres – a feverish crowd at Princeton sitting up till three discussing pragmatism or the immortality of the soul – for the glitter of New York with a tea dance at the Plaza or lunch at Sherries – for the quiet respectable boredom of St Paul.

Father Fay – newly become a Monsignor and looking, he said, like a Turner sunset in his full regalia – caught Fitzgerald's mood and tried to steady him. 'The fear of God,' wrote Fay, 'is your greatest protection – as it is mine, nor could you rid yourself of it if you would – it will all ways be there. As to women – It is not a convention that holds you back as you think, but an instinct that if you begin you will run amuck.' Fitzgerald made a grave mistake, said Fay, to believe he could be a romantic without religion. 'The secret of our success is the mystical element in us. Something flows into us that enlarges our personalities and when that flows out of us our personalities shrink. I should call your last two letters rather shrivelled.'

Fay thought Fitzgerald's faith would eventually clarify, but Fitzgerald wasn't so sure. He felt rather pagan at the moment. Religion seemed to have so little connexion with life.

The dancing class was giving its annual carnival at the Grand Theatre in Montgomery. Three little girls in white Pierrot costumes, their pointed hats made tall and stiff with buckram, came out of the wings skipping rope. One of them skipped across the stage without a *faux pas*. A second knocked her hat over her eyes and fled weeping into the arms of her mother. The third, whose name was Zelda Sayre, knocked her hat completely off, got her feet caught in the rope, fell down, and proceeded to get worse entangled. But she seemed to be enjoying herself. She made it appear that her predicament had been rehearsed, and she brought the house down.

Zelda – so-named for a gypsy queen who had turned up in her mother's reading – came from distinguished forebears on both sides. Her father's uncle, John Tyler Morgan, had been a general in the Civil War and afterwards one of Alabama's most illustrious senators, while her father, Anthony Dickinson Sayre, was a judge on the Alabama Supreme Court. A Jeffersonian democrat and an idealist, this strait-laced old Roman and pillar of his profession had married Minnie Machen, daughter of a Kentucky senator. In Montgomery the Sayres were respected burghers who made no effort in society. Mrs Sayre was musical and had once aspired to the opera, but now she devoted herself to her family and her garden and wrote poems for the local newspaper, while the judge lived in the law and read history for amusement.[12]

Zelda was the baby in a family of five children. As with Fitzgerald, her parents seemed almost old enough to be her grandparents. She inherited her father's brilliance and her mother's generosity, but in other respects she was completely unlike her staid, conservative parents who did not know what to make of their beautiful duck egg. A child of nature, her spirit had something in common with the Greek poetic idea of the demigod or super-human, who is freed from that terror of environment which makes for conformity. Her mother's adored, she stood up to the judge from her earliest years. He would tell her to do something and she would say, 'Look here, "old Dick" [her mother's name for him], I'm not going to do that' – and get away with it. As a bored little girl of ten or eleven, she had telephoned the fire department to say a child was stranded on the Sayres' roof. Then she climbed the roof and kicked away the ladder, so as not to disappoint the firemen when they came.

If people criticized her, they were also amused, and everyone agreed she was 'smart and keen as a brier'. During her senior year at Lanier High she played the part of England in a pageant of the Allied Nations, enacted before the Montgomery Rotary Club. Midway in her speech she was supposed to say, 'Interrupted in these benevolent pursuits, for three years I have been engaged in bloody warfare,' but after 'interrupted' her memory failed. She repeated the word several times and then with a dazzling smile said, 'Gentlemen, I have been permanently interrupted,' and left the hall amid thunderous applause.

Zelda was brave as any boy. Playing foxes and hounds, she jumped over fences with the best of them, while at the gravel pit she dove off the crane which few dared even to climb, ducking the other swimmers as she rose. On picnics, rather than ride in a car with the girls, she got a boy to take her on his motorcycle. Sitting on a pillow (rear seats had not been invented), she would urge him to go faster, and if they hit a bump which sent them sprawling, her enthusiasm was no less. Her admirers were constantly put to the test; the only justification for women, she used to say, was the need for a disturbing element among men.

The first thing one noticed about her looks was the exquisite colouring. Her skin was pink and white and flawless, and her honey-gold hair, very thick and live, grew beautifully around her face. If her sharp nose was perhaps a little beaky, her thin mouth was sensual and alluring, and her deep blue eyes challenged and taunted, the modelling of chin and cheek and brow giving the whole a fragile force.

Clothes meant nothing to Zelda. Supple and boyish, she looked her best in a drenched bathing suit with her hair streaming down. But she also looked well in the ragged middy blouses she wore to school, not to mention the evening dresses her mother made for her. Decked in fluffy organdy beneath a wide-brimmed hat with streamers, Zelda was the very incarnation of a Southern belle. She had a tendency to slouch and sometimes her slip would be showing or a strap hanging down, but such minor defects were obliterated by her golden softness, her lilting grace, the sparkling devilry in her eye. Zelda had a sweet side too, she was gracious and feminine, though underneath was that touch of the hoyden which accents a woman's character, giving it piquancy and strength.

Her flaw was lack of discipline. She wanted to romp, and in her eagerness to sample life she was like a bucking bronco or a heap of bees. Lazy, provincial Montgomery was a pillow over her face, and going to sleep at night in her ward-like room with the white bedspread and curtains, she dreamed of being important, of being noticed, though which of her many talents would make her noticeable she had not ascertained.

During her last year at school she began going out with the soldiers from Camp Sheridan. She smoked when it was still taboo for women, and she was not above taking a swig of corn liquor when the men circulated the bottle. She had no prejudice against necking, or 'boodling', as it was known in the local patois, but sitting in a car with an amorous male was hardly her idea of the way to spend an evening, and men who bored her quickly found it out. Though her parents let her do pretty much as she pleased, occasionally the judge would complain. Meeting her at the door one evening, he said, 'What do you mean by coming home this hour of night, you hussy!'; to which Zelda replied, 'Isn't that what hussies do?' He forbade her to go to the next party, but she was there.

Zelda met Scott Fitzgerald at a Country Club dance in July 1918, a few weeks before her eighteenth birthday. The moment his eye rested on her he went up and introduced himself. There was something enchanted, as if predestined, about the coming together of this pair, whose deep similarity only began with their fresh, scrubbed beauty. People remarked that they looked enough alike to be brother and sister, but how much more they resembled each other beneath the skin! For the first time Fitzgerald had found a girl whose uninhibited love of life rivalled his own and whose daring, originality, and repartee would never bore him. With Ginevra, part of the attraction had been the society she came from; with Zelda, it was she alone who made an overwhelming appeal to his imagination. She pleased him in all the surface ways, but she also had depths he fell in love with, without understanding why.

In his free time Fitzgerald was forever going to and from the Sayres' rented house in not the best section of town, for the judge's salary was a mere $6,000 and he was used to helping relatives. At the start, he and Mrs Sayres were favourably impressed by the handsome, polite young officer, who monopolized the porch swing with Zelda and took her for walks down the sandy, rustling roads fragrant with honeysuckle. He often read her things he was working on and profited from her advice. He told her repeatedly that he would be famous. Remembering him at this time, Zelda wrote in after years, 'There seemed to be some heavenly support beneath his shoulder blades that lifted his feet from the ground in ecstatic suspension, as if he secretly enjoyed the ability to fly but was walking as a compromise to convention.'

Meanwhile his military career had been prospering less than his romantic one. The headquarters company he commanded was made up of tough immigrants from metropolitan New York, whom it was necessary to dominate.

Fitzgerald acquired a notorious strut. A stickler for enunciation, he barked out the orders to his marching men with a ginger that amused some and irritated others. He had a conscientious objector under him and did not realize that he was being gulled when another officer said, 'Fitz, if I had that S.O.B. in my outfit I'd get my .45 and take him out alone and make him drill.' Fitzgerald did precisely that, unaware that he might have been court-martialled for turning a gun on an enlisted man.

One day, when his troops complained about the food, Fitzgerald mounted a horse and marched them double time through the sweltering heat. This extraordinary punishment caused a near mutiny, and Fitzgerald was relieved of his command and put in charge of a stokes mortar platoon. During manoeuvres he fired shells – fortunately duds – into a group on the opposite side of a hill, but he distinguished himself when a leaky barge sank in the Tallapoosa River and the men who couldn't swim had to be rescued. On the whole, he was a conscientious officer, concerned in a dreamy way with the safety and welfare of his platoon, but his good intentions had a way of going awry. For example, enlisted men were not supposed to spend more than $5 a month on Liberty Bonds. During a drive, Fitzgerald got so carried away that he sold some of them bonds amounting to twice their monthly pay, and a superior devoted several days to straightening out the mess. 'The prevailing attitude towards Fitzgerald,' a fellow officer recalled, 'was that if we were given an important task and told he would be assigned to help us, we would prefer to do it alone. This attitude implied on hostility towards Fitzgerald. Indeed most of us liked him.'[13]

In August Scribners returned his novel, praising its originality and making concrete suggestions for improvement. Fitzgerald immediately set to work, and by mid-October a revision of *The Romantic Egotist* was back at Scribners. It was now turned down definitively, despite the enthusiasm of an editor named Maxwell Perkins. For the time being Fitzgerald would have to content himself with love rather than fame.

Going around with Zelda, to be sure, had brought him a certain notoriety. In any group she made herself the centre of attention. If a dance was sluggish, she would turn cartwheels down the floor, or tell the orchestra to play the Highland Fling and do a solo. On a weekend at Auburn she borrowed her escort's tennis shoes because she was suffering from blisters, and chosen queen of the ball, she waltzed around in the spotlight with her feet flapping in enormous sneakers. But if she was a show-off in one sense, in another she wasn't at all. Her high jinks were gay outlets, pure self-expression – the more refreshing because she seemed to be playing to the gallery of herself alone.

In Europe the war was petering out and Fitzgerald wanted desperately to get into it. John Peale Bishop, just arrived at the front, wrote him a letter describing 'a patrol that secured three prisoners in a very real fistfight'. In October Fitzgerald's division was ordered overseas, and on the 26th he went north as the supply officer of an advanced detachment. Because he stopped off at Princeton and was absent during the unloading in Hoboken, several thousand dollars' worth of equipment was lost. The flu epidemic delayed embarkation, but finally Fitzgerald marched on board a transport with a steel helmet slung at his side, then orders were reversed and he marched off again and back to quarters at Camp Mills, Long Island. Then the Armistice was signed and there wasn't any more war. To his everlasting regret, Fitzgerald had missed it.[14]

John Peale Bishop saw it otherwise from the trenches. 'We are alive . . .,' he wrote.

We shall live, we shall be poor perhaps but O Christ! we shall be *free.* . . . Will you honestly take a garret (it may be a basement but a garret sounds better) with me somewhere near Washington Square? Shall we go wandering down to Princeton on fragrant nights of May? . . . We'll . . . climb the stairs of Witherspoon and bellow down the Nass. We'll chant Keats along the leafy dusk of Boudinot Street and come back to talk the night away.

Fitzgerald's behaviour at Camp Mills had been so erratic

that his commanding officer confined him to quarters, and when it came time to return to Camp Sheridan, he was nowhere to be found. It was rumoured he had gone to Princeton the day before. Pulling into Washington in the small hours, his detachment was surprised to see him sitting on an adjacent track with two girls and a bottle. He gave out the story that he had commandeered a private locomotive to take him to Washington by telling the authorities that he had confidential papers for President Wilson. It was one of many fabrications about himself that passed into legend.

Despite his misconduct he now became aide to General J. A. Ryan, commanding the Seventeenth Infantry Brigade. For this 'pleasant & chatty sinecure', as he later called it, he had his good looks and his Princeton background to recommend him; in effect he was the general's social secretary. During a parade he was thrown from his horse and the general appointed a sergeant to give him riding lessons, but on the whole the job proved congenial.

In January Monsignor Fay died suddenly of pneumonia, and Fitzgerald wrote Shane Leslie that 'my little world made to order has been shattered by the death of one man.' How he would miss Fay's comforting presence, the warmth and glow he cast over youth, the perfect understanding! 'I feel,' he wrote Leslie, 'as if in a way his mantle had descended upon me – a desire or more, to some day recreate the atmosphere of him.'

When Fitzgerald's regiment began demobilizing its officers in February, the first to go was a lieutenant who had been caught defrauding the government of a small sum of money. The second was Fitzgerald. Not that he had done anything disgraceful, it was just so easy to get along without him. 'As an officer,' said a comrade-in-arms, 'Fitzgerald was unusually dispensable.'

His discharge came through 18 February, and immediately he set off for New York to make his fortune. He had asked Zelda to marry him, but she was holding out until she was sure he would be able to support her; meanwhile she encouraged the attentions of other men. She was a favourite at proms, and some of Fitzgerald's most dreaded competition came from the aviators at Camp Taylor who stunted their planes over her house.[15]

On his arrival in New York he wired her, DARLING HEART AMBITION ENTHUSIASM AND CONFIDENCE I DECLARE EVERYTHING GLORIOUS THIS WORLD IS A GAME AND WHILE I FEEL SURE OF YOUR LOVE EVERYTHING IS POSSIBLE I AM IN THE LAND OF AMBITION AND SUCCESS AND MY ONLY HOPE AND FAITH IS THAT MY DARLING HEART WILL BE WITH ME SOON.

[7]

FITZGERALD called the next four months the most impressionable of his life. 'New York had all the iridescence of the beginning of the world. The returning troops marched up Fifth Avenue, and the girls were instinctively drawn East and North towards them – this was the greatest nation and there was gala in the air.'

With his Triangle scores under his arm he made the rounds of the newspapers but failed to get a job. Then he met an advertising man who steered him to the Barron Collier Agency, where a light verse writer was needed in the copy department. At ninety dollars a month Fitzgerald was put to work writing slogans for streetcar cards. In later years he laughed over the hit he made with a slogan for the Muscatine Steam Laundry in Muscatine, Iowa: 'We keep you clean in Muscatine'. 'I got a raise for that,' he recalled. ' "It's perhaps a bit imaginative," the boss said, "but still it's plain there's a future for you in this business. Pretty soon this office won't be big enough to hold you." '

Fitzgerald was living at 200 Claremont Avenue in Morningside Heights – 'one room in a high, horrible apartment-house in the middle of nowhere' – while in his imagination he already occupied a honeymoon suite with Zelda. She would join him as soon as he was ready, by which she meant able to support her with a margin of comfort. 'I'd just hate to live a sordid, colourless existence,' she wrote, – 'because you'd soon love me less – and less.' Fitzgerald had written to her parents of his intentions, and she, in turn, wrote to his mother, getting back 'just a nice little note, untranslatable, but she called me "Zelda".' In March Fitzgerald sent Zelda a ring.

But as the weeks of their separation stretched into months, his life became intolerable. His job bored him, and he couldn't sell the plays, stories, poems, sketches, lyrics, jokes which he composed in his off hours. Each evening he hurried back to his room to find a rejected manuscript which he immediately mailed to another magazine. Then he wrote something new and sent that off, and concluded his day by getting more or less drunk.

Running into Paul Dickey, his musical collaborator on the Triangle, Fitzgerald suggested they take a fling at Tin Pan Alley, but Dickey had decided to settle down in his father's business. Fitzgerald often ate at the Yale Club, with which the Princeton Club had temporarily merged, and one day, drinking martinis in the upstairs lounge, he announced that he was going to jump out of the window. No one objected; on the contrary, it was pointed out that the windows were French and ideally suited for jumping, which seemed to cool his ardour. After another cocktail the incongruities of his life began to pour out of him. The twenty-odd dollars he earned in a week barely sufficed to pay for a piece of lingerie he was sending Zelda. Someone said he probably wasn't worth twenty dollars a week, and that if the lingerie seemed expensive, he shouldn't have bought it. But Fitzgerald felt victimized, and during an entire meal he regaled his companions with the stupidities and sterilities of the advertising business.

One of his diversions was apartment hunting, and when a blowsy landlady in Greenwich Village told him he could bring girls to his room, the idea filled him with dismay. Why should he want to bring girls to his room? He *had* a girl – or did he? – Zelda's letters left room for doubt. She mentioned other men and described parties at which she seemed to be enjoying herself. 'I used to wonder why they locked princesses in towers,' Fitzgerald wrote her, and in April Zelda replied,

Scott. you've been so sweet about writing – but I'm so damned tired of being told that you 'used to wonder why they kept princesses in towers' – You've written that verbatim in your last *six* letters! It's dreadfully hard to write so very much – and so many of your letters sound forced – I know you love me, Darling, and I love you more than anything in the world, but if it's going to be so much longer we just *can't* keep up this frantic writing.

Next day Fitzgerald went to Montgomery, accomplishing nothing. Though Zelda was very much in love, she wouldn't marry him. He returned to Barron Collier's in a state of nervous exhaustion, carrying a revolver which someone in the office spirited away. Having told the boss that a family emergency had required his presence in St Paul, he now confessed the truth and asked to be fired. 'You've been more than kind,' Fitzgerald said, 'but I can't adjust to business routine and I don't deserve another chance.' The boss told him to go home and get some sleep. Next morning he came to work revivified.

Zelda's letter thanking him for his visit renewed his hopes. 'I've spent today in the graveyard . . .' she wrote,

trying to unlock a rusty iron vault built in the side of the hill. . . . It's all washed and covered with weepy, watery blue flowers that might have grown from dead eyes – sticky to touch, with a sickening odour. . . . I wanted to *feel* 'William Wreford, 1864'. Why should graves make people feel in vain? I've heard that *so* much and Grey is *so* convincing, but somehow I can't find anything hopeless in having lived – All the broken columns and clasped hands and doves and angels mean romances – and in a hundred years I think I shall like having young people speculate on whether my eyes were brown or blue – of course, they are neither – I hope my grave has an air of many, many years ago about it – Isn't it funny how, out of a row of Confederate soldiers, two or three will *make* you think of dead lovers and dead loves – when they're exactly like the others, even to the yellowish moss? Old death is so beautiful – so very beautiful – We will die together I know – Sweetheart.[16]

When Fitzgerald wrote that the Jazz Age began about the time of the May Day riots in 1919, he was thinking less, perhaps, of those anti-Socialist demonstrations than of an all-night binge of his own which signalled the decade he chronicled. After a Yale fraternity dance at Delmonico's, he and a Princeton junior named Porter Gillespie went to Child's Restaurant at 59th and Broadway where the dance crowd was sobering up. At first Fitzgerald sat off by himself, mixing hash, poached eggs, and catsup in Gillespie's derby. Tiring of this, he would go up to a Yale man and while addressing him earnestly, would scrunch his fried eggs or shredded wheat, then shake hands as they parted. Soon food was being thrown and Fitzgerald was expelled. While Gillespie finished eating, he watched Fitzgerald trying to sneak back in on hands and knees each time the restaurant door opened.

In the early dawn the two of them returned to Delmonico's, where they took the 'In' and 'Out' signs off the coatroom doors and fixed them to their shirt fronts, thenceforth introducing each other as 'Mr In' and 'Mr Out'. After waking their friends at the Biltmore on the house phone, they crossed over to the old Manhattan Hotel and ordered champagne for breakfast. 'You buy it,' Fitzgerald told Gillespie. 'Your father has the money to pay for it' – his way of finding out whether Gillespie's father did. When the champagne was refused them, Fitzgerald went up to a priest and said, 'Father, can you imagine anything more embarrassing than being refused champagne on Sunday morning?' They finally got some at the Commodore and ended up rolling the empty bottles among the churchgoers on Fifth Avenue.

Later Fitzgerald put the antics of Mr In and Mr Out in a story called 'May Day', which also caught his feelings of failure and frustration. Unable to get started as an illustrator, Gordon Sterrett is a dissipated wreck sponging off friends (a depth to which Fitzgerald never descended). Sterrett embodies Fitzgerald's horror of poverty – a poet's horror – reminiscent of Poe's remark that he wouldn't put the hero of 'The Raven' in poor surroundings because 'poverty is commonplace and contrary to the idea of Beauty'. 'May Day', a brilliant bit of social history, ranges far and wide over the city's fevered life. Here are the college boys and debutantes Fitzgerald knew so well but also clerks, waiters, shop girls, policemen, and returning soldiers. The mob assault on the Socialist newspaper was inspired by an actual raid on the *New York Call*. And Sterrett's suicide at the end echoes that of a young Princetonian who shot himself in similar circum-stances.

Later Fitzgerald could see the large pattern of events, but at the time all he cared about was winning Zelda. Her letters, full of Junior League shows and trips to men's colleges, brought little encouragement. He was caught between two worlds. 'As I hovered ghost-like in the Plaza Red Room of a Saturday afternoon,' he remembered,

or went to lush and liquid parties in the East Sixties or tippled with Princetonians in the Biltmore Bar, I was haunted always by my other life – my drab room in the Bronx, my square foot of the subway, my fixation upon the day's letter from Alabama – would it come and what would it say? – my shabby suits, my poverty, and love.

Fitzgerald made a second trip to Montgomery in May and a third one in June, but Zelda was not to be stampeded. He pleaded with her, even stooping to a long monologue of self-pity, and finally she decided to break it off. His wild rush and her knowledge that his work was distasteful to him made her afraid. Then too she was ambitious, and the prospect of liv-ing in a two-room flat and shopping at the A & P did not intrigue her. She loved Fitzgerald, and it cost her to say no, but after their rupture she went back to her proms and theatricals without visible sadness or depression.

Fitzgerald wrote a friend that it was a great tragedy and that unless Zelda changed her mind he would never marry. Back in New York, he quit his job – he had already given a month's notice – and went on a drunk that lasted several weeks and gave him one of the most vivid episodes in *This Side of Paradise*. Early in July he came to his senses and began to consider his next move. One incident had mitigated the despair of the past month. After collecting a hundred and twenty-two rejection slips which were pinned in a frieze around his room, he had sold a story to *Smart Set* for thirty dollars. The story, however, had been written for the *Nassau Lit* two years before, and since his more recent efforts had been rejected, the implication seemed to be that he was on the downgrade at twenty-two.

He still had hopes for his novel, but all spring he had been in the position of the fox and the goose and the bag of beans: if he stopped to rewrite the book he lost his girl. Now, having lost the girl anyway, he decided to live off his parents in St Paul and concentrate on the book.

His poverty was relative after all since his parents were there to fall back on. At school and college they had given him the money he needed, which was only a fraction of the money he wanted, for he dreamed of splurging like a Renaissance prince. His mother had hoped he would make a career of the army, and his father wanted him to enter business, but they backed him now in his dubious venture – keeping the purse strings tight, however, lest he go off on one of his escapades. His desire to break away from his humiliating dependence strengthened him in his work.

He wasted no time and proceeded systematically, with a schedule of chapters pinned to the curtain of his top-floor room. For some one so youthful and impulsive he was already surprisingly organized and professional about his work. He refurbished the old material and wove in new, some of it drawn from stories written and rejected during the spring. The cigarettes accumulated under the corners of his rug where he put the butts and stamped on them; when he ran out, he would salvage a butt and relight it. His head became a kaleidoscope of marvellous shapes and colours as inspiration drove him on he knew not how. When a friend, reading his manuscript, asked what a certain word meant, Fitzgerald said, 'Damn if I know, but doesn't it fit in there just beautifully?' He worked around the clock, skipping meals and having sandwiches and milk brought to his room. His parents stayed out of his way – that was one thing he would say for them – his mother taking his phone calls and keeping his friends from interrupting him.

By the end of July he had finished a first draft. 'While [*The Romantic Egotist*],' he wrote Scribners, 'was a tedious, disconnected casserole, this is a definite attempt at a big novel and I really believe I have hit it. ... If I send you the book by 20 August and you decide you could risk it's publication (I am blatantly confident that you will) would it be brought out in October, say, or just what would decide its date of publication?'

That summer he was seeing a good deal of Father Joe Barron, the youngest priest ever ordained in the diocese of St Paul. At twenty-four Barron had been made Dean of Students at the St Paul Seminary, and now at thirty-one he was a compact, florid man with blue eyes and reddish, wavy hair. During the winter Fitzgerald stayed home from Princeton, he had often gone out to the Seminary to consult Father Joe about things he was writing. Leaning back in his deep leather chair with his cassock wrapped around his legs against the cold, Father Joe would hold forth on all manner of subjects, sacred and profane. His darting, journalistic mind appealed to Fitzgerald; he was witty and sociable yet inflexible on matters of religion. It seemed to him that this brilliant, unstable youth was straying from the Church at his peril. When Fitzgerald got off one of his iconoclasms – oblique yet loaded with a delicate scorn – Barron would hear him out and then say quietly, 'Scott, quit being a damn fool.'[17]

Fitzgerald's current religion was his novel. As he wrote Edmund Wilson, 'My Catholicism is scarcely more than a memory – no that's wrong it's more than that; at any rate I go not to Church nor mumble stray nothings over chrystaline beads.' Wilson was planning a volume of stories about the war, to be written by different authors from different points of view, and he asked Fitzgerald if he would like to contribute. 'For God's sake, Bunny,' Fitzgerald wrote back, 'write a novel & don't waste your time editing collections. It'll get to be a habit. That sounds crass & discordant but you know what I mean.' The crass discordancy did not sit well with Fitzgerald's former mentor on the *Nassau Lit.* 'Don't worry about me,' Wilson replied. 'I'm not writing a novel, but I'm writing almost everything else, – and getting some of it accepted. – I hope your letter isn't a fair sample of your present literary methods: it looks like the attempt of a child of six to write F.P.A.'s column. . . . I don't think any of your titles are any good.' (Fitzgerald had asked Wilson's advice on three: *The Education of a Personage*, *The Romantic Egotist*, and *This Side of Paradise*.)

On 3 September Fitzgerald sent his novel to Scribners with a feeling of elation. 'It is a well-considered, finished *whole* this time,' he said, 'and I think its a more *crowded* (in the best sense) piece of work than has been published in this country for some years.' While waiting for Scribners to decide, he found employment at the shops of the Northern Pacific Railroad. Told to wear old clothes, he came in a polo shirt and dirty white flannels, which seemed rather exotic to the other labourers appropriately dressed in overalls. One of his jobs was roofing freight cars, and when he sat down, instead of kneeling, to hammer the nails, the foreman scolded him for loafing.

The ordeal was soon over. On 16 September he received a special delivery from Scribners accepting *This Side of Paradise*. 'The book is so different,' wrote Maxwell Perkins, 'that it is hard to prophesy how it will sell but we are all for taking a chance and supporting it with vigour.' That day Fitzgerald was drunk, but not on wine. He was full of a sense of life-intoxicated youth bursting. He quit work at the Northern Pacific and ran along the streets stopping automobiles and telling anyone who would listen about his good fortune. A few days later he reeled off the following letter to Alida Bigelow, a friend at Smith College:

1st Epistle of St Scott to the Smithsonian
Chapter the I
Verses the I to the last –

> (599 Summit Ave)
> In a house below the average
> Of a street above the average
> In a room below the roof
> With a lot above the ears
> I shall write Alida Bigelow
> Shall indite Alida Bigelow
> As the worlds most famous gooph
> (This line don't rhyme)

(September 22nd 1919)

Whats a date!		Stop this rot.	
Mr Fate		Keep a date,	What's a date?
Can't berate		Father time,	Mr Fate?
Mr Scott.		Such a lot	S'ever
He is not		To berate;	Scott
Marking time:		Tho I hate	
Its too late		To the dot!	
So in rhyme,			

Most beautiful, rather-too-virtuous-but-entirely-enchanting Alida:

Scribner has accepted my book. Ain't I smart!

But hic jubilatio erat totam spoiled for meum par lisant une
livre, une novellum, (novum) nomine 'Salt' par Herr C. G. Mor-
ris – a most astounding piece of realism ut makes Fortitude look
like an antique mental ash-can and is quite as good as 'The Old
Wives Tale.'

Of course I think Walpole is a weak-wad anyhow.

Read *Salt* young girl so that you may know what life B.

In a few days I'll have lived one score and three days in this
vale of tears. On I plod – always bored often drunk, doing no
penance for my faults – rather do I become more tolerant of
myself from day to day, hardening my chrystal heart with blasphemous humor and shunning only toothpicks, pathos, and poverty as being the three unforgivable things in life.

Before we meet again I hope you will have tasted strong liquor
to excess and kissed many emotional young men in red and yellow moonlights – these things being chasterners of those prejudices which are as gutta percha to the niblicks of the
century.

I am frightfully unhappy, look like the devil, will be famous
within 1 12 month and, I hope, dead within 2.

Hoping you are the same

I am

With Excruciating respect

F. Scott Fitzgerald

P.S. If you wish you may auction off this letter to the gurls of
your collidge – on condition that the proceeds go to the *Society
for the drownding of Armenian Airdales.*

Bla!

F.S.F.

Every morning now he awoke into a world of 'ineffable top-loftiness and promise'. He pleaded with Scribners to publish his book at once – by Christmas at the latest – 'because I'm in that stage where every month counts frantically and seems a cudgel in the fight for happiness against time.' Meanwhile he poured out short stories which he sold to *Smart Set* and *Scribners* magazine. Hoping to break into the top-priced *Saturday Evening Post,* he sent some of his output to Paul Revere Reynolds, a New York literary agent.

At one point during the excitement he had written Zelda and asked to visit her. Her reply was friendly but self-possessed. As she was just recovering from a 'wholesome amour with Auburn's "startling quarterback",' her health and her disposition were excellent though mentally he would find her somewhat deteriorated. She would love to see him and told him to bring a bottle of gin, as she hadn't had a drink all summer. After his last visit every corner the maid started cleaning had yielded up a bottle, or bottles, so his reputation was already ruined in this respect.

In November Fitzgerald went to Montgomery and Zelda agreed to marry him. There was an ecstatic moment when they wandered into a cemetery, and as they lingered among the headstones of the Confederate dead, Zelda said Fitzgerald would never understand how she felt about those graves, but he said he understood so well he would write about it – and did in his story 'The Ice Palace'. After he left, Zelda wrote him, 'I hate to say this, but I don't *think* I had much confidence in you at first. I was just coming [to New York] anyway. It's so nice to know you really *can* do things – *anything* – and I love to feel that maybe I can help just a little.'

Victory was sweet, though not as sweet as it would have been six months earlier before Zelda had rejected him. Fitzgerald couldn't recapture the thrill of their first love, and now that he was a professional writer, his enchantment with certain things Zelda felt and said was already paced by his anxiety to put them in a story. When he wrote her as if they were two old people who had lost their most precious possession, she answered that they hadn't really found it yet.

All the fire and sweetness – the emotional strength that we're capable of is growing – growing – and just because sanity and wisdom are growing too and we're building our love-castle on a firm foundation, nothing is lost. That first abandon couldn't last, but the things that went to make it are tremendously alive – just like blowing bubbles – they burst, but more bubbles just as beautiful can be blown – and burst – till the soap and water is gone – and that's the way we'll be, I guess.

From Montgomery Fitzgerald went to New York where he lived in state at the Knickerbocker Hotel, having by now sold his first story to the *Saturday Evening Post*. One afternoon three Princeton boys he had known in St Paul called on him in his room and found him pleasantly intoxicated, with several bell-hops helping him get dressed. Twenty and fifty dollar bills were scattered about, and on his way downstairs Fitzgerald inserted one in each vest and coat pocket, so that they protruded for all to see. Before leaving the hotel, his friends got most of them away from him and left them with the cashier. Fitzgerald insisted on taking them to 'his bootlegger' – bootleggers were still a rarity – and buying each a bottle of Scotch. When he got back to the hotel, the management was incensed because he had left the tap running and caused a minor flood.

People and parties were a constant temptation to Fitzgerald, who nevertheless knew the meaning of discipline. During Christmas week in St Paul he stayed home from a fancy-dress ball in order to write, though his friends kept phoning to tell him what he was missing. A well-known man-about-town had disguised himself as a camel, and with a taxi driver as his rear half had managed to attend the wrong party. Fitzgerald spent the next day collecting the facts, which he later expanded into a 12,000-word story in twenty-one consecutive hours. Beginning at eight in the morning, he finished the first draft at seven in the evening, copied it over between seven and half-past-four, and mailed it at five. The *Post* bought 'The Camel's Back' for five hundred dollars. It was as easy as that.

By now Edmund Wilson and John Peale Bishop had read the manuscript of *This Side of Paradise*. 'The most poetic thing in the novel is the title,' said Bishop, ' – couldn't be better.' He called the over-all performance 'damned good, brilliant in phases and sins chiefly through exuberance and lack of development.' Wilson was less enthusiastic. 'Your hero as an intellectual,' he wrote,

is a fake of the first water and I read his views on art, politics, religion and society with more riotous mirth than I should care to have you know. . . . It would all be better if you would tighten up your artistic conscience and pay a little more attention to form. . . . I feel called upon to give you this advice because I believe you might become a very popular, trashy novelist without much difficulty. . . . Cultivate a universal irony and do read something other than contemporary British novelists: this history of a young man stuff has been run into the ground and has always seemed to me a bum art-form, anyway. . . . I really like the book though; I enjoyed it enormously and I shouldn't wonder if a good many other people would enjoy it, too.

The split in Fitzgerald's ambition was already apparent – the dilemma he had mentioned to Alfred Noyes. He wanted to be a serious artist yet make a great deal of money, and the astringent, pessimistic tales which came naturally to his pen were out of keeping with the bland optimism of the high-priced popular magazines. He asked his agent whether there was 'any market at all for the cynical or pessimistic story except *Smart Set,* or does realism bar a story from any well paying magazine no matter how cleverly it is done?' With regard to the new novel he was contemplating, he raised the same question: 'Do you think a story like C. G. Norris' Salt or Cabell's Jurgen or Dreiser's Jenny Gerhard would have one chance in a million to be sold serially? I'm asking you for an opinion about this beforehand because it will have an influence on my plans.'

In January he went off to New Orleans and holed up in a boarding house to write, but his powers had begun to flag after the crescendo that followed his book's acceptance. Twice he went to see Zelda in Montgomery. To celebrate the sale of his first story to the movies he gave her a diamond-and-platinum watch and a flame-coloured ostrich fan. These fans were the last word in chic; Fitzgerald had eyed them longingly in the rich stores during his impecunious spring in New York.

As soon as the book came out, he and Zelda would be married. Mrs Sayre was reconciled though she thought them fearfully young and irresponsible. 'As you know,' she wrote Fitzgerald with brilliant understatement,

Zelda has had several admirers; but you seem to be the only one to make anything like a permanent impression. . . . Your church is all right with me [the Sayres were Episcopalians]. A good Catholic is as good as any other good man and that is good enough. It will take more than the Pope to make Zelda good: you will have to call on God Almighty direct. . . . She is not amiable and she is given to *yelping*. But when she yelps just give her your sweetest smile and go quietly about your business and in a little while you will hear that tuneless song 'Bum-bum-bom-bom-bom' and everything will be all right again.

Fitzgerald went north in mid-February and installed himself at the Cottage Club to await Zelda's arrival. On 26 March *This Side of Paradise* was published. Struthers Burt, an author living in Princeton, never forgot a bright cold day when 'shortly before noon, the front-door bell rang and a young man walked in. He looked exactly like an Archangel, and he had the strange aloofness and evasiveness you associate with Archangels. He was beautiful and a little eerie.' As an admirer of Burt's short stories, Fitzgerald said he had come to present him with the first copy of *This Side of Paradise*. If Fitzgerald was being accurate and not just charming, it was the first of countless books inscribed, usually with some personal or idiosyncratic flourish, for few occupations delighted him more.

Zelda wrote him that 'our fairy tale is almost ended, and we're going to marry and live happily ever afterward just like the princess in her tower who worried you so much – and made me so very cross by her constant recurrence.' The night before she left Montgomery she lay awake with a friend plotting ways to attract attention in New York, such as sliding down the banisters of the Biltmore where she and Scott would be staying. As soon as she reached New York, Fitzgerald sent her shopping with a girl whose taste in clothes he admired, for the frills and furbelows that constituted Zelda's idea of style would never do in present surroundings. They were married the morning of 3 April in the rectory of St Patrick's Cathedral, with Ludlow Fowler, a Princeton classmate of Scott's, as best man. Zelda's sisters, Marjorie and Clotilde, were present, but no parent on either side.

When Fitzgerald left St Patrick's that April noon, his prospects were boundless. He had won the girl of his dreams, and *This Side of Paradise* was already in a second printing. Not only that, but the boom was in the air, America stood on the verge of 'the greatest, gaudiest spree in history', and Fitzgerald would be there to tell about it.

[8]

THOSE who had known Fitzgerald at Princeton and around New York after the war were inclined to scepticism. 'We were all egomaniacs then,' one of them recalled, ' – all wrapped up in our own little concerns – and to think that this guy who had written songs for the Triangle should blossom out with a book that would make him famous! It was fantastic. I didn't have time to read it. *This Side of Paradise couldn't* be any good.'

But the gusto of the critics made one reconsider. Here, it seemed, was a writer of uncanny gifts and enormous promise whose very defects – brashness, arrogance, immaturity – were part of his charm. What mattered his carelessness, his lack of form? Wasn't exuberance to be prized above technique in a young man's book? Tarkington's *Seventeen* and Johnson's *Stover at Yale*, both of which Fitzgerald had pored over and admired, were called mere superficial sketches by comparison. He found his name mentioned in the same breath with Byron, Kipling, the early Dreiser, and the words 'artist' and 'genius' leapt out at him from the reviews.

For a while he lived in a state of pleasant madness, thinking only of his book's reception. He knew the parts of the country where it was selling best and could tell you its approximate earnings at any moment. He lingered in bookstores, hoping to hear it praised, and when he met someone who didn't know of it he was crushed. It amused him that Puritans were shocked by his accounts of drinking and necking. The strictures of the Catholic press also gave him wry satisfaction, though the priest, Father Darcy, seemed to him the most sympathetic character in the book.[18]

Less easy to shrug off was the criticism of Heywood Broun, the *New York Tribune*'s influential reviewer. 'We are afraid,' wrote Broun of Fitzgerald's hero, 'that not a few undergraduates are given to the sin of not kissing and then telling anyway.' When the gibes continued in succeeding columns, Fitzgerald invited the big, ramshackle ex-sports-reporter to lunch and told him in a kindly way that it was too bad he had let his life slip by without accomplishing anything. (Broun had just turned thirty.)[19]

Let us remember Fitzgerald in his first glory, happier than he would ever be again, though for six or eight years his life would be relatively unclouded. A faun, with waving blond hair parted in the middle and an expression half-serious, half-humorous, he radiated a perceptiveness, a sense of discovery that made you tingle when you were with him. He was living the American dream – youth, beauty, money, early success – and he believed in these things so passionately that he endowed them with a certain grandeur. He and Zelda were a perfect pair, like a shepherd and shepherdess in a Meissen. You could hardly imagine one without the other and you wanted to preserve them and protect them hoping that their idyll might never end.

That is, when they were behaving themselves. There were times when you wished they would sober up or go away. In April they went to Princeton to 'chaperon' houseparties. 'We were there three days,' Fitzgerald wrote a friend. 'Zelda and five men in Harvey Firestone's car and not one of us drew a sober breath. ... It was the damndest party ever held in Princeton & every one in the University will agree.' Zelda, whom Fitzgerald introduced all around as his mistress, turned cartwheels down Prospect Street and came to breakfast at Cottage with a demi-john of applejack, which she poured over the omelettes to make *omelettes flambées*. Fitzgerald got into brawls and people began to speak of him as a boisterous 'run-it-out' drunk – 'running it out' being the pejorative term for someone who made a spectacle of himself.

The following weekend Fitzgerald, John Peale Bishop, Edmund Wilson, and Stanley Dell descended on Princeton in Dell's Buick for a banquet honouring the *Nassau Lit*'s former editors. Equipped with props from the Greenwich

Village Playhouse, they drove up Fifth Avenue which had been cleared of traffic for the May Day parade. Fitzgerald and Bishop in the back were making signs and hanging them out the window; the policeman who chased them away took particular offence at 'We Are the Reds from Parnassus'. On the way to Princeton more signs were displayed, such as, 'Here's to John Grier Hibben [president of Princeton]. He ought to be selling ribbon'. They stopped first at Christian Gauss's, and when the professor met them at the door, they crowned him with a laurel wreath and Fitzgerald delivered an oration ending with the sentiment, 'We are going to give literature the greatest boost it has ever known.' 'Who knows,' said Gauss, 'you may give it the fatal shove.' Then Fitzgerald, wearing a halo and wings and carrying a lyre, went to Cottage where he was symbolically ejected from a rear window.[15] It was the first he knew of his suspension from the club.

Apparently his and Zelda's misbehaviour during houseparties had since become a scandal, and some of those who had aided and abetted them at the time had voted for Fitzgerald's suspension. Not only was he hurt, but the hypocrisy of the proceedings hardened his contempt for uplift and reform.

Several weeks later he was honoured to receive a letter from President Hibben, congratulating him on 'The Four Fists', a didactic story which Fitzgerald was ashamed of, but which, according to Hibben, showed 'human nature at its best'. Hibben had been distressed by certain aspects of *This Side of Paradise*; he thought it made Princeton seem too much like a country club where a spirit of calculation and snobbery prevailed. 'The Four Fists' pointed to the instinctive nobility of man, and Hibben hoped Fitzgerald would pursue this philosophy in his future writings. Fitzgerald's reply was respectful but uncompromising. While appreciating President Hibben's interest in his work, he said he had written 'The Four Fists' when it was financially necessary to give the magazines what they wanted, and he was surprised by the plaudits it had received.[20]

New York in 1920. 'The first speakeasies had arrived, the toddle was *passé*, the Montmartre was the smart place to dance and Lillian Tashman's fair hair weaved around the floor among the enliquored college boys.' New York, the playground of a younger generation that was tired of Great Causes, at odds with its elders, full of energy stored up by the war, and determined to be amused. Fitzgerald's blend of flippancy and glamour caught the mood of the moment, and so he became, in the words of a contemporary, 'our darling, our genius, our fool'. He was not the first spokesman for insurgent youth – that honour belonged to Randolph Bourne or possibly Edna Millay – but with the talents of an actor wedded to those of an author, he dramatized a point of view that was second nature to him. It had long been apparent that his own parents were incompetent and unknowing. He extended the notion to the parents of everyone else, and the mystique of the Younger Generation caught hold.

Fame altered him surprisingly little. He took it with a light touch, making fun of it in a way that scarcely concealed his satisfaction. 'You can't treat me like this,' he would say with a twinkle, 'I'm an important person'; or 'Let's go down to the Plaza for lunch – they'll swoon when they see me come in.' With naïve enthusiasm he would tell how much he was getting for a short story or a movie right, and at lectures, after captivating his audience with nervous young ramblings about the flapper, he succumbed to the autograph seekers with embarrassed delight.

Around New York he remained the incorrigible undergraduate. He and Zelda surrendered to impulses which wouldn't even have occurred to more prosaic souls. The two of them taking hands after a Carnegie Hall concert and running like the wind – like two young hawks – down crowded 57th Street, in and out of traffic. Scott doing handstands in the Biltmore lobby because he hadn't been in the news that week, and, as Oscar Wilde said, the only thing worse than being talked about is being forgotten. Scott and Zelda at the theatre sitting quietly during the funny parts and roaring when the house was still. Scott whimsically divesting himself of coat, vest and shirt in the sixth row of the *Scandals*, and being helped out by a posse of ushers. Scott and Zelda going to a party, one of them on the roof of the taxi and the other on the hood.

They got away with it because of their air of breeding and refinement. They seemed so much a lady and gentleman that it was hard to credit the more outlandish tales about them until they began to happen right before one's eyes. Then too their devilment stopped short of vulgarity; without being prudes, they shared a disdain for smut or grossness of any kind.

After several weeks of honeymooning at the Biltmore, the Fitzgeralds were asked to leave, the continuing hilarity of their presence being considered prejudicial to good order and restful nights. They moved to the Commodore and then decided to spend the summer in the country, where Zelda could swim and Scott could write undisturbed. In their second-hand Marmon they set out for Lake Champlain, but the first day on the road someone told them the lake was too cold to swim in, so they bore east till they came to Westport, Connecticut. Here they rented the grey-shingled Wakeman 'cottage', almost in sight of Long Island Sound. The original house dated from revolutionary times, and nearby a stone monument of a Minute Man stood watch over the placid fields.

The Fitzgeralds joined the beach club, but soon the quiet of their days became oppressive, and they made trips to New York in search of excitement. They sloshed down gin-and-fruit-juice concoctions in various bachelor apartments, and they travelled the popular routes from dinner to the theatre, thence to the Midnight Frolic, or, at Zelda's urging, to one of the cellars in Greenwich Village where the 'new poetry' movement was having its short-lived boom. Weekends they gave over-stimulated parties in Westport at which Scott's Princeton friends rubbed elbows with the artists, writers, and theatre people of their new milieu.

By now Fitzgerald realized what he must previously have guessed: that Zelda was no housekeeper. Sketchy about ordering meals, she completely ignored the laundry, much to the chagrin of Scott, who liked to change his shirt several times a day. Her carelessness with money was partly his fault, for when a cheque came in from his agent, he gave her huge wads of bills for the most trifling expenditures. But there were compensations; living with Zelda was like a poem. Always dainty and appetizing in her fresh cotton dresses, she had what Fitzgerald called 'a flower-like quality of blooming and hibernating with the seasons.' She was earthier than he and brought him back to nature and the senses from which his imagination was constantly transporting him. He was proud of her attractiveness to men – of the way they flocked around her in rowdy groups warming themselves with her vitality. Had they loved each other less there would have been occasion for a good deal of jealousy.

But, as Fitzgerald wrote in *The Beautiful and Damned*, 'of the things they possessed in common, the greatest of all was their almost uncanny pull at each other's hearts.' Moments in that novel carry the imprint of their early devotion. On leaving a hotel where they have been happy together, the wife in the story begins to cry, and when her husband tries to comfort her she says,

'Everywhere we go on and move and change, something's lost – something's left behind. You can't ever quite repeat anything, and I've been so yours here – '
He held her passionately near, discerning far beyond any criticism of her sentiment a wise grasping of the minute . . .
Later in the afternoon when he returned from the station with the tickets he found her asleep on one of the beds, her arm curled about a black object which he could not at first identify. Coming closer he found it was one of his shoes, not a particularly new one, nor clean one, but her face, tear-stained, was pressed against it, and he understood her ancient and most honourable message. There was almost ecstasy in waking her and seeing her smile at him, shy but well aware of her own nicety of imagination.

Or take the letter in *The Beautiful and Damned* that is but a slight re-wording of the following, written by Zelda after one of their fights:

I look down the tracks and see you coming – and out of every haze & mist your darling rumpled trousers are hurrying to me – without you dearest, dearest, I couldn't see or hear or feel or think – or live – I love you so and I'm never in all our lives going to let us be apart another night. It's like begging for mercy of a storm or killing Beauty or growing old, without you. . . . Goofo, you've *got* to try to feel how much [I love you] – how inanimate I am when you're gone – I can't even hate these damnable people – Nobody's got any right to live but us – and they're dirtying up our world and I can't hate them because I want you so. Come Quick – Come Quick to me – I could never do without you if you hated me and were covered with sores like a leper – and if you ran away with another woman and starved and beat me – I still would want you *I know*.

If Scott had begun by being the more in love, after their marriage Zelda gave herself so completely that such comparisons were meaningless. And yet the precariousness of their situation was apparent from the start, as one learns from the diary of Alexander McKaig, an advertising man with literary ambitions who had been a classmate and close friend of Scott's at Princeton.[21]

12 April [*1920*]. Called on Scott Fitz and his bride. Latter temperamental small town Southern Belle. Chews gum – shows knees. I do not think marriage can succeed. Both drinking heavily. Think they will be divorced in 3 years. Scott write something big – then die in a garret at 32.

13 June Visit Fitz at Westport. . . . Terrible party. Fitz & Zelda fighting like mad – say themselves marriage can't succeed.

15 Sept. In the evening Zelda – drunk – having decided to leave Fitz & having nearly been killed walking down RR tracks, blew in. Fitz came shortly after. He had caught same train with no money or ticket. They threatened to put him off but finally let him stay on – Zelda refusing to give him any money. They continued their fight while here. . . . Fitz should let Zelda go & not run after her. Like all husbands he is afraid of what she may do in a moment of caprice. . . .

Trouble is, Fitz absorbed in Zelda's personality – she is the stronger of the two. She has supplied him with all his copy for women – Fitz argued about various things. Mind absolutely undisciplined but guesses right – intuition marvellous. ... Senses the exact mood & drift of a situation so surely & quickly – much better at this than any of rest of us.

27 Sept. John [Peale Bishop] spent weekend at Fitz – new novel sounds awful – no seriousness of approach. Zelda interrupts him all the time – diverts in both senses. Discussed his success complex – artist's desire for flattery & influence – member of financially decadent family – Fitz bemoaning fact [that he] never can make more than hundred thousand a year – to do that have to become a Tarkington.

12 Oct. Went to Fitzgeralds. [By now they had moved back to New York.] Usual problem there. What shall Zelda do? I think she might do a little housework – [apartment] looks like a pig sty. If she's there Fitz can't work – she bothers him – if she's not there he can't work – worried of what she might do. ... I told her she would have to make up her mind whether she wanted to go in movies or get in with young married set. To do that would require a little effort & Zelda will never make an effort. Moreover, she and Fitz like only aristocrats who don't give a damn what the world thinks or clever bohemians who don't give a damn what the world thinks. ... Fitz makes a good criticism of himself – does not see more than lots of people but is able to put down more of what he sees.

13 Oct. Fitz made another true remark about himself – draw brilliant picture of [George Jean] Nathan sitting in chair but how Nathan thinks he cannot depict – cannot depict how any one thinks except himself & possibly Zelda. Find that after he has written about a character for a while it becomes just himself again.

16 Oct. Spent evening at Fitzgeralds. Fitz has been on wagon 8 days – talks as if it were a century. Zelda increasingly restless – says frankly she simply wants to be amused and is only

good for useless, pleasure-giving pursuits; great problem –
what is she to do? Fitz has his writing of course – God knows
where the two of them are going to end up.

20 Oct. Fitz is hard up now but Zelda is nagging him for a
$750 fur coat & she can nag. Poor devil.

21 Oct. Went up to Fitzgeralds to spend evening. They just
recovering from an awful party. Much taken with idea of
having a baby. Have just planned a good baby & a bad baby
– former has Scott's eyes, Zelda's nose, Scott's legs, Zelda's
mouth etc. Latter has Zelda's legs, Scott's hair etc. Scott hard
up for money in spite of fact he had made $20,000 in past 12
months.

25 Oct. Follies with Scott & Zelda. Fitz very cuckoo. Lost
purse with $50.00 & then after every one in place hunted for
it, found it. He did not have enough money to pay cheque of
course.

27 Nov. I spent evening shaving Zelda's neck to make her
bobbed hair look better. She is lovely – wonderful eyes and
mouth.

28 Nov. Scott said – to go through terrible toil of writing
man must have belief his writings will be eagerly bought
and forever.

11 Dec. Evening at Fitz. Fitz & I argued with Zelda about
notoriety they are getting through being so publicly and
spectacularly drunk. Zelda wants to live life of an 'extravagant'. No thought of what world will think or of future. I
told them they were headed for catastrophe if they kept up
at present rate.

18 Dec. [John Peale Bishop and I] discussed glamor of Fitz
phrases. I mentioned his intuition. Also his dissipation all
aimed to hand down Fitzgerald legend. His claiming to be
great grandson of Francis Scott Key is part of it. Never
claimed that till recently – now it is being press agented. I
think he is really a grand nephew.

17 April [*1921*] Fitz confessed this evening at dinner that

Zelda's ideas entirely responsible for 'Jelly Bean' & 'Ice Palace'. Her ideas largely in this new novel. Had a long talk with her this evening about way fool women can rout intelligent women with the men. She is without doubt the most brilliant & most beautiful young woman I've ever known.

5 May Fitzgeralds gone gloriously to Europe on the Aquitania. I miss them dreadfully – used to see them every day.

To go back a little, after their summer in Westport the Fitzgeralds had rented an apartment near the Plaza where they could benefit from the hotel's room service without being subject to its rules. One day Lawton Campbell, Scott's friend of Triangle days, was invited to join them for lunch. Arriving promptly at one, Campbell found their room a shambles; overflowing ashtrays and half-filled glasses from the night before, breakfast dishes on the unmade bed, books and papers scattered everywhere. Scott was dressing while Zelda luxuriated in the tub with the door ajar. 'Scott,' she would call, 'tell Lawton 'bout. . . . Tell Lawton what I said when. . . . Now tell Lawton what I did . . .' Before Scott could elaborate, Zelda would give her own version. Scott cued her and chuckled as she told of spinach and champagne, of going back to the kitchen at the Waldorf and dancing on the table tops, of crashing dishes and being escorted out by the house detectives. The anecdotes rippled on until she appeared in the door buttoning her dress and Campbell, glancing at his watch, saw it was almost two and his lunch hour was over.

Such were the Fitzgeralds of legend. From this period Scott remembered 'riding in a taxi one afternoon between very tall buildings under a mauve and rosy sky; I began to bawl because I had everything I wanted and knew I would never be so happy again.' It wasn't till much later that they realized how lonely they had been amid the carnival of New York – 'like small children in a great bright unexplored barn.' They were not altogether what they seemed. Over the din of a night club Scott would start talking literature, and suddenly one realized that behind his collegiate façade was someone finer and quieter, someone very much harassed by a gift. Sensitive as a young leaf, he trembled to all his surroundings. He registered every emotion, noticed every change of manners, and put it in his fiction which he wrote almost like journalism with a dash of poetry added. Thus he recorded the age he was helping to form, and his work and his play became hopelessly intertwined.

In this difficult game Zelda was both an inspiration and a torment. Her pranks gave him much of his material, but then again he would have to force her to leave him alone so he could make use of what he had before the next onslaught began. Her touch of fantasy, her shrewd strangeness added spice to his wonderful perceptiveness – his ability to catch an earthly manifestation on the wing and give it life and fire. At the same time the standards he had set himself were beyond her comprehension. Basically an artist, he chafed at having to write *Saturday Evening Post* potboilers with what he called 'the required jazz ending'. Long afterwards Zelda said, 'I always felt a story for the *Post* was tops, a goal worth seeking. It really meant something you know – they only took stories of real craftsmanship. But Scott couldn't stand to write them.' Fitzgerald, by his own admission, was 'a man divided'. Zelda wanted him to work too much for her and not enough for his dream.[22]

During the summer he had begun a novel which he continued in spurts through the fall, giving out enthusiastic reports of his progress. 10 November: 'The novel goes beautifully. Done 15,000 words in the last three days which is very fast writing even for me who write very fast.' In *The Flight of the Rocket*, his provisional title for *The Beautiful and Damned*, he was describing how a young man with the tastes and weakness of the artist but with no actual creative inspiration – how this young man and his beautiful wife are wrecked on the shoals of dissipation. 'This sounds sordid,' he wrote his editor, 'but it's really a most sensational book & I hope won't dissappoint the critics who liked my first one.'

In August, Scribners had published a volume of his stories, *Flappers and Philosophers*. Over them glittered the sun of his early success – 'a wealthy happy sun' that 'shyed little golden discs at the sea' or 'dripped over the house like gold paint over an art jar' – but there was also terror in the imprisoning chill of 'The Ice Palace' and the mesmeric doom of 'The Cut-Glass Bowl'. The critics, on the whole, did not feel that the collection fulfilled the promise of *This Side of Paradise*. They warned of a slick commercialism, an ad-man's glamour, and Fitzgerald's cocky tone seemed of a piece with his errors in grammar and syntax, though few could deny his charm. Through his tales ran a lyric beat, a fox-trot, a melody. Fitzgerald was a born romancer and illusionist, whose ever-beautiful, ever-witty young people did not exist outside his pages although later they seemed to typify the age.[23]

The early twenties was a thrilling time in American letters. The renaissance, heralded in the work of Dreiser, Anderson, and others, had gained momentum with the war. As America, the most powerful of nations, broke its subservience to European culture, new voices sprang up on every hand. The writers of the post-war generation were united in their opposition to Victorian ideals but intensely competitive among themselves, and under the circumstances not the least attractive thing about Fitzgerald was his professional generosity. He promoted the work of his fellows and took pride in their success. Zelda would remember him sitting up at night to wrestle with a friend's manuscript when his own was unfinished. 'No one knows how much Scott did for others,' said Maxwell Perkins of Scribners. 'He was so kind, and with his ability to spot new writers he would have made a good publisher if he hadn't written.'

Publishing Fitzgerald had been a departure, one might say a break-through, for the house of Scribners, whose lists in recent years had featured such dignitaries as Edith Wharton and Henry James. Known also for their British authors – Meredith, Stevenson, Galsworthy, and Barrie – Scribners had thus far eschewed the realism of the 'American renaissance'. Fitzgerald's realism, to be sure, was sweetened with romance, but Charles Scribner, Sr. had hesitated to put his imprint on *This Side of Paradise*, which struck him as frivolous. When he yielded to the enthusiasm of Maxwell Perkins, his most far-seeing editor, the monarchy of Scribners went over to the revolution.

Perkins was deceptive; at first glance he seemed spare New England and perfectly in the Scribners tradition. With his roots in Boston and Vermont, he had gone to St Paul's and Harvard and come to publishing by way of journalism, with a suppressed desire to write. A courtly, seemingly withdrawn, yet listening man in his middle thirties, he was given to pregnant silences, during which he stood gently rocking with thumbs behind his lapels, or doodled profiles of Napoleon and his other boyhood hero, Shelley – profiles that oddly resembled his own in their antique beauty. Some said Perkins was shy, but others disagreed on the grounds that a shy man would not sit in your presence and say absolutely nothing; at some point he would babble from sheer embarrassment. Perkins was a unique blend of the Puritan and the artist, of granite and warmth, of shrewdness and imagination. He used to say that the best part of a man is a boy, and back of his blue eyes – 'full of a strange misty light', Thomas Wolfe remembered, 'a kind of far weather of the sea in them' – one felt the perpetual boy, the romantic adventurer. 'His passion,' said a colleague, 'was for the rare real thing, the flash of poetic insight that lights up a character or a situation and reveals talent at work.' Modern and experimental in his literary taste, he was still old-fashioned enough to believe that honour, loyalty, and fortitude were the important things, and that to be born knowing this was a step towards becoming a great writer in more than the technical sense. If one of the signs of talent is the instinct or capacity for meeting the right helper at the right time, surely Fitzgerald's meeting with Perkins was a case in point.

Around the offices of Scribners, sedately reminiscent of the last century, Fitzgerald's presence was as exotic as his prose. He gave the atmosphere a perceptible lift when he blew in after a night of writing or carousing, eager and responsive, a smile or a quip for everyone despite the circles under his eyes. An editor would be working at his desk when a hat landed plop in the middle of it, meaning that Fitzgerald, passing by in the corridor, had tossed it over the partition – his way of saying hello.

Occasionally he looked in at *Vanity Fair* where editors Edmund Wilson and John Peale Bishop were enjoying a youthful authority: Bishop urbane and dignified, talking a little as if he had a hot potato in his mouth; Wilson absentminded and detached, so that at the mention of a current happening known to everyone he might register surprise. In their lighter moments Wilson and Bishop spoke Latin to each other, or played a game called 'The Rape of the Sabines', which consisted of hoisting their secretary on to one of the file cabinets. They were Fitzgerald's link with his intellectual past, with the Princeton he cherished, and their reaction to his success had been a mixture of surprise, delight, amusement, and – on Wilson's side – a touch of envy, for he was more ambitious than Bishop.

In any event, neither Wilson nor Bishop had foreseen Fitzgerald's easy jump to prominence. At Princeton they had taken each other seriously, while Fitzgerald was on the fringes of what they believed in. Even now they had a feeling, shared by a good many others, that his *Saturday Evening Post* effulgence was all very well, but a little trashy (a favourite epithet of Wilson's) and not likely to last. Teasing him, they drew up an exhibit of Fitzgeraldiana for the Scribners window, which would contain among other items:

– Original copy of Rupert Brooke's poems (Borrowed from J.P.B.) from which the title [*This Side of Paradise*] was taken
– Overseas cap never worn overseas
– Copy of Sinister Street (borrowed from E.W.) used as inspiration for T.S. of P.
– Entire Fitzgerald library consisting of seven books, one of them a notebook and two made up of press clippings
– Photograph of the Newman foot-ball team with Fitzgerald as half-back (with certificate signed by the Headmaster and vouching for the genuineness of the photograph)
– First Brooks suit worn by Fitzgerald
– Mirror

While Fitzgerald would never be as close to Wilson as he was to Bishop, Wilson's eminence as a critic was to make him the greater influence as time went on. Already Wilson had a settled air, and his essays and reviews suggested the weight and skill of a much older man. At Princeton people had thought him funny, queer, distant, but he had gone his way with briery independence. One had imagined him rising to the top in a distinguished university, yet with sound instinct he had bucked a naturally withdrawing temper and taken, for him, the harder road out into journalism.

At bottom he and Fitzgerald remained two sides of a coin, in stimulating opposition. Though Wilson could appreciate romanticism intellectually (his first book of criticism, *Axel's Castle*, would be a study of the Symbolists whom he treated as more sophisticated Romantics), he himself was eighteenth century in his sturdy rationalism, his omnivorous curiosity, the sane balance of his mind and style. He had in him some of the crusading vigour of the French Enlightenment, the same willingness to fight for a cause or an idea he believed in, and his discursive and expository talents belonged to an age of prose. 'Your poems I like less than your prose,' Fitzgerald presently wrote him, '. . . . all your poetry seems to flow from some source outside or before the romantic movement even when its intent is most lyrical.' It was Fitzgerald who, by comparison belonged with the Romantics – with Byron, Keats, and Shelley, each of whom he resembled in facets of his nature (Byron's dash, the sweetness of Shelley, Keats's yearning for artistic perfection). Wilson liked to deflate Fitzgerald by pricking his dreams and illusions with common sense, yet Wilson who also wanted to write imaginative literature had much to learn from Fitzgerald if it could ever be taught. Wilson's problem had always been an inability to engage with life, to experience it at first hand. He understood books better than people, who did not greatly interest him unless they were artists or intellectuals and could meet him on his own ground. Even as a reporter he remained essentially the student, the brilliant outsider, getting up on this or that subject from which his temperament seemed to exclude him. At parties where Fitzgerald would be mixing with everyone or generally misbehaving, Wilson was likely to be in a corner talking earnestly – still so shy that he might not even look at you, and then as you turned away, you were conscious of his brown eyes, choleric and watchful climbing your face like squirrels.

Wilson's shyness, however, was that of a man who could also be very bold. He was sure of his values and opinions, he knew where he stood, and his early criticism of Fitzgerald's work betrays a somewhat patronizing tone. Wilson sounds the note of the schoolmaster whose exceptional but wayward pupil has fallen short of his best. Though Fitzgerald is 'exhilaratingly clever', *This Side of Paradise* is 'very immaturely imagined', illiterate, and almost devoid of intellectual content. Not only is it highly imitative, in Compton Mackenzie it imitates an inferior model. It has almost every fault and deficiency that a novel can possess except the cardinal one of failing to live. Wilson's praise, when it comes, is backhanded. He is more intent on showing the minus than the plus. But if he did less than justice to the book's freshness and beauty, if he failed to communicate its excitement for its day, he pointed knowingly to its flaws and Fitzgerald respected him for it. 'Wilson's article about me in the March [*Bookman*] is superb', Fitzgerald wrote Perkins. 'It's no blurb – not by a darn sight – but its the first time I've been done *at length* by an intelligent & sophisticated man and I appreciate it – jeers and all.'

Wilson, of course, was still a fledgling. Among the more established critics Fitzgerald looked up to H. L. Mencken and George Jean Nathan. Co-editors of *Smart Set*, the first magazine to publish his work, Mencken and Nathan were dynamiters of Puritanism and the 'Genteel Tradition' in American literature. Nathan, a cynic and dandy with dark eyes and a sensitive, sullen mouth, was making a name as a theatre critic, and sometimes he took the Fitzgeralds to first nights bristling with celebrities. During the summer, he had visited them in Westport, professing his ardour for Zelda in a series of *billets-doux* of which the following is a fair sample:

'Dear Blonde: Why call me a polygamist when my passion for you is at once so obvious and so single? Particularly when I am lit.' Or this: 'Dear Misguided Woman: Like so many uncommonly beautiful creatures, you reveal a streak of obtuseness. The calling of a husband's attention to a love letter addressed to his wife is but part of a highly sagacious technique. . . . It completely disarms suspicion. . . I have bought five more cases of Miltshire gin.'

In Westport the Fitzgeralds had had a tiny Japanese butler, Tana, whom Nathan insisted was a German spy. He sent Tana a postcard addressed to Lt Emile Tannenbaum, commanding him to investigate the Fitzgerald's cellar and report in code cipher 24-B whether the floor was solid enough to hold a two-ton cannon in the event of war. There were subsequent communiqués in oriental calligraphy. Fitzgerald always handed them to Tana without a smile, and hours later the butler would be found puzzling over them in the kitchen, protesting that the symbols weren't Japanese, nor anything resembling Japanese. Meanwhile Mencken added his touch. 'I have sent Tannenbaum five copies of the *Berliner Tageblatt* each plastered with German stamps,' he wrote Nathan. 'Let me know if Fitzgerald is killed when the Westport American Legion raids his house.'

Mencken was Fitzgerald's special delight. The Teutonic *bon vivant*, with the taste for beer, seafood, and Uncle Willy cigars, with the racy talk and snapping blue eyes under sardonically arched brows – who could resist his enchantment with the everlasting spectacle of human folly? His railing at the Establishment – whether it be the 'rev. clergy' or the professors, Democracy or Prohibition – brought Fitzgerald's grateful applause. When Fitzgerald told Mencken he was basing one of the characters in his novel on Nathan, Mencken proposed a secret conference. 'There are certain episodes in Nathan's life,' he wrote,

that, while extremely discreditable, are very effective dramatically, and I'd like to impart them to you. There was, for example, the Schapiro case in 1904. I am surely not one to credit the Schapiro girl with anything approaching innocence, but, nevertheless,

Nathan's treatment of her could not and cannot be defended. And no one sympathized with him very much when he was forced to leave town for two months and hide in Union Hill, New Jersey.

In April 1921, with the novel completed and Zelda pregnant, the Fitzgeralds decided to go abroad. They were tired of their New York apartment with its stifling atmosphere of liquor, smoke, open trunks, too many callers, and eternal laundry bags, and there were indications that New York was tiring of them. One evening in the Jungle Club, an elaborate speakeasy, Lawton Campbell noticed a somewhat wobbly Fitzgerald arguing with the enormous bouncer at the door to the inner bar. The bouncer thought Fitzgerald had had enough to drink, and fearing a scene Campbell intervened and persuaded Fitzgerald to join his table. Moments later Zelda appeared at the door looking for Scott. Campbell ushered her to the table also, but she refused to sit down, saying Scott had walked out on her. Hoping to change her mood, Campbell asked her to dance. No thank you, she was going back to the bar and Scott was going with her. No so-and-so bouncer could tell him what to do.

Heads high, the Fitzgeralds returned to the fray. The bouncer let Zelda pass, but not Scott, who on a word from Zelda swung at him and missed. After another phantom blow, the bouncer lost patience and gave Fitzgerald a shove that sent him crashing into a table halfway across the room. Campbell went over and persuaded him to leave. As Zelda had disappeared, Campbell decided to come back for her after getting Scott outside. They were signalling a taxi when Zelda rushed out on the pavement, hatless and wrapless, crying, 'Scott, you're not going to let them get away with that! If you want a drink why shouldn't you have one?' – and Fitzgerald staggered back in over Campbell's protests.

Next day Campbell was getting a haircut at the Plaza when the barber said, 'Have you seen your friend Fitzgerald? You wouldn't recognize him.' The barber had been summoned to give Fitzgerald a shave – somewhat pointlessly as he was in bed with his head bandaged and one eye completely closed. There were scars and bruises on his body that indicated a brutal beating. When Campbell went to see him, Fitzgerald was unable to remember what had happened. Campbell asked after Zelda. 'Oh, she's fine,' Fitzgerald whispered through the gauze. 'She's gone to exchange our tickets. We were sailing for Europe today.'

They got off a week later on the *Aquitania*. Fitzgerald went down the passenger list checking the names of the people he had heard of, and beside 'Mr and Mrs Francis S. Fitzgerald' he put, 'Disguise! Sh!' Zelda wrote Max Perkins that the main object of the crossing seemed to be 'to gaze furtively & impressedly at Colonel House & answer your horrible dinner partners in monosyllables. However, I suppose it amuses the people that think "there's something in every fellow if you can just get at it." '

The first stop was London. *This Side of Paradise*, now in its eleventh American printing, was about to be published there, and Fitzgerald, eager to make a good impression, heeded Shane Leslie's warning that English intellectuals did not drink. When John Galsworthy invited them to dinner with St John Ervine, Scott told his host that he was one of the three living authors he admired most – the other two being Conrad and Anatole France. Later asked what Galsworthy had replied, Fitzgerald said, 'I don't think he liked it much. He knew he wasn't that good.'

Fitzgerald found Oxford just as beautiful as he had imagined it from Compton Mackenzie's *Sinister Street*, and Zelda enthused to Shane Leslie over 'the Town Hall with the Redskins walking around it' – by which she meant Buckingham Palace during the changing of the Grenadier Guards in their scarlet tunics. Leslie would remember Zelda as 'a toy, a little geisha, a lovely thing'. He took the Fitzgeralds on a tour of the river slums, of Limehouse and Wapping, showing them where Jack the Ripper had slain his victims, and they were enthralled. But on the whole, sightseeing was not their dish. People were their nutriment, and when they got to France they couldn't even speak the language. In Paris they sat for an hour outside Anatole

France's house hoping to catch a glimpse of the old gentleman, but he failed to oblige. Presently they were asked to leave their hotel because of Zelda's penchant for lashing the elevator at her floor with her belt, so as to have it on hand when she had finished dressing for dinner. After a jaunt through Italy, which to their American palates was even more distasteful than France, they returned to London the end of June. Scott had thought of settling there, but now he changed his mind, chilled perhaps by the unflattering reviews of *This Side of Paradise*.

Returning to America, the Fitzgeralds went to Montgomery with the idea of buying a house and putting down roots. At the last minute, however, they decided to have their child in St Paul.

[9]

FITZGERALD returned to St Paul in triumph. He carried within him a great excitement, and the crest of fame sat lightly on his young head. Going up to an older writer – Charles Flandrau – at a dance, he said, 'Oh, Charlie, how wonderful it is to be young and beautiful and a success!' When interviewed for the *St Paul Daily News* at White Bear Lake where he had rented a house, he came down in his pyjamas, and his eyes were 'blue and domineering', his nose 'Grecian and pleasantly snippy', as he held forth on American letters. Mencken was the one man for whom he had complete respect. Floyd Dell had touched the depths of banality in *The Mooncalf*. Carl Sandburg was less of a poet than Charlie Chaplin. Fitzgerald claimed to have three novels in his head and gave the impression of great buoyancy, though even now he was subject to despair.

The past five months of loafing had demoralized him, the underside of his creativity being a destructiveness which tore at himself and others. 'I should like to sit down with ½ dozen chosen companions,' he wrote Perkins, '& drink myself to death but I am sick alike of life, liquor and literature. If it wasn't for Zelda I think I'd disappear out of sight for three years. Ship as a sailor or something & get hard – I'm sick of the flabby semi-intellectual softness in which I flounder with most of my generation.'

With fall coming on, he and Zelda moved to a house on Goodrich Avenue in St Paul. When their child was born 26 October, Fitzgerald wired Zelda's parents, LILLIAN GISH IS IN MOURNING CONSTANCE TALMADGE IS A BACK NUMBER A SECOND MARY PICKFORD HAS ARRIVED. Fitzgerald had been the most anxious of prospective fathers, though not too anxious to record Zelda's remarks as she came out of ether: 'Oh God, goofo, I'm drunk. Mark Twain. Isn't she smart –

she has the hiccups. I hope it's beautiful and a fool – a beautiful little fool.' (The last sentiment would reappear in the mouth of Gatsby's sweetheart.)

Living in St Paul threw Fitzgerald with his parents for the first time since his marriage, and he was more critical of them than ever. In his eyes his mother remained a grotesque, while his father, natty as ever with his Vandyke and the white piping on his vests, seemed bland and uninteresting. The parents were a study in contrast; picturing his father as an attractive gentleman who had never amounted to anything, Fitzgerald gave the impression that his mother took in boarders and did the wash. He liked to dramatize the incongruities of his background in a manner more literary than accurate.

After recent excitements, St Paul was a come-down. The Victorian splendour of Summit Avenue no longer seemed grand but merely heavy. One missed the tempo of New York, where skirts were climbing rapidly to the knee and Macy's displayed cigar cases that turned out to be flasks. But the urge to startle and amuse, to shake life out of its conventional wrappings and give it some of the colour of fiction, was ever-present in Fitzgerald, who did what he could with the materials at hand. Running into an old girl, Margaret Armstrong, he reminisced with her – Fitzgerald had great nostalgia for his early friendships – after which he went down the block for a shave. When Margaret passed the barbershop moments later, Fitzgerald was in a chair with a cloth around his neck and lather all over his face, but he rushed out in the street exclaiming, 'Margaret, how are you! I'm so glad to see you!' as if they hadn't met for years. If it was partly done for the effect on passers-by, part of it too was his talent driving him. 'Reporting the extreme things as if they were the average things,' he once noted, 'will start you on the art of fiction.'

Determined to order his life, Fitzgerald rented a room downtown where he wrote his daily stint, afterwards going to the Kilmarnock Bookshop at Fourth and Minnesota for relaxation. You stepped off the street through a corner door into what looked like an old billiard room, dark and faintly dirty, the walls lined with books from floor to ceiling, and the new arrivals, chiefly fiction, on two long centre tables. Glancing at these, Fitzgerald would proceed to the rear room, where a fire blazed in cold weather and a sprinkling of comfortable chairs held out their arms to visitors. Here there was always good talk. One of the proprietors had come back from England with bootleg copies of James Joyce's *Ulysses*, which was causing a great stir. The other proprietor, Tom Boyd, edited the literary page of the *St Paul Daily News*, which helped to keep Fitzgerald before the public eye. Two years younger than Fitzgerald, Boyd was handsome, lusty, excitable, rough-smart, his education having stopped with high school. A hero in the Marines, he was soon to write a considerable war novel, *Through the Wheat*, which Fitzgerald got Scribners to publish.[24]

Distinguished visitors dropped in at the bookshop from time to time, and one day Fitzgerald met Joseph Hergesheimer, then approaching the height of his lucrative fame.

'Mr Hergesheimer,' said Fitzgerald, 'a writer's life is full of bitterness, frustration, and despair. Don't you think it would be better to be born with a talent for, say, carpentry?'

Hergesheimer's eyes twinkled behind horn-rimmed glasses.

'For Christ's sake!' he snapped, 'I lived for years in the mountains of Virginia, eating hominy grits and black-eyed peas and writing on a broken-down machine before I sold one God-damned line. And you talk to me about despair!'

A regular at the bookshop was Father Joe Barron, still a close friend of Fitzgerald's, though the latter had had nothing to do with the Church since his marriage. (His daughter, however, had been baptized a Catholic with Barron as godfather.) Barron used to say the Church was well rid of Fitzgerald, secretly believing he would return to it some day because he was intelligent. Barron liked Zelda, much as they disagreed. One evening, when she advanced the proposition

that most people – especially writers – took money too
seriously, Father Joe queried 'All right, Zelda – supposing
Scott's stuff stopped selling and you saw a dress that you
wanted more than anything in the world, and to get it you'd
have to spend your last hundred dollars. What would you
do?'

'I'd buy the dress,' said Zelda.

Barron said she just thought she would; she was posing.
Zelda flared back, and the argument went on until Barron
declared she couldn't be that tough because nothing in her
life had conditioned her for toughness. Scott listened in
silence, holding his drink and smiling.

During the fall and winter he polished the proofs of *The
Beautiful and Damned,* which Zelda criticized with tangible
results. She maintained, for example, that the new ending he
had written was a piece of morality and ought to be cut.
Fitzgerald, undecided, asked Perkin's advice. Perkins said
that from an artistic point of view he agreed with Zelda, and
the book was concluded as it now stands. A passage Zelda
particularly liked was Maury Noble's debunking of the Old
Testament as the work of some ancient sceptics, whose sole
aim had been the literary immortality they achieved.
Mencken also liked this bit of irreverence, and when Perkins
denounced it, Fitzgerald was upset. He wrote a long letter,
invoking Samuel Butler and Anatole France, Voltaire and
Bernard Shaw, Mark Twain and George Moore, as great writers who had refused homage to the Bible and its God. 'I do
not expect in any event,' he wrote Perkins, 'that I am to have
the same person for person public this time that *Paradise*
had. My one hope is to be endorsed by the intellectually élite
& thus be *forced* on people as Conrad has. ... If I cut this
out, it would only [be] because I would be afraid and I
haven't done that yet & dread the day when I'll have to.'

Perkins stuck to his guns. Granted that most people under
forty would agree with Fitzgerald in substance, he did not
think the Old Testament should be treated in such a way as
to dismiss its immense historical importance. In the end,
Fitzgerald softened a few words but let the passage stand.

Another fret was the illustration on the dust jacket. 'I hope to God that Hill draws a good-looking girl,' Fitzgerald wrote Perkins, 'also' (remembering the art work for *This Side of Paradise*) 'that if there's a man he'll keep his tie outside his collar.' When the dusk jacket arrived, it confirmed Fitzgerald's worst fears. The *prima donna* in him was hypersensitive to his public image. 'The girl,' he wrote Perkins,

is excellent of course – it looks somewhat like Zelda but the man, I suspect, is a sort of debauched edition of me. . . . I do not understand an artist of Hill's talent and carefullness going quite contrary to a detailed description of the hero in the book. . . . Anthony is 'just under six feet' – Here he looks about Gloria's height with ugly short legs. . . . Anthony is dark haired – this bartender on the cover is light haired. . . . He looks like a sawed-off young tough in his first dinner-coat. . . . Everybody I've talked to agrees with me and I'm a little sore.

The Beautiful and Damned, published 3 March 1922, brought Fitzgerald accolades from those whose opinions he valued. Mencken congratulated him for staking out new ground instead of rewriting *This Side of Paradise*, which would have assured him financial success as well as a good deal of uncritical praise. Nathan called the book 'a very substantial performance – a first-rate job' and Edmund Wilson, who had read the manuscript and persuaded Fitzgerald to prune some of its excesses, thought it a distinct advance over *This Side of Paradise*. Fitzgerald was aiming high; he only wanted to be the best novelist of his generation. 'You cannot hurt my feelings about the book,' he wrote Bishop, 'tho I did resent in your Baltimore article being definately limited at 25 years old to a place between [Compton] Mckenzie who wrote 2½ good (but not wonderful) novels & then died – and Tarkington who if he has a great talent has the mind of a schoolboy. I mean, at my age they'd done nothing.'

Mencken was right. Fitzgerald, with the instinct that distinguishes the artist from the self-repeating hack, had tried something new. In a sense, *The Beautiful and Damned* was a repudiation of the Younger Generation thesis that had brought him to power; Gloria and Anthony Patch – young, glamorous, emancipated – live selfishly and hedonistically after the mode of rebellious youth and end up desperate and degraded. The bleakness of the theme put off many readers and caused sombre speculations about the author's private life. Gloria and Anthony, however, were not literal renderings of Scott and Zelda. 'Gloria was a much more trivial and vulgar person than your mother,' Fitzgerald wrote his daughter in after years. 'I can't really say there was any resemblance except in the beauty and certain terms of expression she used, and also I naturally used many circumstantial events of our early married life. However the emphases were entirely different. We had a much better time than Anthony and Gloria had.'

Still, an imagined kinship remained. *The Beautiful and Damned* was a projection of what Fitzgerald had come to consider the decayed part of their lives, and his amazing prescience, as we read the book today, gives a touch of heartache to its brassy prose. The jaunty epigraph – 'The victor belongs to the spoils' – might have been the epigraph for Fitzgerald's whole career, while the final glimpse of Gloria with her looks gone and of Anthony sunk in alcoholism is all too prophetic. After a fight in which Anthony breaks Gloria's spirit, he muses that 'it was yet problematical whether Gloria without her arrogance, her independence, her virginal confidence and courage would be the girl of his glory, the radiant woman who was precious and charming because she was ineffably, triumphantly herself.' Gloria recovers from the fight, but what if her spirit were permanently submerged in mental illness? So much of what Scott loved in Zelda depended on verve.

The Beautiful and Damned, while more consciously wrought and constructed than *This Side of Paradise,* was in some ways a weaker book. The earlier work was a portent, and as a picture of American college life it has never been surpassed. Fitzgerald told Shane Leslie he had written it, as Stevenson wrote *Treasure Island,* to satisfy his craving for a certain kind of novel. It has in spots the grace, the inevitability, the poetry of Fitzgerald's deepest vein. *The Beauti-*

ful and Damned, for all its wealth of irony and satire, seems a bit laboured by comparison.[25]

In March the Fitzgeralds went to New York to celebrate the book's publication. On their return Scott wrote Edmund Wilson, 'I was sorry our meetings in New York were so fragmentary. My original plan was to contrive to have long discourses with you but that interminable party began and I couldn't seem to get sober enough to be able to tolerate being sober. In fact the whole trip was largely a failure.'

While getting together a collection of his short stories (it was Scribners' policy to follow each novel with such a collection), Fitzgerald found time to write the St Paul Junior League Show, and did it with a good grace and accommodation unlooked for in a professional of his standing. He and Zelda and the baby spent the summer at the White Bear Yacht Club while he toyed with the idea of a novel set in the Midwest and New York of 1885, though before starting it he wanted to accumulate enough money so as not to be interrupted. The four stories he had written since coming to St Paul hadn't begun to meet expenses, and it had been necessary for Scribners to advance him $5,643 on *The Beautiful and Damned*. Its sales proved disappointing: 43,000 the first year, as against the 60,000 Fitzgerald had predicted. (*This Side of Paradise* had sold 44,000 during the same period, a good though not a startling sale considering its vogue.)

In July Fitzgerald weighed an offer to make a movie of *This Side of Paradise*, with him and Zelda in the leading roles, turning it down much to Perkins' relief. His great hope now was a play he had written. He called it 'a sure-fire money-maker' and counted on having it produced when he and Zelda moved East in the fall, for they were tired of St Paul.[26]

Meanwhile the baby was adorable, and, said Fitzgerald, '. . . we dazzle her exquisite eyes with gold pieces in the hopes that she'll marry a millionaire'.

Mid-September found the Fitzgeralds at the Plaza. When

they weren't house-hunting in the suburbs, Scott was writing a story, 'Winter Dreams', which he later called 'a sort of first draft of the Gatsby idea', or soberly transacting business in connexion with his play. He and Zelda were on the wagon, having made up their minds to steer clear of the ever-impending bacchanalia around New York.

Early in October they rented a house at 6 Gateway Drive in the incorporated village of Great Neck Estates near Great Neck, Long Island. While Fitzgerald was at Princeton, he had gone with Shane Leslie to visit the Bourke Cochrans at nearby Port Washington and had carried away vivid memories of the great estates clustering that part of the Island. Because Great Neck was half an hour from Broadway by the Long Island Express, a new element had been moving in of late: actors, song-writers, comedians, producers – celebrities like Lillian Russell, Goerge M. Cohan, and the great Ziegfeld himself. Their presence augured a good time, and having hired a couple to keep house and a nurse for the baby, the Fitzgeralds settled down to a riotous year which provided the background for *The Great Gatsby*.

The flavour of that year is suggested by these excerpts from Zelda's letters to the Kalmans – Sandra and 'Kallie' – a couple they had known in St Paul:

13 October 1922. Are you really coming east for the football games? If you are you *must* come stay with us in our nifty little Babbit-home at Great Neck. We seem to have achieved a state of comparative organization at last and, having bought loads of very interesting flour sieves and cocktail-shakers, are in a position to make a bid for your patronage on your next trip. We have had the most terrible time – very alcoholic & chaotic. We behaved so long that eventually we looked up Engalichoff which, needless to say, started us on a weeks festivity, equalled only by ancient Rome *and* Nineveh! For the rest we find ourselves diving into a fountain on the Greenwich Village Follies Curtain, getting drunk with Zoë Akins & George Nathan and hiring Swedish servants – having come all the way from Minnesota to avoid them.

Early November 1922. And now for the weather: it is perfectly delicious here and you and Kallie *must* come for the games. Think of the ride through the dusty blue twilight back to New York and the crysanthemums and the sort of burnt smell in the air – and the liquor. And then think of the Mont Matre afterward and the theatre . . .

Late November 1922. For a while I was consumed with a burning wrath at you two for not coming East, but after the game I began to see the wisdom of your decision. It was very spectacular and very dull, and doubtless you may have heard that Yale lost 3–0. That is all I know about the game part. After it was over, we went around to the clubs and I felt like Methusalah and all the kids were Peggys age so we ate dinner at 'The Baltimore Lunch' – a place like Child's, only not so exclusive. Then we took our drunken and very gay friends to call on a Presbyterian gentleman named Agar. There we met countless deans and proctors and professors daughters and our friends danced and sang for them, much to their horror and incomprehension.

5 January 1923. I suppose you had a glorious New Years. We saw ourselves out and the Year in between drinks at a dull party which I succeeded in ruining by throwing everybody's hat into a centre bowl-shaped light. It was very exhilirating and I wish you had been here to help me.

21 June 1923. First of all I feel perfectly awful about not seeing you on Monday – or whatever day it was. Everything beginning Friday and ending today has lost itself in the dimness and shadiness of my past and the Gregorian Calendar has lost all significance to me. It seems awful now that I have come to and discovered you gone that I never even got a good look at Sandy. Monday night when I returned from regions unmentionable because unknown and got your message I called the Ritz and had some faint difficulty with the clerk. I'm not sure that I told my right name but if I did, did you get word. . . . But Scott now has a flash of clairvoyance and informs me that I rode out of your room in a laundry wagon – and that Sandy became very high hat about it – so maybe you hope you will never seen us again.

July 1923. Scott has started a new novel and retired into strict seclusion and celibacy. He's horribly intent on it and has built up a beautiful legend about himself which corresponds somewhat to the old fable about the ant & the grasshopper. *Me* being the grasshopper.

The Fitzgeralds had moved to Great Neck hoping to settle down and be normal, but despite the hired help their *ménage* was erratic. Zelda told an interviewer that breakfast and lunch were 'extremely moveable feasts', and dinner guests would find that the wrong food had been ordered, or else that there was too much of one thing and not enough of another. The house lacked a central command; Scott and Zelda gave overlapping instructions and in the end little got done.

There was a memorable dinner for Rebecca West at which she failed to appear. Fitzgerald got a pillow, painted a face on it, crowned it with an enormous plumed hat, and put it in the seat of honour. All during the meal he insulted this effigy of the authoress and teased it about her books. When a delivery boy rang the bell, Fitzgerald went to the door and said in a loud voice, 'No, Miss West, you can't come in. We don't want you now.' Rebecca West, lecturing in this country, had received the invitation through a third party, and at the last minute had been unable to find Fitzgerald's address or even the name of the town where he lived. When they met later on, they liked each other. Rebecca West always remembered Fitzgerald for his graciousness and charity.

It is interesting to speculate on the Great Neck parties that might have been a model for Gatsby's. There were those of Herbert Bayard Swope, the well-known sportsman-journalist; on his croquet course, illumined by car headlights, games were played for $2,000 stakes. There were those of Gene Buck, Ziegfeld's right-hand man. Buck's house had been decorated by the *Follies'* stage designer, and Ring Lardner described the living room as looking like 'the Yale Bowl – with lamps'. The Fitzgeralds also entertained in a somewhat garish manner. They were usually 'on' in the theatrical sense, and they liked their captive audience to be as large and illustrious as possible. They 'knew every one', which is to say most of those whom Ralph Barton, the cartoonist, would have represented as being in the orchestra on opening night. After one of their brawls they framed a set of house rules which were only partly facetious. Item: 'Visitors are requested not to break down doors in search of liquor, even when authorized to do so by the host and hostess.' Item: 'Week-end guests are respectfully notified that invitations to stay over Monday, issued by the host and hostess during the small hours of Sunday morning, must not be taken seriously.'

Fitzgerald was given to pet expressions. At Princeton all his enthusiasms had been 'knock-outs', and now the magic word was 'egg'. People he liked were 'good eggs', or 'colossal eggs', and people he didn't like were 'bad eggs' or 'unspeakable eggs'. One evening the actress, Laurette Taylor, happened in on a Fitzgerald party. As she entered the room, Scott recognized her, and dropping to his knees he took her hands in his and said, 'My God, you beautiful egg! You beautiful egg!' He led her to a couch before which he knelt and resumed his incantation: 'You beautiful, beautiful egg!' When Laurette Taylor got home she summoned her husband, the playwright Hartley Manners, from his Saturday night poker game. 'Oh, Hartley' – she began to cry – 'I've just seen the doom of youth. Understand? The doom of youth itself. A walking doom.'

Despite their hospitality, the Fitzgeralds made few friends in Great Neck where their only real intimates were the Lardners. During the year Scott was meditating *Gatsby*, and the first six months of writing it, the supreme influence in his life was 'Ring'. Lardner had a wondrous courtliness and consideration, though like Fitzgerald he was a practical joker of slightly sinister intent. One day the two of them lunched with Rube Goldberg, the cartoonist, and afterwards sat around drinking while Goldberg kept insisting he needed a haircut. Finally they adjourned to the local barber, who was about to go home and left the shop in their hands. Goldberg was inveigled into a chair where he promptly fell asleep, and when he woke up, his friends were gone and his hair was cut in patches. He was less amused than they, for he had to attend a family gathering that evening. On another occasion Lardner and Fitzgerald did a tipsy dance on the lawn of the Doubleday estate, hoping to attract the attention of Joseph Conrad who was staying there, but they only attracted the caretaker who expelled them.

There is a brotherhood of the intemperate which helps to explain the bond between Lardner and Fitzgerald, different as they were on the surface: the light and the dark, the short and the tall, the expansive and the reticent, the merry and the dismal. Fitzgerald described Lardner's face as resembling a cathedral. The high cheekbones and swarthy complexion gave it an Indian cast, and the heavy eyebrows would have been fierce but for the sadness of the large, dark, hypnotic eyes. Lardner's dignity and authority made one proud to be his friend. Not infrequently he and Fitzgerald talked the night away over a case of Canadian ale or something stronger, until Ring, yawning and blinking at the early sun, would say, 'Well, I guess the children have left for school by now – I might as well go home.'

Mildly self-deprecating, Lardner considered himself a reporter rather than a literary man. His bailiwick was sports and popular entertainment, and he remained a little leery of the critics who were booming his work. What he gave Fitzgerald was intangible but invaluable – a fountain of wit, a cockeyed inner sense of truth, a feeling of being in cahoots with the world in general – while Fitzgerald, on his side, helped Lardner collect his first book of short stories which Scribners published. ('Readers,' said Lardner of the reviews, 'might think I was having an affair with some of the Critics.'

But already there had fastened on Lardner the despair which deepened until his death in 1933. Then Fitzgerald summed up his affection for this proud, shy, inscrutable man in an obituary memoir which concludes, 'Let us not obscure him by the flowers, but walk up and look at that fine medallion, all abraded by sorrows that perhaps we are not equipped to understand. Ring made no enemies, because he was kind, and to many millions he gave release and delight.'

In June Eleanor Browder, a friend of Zelda's from Montgomery, spent a week with the Fitzgeralds and never forgot the day she and Zelda met Scott at the Plaza for tea. He came in carrying a bottle of champagne with which he had fortified himself for a dentist appointment, and now, with Anita Loos in tow, he was celebrating the fact that the appointment was over. The four of them went into the Palm Room where the waiter refused to serve them because of Scott's condition, so presently they were driving out to Great Neck in a rented car, quaffing warm champagne from a case of it at their feet. Cocktails awaited them at Gateway Drive, followed by a candlelight supper. They had finished the first course when a woman who had been pursuing Scott came to the front door. He got rid of her, but when he sat down again Zelda made a remark. One word led to another, and suddenly Scott was on his feet wrenching the cloth from the table and striding out of the room amid the crash of china and glass.

'Shall we have our coffee in the next room?' said Zelda. The three women picked their way through the debris and sipped *demitasses* while Scott fell asleep under a tree. Later he came in, all politeness, and the incident was not referred to during the rest of Eleanor's stay.

Despite such strangeness, the Fitzgeralds were still the golden couple of American letters. When a New York reporter called on them at home and Scott was asked to describe his wife, he said, 'She's the most charming person in the world.' Pressed for details, he added fervently, 'That's all. I refuse to amplify – excepting she's perfect.'

'You don't think that,' Zelda put in. 'You think I'm a lazy woman.'

'No,' said Scott. 'I like it. I think you're perfect. You're always ready to listen to my manuscripts at any hour of day or night. You're charming – beautiful. You do, I believe, clean the ice-box once a week.'

Van Wyck Brooks has written affectingly of the Fitzgeralds as they seemed to him during this period. Brooks went to a dinner

at which Fitzgerald and Zelda, his wife, arriving an hour late when the others had finished, sitting at table fell asleep over the soup that was brought in, for they had spent the two previous nights at parties. So Scott Fitzgerald said as he awoke for a moment, while some one gathered Zelda up, with her bright cropped hair and diaphanous gown, and dropped her on a bed in a room near by. There she lay curled and asleep like a silky kitten. Scott slumbered in the living-room waking up suddenly again to telephone an order for two cases of champagne, together with a fleet of taxis to take us to a night club. That moment and scene bring back now a curious note of the twenties that one did not connect with insanity and tragedy then, while I was drawn to the Scott Fitzgeralds, whom I never really knew but who seemed to me, so obviously, romantic lovers.

Around New York Fitzgerald was still the awesome, successful, young genius whose name was news. When he hit a plain-clothes man who insulted Zelda at a Webster Hall dance, he read in the paper next day, 'Fitzgerald Knocks Officer This Side of Paradise'. But notoriety and success no longer satisfied – now that he had them he was inclined to think, 'Is *this* all!' – and the writing he had to do to maintain himself had grown increasingly irksome. He found himself repeating the matter of an earlier period without being able to recapture the exuberant manner. It rankled him that a cheap story like 'The Popular Girl', tossed off the week the baby was born, should bring $1,500 from the *Post*, while 'The Diamond as Big as the Ritz', a genuinely imaginative thing to which he had devoted three weeks of enthusiasm, had to be sold to *Smart Set* for $300.

To liberate himself from the *Post*, but also because the theatre enticed him, he had written *The Vegetable, or from President to Postman*. It was a farce in which Jerry Frost, a henpecked railroad clerk, is persuaded to run for President. The second act, a fantasy with Frost dreaming he *is* President, gave Fitzgerald his chance to spoof the Harding régime, while the third act concluded happily with Frost becoming the postman he had always wanted to be. Fitzgerald thought it the funniest play ever written; he was sure it would make him rich, though three producers turned it down before Sam Harris agreed to undertake it.

The play opened in Atlantic City on 20 November 1923. The Fitzgeralds went down with the Lardners and Allen Dwan the movie director, and there was a gala audience including Mayor Hylan of New York. The first act went well enough, but the dream sequence in the second act confused the audience, who got bored and walked out in droves. 'It was,' said Fitzgerald, 'a colossal frost. . . . I wanted to stop the show and say it was all a mistake but the actors struggled heroically on.' During the second intermission Fitzgerald and Lardner asked Ernest Truex, the lead, 'Are you going to stay and do the last act?' Truex said he was. 'Don't be silly,' they laughed, 'we've met a bartender down the street who's an old friend of ours' – and that was the last Truex saw of them.

After a fruitless week of patching and revising, the play was abandoned. Fitzgerald had been mistaken in thinking that his fictional talents were immediately transferable to the stage.

The sale of the movie rights to *This Side of Paradise* for $10,000 the previous spring had given him a false sense of security. He now had $5,000 worth of pressing obligations. His finances had always been a rearguard action, even during the first year of his success, when his income was doubling every month and he felt a little patronizing towards the millionaires riding down Park Avenue in their limousines. In 1919 he had made $879; in 1920, $18,850; in 1921, $19,065; in 1922, $25,135; and in 1923, $28,760. Not a cent of it had been saved, however, and investments were out of the question. He joked about something he called 'his bond', an unlisted security which he had bought just before his marriage and which he could never sell in moments of crisis. (Once it was turned in at the Subway Office when he accidentally left it in one of the cars.) He was always in debt to his agent, for when he submitted a story he was used to collecting the money for the next unwritten one. Scribners, too, had been giving him large advances. He was humorous about it, signing his letters to Perkins 'the Inevitable Beggar', and offering to pay interest, but the fact remained that he couldn't live within his income, and where the money went no one knew. Eleanor Browder, when she visited the Fitzgeralds, found some of it stuffed in the side pockets of their Rolls-Royce coupé.

With the play a failure and no book in sight, Fitzgerald had only one recourse. He retired to the large bare room with oil stove over his garage and emerged next afternoon with a 7,000 word story. It took him twelve hours a day for five weeks 'to rise from abject poverty back into the middle class', and several more months at an easier gait before he had enough margin to resume work on *Gatsby*. Meanwhile the strain was giving him coughs, itches, stomach aches, insomnia. 'I really worked hard as hell last winter,' he said in retrospect, ' – but it was all trash and it nearly broke my heart as well as my iron constitution.'

Fitzgerald did not condone his improvidence. A stern self-critic, he deplored it and atoned for it with orgies of work. The sweat that went into his least productions has been underestimated. People said he was facile, and certainly he had that side to him, but he made his writing seem easier than it was by taking immense pains, by struggling with it until he got it precisely the way he wanted it.

At Great Neck a macabre note had entered the Fitzgeralds' revels. The year after their marriage their drinking around New York had been a gay, irresponsible, left-over-from-college affair, but now their fun was turning destructive. Fitzgerald vanished into the city on two-and three-day drunks, after which neighbours would find him asleep on his own front lawn. At dinner parties he crawled around under the table, or hacked off his tie with a kitchen knife, or tried to eat soup with a fork. Once, when the Max Perkinses were along, he drove them into a pond because it seemed more fun – then he and Zelda got out in water up to their waists and tried to push the car ashore.

It is hard to say whether he or she was the leader in this chaos. They complemented each other like gin and vermouth in a martini, each making the other more powerful in their war with dullness and convention. Perkins blamed their extravagances on Zelda, when actually Scott was the more idiotically extravagant of the two. His pride demanded that Zelda have the best of everything, and he was always buying her expensive jewellery which she sometimes threw away in a moment of pique. Both were unstable; when they should have called a halt, they egged each other on. They faced life not ignobly but with a mad sort of daring, committed to doing as they pleased and never counting the cost.

Clearly, they needed a change. Scott complained that friends from New York were turning his home into a roadhouse, and he was tired of being publicized as the Homer of the flapper. He would take the atmosphere of Long Island – the starlight, the wealth, the magnificent estates, the glimpses of the Sound – and materialize it under foreign skies. He would go to Europe and stay there until he had accomplished some great things.

Uprooting Zelda was no problem. 'I hate a room without an open suitcase in it,' she used to say, ' – it seems so permanent.'

In April the Fitzgeralds sailed on the *S.S. Minnewaska*, intending to settle near Hyères on the French Riviera. Their departure brought this tribute from Ring Lardner:

TO ZELDA

Zelda, fair queen of Alabam',
Across the waves I kiss you!
You think I am a stone, a clam:
You think that I don't care a damn,
But God! how I will miss you![27]

For months and months you've meant to me
What Mario meant to Tosca.

You've gone, and I am all at sea
Just like the Minnewaska.

I once respected him you call
Your spouse, and that is why, dear,
I held my tongue – And then, last Fall,
He bared a flippancy and gall
Of which I had no idear.

When I with pulmonary pain
Was seized, he had the gumption
To send me lives of Wilde and Crane,
Two brother craftsmen who in vain
Had battled with consumption.

We wreak our vengeance as we can,
And I have no objection
To getting even with this 'man'
By stealing your affection.

So, dearie, when your tender heart
Of all his coarseness tires,
Just cable me and I will start
Immediately for Hyeres.

To hell with Scott Fitzgerald then!
To hell with Scott, his daughter!
It's you and I back home again,
To Great Neck, where the men are men,
And booze is ¾ water.

[10]

ZELDA wrote Max Perkins of their weird crossing, 'haunted by such tunes as "Horsey keep your tail up, keep the sun out of my eyes" played by an aboriginal English orchestra'. In Paris they lunched with John Peale Bishop at an expensive restaurant in the Bois where it was difficult to order for little Scottie, and Fitzgerald gave her one of his shoelaces and a handful of coins which she played with on the gravel under the tables. Having hired an English nanny, the Fitzgeralds went on to Hyères where – Zelda's letter continued – 'Scott reads nothing but lives of Byron & Shelley and shows the most romantic proclivities.' They were living in a hotel 'surrounded by invalids of every variety and all the native Hyèrsans have goiters'. The menu featured goat's meat, a state of affairs not to be endured.

Early in June they moved up the Riviera to St Raphael where they rented the Villa Marie, set back in a wood of cypress and parasol pines. Here they began their new life with the usual well-meaning, hopeful gaiety. Scott grew a moustache and rented a baby Renault in which he and Zelda ranged along the coast. On mornings after late evenings in St Raphael, when the details of their homecoming had been hazy, Scottie would be sent to the garage to report on the condition of the car and would bring back the intelligence, for example, that the tyres were round on the top but flat at the bottom.

The deep Greek of the Mediterranean licked its chops over the edges of our febrile civilization. Keeps crumbled on grey hillsides and sowed the dust of their battlements beneath the olives and the cactus. Ancient moats slept bound in tangled honeysuckle; fragile poppies bled the causeways; vineyards caught on jagged rocks like bits of worn carpet. The baritone of tired medieval bells proclaimed disinterestedly a holiday from time. Lavender bloomed silently over the rocks. It was hard to see in the vibrancy of the sun.

Thus Zelda would recall the *mise en scène* of her love affair.

Like Scott she had left America wanting a deep spiritual change, but unlike him she had no prospect of writing a great novel. At twenty-three – almost twenty-four – she may have begun to fear her looks were going, or she may have felt insufficient basking in her husband's glory. Perhaps she was trying to make him jealous, or perhaps she was bored and the seduction of the moment proved too strong. There is no single explanation for her involvement with a French naval flyer named Edouard Josanne.[28]

Fitzgerald was used to men falling in love with Zelda. Caught up in his book, he was glad not to have her bothering him, and at first he didn't suspect what was going on. In a piece of journalism he wrote at this time he described how

in half an hour, René and Bobbé [Edouard Josanne], officers of aviation, are coming to dinner in their white ducks. . . . Afterwards, in the garden, their white uniforms will grow dimmer as the more liquid dark comes down, until they, like the heavy roses and the nightingales in the pines, will seem to take an essential and indivisible part in the beauty of this proud gay land.

Zelda, in her descriptions of Josanne in her novel *Save Me the Waltz*, stressed the muscularity of his lean, bronzed body under the starched uniforms. He was handsome – in feature not unlike Scott – but he was 'full of the sun' while Scott was 'a moon person'. Josanne was daring and zoomed his plane perilously low over the Villa Marie.

Matters had gone far when Scott caught on, and momentarily he was shattered. He really believed in love, in what two people can build against the world's cheap scepticism. 'Upon the theme of marital fidelity,' said his friend Ernest Boyd, the critic, 'Fitzgerald's eloquence has moved me to tears. . . . Where so many others are conscious only of sex, he is conscious of his soul. His Catholic heaven is not so far away that he can be misled into mistaking the shoddy dream of a radical millennium as a substitute for Paradise.'

Fitzgerald forced a showdown and delivered an ultimatum which banished Josanne from their lives. The crisis took place 13 July; in August Fitzgerald wrote in his Ledger, 'Zelda and I close together,' and in September, 'Trouble clearing away.' But the episode was a rent in their armour which he would never forget.

In a letter to Perkins he called it 'a fair summer. I've been unhappy but my work hasn't suffered from it. I am grown at last.' His work may even have profited. Who can say but that Fitzgerald's jealousy sharpened the edge of Gatsby's and gave weight to Tom Buchanan's bullish determination to regain his wife? In any case, Fitzgerald's prose was sparkling as never before, and as an artist he had shot up. In July 1922, before moving to Great Neck, he had said he wanted 'to write something *new* – something extraordinary and beautiful and simple & intricately patterned'. Of such idealism *The Great Gatsby* had been born, and the lashing his published play received at the hands of the critics had sent him back to the novel in a chastened mood.

It is only in the last four months [he wrote Perkins just before leaving America], that I've realized how much I've – well, almost *deteriorated* in the three years since I finished the Beautiful and Damned. The last four months of course I've worked but in the two years – over two years – before that, I produced exactly *one* play, *half a dozen* short stories and three or four articles – an average of about *one hundred* words a day. If I'd spent the time reading or travelling or doing anything – even staying healthy – it'd be different but I spent it uselessly, neither in study nor in contemplation but only in drinking and raising hell generally. If I'd written B&D at the rate of 100 words a day it would have taken me *4 years* so you can imagine the moral effect the whole chasm had on me.

What I'm trying to say is just that I'll have to ask you to have patience about the book and trust me that *at last*, or at least for the 1st time in years, I'm doing the best I can. I've gotten in dozens of bad habits that I'm trying to get rid of

1. Laziness
2. Referring everything to Zelda – a terrible habit, nothing ought to be referred to anybody until it's finished
3. Word consciousness & self-doubt
                    ect. ect. ect. ect.

I feel I have an enormous power in me now, more than I've ever had in a way but it works so fitfully and with so many bogeys because I've *talked so much* and not lived enough within myself to develop the necessary self reliance. Also I don't know any one who has used up so much personal experience as I have at 27. Copperfield & Pendennis were written at past forty while This Side of Paradise was three books & the B&D was two. So in my new novel I'm thrown directly on purely creative work – not trashy imaginings as in my stories but the sustained imagination of a sincere yet radiant world. So I tread slowly and carefully & at times in considerable distress. This book will be a consciously artistic achievement & must depend on that as the 1st books did not.

In 1934 Fitzgerald would say that never had he tried to keep his artistic conscience so pure as during the ten months of writing *Gatsby*. Before beginning it he had reread the preface to *The Nigger of the Narcissus*, and Conrad's dictum that a work of art should carry its justification in every line had been his guide.

In September the Lardners, touring Europe, spent a few days with the Fitzgeralds at St Raphael. The 'pulmonary pain' Ring had joked about in his poem to Zelda was a reality; he was suffering from tuberculosis, and during most of the visit he reclined on a Louis XV sofa in his bathrobe and prodded Fitzgerald with dry, unexpected remarks. The manuscript of *Gatsby* went to Scribners the end of October. Perkins wrote back at once, praising the book's vitality, style, *glamour*, and the unusual quality of its underlying thought. Later came a detailed analysis of its flaws which Fitzgerald took pains to remedy, especially the sag of interest in Chapters Six and Seven and the undue vagueness of Gatsby and his origins (some of the vagueness was intended – to give him an air of mystery). Perkins ended by saying that the description of the Valley of Ashes and the catalogue of those who attended Gatsby's parties were such things as make men famous, while the eyes of Dr T. J. Eckleburg and the glimpses of city, sea, and sky brought in a note of eternity.

Fitzgerald was overjoyed. His confidence was renewed, and for the first time since *The Vegetable* failed he thought himself a wonderful writer. Predicting a sale of 80,000, or twice that of his previous novels, he wrote Perkins that the proofs, because of the intricate changes he had in mind to make it a perfect book, would be the most expensive since *Madame Bovary*. Meanwhile he told his agent that after rehabilitating himself financially with three or four short stories, he was starting another novel. 'My loafing days are over – I feel as though I'd wasted 1922 & 1923.'

For no more apparent reason than that Zelda had been reading Henry James, the Fitzgeralds decided to winter in Rome. *Ben Hur*, starring Ramon Navarro and Carmel Myers, was filming there 'in bigger and grander papiermaché arenas than the real ones', and Scott and Zelda amused themselves with the cast, but after hitting a policeman in an argument over a taxi fare, Scott was beaten up and jailed. He once said that coming from the Midwest he had only the vaguest race prejudices. This experience, however, gave him a hatred of Italians that extended to the country itself – 'a dead land', he called it, 'where everything that could be done or said was done long ago, for whoever is decieved by the pseudo activity under Mussolini is decieved by the spasmotic last jerk of a corpse'. In January he and Zelda moved to Capri, liking it no better. They had been sick a good deal, especially Zelda, and her affair had left a bitterness between them. Nevertheless, Fitzgerald wrote Bishop that they were still enormously in love and about the only truly happily married people he knew.

In April they started north, having decided to make Paris their headquarters. On the tenth of the month *Gatsby* would be published, and as the day approached Fitzgerald's confidence waned. What if women didn't like it because it contained no important female character, and what if the critics didn't like it because it dealt with the rich instead of the farm types then in vogue? Fitzgerald stewed over the advertising, fearful lest his book be mistaken for just another jazz-and-society novel. He had never been sure of the title, and as late as 19 March, he had wired Perkins, CRAZY ABOUT TITLE UNDER THE RED WHITE AND BLUE WHAT WOULD BE DELAY? (Perkins talked him out of this brainstorm.) The day before publication he wired for news, and the first bulletin came back, 'SALES SITUATION DOUBT-FUL EXCELLENT REVIEWS.'[29]

The reviews – and they *were* excellent, the most impressive he had ever received – struck a common note: his meta-morphosis from adolescent prodigy into mature artist. There were also letters from Willa Cather and Edith Wharton; from Gertrude Stein, who said Fitzgerald was creating the contemporary world as much as Thackery had created his in *Pendennis* and *Vanity Fair*; from T. E. Eliot (Fitzgerald thought him the greatest living poet), who said that *Gatsby* was the first step American fiction had taken since Henry James. Lunching with Gilbert Seldes some months after re-ceiving Eliot's letter, Fitzgerald produced it, saying he just happened to have it with him, and when a friend came over to speak to them, he unabashedly drew it out a second time.

The Great Gatsby was indeed a more conscious work of art than Fitzgerald's first two novels, just as its hero was less obviously an autobiographical projection than either Amory Blaine or Anthony Patch. Gatsby had been created, Fitz-gerald said later, on the image of some Minnesota farm type, known and forgotten and associated with a sense of romance. With Gatsby in mind he had studied bootleggers of his ac-quaintance, and Gatsby's financial intrigues were perhaps modelled on the Fuller-McGee case which had filled the papers in 1922. The essential Gatsby, however – he of the heightened sensitivity to the promises of life, of the extra-ordinary gift of hope and the romantic readiness – was Fitz-gerald himself. In the figure of Gatsby, he had been able to objectify and poetize his early feelings about the rich: that they were a race apart with a better seat in life's grandstand, that their existence was somehow more beautiful and intense than that of ordinary mortals. Barricaded behind their fortunes, they had seemed to him almost like royalty. Fitzgerald's snobbery was romantic – graced and to some extent redeemed by the imagination in a way that is peculiarly Irish. One finds the same point of view in Yeats or Oscar Wilde.

But also Fitzgerald sensed a corruption in the rich and mistrusted their might. 'That was always my experience,' he wrote near the end of his life,

– a poor boy in a rich town; a poor boy in a rich boy's school; a poor boy in a rich man's club at Princeton. . . . I have never been able to forgive the rich for being rich, and it has colored my entire life and works.' He told a friend that 'the whole idea of Gatsby is the unfairness of a poor young man not being able to marry a girl with money. This theme comes up again and again because I lived it.' [30, 31]

Thus Gatsby's love for Daisy was Fitzgerald's love for Zelda – and before her, Ginevra – decked out in a Keatsian prose. Keats stands back of the book's tactile and sensuous imagery, just as Conrad stands back of its brooding terror and the device of the bemused narrator. Another influence, surprisingly, was *The Brothers Karamazov*, which had overwhelmed Fitzgerald when he read it in 1922. But *Gatsby*'s pervasive and memorable quality was non-derivative – was Fitzgerald finding within himself new depths of tenderness and understanding. Since *The Beautiful and Damned* his sensibility had undergone a mysterious change, which can only be explained as phenomenon of growth. He had put away the harsh smartness which he considered the greatest flaw of his earlier work. Here in its place was a taut realism but also a gossamer romance, a yearning and straining after the beauty that hangs by a thread, a lyric compassion. Fitzgerald had found his voice and at last done something truly his own. [32, 33, 34]

Financially the book was a disappointment. Its sale of 22,000 little more than cancelled his advance from Scribners.

Perkins explained that the trade was sceptical because *Gatsby* seemed short for a novel, because it was over the heads of more people than Fitzgerald would suppose, because the idea of so many parties and drinks was somehow prejudicial. The trend in fiction was towards the delineation of the American 'peasant' who did not exist, said Fitzgerald angrily, except in the minds of certain critics and fourth-rate novelists. 'Some day they'll eat grass, by God!' he wrote Perkins. 'This thing, both the effort and the result have hardened me and I think now that I'm much better than any of the young Americans *without exception.*'

His plan was still to get ahead on short stories and then begin another novel – 'something really NEW in form, idea, structure – the model for the age that Joyce and Stein are searching for, that Conrad didn't find.' If the proceeds from it would support him with no more intervals of trash, he would continue as a novelist. Otherwise he was going to Hollywood to learn the movie business.

I can't reduce our scale of living and I can't stand this financial insecurity. Anyhow there's no point in trying to be an artist if you can't do your best. I had my chance back in 1920 to start my life on a sensible scale and I lost it and so I'll have to pay the penalty. Then perhaps at 40 I can start writing again without constant worry and interruption.

Early in May the Fitzgeralds reached Paris, where they rented a fifth-floor walk-up at 14 rue Tilsit, a block from the Etoile. When Scott stepped to the corner of the Avenue Wagram, the Arc de Triomphe faced him end on, breathing the Napoleonic legend. That great commander had always fascinated Fitzgerald, a chronic hero-worshipper, who sought in others the qualities he lacked.

The previous fall he had written Max Perkins about a young writer named Ernest Hemingway, whose stories, appearing in *avant-garde* magazines, were making a stir. 'I'd look him up right away,' Fitzgerald advised Perkins. 'He's the real thing.' Soon after he got to Paris, Fitzgerald tracked Hemingway down in one of his Left Bank haunts, and different as they were in everything except their Midwestern background and their passion for writing, they quickly became friends. In place of college Hemingway had worked on a Kansas City newspaper, had gone to Italy at eighteen to drive an ambulance and almost had his leg blown off by an Austrian mortar. Returning to America, he had married and had veered back to Europe as a correspondent for the *Toronto Star*, covering, among other spectacles, the Lausanne Conference and the Greco-Turkish War. Schooled in combat and journalism, he knew the world in a way Fitzgerald did not and seemed on the whole more mature, though actually he was three years younger.

Hemingway was a big, self-assured, engaging fellow with black hair and a small moustache, with a boyish grin that bared a good set of teeth, and dark eyes that glanced about him with a hunter's acumen. Lounging in the bistros of Montparnasse, he seemed a bit of a roughneck, but he was genial and relaxed. He revelled in his senses; the world of sport and nature was open to him as it never could be to an essentially indoor person like Fitzgerald. Hemingway was an expert fisherman, a good skier and boxer. A shade awkward in games like tennis or baseball, he had developed a swiftness in the ring that was surprising in one of his bulk. As he paddled about the streets in a patched coat and sneakers, he would often be feinting and jabbing, but no one noticed him except to smile. If you were his companion, you didn't josh him either. He would ask you whether you wanted to make something out of it if you did.

Dean Gauss was in Paris that summer, and he and Hemingway and Fitzgerald lunched together a few times. Gauss found Hemingway a naïf, earnest Balzacien type boy, without 'pretensions or flub-dub' and regretted he was unable to like what Hemingway wrote. Fitzgerald had no such difficulty. He marvelled at the freshness of the young man's world evoked in Hemingway's stories and sketches, and respected the discipline back of the mosaic prose. Hemingway had given up a promising career in journalism to write unprofitable fiction, doing his paragraphs over and over as if they were five-finger exercises. He was living in a bare apartment overlooking a lumber yard, and though his inner certitude didn't require much encouragement he was getting it from such experts as Ezra Pound and Gertrude Stein.

One day Hemingway took Fitzgerald to call on Miss Stein at her studio in the rue Férou, and Fitzgerald charmed and was charmed by the priestess of the arts with her beefsteak laugh and quick perceptions. He looked up to her and played up to her, and she made him feel at ease, so that he wasn't tongue-tied as he had been when he met Theodore Dreiser – and would be presently on a visit to Edith Wharton.

Mrs Wharton's letter praising *Gatsby* had concluded with an invitation to her eighteenth-century villa north of Paris, and one afternoon Fitzgerald drove out with Teddy Chanler, whose mother was an intimate of the distinguished authoress. Fitzgerald was nervous and stopped for several bracers along the way while Chanler sat in the car. His drinking at such times was something he went off and did by himself, like taking a pill. It had no connexion with anyone else.

Arrived at the Pavillon Colombe, Fitzgerald and Chanler were ushered into a salon where Mrs Wharton, the confidante of Henry James, sat behind her tea set in shy majesty. There was one other guest, an American-born Cambridge don named Gaillard Lapsley. Mrs Wharton, so witty and delightful when one got to know her, was notoriously ill at ease on first acquaintance and inclined to take refuge behind the haughty mien of an aristocratic New Yorker. Since Chanler and Lapsley were unable to break the ice, Fitzgerald descended to such platitudes as 'Mrs Wharton, you have no idea what it means to me to come out here.' Finally, in desperation, he suggested telling 'a couple of – er – rather rough stories.' Permission having been granted by a queenly nod, a fixed smile, he began one and switched to another about an American couple who had spent three days in a Paris bordello, which they mistook for a hotel. As he faltered to a conclusion, Mrs Wharton said, 'But Mr Fitzgerald, your story lacks data' – whereupon he tried to patch it up without success.[35]

When he had gone, Mrs Wharton said to Lapsley, 'There must be something peculiar about that young man.' Lapsley explained that Fitzgerald had been drinking. Mrs Wharton wrote 'Horrible' beside his name in her diary; of course he would never be asked again. But as someone remarked – someone who had met with a similar reception at the Pavillon Colombe – 'Mrs Wharton has the grand manner that triumphs over a situation when another person might save it.'[35]

It was, Fitzgerald wrote in his Ledger, a time of '1000 parties and no work.' He was polishing a story called 'The Rich Boy', written on the heels of *Gatsby*, but concentration was difficult with a new world opening out before him. He still had something in common with Amory Blaine, who got distracted when he started writing – 'get afraid I'm doing it instead of living – get thinking maybe life is waiting for me in the Japanese gardens at the Ritz or at Atlantic City or on the lower East Side.'

On their way through Paris the previous spring, the Fitzgeralds had met Gerald and Sara Murphy with whom they were now establishing a real *entente*. Independently wealthy, the Murphys had moved abroad after the war and taken up with the artists and literati. Fitzgerald had found the rich disappointingly dull since success had opened their doors to him, but now the Murphys came along to revive his hopes. Gerald was an *élégant* – slender, fit, and dressed to the nines. He affected long sideburns and carried a gold-headed cane and wore a special hat with a wide, swooping brim, humorously insisting that an ordinary hat looked silly with his 'Irish mug'. A man of exceptional taste and sensitivity, he had a knack for making life vivid and surprising. If you climbed the Eiffel Tower with him, he would point out a sight no one had noticed and tell you an amusing story about it into the bargain. He painted, and had done some sets for the Russian Ballet (once he and Sara had given a party for the whole Diaghilev troupe). They also gave dinners for as many as forty people at Maxim's, and it was known that the tip for the hats was paid in advance, lest the sum prove embarrassing to some of the poorer artists present. Sara kept more in the background than Gerald, but her quiet, intelligent charm was felt nonetheless. In this perfect team, as one of their friends recalled, Sara was the wind and Gerald the sail.

The Murphys really invented the summer colony at Antibes. Traditionally, one wintered on the Riviera and summered at Deauville, even though the swimming was reminiscent of the coast of Maine. The summer of 1922, however, the Murphys had rented the first floor of the Hôtel du Cap d'Antibes for themselves and their friends, after the proprietor had closed the rest of it and gone north. The villas along the cape were shuttered and empty. One felt an air of desertion, almost of savagery, under the brutal sunshine, amid the hard, bright colours of mountains and sea. Because of the dryness the heat was quite bearable, and when the Murphys discovered there wasn't any beach they set out to make one. With a mattock Gerald removed the packed, red seaweed from the Plage de la Garoupe until a few hundred yards of sand had been laid bare. The natives, peeking through the trees, thought these Americans who swam and doused themselves with banana oil must be crazy; there was a superstition among them that sea bathing was bad for the kidneys.

The Murphys liked Antibes so much they decided to build. Their house, the Villa America, was set in a garden of oranges, lemons, mimosas and cedars of Lebanon, and from the terrace out back one had a view of the Golfe Juan with the Estérelles rising beyond. In the living room, with its black-and-white tiled floor and its furniture made of aluminum tubing, the Steinway had just one ornament: a ball bearing which Gerald had spotted somewhere and liked the looks of. On the music rack would be the latest Stravinsky; no one noticed it, perhaps, but it was there. When you went to the Murphys for dinner, their attractive children appeared in blue matador pants with a red arrow at the leg. The food was always perfection. There would be whole peaches floating in brandy, and pheasants elaborately garnished, and the French guests would delight in the Americanism of a heaping plate of corn off the cob, topped by a poached egg. Everything was thought out with almost Oriental precision, and the Murphys themselves were the warmest and most genial of hosts. Like all formal people, however, they had a certain reserve. You didn't just drop in on them – you were invited, and you went away feeling it had been a treat.

The Fitzgeralds spent the month of August on the Riviera under the Murphys' wing. There was much talk of their coming; first they were, then they weren't. Then one morning they showed up at the Plage de la Garoupe already badly scorched from tennis the day before. Everyone was solicitous, telling them to keep their shoulders covered and rub on ointment. Too burned to go in swimming, Scott chatted with a reporter who chronicled their arrival. He claimed to be feeling old that summer, but the reporter found him stocky, muscular, clear-skinned, with wide fresh green-blue eyes – no touch of grey, no lines or sagging anywhere. Nor did Zelda show her age; she might have been in her teens. Perhaps Scottie did. Yes, there was no denying she looked her four.

The only people at Antibes that summer, Fitzgerald wrote Bishop, were 'me, Zelda, the Valentinos, the Murphys, Mistinguet, Rex Ingram, Dos Passos, Alice Terry, the Mclieshes, Charlie Bracket, Maude Kahn, Esther Murphy, Marguerite Namara, E. Phillips Openhiem, Mannes the violinist, Floyd Dell, Max and Chrystal Eastman, ex-Premier Orlando, Ettienne de Beaumont – just a real place to rough it, an escape from all the world.' In the opening chapters of *Tender Is the Night* Fitzgerald scrambled the geography of Antibes, but he caught its atmosphere. It was a world of nannies and beach umbrellas and *espadrilles*, of hot gusts filtering through closed shutters and faded cars cooking on driveways. Gerald Murphy dominated the beach like Dick Diver in his jockey cap, the others sending out 'antennae of attention' to whatever he was doing.

When Scottie said she wished she were married, Murphy suggested, 'Why not marry me?' He made a real occasion of it, trimming his Renault with satin and decking it with flowers, and Scottie wore a white dress and a veil, and carried a bridal wreath. Fitzgerald was on hand to give his daughter away, though there wasn't an actual ceremony; it mostly had to do with the cake. Afterwards, Murphy drove Scottie around in his car for an appropriate length of time and presented her with a ring from the local Five and Ten – supposedly a diamond – though Scottie said it wasn't real.

Fitzgerald, too, had a way with children. One afternoon in the garden of his house at Cannes he staged a crusade with toy soldiers and a cardboard castle made by Zelda. He flooded a hollow for the Mediterranean, and across the water a large black beetle, representing a dragon, lived in an improvised cave. Fitzgerald told a story which ended with the castle being stormed and the right people winning, and the children followed breathlessly as this adult crawled around under the eucalyptus, completely lost in their world.

Zelda was choosy about people, but she loved the Murphys, and as for Scott, he would gaze across the table at Sara – his chin resting on his palm in a characteristic, dreaming pose – and say, 'Sara, look at me,' and when she did he would say, 'Thank you,' like a mooning schoolboy. Sara was pert and trim and went swimming with a string of pearls around her neck ('her brown back hanging from her pearls,' Fitzgerald wrote in *Tender Is the Night*). What he admired about Gerald he put into the character of Dick Diver: the elegance, the turns of phrase, the flare for entertainment, above all Murphy's appreciation of others, his power to draw them out and see the best in them. It was a quality Murphy shared with men as unlike him as Father Fay, Max Perkins, and Dean Gauss – a quality prized by Fitzgerald, who had a great deal of it himself.

The Fitzgeralds were on their best behaviour that summer, but the Murphys spent a harrowing evening with them at St Paul de Vence, in the mountains back of Nice. The four of them had been dining on the terrace of an inn built on a spur between two valleys, with the old town rising behind them. Murphy had been saying that this was the site of one of the Roman chain fires, announcing the conquest of Gaul. Isadora Duncan, in purple robes, happened to be at a nearby table with three men, and on an impulse Fitzgerald went over and sat at her feet and told her about the Romans while she ran her hands through his hair and called him her centurion. The interlude was poetic rather than amorous, but suddenly Zelda rose and flung herself down a flight of stone steps into what looked like darkness and oblivion. Only when Murphy and Fitzgerald rushed after her were they conscious of the door at the bottom. Giving no explanation, Zelda went inside to wash her skinned knees and came out composed.

Driving home, she and Scott turned on to a trestle instead of following the road and fell asleep when their car stalled. They might have been hit by the morning trolley as it sped down to Nice had not a peasant seen them and carried them to safety. The same obliging peasant hooked his oxen to the car and rescued that too.

In September the Fitzgeralds returned to Paris healthy and brown, Scott enthusing over a novel he had begun but depressed at having to do potboilers for the *Post* when all the talk was of art. The *Post* had quintupled his price in six years; though he was now getting $2,500 a story, the more he was paid for his 'trash', he wrote Perkins, the less he could bring himself to write it.

His private disgruntlement increased his admiration for the incorruptible Hemingway. One day on the beach at Antibes Fitzgerald had taken Glenway Wescott into the shadow of a rock and lectured him about this young phenomenon, obviously the one true genius of the decade. He thought Wescott would agree that his own novel and *Gatsby* were somewhat overrated just then, while Hemingway was being neglected, misunderstood, insufficiently remunerated. What could Wescott do to help him, Fitzgerald wanted to know, shaking him by the elbow. Would he write a laudatory essay? (Fitzgerald wrote one himself in the course of the fall.) What struck Wescott was Fitzgerald's naïveté and lack of calculation. It simply had not occurred to him that unfriendliness or pettiness on Wescott's part might inhibit his enthusiasm for the work of a competitor.

The fall of 1925, though Hemingway had yet to publish his first novel, his achievement was impressive. At twenty-six he had 'broken the language', as the French say; out of the old shop-worn words and phrases he had forged a shining instrument. The Saxon hammer-strokes of his prose had a power and novelty that made Fitzgerald, with a style formed under more traditional auspices, seem almost a late-flowering Victorian. Eager for Hemingway to become a Scribners author, Fitzgerald began smoothing his path and facilitated his transfer to Scribners from his first publisher, Boni & Liveright.

Much as Fitzgerald was drawn to Hemingway the writer, he was even more drawn to Hemingway the man – this athlete of letters, at once so nice and so bitter, so modest and so bluff. Hemingway was a complex individual who had adopted the stance of a simple one. He would discuss art as long as one avoided the precious, but preferred the masculine topics of sport and war. Anything emotional or gushing was 'damn female talk', and when the conversation took that turn, he was apt to get up and leave. Like anyone with a great deal of fire, he was moody. His *bonhomie* concealed a natural shyness and sensitivity, yet at bottom he was the type of the *condottiere*, of the adventurer used to living by his wits and cunning with a soldierly contempt for weakness in all its forms. He was a competitor who would have battled to the top in any enterprise, and underlying his whole character and giving it dignity was an exemplary courage – the true courage of the intelligent and imaginative man who feels fear but overcomes it by an act of will.

Fitzgerald's association with Hemingway revived his regrets that he hadn't been in the war. He would spend whole days in the basement of Brentano's poring over their stereopticon slides of stagnant trenches and torn bodies, and Ludendorff's *Memoirs* became a treasured work. A trip to Verdun in October was the basis for his moving description of an overgrown battlefield in *Tender Is the Night*. He listened to Hemingway preaching his doctrine that war was the greatest subject, because 'it groups the maximum of material and speeds up the action and brings out all sorts of stuff normally you have to wait a lifetime to get.' But Hemingway and Fitzgerald were very different, and one may doubt that war was the ideal subject for Fitzgerald as it was for Hemingway, or as it had been for Stephen Crane – so obsessed by it that he wrote his masterpiece without having seen any action at all. The sort of violence that concerned Fitzgerald required a social rather than a martial setting.[36]

That fall the Murphys were living at St Cloud in a house that had belonged to the composer Gounod, and one night Fitzgerald went to sleep under a bush on their lawn. Another night he phoned them at 3 a.m. to say he and Zelda were sailing next day on the *Berengaria*. They weren't, of course. It was a device to pry the Murphys out on a party, but Scott was getting out of hand as far as the Murphys were concerned. He wanted each evening to be adventurous, spectacular, unpredictable, and when nothing happened, as was usually the case, he either fell asleep or made a scene.

Once when the four of them were driving to Les Halles, Fitzgerald, who didn't much care for the colour of the old market, created a little colour of his own by chewing hundred franc notes (the equivalent of twenty-dollar bills) and spitting them out the taxi window. 'Oh Scott, they're so dirty!' Sara protested, but Fitzgerald went right on. Finally the driver could stand it no longer. Stopping the cab, he ran back to retrieve some of the money. Fitzgerald jumped into the driver's seat and headed for the Seine, saying he was going to plunge them into it. As he came to one of the ramps, they managed to get the wheel away from him and return it to the terrified driver, who came flapping up behind them in his long coat.

Another time Fitzgerald stole a *tri-porteur* – a three-wheeled delivery wagonette – and scooted crazily around the Place de la Concorde while policemen whistled and motorists swore. If anyone could control him, it was Murphy, for Scott stood in awe of Gerald's unfailing propriety. Once when they were leaving a nightclub, Scott slipped to the floor and pretended to pass out. 'Scott,' said Gerald, 'this is *not* Princeton and I am *not* your roommate. Get up!' Fitzgerald obeyed.

The Fitzgeralds disliked their flat on the rue Tilsit. Zelda described it as smelling like a church chancery, and the furniture was imitation Louis XV from the Galeries Lafayette. When Louis Bromfield called on them, it seemed to him that they were camping out between two worlds.

In November they visited London where they 'went to some very high tone parties with the Mountbattens and all that sort of thing. Very impressed,' Fitzgerald wrote Perkins, 'but not very as I furnished most of the amusement myself.' December found them back in Paris, and Zelda wrote that they were 'passing the winter agreeably among plagiarists who are always delightful and [had] spent a good deal of time in taxis if you know what I mean. ... Now once again the straight & narrow goes winding & wobbling before us and Scott is working.' In January they went to a resort in the Pyrenees where Zelda, ailing for over a year, took a cure. When they rented a villa at Juan-les-Pins the end of February, Fitzgerald wrote Perkins that being back on his beloved Riviera with his novel absorbing him made him happier than he had been for years. He was cheered by the reviews of his third book of stories, and his finances had taken a lucky turn. *Gatsby* had made a successful Broadway play and would presently be sold to the movies, windfalls which netted him more than $22,000. As a result he wrote not a single short story between February 1926 and June 1927. His most recent effort, 'Your Way and Mine', he considered too lowly for the *Post*. 'It hasn't one redeeming touch of my usual spirit in it,' he told his agent. '... I'd rather have

$1,000 for it from some obscure place than twice that & have it seen. *I feel very strongly about this!*'

In June the Fitzgeralds went to Paris so Zelda could have an operation. During her two weeks at the American Hospital in Neuilly, Fitzgerald lived in a neighbouring hotel and went out on the town every night with James Rennie, who had played the lead in the Broadway production of *Gatsby*. One dawn as they were leaving a café on Montmartre, they saw a shabby little figure crossing the street ahead of them. Fitzgerald gripped Rennie's arm. 'Watch him,' he said, 'he's making for that garbage can over there.' Sure enough, the man began rooting around in it. 'Come on,' said Fitzgerald, 'let's have some fun.'

He sprinted the intervening block and joined the scavenger shoulder to shoulder. The going was a bit crowded now. At one point they stopped to argue, apparently reaching an agreement, for the search was renewed. Without the other noticing, Fitzgerald flipped a coin in the can, and when they both appeared to see it at the same time, the fight was really on. Fitzgerald fumbled so that his rival got it. Repeating the trick, he let himself be beaten a second time. Suddenly he froze as he picked up a spray of withered smilax. Coins were forgotten now; here was a treasure beyond compare. Holding it reverently, he made a speech in his broken French – then handed it to the Frenchman with an elaborate gesture. 'Go to him,' he said, pointing to Rennie, and added in English, 'He's a collector, he'll pay you for it.'

Taking his cue, Rennie gave the Frenchman five francs, wrapped the smilax in his handkerchief, and he and Fitzgerald proceeded on their way.

Wherever they went Fitzgerald insisted on being host, and Rennie was appalled by the size of the tips which were sometimes as large as the bill itself. Realizing it would be fruitless to argue, he adopted the strategy of calling Fitzgerald's attention to something behind him and pocketing the overtip while his back was turned. On their last evening together Rennie explained the ruse and returned the extra money. At first Fitzgerald was put out, but then he smiled. 'This is wonderful,' he said, 'and tomorrow you're leaving. Let's go some-where quickly and spend it.'

For once Rennie left the tips alone. He had the feeling that he was being watched.

When the Fitzgeralds returned to the Riviera the middle of June, they rented a villa next to the casino at Antibes, for Juan-les-Pins seemed a bit remote with the season in full swing under the Murphys' auspices. The Murphys' en-tourage that summer included the Fitzgeralds, the Archi-bald MacLeishes, the Philip Barrys, the Charles Bracketts, and several non-literary couples. There were also transients like the John Peale Bishops and the Donald Ogden Stewarts, Ernest Hemingway and Alexander Woolcott, but the Plage de la Garoupe remained a closed corporation, and when strangers appeared, the children were trained to throw sand at them.

Hoping to return to America in the fall with his novel completed, Fitzgerald spent much of the day writing and came down to the beach tense and preoccupied. His indoor pallor distinguished him from the others though he still seemed vital and robust. His physique had been excellent to begin with: remembering his sturdy legs, lean torso, good arms and shoulders, a friend of college days spoke of his 'ar-row collar head on a longshoreman's body'. There was rug-gedness mixed with his delicacy, and his refined, almost pretty features conveyed a certain force, the virile domi-nance of someone who knows what he is about. In con-versation he was always generalizing – having a theory, an attitude, a 'hunch' (to use his favourite expression) about everything. He would contradict simply to start debate, and if he wasn't restful, neither was he dull, even when dis-cussing hair, about which he knew a great deal that summer. He had set out to read the Encyclopedia Britannica cover to cover and had got as far as the letter 'H'.

Despite two years abroad he still had the air of a tourist. Historical landmarks excited him, as did everything that had a human story connected with it, but for the most part he was indifferent to the foreign culture which the rest of the group were doing their best to absorb. MacLeish, for example, would get Italians to read Cavalcanti in the original, so he could savour the rhythms. That was not Fitzgerald's approach at all. His tastes were incorrigibly American, and when offered the English 'Abdullah' cigarettes that many of his friends were smoking, he would apologize with a sort of pride for being a Midwesterner who preferred Chesterfields. He made no effort to improve his stumbling French, nor did he concern himself with French art, architecture, or theatre, though once, it is true, a production of Racine's *Phèdre* caused him to exclaim, 'My God, all modern psychology is there! That man knew everything Freud discovered later and much more clumsily.' Most Europeans, however, considered him a sensitive boor, without real cultivation or finesse. He used to infuriate the waiters at the casino by praising the German military, saying such things as, 'Those Germans are going to come through here some day and wipe you up.'

In contrast to the previous summer, he and Zelda were behaving their worst. When they exploded into the casino, people would groan, 'Here come the Fitzgeralds!' If things were dull at Scott's table, he would pick up an ashtray and flip it quoit-like to the table adjoining. It didn't matter whether it had ashes in it or not; the whole idea was to get a reaction. He threw furniture about and heaved salt cellars at the windows, for a little breakage was part of the evening's entertainment. Once he crawled under the coconut matting in front of the main door, making a huge lump that resembled some monstrous turtle and emitting strange sounds.

When introduced, he would say in his nicest Princeton manner, 'I'm very glad to meet you, sir – you know I'm an alcoholic.' His drinking was much on his mind; he inscribed a book for a friend, 'You can drink some of the cocktails all of the time and all of the cocktails some of the time but – (Think this over, Judah).' Once he deliberately kicked over an old woman's tray of nuts and candies all prettily laid out for sale, and by way of recompense emptied his pockets of the soggy roll of bills he usually had with him. On a visit to Monte Carlo, when the doorman refused to let him gamble without his American passport, Fitzgerald said, 'Très bien, you son-of-a-bitch,' and passed out at the doorman's feet.

Egged on by Charlie MacArthur, who had a Scotch elfin quality and a touch of the hoodlum in him, Fitzgerald did things which might have led to serious consequences. Late one evening he and MacArthur were alone in a bar disputing the possibility of sawing a man in half. Fitzgerald said it couldn't be done, MacArthur said it could. 'There's one way of finding out,' MacArthur said at length. They persuaded the barman to lie down on a couple of chairs to which they tied him with ropes, and while MacArthur was out getting a two-man saw, the barman made such a commotion that the police arrived. The incident was embroidered in *Tender Is the Night*, where Abe North plans to saw the waiter in half with a *musical* saw, to eliminate any sordidness.

Zelda, too, was acting strangely. With her angry sidelong glances and barbed remarks there was something crouching and inimical in her posture. She was a wily antagonist who lay in wait for you conversationally and gave compliments that turned out to be brickbats. 'Did you ever see a woman's face with so many fine, large teeth in it?' she might say of someone she didn't like – after which she would retreat into herself. But the Murphys remained fond of her and she of them.

'She was very beautiful in an unusual way,' Gerald recalled.

She had a rather powerful, hawk-like expression, very beautiful features, not classic, and extremely penetrating eyes, and a very beautiful figure, and she moved beautifully. She had a beautiful voice as some – I suppose most – Southern women do have. She had a slight Southern accent. She had a great sense of her own appearance and wore dresses that were very full and very graceful and her sense of the colour that she should wear was very keen. [Murphy particularly remembered certain dusty pinks and reds.] She had a great head of tousled hair which was extremely beautiful, neither blonde nor brown, and I always thought it was remarkable that her favourite flower was a peony. They happened to grow in our garden and whenever she came to see us she would take a great bunch of them and do something with them and pin them on her bodice and they somehow were very expressive of her.

When you knew Zelda as well as the Murphys did, you discovered that in her way she was just as rare a person as Scott. She had a sweet, lasting quality that inspired affection despite her erratic, sometimes terrifying, behaviour. Driving along the Grande Corniche one evening, she said to her companion, 'I think I'll turn off here,' and had to be physically restrained from veering over a cliff. Another time she lay down in front of a parked car and said, 'Scott, drive over me.' Fitzgerald started the engine and had actually released the brake when someone slammed it on again. Zelda was bold – bolder than Scott – though the cool madness with which she performed her outrages seldom offended good taste. Late one evening at the Casino, when everyone had gone home except the Murphys and a scattering of Frenchmen, Zelda emerged from the dressing room on to the dance floor with her skirts held so high one could see her bare midriff. The Frenchmen's faces went cold with surprise, then warmed with interest and delight as she pirouetted about the hall, completely dignified and self-absorbed. The orchestra got into the swing of it and when she sat down at the end of three or four minutes, she was in such a trance that she scarcely heard the Murphys' congratulations.

'Why do you do it?' friends would ask the Fitzgeralds mornings after on the beach. 'How do you stand these awful hangovers? Besides, you're so much more attractive when you're sober.'

The Fitzgeralds agreed, but every night was the same, and you went out with them at your own risk. In September the Murphys gave a dinner at which Scott went further than even their leniency would permit. Dessert consisted of figs with pineapple sherbet, and he picked up a fig and threw it at the bare back of a French countess. The countess stiffened as the icy fruit slid down her *décolletage*, but she never said a word, thinking no doubt that a waiter had been careless.

After dinner, when the guests had got up to stroll about the garden, Fitzgerald was drifting among the tables with a dream in his eye. Suddenly, without calling attention to it, he picked up one of the Venetian glasses with white and gold spinning which the Murphys were specially fond of and tossed it over the high wall that surrounded the garden, listening to it break on the bricks outside. The gesture had an eighteenth-century extravagance and impromptu reminiscent of gentlemen dashing their glasses on the hearth after a single drink. Fitzgerald wasn't trying to be ugly; it was as if he thought this a fitting death for such exquisite goblets. He had sent two more into the night before the Murphys stopped him and forbade him to enter their house for three weeks. His mouth was a line of resentment as the sentence was passed, and exactly three weeks later he appeared at their door, without, however, alluding to the reason for his absence.

The Fitzgeralds stayed at Antibes through the autumn. 'Now all the gay decorative people have left,' Zelda wrote Perkins at the end of September, 'taking with them the sense of carnival & impending disaster that colored this summer. Scott is working and still brooding about the war. Ernest Hemingway was here for a while – seeming sort of a materialistic mystic. ... It's heavenly here when its burnt & dusty and the water crackles in the fall. Scott's novel is going to be excellent.' But before they sailed for America 10 December, Fitzgerald wrote Perkins that the novel was 'not nearly finished'.

On shipboard with them was Ludlow Fowler, who had been best man at their wedding. He sat with the Fitzgeralds at a large uproarious table, and after the meals Scott would lead discussions in the lounge. 'You stay out of this because you're on your honeymoon,' he would tell Ludlow. Then turning to the others he would ask, 'Is there any man present who can honestly say he has never hit his wife in anger?' In the ensuing attempt to define the word 'Anger', Fitzgerald was the moderator. He loved to be the cynosure of a group.

Meanwhile Zelda was telling Fowler, 'Now Ludlow, take it from an old souse like me – don't let drinking get you in the position it's gotten Scott if you want your marriage to be any good.'

[11]

WITH Europe and the Murphys Fitzgerald came as close as he ever would to finding perfection in the real world, and in a way the rest of his life was a retreat from this summit. He inaugurated 1927 with a trip to Hollywood. Needing the cash and curious about his potential as a scriptwriter, he accepted an offer from United Artists to do an original story for Constance Talmadge.

During their two months in the film capital Scott and Zelda lived at the ultra-fashionable Ambassador Hotel, in a four-apartment bungalow with John Barrymore, Carmel Myers, and the author Carl Van Vechten. A woman reporter who called on them was met at the door by a restless young man with 'Prince-of-Wales hair' and a 'sensitive, taut, faintly contemptuous mouth'. The reporter wanted to know how the flappers of the screen differed from the original flapper Fitzgerald had created.

'Well, I can only' – he lit a cigarette, put it out, and crossed to another chair – 'speak about the immediate present. I know nothing of their evolution. You see, we've been living on the Riviera for three years. In that time, the only movies we've seen have been a few of the very old pictures or the Westerns they show over there. I might' – his face brightened – 'tell you what I think of Tom Mix.'

'Scott!' Zelda cautioned.

'Oh well.'

Having exhausted the available chairs, he returned to the first one and obligingly analysed the stars playing flapper rôles – Clara Bow, Constance Talmadge, Colleen Moore. It seemed as though the Flapper, that stereotype he had gone to Europe to escape, was irrevocably linked to his name.

Fitzgerald described Hollywood as 'a tragic city of beautiful girls, – the girls who mop the floor are beautiful, the shop ladies. You never want to see any more beauty' – and to him one was more beautiful than all the others. Lois Moran – fresh, blonde, blue-eyed, just seventeen and unspoiled by her success as an actress – was the perfect antidote to what, at thirty-one, he considered his approaching middle-age. Recently returned from four years abroad, she spoke French almost as fluently as English and kept a chapbook full of poetic quotations. Fitzgerald put his first emotion for her into a story called 'Magnetism', where Lois is Helen Avery, the young movie star who causes the happily married George Hannaford to waver. Like Hannaford, Fitzgerald felt that he and Lois 'each knew half of some secret about people and life, and that if they rushed towards each other there would be a romantic communion of almost unbelievable intensity.' It was all very pure and idealistic – never anything more than a delicate flirtation, with Lois wanting Fitzgerald to be the lead in her next picture. The charmer on the edge of girlhood would be a recurring figure in Fitzgerald's fiction of the next few years, and he did Lois once and for all as Rosemary Hoyt in *Tender Is the Night*.

Zelda, meanwhile, had been taking Black Bottom lessons and having her fortune told by Santa Monica seers. At first she liked Hollywood, but soon its newness – the feeling that everything was mere decoration – began to pall. Since the movie colony wasn't as gay as she had hoped, she and Scott tried to enliven it with their pranks. They went to one party in nightgown and pyjamas, parodying the actors' habit of going everywhere in the costumes they wore on the sets. At another, the guests' nostrils were assailed by a strange odour, and out in the kitchen the hostess found Fitzgerald brewing the ladies' compacts and handbags in tomato sauce.

Most of the time, however, he was incarcerated with his script and ate his meals in his room. One morning Carl Van Vechten saw him pacing outside the bungalow with his eyes on the distant hills.

'Scott, come here!' called Van Vechten.

'I can't,' said Fitzgerald over his shoulder, ' – I've got scarlet fever.'

He and Zelda drove out in the country to see a movie being made in a replica French village. There were hundreds of extras dressed as peasants and soldiers, and when one kind of whistle blew they all ran off to war and when another kind blew they all ran back again. It was odd to hear the director say, 'I'll take twenty peasants down here,' but it gave Fitzgerald an inkling of that 'more glittering, grosser power' which, after the relative failure of *Tender Is the Night*, he would come to regard as fatal competition for the novelist. He didn't like movie people in general – what he called their 'almost hysterical egotism and excitability hidden under an extremely thin veil of elaborate good-fellowship' – and scriptwriting was a disappointment. He later admitted that he had gone to Hollywood confident to the point of conceit. 'I had been generally acknowledged for several years as the top American writer both seriously and, as far as prices went, popularly. . . . I honestly believed that *with no effort on my part* I was a sort of magician with words – an odd delusion when I had worked so desperately hard to develop a hard, colorful prose style.' United Artists had paid him $3,500 down, but he never got the $12,500 due him on completion of the picture because his script was rejected. Writing the trip off as an experience, he went back to his real *métier* of prose fiction.

He needed a quiet place to finish his novel. Max Perkins had suggested Wilmington, thinking that the kind of feudality that existed there under the DuPonts would interest Fitzgerald and give him material for future work. With the help of his college room mate, John Biggs – now a Wilmington attorney – Fitzgerald rented Ellerslie, a large, high-ceilinged house romantically situated on the banks of the Delaware. Built in 1842, it was shaded by old oaks, beeches and horse chestnuts, and the Greek-columned portico behind commanded a sweeping view of the river. The house was said to be haunted; Fitzgerald sometimes tried to frighten guests by impersonating the ghost. The low rental was an attraction, for until he finished his novel he would need to economize.

Nevertheless he and Zelda continued to live their legend,

though Wilmington was a more restricted stage than Paris or New York. They renewed their friendship with Tommy Hitchcock, the polo star, whom they had known on Long Island where he had suggested the kind of glamour Fitzgerald bestowed on Tom and Daisy Buchanan in *The Great Gatsby*. Fitzgerald admired Hitchcock more than Lindbergh, the national idol of 1927, whom he called 'a woman's idea of a man'. Perhaps it was only that Hitchcock's adventures made a better narrative in the Fitzgerald vein. He had flown in the Lafayette Escadrille with Hobey Baker, and after being shot down and made prisoner, had escaped by jumping from the window of a moving train. Returning to America with the *Croix de guerre* and a great name in polo, he had had the humility to enter Harvard as a freshman. 'That combination [of qualities],' wrote Fitzgerald, 'is what forever will put him in my pantheon of heros' – and a Fitzgerald hero was someone to emulate. During a houseparty at Elleslie a polo match was staged with the contestants swinging croquet mallets while mounted on plough horses from a neighbouring field.

In August, Scott and Zelda visited the Chanlers at their summer home in upstate New York. Teddy Chanler had accompanied him on the unfortunate visit to Mrs Wharton, and Scott was especially fond of Teddy's mother, the writer Margaret Winthrop Chanler, whom he once described as the most charming older woman he had ever met. She called him her 'imprudent angel' and told him stories about Prince Borghese and other fashionables she had known during a girlhood abroad. When she asked him his ambition, he replied, 'To stay married and in love with Zelda and write the greatest novel in the world.' 'Then you'll have to do something about your drinking,' she said, but Fitzgerald only shrugged. The Chanlers' small bootleg stock was presided over by their Italian butler, on whom Fitzgerald exercised his wiles. Going out to the kitchen, he would confide in Venturino, 'Mrs Chanler is so brilliant that I simply have to have another drink to keep up with her.'

At Christmas the Fitzgeralds gave a party that was a par-able of their whole lives. They had planned it as a quiet affair focused on Scottie, for whom they had bought innumerable presents and trimmed an exotic tree. They asked a few friends, but then the unexpected guests began to arrive: a newspaperman who passed out; a theatrical agent who came with his mistress and knocked her unconscious. Others dropped by and behaved no better. When a group of villagers appeared singing carols, they had to be asked in and feted, until finally everyone's nerves snapped and what was to have been the perfect Christmas turned into a Witch's Sabbath.

Fitzgerald could always detach a part of himself from these fiascos. Next day when they were picking up the debris and Scottie was crying and nerves were still frayed, he smiled and said, 'Just think – it's like this now all over the country.'

But there were also joyous, luminous times with Scottie such as the one he described in his sketch, 'Outside the Cabinet-Maker's'. While Zelda was in the shop ordering a surprise doll's house, Fitzgerald sat with his little daughter in the car, extracting drama and excitement from a dingy Wilmington intersection. He had an instinct for quickening life, for taking the slag out of it and making it what in our dreams we think it should be. Thus the room with the banging shutter in the drab house across the street was where the Ogre had imprisoned the Fairy Princess because he wasn't invited to the christening. The Prince would be able to release her when he had found the three stones, one of which had already turned up in President Coolidge's collar-box. He was looking for a second one in Iceland, and as Scottie turned away, Fitzgerald announced that the room had turned blue, meaning the Prince had found the second stone. The small boy walking towards the house with enormous strides was the Ogre in disguise, and the chalk marks he made under the doorbell were magic signs. Two men crossing the street were the King's soldiers, part of an army that was gathering nearby to surround the house. The banging shutter was being manipulated by the good and bad fairies, who had their private reasons for wanting it opened or closed.

'You're my good fairy,' said Fitzgerald smiling and touching Scottie's cheek.

Later, when the doll's house had been built, Zelda papered and painted it and furnished it so elegantly and completely that one wanted to move in right away.

Since his suspension from Cottage Club in 1920 Fitzgerald had been a little cool towards his Alma Mater, but in 1927, when *College Humor* asked him to do a piece on Princeton, he found he really loved the place. Nostalgia welled up in him when he rode the rocky shuttle from the Junction towards the green and towered retreat that had inspired his first book. Needing colour for a story, he stopped off several times in September to watch football practice, and his passion for the game flared up anew. For the rest of his life he would be an ardent fan and football analyst – though when he saw Princeton wallop Cornell in October his curiosity was not confined to events on the field. Sweeping the opposite stands with his binoculars he was heard to say, 'I wonder how many of those people over there have gallstones.'

In January 1928, Cottage invited him to lecture, and, anxious to atone for previous misconduct, he was unduly nervous beforehand. He made a point of having nothing to drink, but when he rose to speak he couldn't get started. He would mumble a few sentences and then say under his breath, 'God, I'm a lousy speaker!' Finally he sat down and someone began telling dirty jokes. What was to have been an inspirational talk on authorship degenerated into a round of the smoking room stories he abhorred. Later he drowned his sorrows at a party in the home of Edgar Palmer, the donor of Palmer Stadium. At one point Fitzgerald went up to his host – a shy man – and said, 'You know, I've been studying you, and thank God I don't look like that. It must be because you have so much money.'

On the train to Wilmington next day he fell in with some undergraduates who shocked him with their cynicism about the honour system. In his article for *College Humor*, Fitzgerald had called it 'Princeton's sacred tradition . . . something humanly precious.' 'Personally,' he wrote, 'I have never seen or heard of a Princeton man cheating in an examination, though I am told a few such cases have been mercilessly and summarily dealt with.' His companions on the train, however, told him of violations that hadn't been reported, and they weren't even sure such violations *should* be reported. Fitzgerald wrote Dean Gauss at once; he wanted to know how the undergraduates could be awakened to their stupidity. When Gauss replied that his own position was delicate, since the honour system was completely in the hands of the students, Fitzgerald scrawled on Gauss's letter, 'He is probably the greatest educator in the country. Nevertheless he is pulling a Pontius Pilate here – not deliberately but waiting for a cue.'

In February the Fitzgeralds gave the house party which Edmund Wilson has described in his vignette 'A Weekend at Ellerslie'. Now on the staff of *The New Republic*, Wilson had remained a sort of father figure in literature to whom Fitzgerald felt accountable for his progress or lack of it. Wilson had seen very little of Fitzgerald since his departure for Europe in 1924 and was conscious that their relations had 'suffered a certain chill'. Wilson had grown more tolerant and worldly with the years, having by now been through a somewhat self-conscious Bohemian phase of his own, yet he frowned on Fitzgerald's pleasure-seeking abroad as well as on his 'invincible compulsion to live like a millionaire'. At one point during the weekend Fitzgerald invited Wilson and Gilbert Seldes to criticize his character. Seldes told Fitzgerald that if he had a fault it was making life seem rather dull, and, remembered Wilson, 'this quite put him out of countenance till we both began to laugh.'

Just as often it was Fitzgerald who pulled Wilson's leg. One day when they had lunched together in New York, they looked in on T. S. Matthews, Princeton '22 and a colleague of Wilson's at *The New Republic*. 'Fitzgerald was about Wilson's height,' Matthews recalled, 'but otherwise a lively contrast to him; alert, compact, grinning, crackling with nervous energy. Wilson introduced us.

' "What!" said Fitzgerald, opening his eyes wide. "Not *the* Mr Matthews."

' "Oh," said Wilson, looking at him in surprise, "do you know him?"

' "*Know* him! I used to fix his teeth!"

'This assertion,' remembered Matthews, 'pleased me but seemed to alarm Wilson vaguely.'

Fitzgerald had returned from Europe a devotee of Spengler, whose *Decline of the West* was all the rage, and in the prosperous luxury-loving America of 1927 Fitzgerald thought he saw new evidence of Western man's decay. Interviews with him sooner or later worked around to the ineffectuality of the American male, and the need of a war to test America's mettle. The preoccupation with Spengler may also have been linked to Fitzgerald's subconscious sense of his own decline. His writing, so abundant and free-flowing at the start, had become an increasing chore. Mired in his novel, he had had to resume short stories for the *Post* with consequent loss of morale, and Max Perkins was much concerned by what he euphemistically called 'Scott's nerves'. 'The doctors,' he wrote Lardner the fall of 1927,

tell him he must take exercise and must not drink, but that he is really O.K. in every important way. [Yesterday] he worked here for an hour and then got one of his nervous fits, and could not work any more and wanted to go out and have a drink. So we did on condition that it would be only one drink, and that is all we had.

Fitzgerald's drinking wasn't his only problem. Zelda's long-smouldering discontent had made her increasingly difficult to live with. Her wilfulness had modulated into a bizarre pettishness. Out with a group of friends, she would suddenly want fresh strawberries or watercress sandwiches and make everyone thoroughly uncomfortable until she got them. When others were enjoying themselves, she would say she didn't like the orchestra and insist on going home. Her habit of nervously chewing the inside of her mouth had been growing, and recently her looks had begun to go. Her skin had coarsened, and her sharp features now at times seemed graven, stony, a little angular.

She was no longer satisfied to be simply the wife of Scott Fitzgerald. He had written her into his books and made her a legend, but she didn't want to be an artist's model – she wanted to be an artist herself. For a long time Zelda, the artist, had been obstructed by an indolent Zelda, who was equally happy eating an apple, or reading a book, or sitting in the sun perfecting the tan on her slick brown legs. 'I hope I'll never get ambitious enough to try anything,' she had written Scott before their marriage. 'It's so *much* nicer to be damned sure I *could* do it better than other people – and I might not could if I tried – that, of course, would break my heart.' But gradually she had found the ambition to produce essays and sketches, and without much effort had got her by-line into the popular magazines. She frequently pointed out Scott's indebtedness to her; in a review of the *The Beautiful and Damned* she had said, 'Mr Fitzgerald – I believe that is how he spells his name – seems to believe that plagiarism begins at home.' Scott didn't deny it. On the contrary, he used to say he knew nothing about human nature and had to learn it all from Zelda, and there was a measure of truth in his gallantry. Zelda was the realist of the two, the cooler in her appraisals, seeing through people whom Scott in his boyish way had already begun to idealize.

But since Scott had pre-empted the field of letters, Zelda felt she must choose some other art. There was painting which she had taken up semi-seriously the spring of 1925 at Capri. There was dancing; since she was a little girl, she had delighted to kick off her shoes and dance wherever she was. It was therefore no surprise when she began going to Philadelphia for ballet lessons, though her desire to be a professional ballerina twenty years too late was perhaps a bit odd.

In a story she wrote, 'The Millionaire's Girl', the heroine leaves her husband to embark on a movie career because 'ever since I met him everything I do or that happens to me has seemed because of him. Now I am going to make a hit so I can choose him again.' Zelda wanted to prove herself. In the past Scott had reproached her for being lazy and wasting her talents, pointing out that Lois Moran had made the most of hers. Well, Zelda would show him . . .

Her letters to Carl Van Vechten during the first year at Ellerslie had flashes of the old gaiety, but a forced, hectic quality prevailed, as in the following excerpts:

27 May 1927. 'From the depths of my polluted soul, I am sorry that the week-end was such a mess. Do forgive my iniquities and my putrid drunkenness. This *was* such a nice place, and it should have been a good party if I had not explored my abyses in public. – Anyhow, please realize that I am sorry and contrite and thoroughly miserable with the knowledge that it would be just the same again if I got so drunk.'

14 June 1927. 'I have painted a superb portrait of Lavinia, a very black and wizened ferret who lives under the bed upstairs I think but as she is always darting about behind corners I can't swear that she actually exists at all. – But the portrait does – I want the Anderson Galleries to exhibit it.'

6 September 1927. [Answering Van Vechten's suggestion that the Fitzgeralds take a trip with him through New England.] 'There is scarcely a pullman on the N.Y. Central in which we have not been taken drunk and Scott simply has to work. – Likewise I am painting again and will have to work if I am to turn two apples and a stick of gum into an affair of pyramids and angles and cosmic beauty before fall. – Also I have a maniac in charge of Scottie since the British Empire [Scottie's nanny] passed out of our life. She came from the top of Mont Matre and rolls into a corner when I speak to her and begins muttering about how droll the vie is. She is a great trial, but I find her philosophy so uplifting and her tongue so sharp that I am afraid to fire her. I will surely have to go to France to get rid of her – Besides, she has the evil eye – and I couldn't leave Scottie here to be turned into a toad while I was flowing down the broad New England valleys.'

14 October 1927. 'Please forgive my not writing sooner. – It seems that life went to pieces. I joined the Philadelphia opera ballet and guests came and every-body has been so drunk in this country lately that I am just finding enough chaos to pursue my own ends in, undisturbed, again. . . . Our house is full of every ghost but Fanny Ward & Conan Doyle imaginable and I hope that I will never again feel attractive.'

23 March 1928. 'Scott is bridging the Atlantic with Post stories. We want to go in May because Wilmington has turned out to be the black hole of Calcutta and I simply must have some Chablis and curry and fraises du bois with peaches in champagne for desert. Also I want to feel a sense of intrigue which is only in Paris, and, maybe, in Monte Negro.'

As forecast above, the Fitzgeralds spent the summer of 1928 in Paris, at 58 rue Vaugirard across the street from the Luxembourg Gardens. One of the excitements of the trip was meeting James Joyce, whom Scott held in such awe that he had never dared approach him. When Sylvia Beach, proprietress of the bookshop Shakespeare & Co., invited Joyce and Fitzgerald to dinner, Fitzgerald threatened to jump out of the window in tribute to Joyce's genius. 'That young man must be mad,' Joyce said afterwards. 'I'm afraid he'll do himself some injury.'

Through Sylvia Beach Fitzgerald met André Chamson, the only foreign writer he really befriended during all his years abroad. Chamson had come to Paris from the depths of the Cevennes, the mountain country north of Nimes, and though his regional novels were highly regarded, he was obliged to eke out his living with a clerical post at the Assemblé Nationale. He lived in a top-floor apartment back of the Panthéon, and one evening Fitzgerald came clomping up the stairs with an enormous ice bucket full of champagne. When Chamson met him on a landing halfway down, Fitzgerald proposed to swim in the ice bucket. He stripped off his shirt, and, remembered Chamson, 'Little Puritan that

I was, I found myself in great anxiety. Scott was getting ready to take off his pants. By dint of much eloquence I persuaded him he would be better off swimming in his ice bucket in my apartment' – where, however, still greater anxieties lay in store. At a point during the evening when Fitzgerald was none too steady on his legs, he stepped on to the ledge outside the balustrade of Chamson's sixth-floor balcony – to be more in touch with the city, so he explained – and holding on with one hand he hopped up and down on one foot, crying, 'I am Voltaire! I am Rousseau! I am Victor Hugo!' You couldn't do anything with him at such moments. He was sardonic, sadistic even, as he tempted fate with the cavalier insouciance that was part of his charm.

Zelda, meanwhile, had been pursuing her ballet, and the few times Chamson saw her at the Fitzgeralds' apartment her face was covered with grease. He got the impression that the relations between her and Scott were tumultuous and unhappy, though by himself Scott was a delightful companion, interested in everyone and everything. He seldom talked shop. 'From time to time,' Chamson recalled, 'he opened the armoire of his art, but he thought the problem of the artist was to live.' Intense living would inevitably lead to creation. To Chamson, then twenty-six, Fitzgerald seemed like a boy of twenty and brought to mind that Prince Charming of French Romantics, Alfred de Musset. Fitzgerald had Musset's vanity, lyricism, and generosity, and the same urge to perpetuate his youth – or at least the illusion of it with drink.

The Fitzgeralds returned to America in September. Scott was now thirty-two and 'sore as hell about it', he wrote in his Ledger. According to Max Perkins, who met him at the boat after a stormy voyage, he 'had wine cheques for about two hundred dollars, and . . . was still moderately intoxicated. On the other hand he looked quite well, and told me his novel was all on paper – it was only a question of straightening out a few parts of it that did not satisfy him.' Embarrassed by his $8,000 advance from Scribners, Fitzgerald had taken to bluffing, and Perkins gave him the benefit of the doubt. Though he had promised to return with the completed manuscript, it wasn't till November that he sent Perkins the first quarter of it, and the second quarter was still outstanding in March 1929, when the Fitzgeralds' two-year lease on Ellerslie expired and they went back to Europe to live. 'A thousand thanks for your patience,' Fitzgerald wrote Perkins in a farewell note, ' – just trust me a few months longer, Max – its been a discouraging time for me too but I will never forget your kindness and the fact that you've never reproached me.'

There was comfort in the Basil Duke Lee stories, nine of which Fitzgerald had written between March 1928, and February 1929. These tales of his boyhood were sincere and spontaneous, the least of them outshining the somewhat flimsy love stories he was used to writing for the *Post*. By 1927 his story price had risen to $3,500 and that year he earned a record $29,738. He and Zelda were living on the same scale as ever, with much the same abandon. 'We don't go in for self-preservation,' they said. 'When we married we made up our minds never to be afraid.'

But during their final months at Ellerslie anyone could see they were skating on thin ice. Zelda was taxing herself to the limit; she painted and wrote and helped Scottie with her lessons, while her incessant ballet practice reminded John Biggs of the dancing madness of the Middle Ages. A change had come over Scott too. Self-contempt was making him overbearing, and he would go up to strangers in public places and provoke them with, 'I'm Scott Fitzgerald, and who are you, and what do you do, and why do you do it?' One evening, when he came home intoxicated and Zelda said, 'Oh Scott, you promised you wouldn't!', he picked up a figurine and smashed it on the floor. To the person she was with, Zelda said, 'He does that because he knows it's my favourite thing in the house.' During the summer abroad he had twice been jailed, and now he went down to the toughest section of Wilmington with his French chauffeur – an ex-pugilist – and got into brawls that ended at the police station. Several times

John Biggs was roused in the middle of the night to extricate him.

Fitzgerald was sincerely and charmingly apologetic for his misdemeanours, which made them easier to forgive. After a party at Ellerslie he wrote a friend,

I'm afraid I was the world's worst bore last night. I was in the insistent mood – you know the insistent mood? I'm afraid I irritated both you and Eleanor, and I wanted to please you more than any one there. It's all very dim to me but I remember a lot of talk about fairies and the managing type of American woman, whatever that means. . . . Please forgive me and tell Eleanor I can be almost human when sober.

[12]

DESCRIBING New York on his return from Europe the end of 1926, Fitzgerald wrote,

The restlessness . . . approached hysteria. The parties were bigger. . . . The pace was faster . . . the shows were broader, the buildings were higher, the morals were looser, and the liquor was cheaper; but all these benefits did not really minister to much delight. Young people wore out early – they were hard and languid at twenty-one. . . . Most of my friends drank too much – the more they were in tune to the times the more they drank. . . . The city was bloated, glutted, stupid with cake and circuses, and a new expression 'Oh yeah?' summed up all the enthusiasm evoked by the announcement of the last super-skyscrapers.

Such sentiments helped drive Fitzgerald back to Europe the spring of 1929, but Americans have a way of leaving their soil only to discover what they love about it. In an otherwise unimportant short story, he presently wrote,

Watching the fading city [New York], the fading shore, from the deck of the *Majestic,* he had a sense of overwhelming gratitude and gladness that America was there, that under the ugly débris of industry the rich land still pushed up, incorrigibly lavish and fertile, and that in the heart of the leaderless people the old generosities and devotions fought on. . . . The best of America was the best of the world. . . . France was a land, England was a people, but America, having about it still that quality of the idea, was harder to utter, – it was the graves at Shiloh and the tired, drawn, nervous faces of its great men, and the country boys dying in the Argonne for a phrase that was empty before their bodies withered. It was a willingness of the heart.

Landing at Genoa early in March, the Fitzgeralds spent a month on the Riviera before going up to Paris. In July they were back at Cannes, conveniently near the Murphys at

Antibes, but that paradise had sadly altered. It was flooded with American tourists, and no one swam any more save for a short hangover dip at noon. Instead people sat around the bar discussing each other.

Scott's relations with the Murphys had grown a little tense. He was using them in his novel, and when he was with them, he dissected them so publicly and relentlessly that Sara finally wrote him,

You can't expect anyone to like or stand a *Continual* feeling of analysis, & sub-analysis & criticism – on the whole unfriendly – such as we have felt for quite awhile. It is definitely in the air, – & quite unpleasant. – It certainly detracts from any gathering, – & Gerald, for one, simply curls up at the edges & becomes someone else in that sort of atmosphere. And last night you even said, 'that you had never seen Gerald so silly & rude.' It's hardly likely that I should explain Gerald, – or Gerald me – to you. If you don't know what people are like it's *your* loss – and if Gerald was 'rude' in getting up & leaving a party that had gotten *quite bad*, – then he was rude to the Hemingways & MacLeishes too. No, it is hardly likely that you would stick at a thing like *manners* – it is more probably some theory you have, – (it *may* be something to do with the book), – But *you ought to know at your age* that *you Can't have Theories about friends.* If you Can't take friends largely, & without suspicion – then they are not friends at all – We *cannot* – Gerald & I – at our age – & stage in life – *be bothered* with sophomoric situations – like last night. We are very simple people – (unless we feel ourselves in a collegiate quagmire) – and we are *literally* & *actually* fond of you both – (There is no reason for saying this that I know of – unless we meant it.) And so – *for God's sake* take it or leave it, – as it is meant, – a straight gesture, *without* subtitles –

Yr old & rather irritated friend
Sara

What often passed for rudeness in Fitzgerald was this kind of curiosity, this attempt to bring people out. Their revelations, however, were only the starting point from which he was going to make something – compose. He didn't run home and write it all down like a newspaperman. Rather he courted a mood, a vision, a state of mind and feeling that would enable him to pluck his impressions out of the air, like an artist.

In October the Fitzgeralds returned to Paris and rented an apartment at 10 rue Pergolèse, off the Avenue de la Grande Armée. That autumn the stock market crashed, but Fitzgerald had more immediate concerns; his own life seemed to be crashing around him as his drinking, long a problem, got completely out of hand.

Old friends like the Kalmans, visiting Paris that year, found him charming yet insufferable. When the Kalmans arrived at their hotel, Fitzgerald was waiting for them in the lobby. 'How did you know we were coming?' they asked. Fitzgerald, out for a stroll, had noticed a truck with four Oshkosh trunks on it and had said to himself, 'Only the Kalmans would have four Oshkosh trunks. Then I saw your initials, so I followed the truck. The trunks will be here in a minute.' After this pleasant beginning Fitzgerald came to the Kalmans for cocktails next day and mortified them before their other guests. When Oscar Kalman forbade him to have any more to drink, Fitzgerald stormed out of the apartment, saying he would never speak to them again, but the following noon he was banging on their door and pleading, 'Kallie, come down to Prunier's with me and have some oysters – I know I was perfectly terrible last night.'

He liked the constant flow of people through his life, and a favourite place for attaching them was the Ritz Bar with its predominantly American clientele. One day he was ordering a drink when the head barman came over and said, 'Mr Fitzgerald, it cost me a hundred francs to get that man a new hat.'

'What man?'

'That man whose hat you smashed.'

'Did I smash someone's hat?'

It developed that Fitzgerald, sitting in the bar the previous evening, had got up without provocation and smashed a stranger's hat as he entered.

'I must tell you,' the barman went on, 'that if anything like that happens again we can't serve you in here.'

'You're absolutely right,' Fitzgerald concurred.

Drink turned him inside out. Beyond a point he became possessed, like some character in Dostoevsky, and yet he seemed marked for alcoholism and his tolerance diminished as the malady increased its hold. Murphy recalled how, in 1926, Fitzgerald would come over the Villa America with the wonderful aloofness he had when he had been writing. He wrote cold sober in those days; he later said – and there is no reason to doubt it – that he did not deliberately mix liquor with his work until 1928 at Ellerslie. But Murphy also recalled how Fitzgerald, having had two martinis and a little wine with dinner, would ask to lie down. One evening he passed out on their sofa and spent the night there, and the maid, alarmed by his bust-like pallor when she found him next morning, said to Sara, '*Madame est sûre que Monsieur n'est pas mort?*'

Originally Fitzgerald had drunk to enhance life, to heighten its possibilities. After a few cocktails he seemed to be mentally skating, but gradually drink had gained the upper hand, and any attempt to explain his submission should perhaps begin with the fact that he was Irish. That race of word-weavers and fantasts has shown an historic weakness for the bottle. Fitzgerald's father was known as a man who drank – so also his two McQuillan uncles. In Scott the tendency was aggravated by the contradictions of a high-strung, artistic temperament. With himself in mind, he wrote, 'Like so many men who are shy because they cannot fit their world of imagination into reality, or don't want to, he had learned compensations.' Fitzgerald was shy and a dreamer, yet people meant more to him than anything, and drinking was a bridge. 'I found,' says an alcoholic in one of his stories, 'that with a few drinks I got expansive and somehow had the ability to please people. ... Then I began to take a whole lot of drinks to keep going and have everybody think I was wonderful.'

There were other conflicts. Though a renegade Catholic,

he was not unspiritual and part of him hated being at odds with the Church. He loved fame but never quite believed in his own because it had come so suddenly. He wanted to earn fantastic sums, yet had to compromise his talent – selling it piece-meal to the magazines – to earn as much as he did. He once told John Biggs that he drank because he felt he could never be a first-rate writer – he would always be 'at the top of the second class'. He suffered from the insecurity of all imaginative creators who can't be sure they'll do it again, and drinking brought him release from a tortured sensitivity, from the unrelenting conflict between his poetic vision and the shock of the world. He drank the way Baudelaire describes Poe drinking – not as an epicure 'but barbarously, with a speed and dispatch altogether American, as if he were performing a homicidal function, as if he had to kill something inside himself, a worm that would not die.' There was a terrible deliberateness about the way Fitzgerald dosed himself with gin.

In June he had written Perkins that he was working on his novel from a new angle which he thought would solve previous difficulties. Then his references to it trailed off. Instead he filled his letters with descriptions of young writers Scribners might be interested in publishing (Erskine Caldwell, Morley Callaghan), though Perkins kept implying that the manuscript they really wanted to see was his own. Three years had elapsed since his last book, but when his agent suggested he bring out the Basil stories as a collection, Fitzgerald replied,

I could have published four lowsy, half baked books in the last five years & people would have thought I was at least a worthy young man not drinking myself to pieces in the south seas – but I'd be dead as Michael Arlen, Bromfield, Tom Boyd ... & the others who think they can trick the world with the hurried and the second rate.

Since *Gatsby* Fitzgerald's standards for his serious work had continued to rise. He was pitting himself now against Hemingway, whose style – with its blocky, workmanlike, brick-and-mortar quality – was utterly different from Fitzgerald's, yet clearly that of a great artist. 'Yes, there's magic in it,' Fitzgerald had said to Gerald Murphy after reading *The Sun Also Rises*, while *In Our Time* had caused him to concede, 'Ernest's book of stories is so much better than mine.' Hemingway had recently published *A Farewell to Arms*, his long-contemplated masterpiece about the war Fitzgerald hadn't fought. It would sell 93,000 copies the first year, more than twice the initial sale of any of Fitzgerald's books, so that popularly as well as artistically he began to feel himself eclipsed.

With success Hemingway's slight early diffidence was vanishing into the restrained bravado of a champ. Comparing him to Fitzgerald at this time would be like comparing a butterfly and a bull; the butterfly has beautiful colours on its wings, but the bull is *there*. Hemingway was a force. His personality overpowered you, making you do the things he wanted to do, making you enthusiastic about the things he was enthusiastic about. The world revolved around *him*, while Fitzgerald – off to one side – was subtler, more insidious, more sympathetic, more like light playing through clouds. Fitzgerald had the dangerous Athenian qualities of facility and grace as against Hemingway's Spartan virtues of ruggedness and perseverance. Both were accomplished artists, but perhaps the ultimate choice lay between Fitzgerald's more sensitive penetration of human lives and Hemingway's harder, more burnished style.

Their friendship had grown a bit prickly since the early days when Fitzgerald had been Hemingway's promoter. Back in 1925–6 their letters had a carefree, spoofing tone. In an advance description of *The Sun Also Rises* Hemingway wrote Fitzgerald that though he had tried to imitate *The Great Gatsby* he felt he had failed, somewhat because of never having been on Long Island.

The hero, like Gatsby, is a Lake Superior Salmon Fisherman. (There are no salmon in Lake Superior.) The action all takes place in Newport, R.I., and the heroine is a girl named Sophie Irene Loeb who kills her mother. The scene in which Sophie gives birth to twins in the death house at Sing Sing where she is waiting to be electrocuted for the murder of the father and sister of her, as then, unborn children I got from Dreiser but practically everything else in the book is either my own or yours. I know you'll be glad to see it. The Sun Also Rises comes from Sophie's statement as she is strapped into the chair as the current mounts.

Here Hemingway was joshing Fitzgerald about his novel in progress, supposedly a study of matricide. But even in those days there was friction, for Fitzgerald's attentions could be burdensome. Out on the town with his friends, he would suddenly decide he had to talk with Ernest, and his intrusions in the small hours were not always welcomed by Hemingway. During the day, when Hemingway was out, Fitzgerald would stop by his apartment and make trouble with the concierge – so much so that when Fitzgerald returned to Europe in 1929, Hemingway wrote Perkins that he did not want Fitzgerald to know his address. Fitzgerald found it anyway, and they saw a good deal of each other, though in his Ledger Fitzgerald now spoke of Hemingway's 'coldness'.

Part of the trouble was Fitzgerald's irritability about his work. When Gertrude Stein remarked that Hemingway's and Fitzgerald's 'flames' were 'not the same', Fitzgerald took her to mean that she thought Hemingway's superior, and Hemingway wrote Fitzgerald assuring him she had meant the reverse. Hemingway said he didn't agree, of course – any comparison between hypothetical 'flames' being pure nonsense and any comparison between him and Fitzgerald being nonsense too. They had started along different paths and wouldn't have met except by accident, and, as writers, had nothing in common except a desire to write well. So why must Fitzgerald make comparisons and talk of superiority? If he had to have feelings of either superiority or inferiority towards Hemingway, well and good, as long as Hemingway did not have to have feelings of either superiority or inferiority towards him. There could be no such thing between serious writers, who were all on the same boat headed towards death. Competition within the boat was as silly as deck sports. The only real competition was the original one of making the boat, but Fitzgerald was getting touchy because he hadn't finished his novel. Hemingway said he understood, and Fitzgerald could be a lot more touchy and he wouldn't mind.

Proud and vulnerable himself, Hemingway was patient with Fitzgerald, yet he was nothing if not a competitor. Back in 1925–6 it was already with a touch of irony that he used to speak of Fitzgerald as his 'patron'. When Fitzgerald met James Joyce the summer of 1928, he had mentioned to Perkins that Joyce wrote 'eleven hours a day to my intermittent 8', and Perkins quoted the remark to Hemingway, who wrote Fitzgerald that he certainly was a worker! Hemingway said he had never been able to write longer than two hours without getting utterly pooped – any longer and the stuff became tripe – but here was old Fitz, whom he once knew, working eight hours a day. He wondered how it felt. What was the secret of Fitzgerald's ability to write for eight hours every day? Hemingway looked forward with some eagerness to seeing the product. Would it be like the effusions of that other great worker and fellow Celt – Joyce? Had Fitzgerald gone in for not making sense? Hemingway called Fitzgerald a dirty lousy liar to say he worked (wrote) eight hours a day.

The spring of 1929 there had been unpleasantness between them because of Hemingway's boxing match with the Canadian writer, Morley Callaghan. Fitzgerald, as timekeeper, had accidentally let a round go overtime when Hemingway was getting the worst of it. Some months later when Fitzgerald, in a drunken quarrel, said he felt a need to smash Hemingway as a man, Hemingway suggested that Fitzgerald had purposely let the round go on. Fitzgerald was so indignant that Hemingway wrote a long letter exonerating him. Meanwhile the *New York Herald Tribune* had printed a false report that Callaghan had knocked Hemingway out. Hemingway prevailed on Fitzgerald to wire Callaghan (now in America) that he, Fitzgerald, was awaiting a correction of the story. Callaghan, who hadn't been responsible for the story in the first place and who had already sent in a correction, was incensed at Fitzgerald until Hemingway wrote him, taking full responsibility for the wire.

More ominous than Fitzgerald's quarrels with his friends was his unending feud with Zelda. Her mania for the ballet, together with his drinking, had brought them to the edge of indifference. Besides her morning classes – at which she was always the first to appear, usually with a bouquet for the teacher – she took private lessons in the afternoon, dieting all the while in the hope of perfecting a body that had begun too late to cope with the intricacies of *entrechat* and *pas-de-bourée*. Her inner torment is described in her novel *Save Me the Waltz*, where the asceticism of the dance becomes a sort of penance for Alabama Knight. Under its discipline she loses interest in material possessions; she isn't trying to gain anything but to get rid of some of herself. 'It seemed to Alabama that, reaching her goal, she would drive the devils that had driven her,' and the thought of stopping makes her sick and middle-aged. Like Alabama, Zelda had hoped for a part in the Diaghilev troupe, but all she got was an offer to be a shimmy dancer in the Folies Bergères.

While it wasn't Scott's nature to interfere, his scepticism was apparent. 'Are you under the illusion that you'll ever be any good at this stuff?' he would say. 'There's no use killing yourself. I hope you realize that the biggest difference in the world is between the amateur and the professional in the arts.' Meanwhile their home life – what was left of it – became unbearable. They 'passed each other in the musty corridors hastily and ate distantly facing each other with the air of enemies awaiting some gesture of hostility.' Their misery was completed by an unhousebroken dog named Adage, which the cook spoiled while neglecting Scott and Scottie.

To stem the poisonous drift, Scott took Zelda on a North African tour in February 1930, and according to Bishop, Scott returned 'with a good ruddy colour, very unlike the winter paleness with which he went away. I take it from his conversation he is in much better shape all around.' But

Zelda went back to her ballet with the same fury. During a lunch party in April she was so fearful of missing her lesson that Oscar Kalman got up from the table to accompany her. Though there was plenty of time, Zelda insisted she was going to be late and began changing into her ballet clothes in the taxi. When traffic held them up, she bolted and ran the remaining distance. Kalman phoned Fitzgerald who went to the studio at once, where they convinced him Zelda was ill.

She spent the next ten days in a hospital at Malmaison. 'Mrs Fitzgerald,' said the doctor's report,

entered 23 April 1930, in a state of acute anxiety, unable to stay put, repeating continually, 'It's frightful, it's horrible, what's going to become of me, I must work and I no longer can, I must die and yet I have to work. I'll never be cured, let me go, I have to see "Madame" (the dancing teacher), she has given me the greatest joy in the world, it's comparable to sunlight falling on a block of crystal, to a symphony of perfumes, to the most perfect strains of the greatest masters of music.'

She was slightly tipsy on her arrival and according to recent reports had drunk a great deal, finding that alcohol stimulated her for her work. Afterwards, the patient experienced several more outbreaks of anxiety similar to the first, especially around nightfall.

In sum, it is a question of a *petite anxieuse* worn out by her work in a milieu of professional dancers. Violent reactions, several suicidal attempts never pushed to the limit. Leaves the hospital 2 May, against the doctor's advice.

Zelda went back to her ballet, the strain intensified by a round of parties connected with a friend's wedding. When she broke down a second time the end of May, her condition was seen to be more serious. After two weeks at the Valmont Clinic in Switzerland, her doctor reported,

at the beginning of her stay Mrs F. said she hadn't been sick and had been brought to the sanatorium under duress. Every day she repeated that she wanted to return to Paris to resume the ballet in which she thinks she finds the sole satisfaction of her life.

From the organic point of view nothing to report, no signs of neurological illness. It became clearer and clearer that a simple rest cure was absolutely insufficient, and that psychiatric treatment by a specialist in a sanatorium was indicated. It was evident that the relations between the patient and the husband had been shaky for some time and that for this reason the patient had tried to create a life of her own through the ballet (since family life and obligations were not sufficient to satisfy her ambition and her artistic leanings).

For years there had been reason to question Zelda's sanity, but Fitzgerald refused to face the issue until it was thrust upon him. The spring of 1925 Gerald Murphy had dropped by Fitzgerald's Paris apartment to find him in a turmoil. 'Ernest has just gone home,' he said. Apparently Hemingway had been invited to meet Zelda, Fitzgerald assuming they would have everything in common and get along beautifully. The *rapport* had been less than instantaneous – their strong personalities did not blend (Zelda's word for Hemingway was 'bogus') – and as Hemingway left, he remarked to Fitzgerald in the hall, 'But Scott you realize, don't you, that she's crazy?' Once, in a flower shop, Zelda had said to Scott quite seriously that the lilies were talking to her, and during their trip to Hollywood in 1927 she had put her dresses in a bathtub and set fire to them. After that, her peculiarities had been somewhat masked by her passion for ballet. But Scott used to wonder about her long silences, during which no one could reach her, and when a friend asked her why she drank, she replied, 'Because the world is chaos and when I drink I'm chaotic.'[37]

Zelda's doctor at Valmont called in the psychotherapist, Oscar Forel, who diagnosed her case as schizophrenia and admitted her to his sanatorium at Prangins, near Geneva. She entered Prangins early in June, and Scott spent the next year drifting from town to town in Switzerland – 'a country,' he said, 'where very few things begin, but many things end.' Occasionally he went to Paris to be with Scottie and her nurse, but Zelda's recovery was now a dedication.

There is a touching letter from Fitzgerald to Dr Forel, written at the time Zelda entered the sanatorium. Fitzgerald accepts the doctor's proscription against seeing her until her attitude towards him changes, but he wants to know if he can have flowers sent her every other day. He wonders when it will be safe to write her little notes that do not mention her illness or their misunderstandings. He speaks of Scribners' plan to publish a book of Zelda's short pieces which, he thinks, will give her a sense of a public and take her mind off ballet.

In July Fitzgerald sent Perkins three stories, subsequently lost, which Zelda had written

in the dark middle of her nervous breakdown. I think you'll see that apart from the beauty & richness of the writing they have a strange haunting and evocative quality that is absolutely new. I think too that there is a certain unity apparent in them – their actual unity is a fact because each of them is the story of her life when things for a while seemed to have brought her to the edge of madness and dispair. In my opinion they are literature tho I may in this case read so much between the lines that my opinion is valueless. [*Scribners* magazine turned them down and the proposed book was abandoned.]

At the doctor's suggestion Fitzgerald wrote Zelda's ballet teacher, Egarova, for an estimate of her potentialities. To cure her, it seemed important to make her realize the futility of her ambitions. Egarova's reply was not as discouraging as Fitzgerald and the doctor might have wished. She said that while Zelda had begun too late to be a star, she had ability and would be capable of handling secondary rôles in a big company such as the Massine Ballet in New York.

During June and July, Zelda fluctuated between hysterical madness and a brilliant lucidity. When she tried to run away the doctor confined her, with salutary effect. Scottie came to visit her, but in August her first meeting with Scott had to be postponed when the thought of it caused her to break out with virulent eczema. The meeting took place in September, only to be followed by another attack of eczema, and Scott began to hope that Zelda's trouble might be physiological. 'I can't help clinging to the idea,' he wrote Forel, 'that some essential physical thing like salt or iron or semen or some unguessed at holy water is either missing or is present in too great quantity.'

Probing Zelda's past, Fitzgerald blamed Mrs Sayre for the way she had coddled her last and favourite child. She had nursed Zelda until, as Zelda said herself, she 'could probably have chewed sticks'. Then Mrs Sayre had waited on her, stood in for her, defended her against the rest of the family, so that there developed, Fitzgerald said, 'the necessity of an arbitrary and unmotivated, often *an even undesired self-assertion* – the contrast between which, and a rationality acquired from her father was later to drive her mad.' Of course, Fitzgerald was conscious of his own rôle in the tragedy. The doctor had told him he mustn't drink for a year, as his drinking was one of the things that had haunted Zelda in her delirium. She was given one chance in four of total recovery – two chances of a partial one – but her progress was slow with frequent setbacks, and Fitzgerald began to learn the pathos of an old appeal:

> Canst thou not minister to a mind diseas'd
> Pluck from the memory a rooted sorrow,
> Raze out the written troubles of the brain,
> And with some sweet oblivious antidote
> Cleanse the stuff'd bosom of that perilous stuff
> Which weighs upon the heart?

Rebecca West caught a glimpse of Fitzgerald about this time – a glimpse which gains significance against the background of his private misfortunes. She and her son were having lunch at Armenonville,

very few people were there and we sat down by the lake. Presently Scott Fitzgerald appeared with a woman from New York whom I knew, called Emily Vanderbilt. She was very handsome, I think she had the most beautifully shaped head and the most cunningly devised hair-cut to show it off that I have ever seen. They sat down at a table still nearer the lake than we were, with their backs to us. She was telling him some long and sad story, and going over and over it. He was leaning towards her, sometimes caressing her hands, showing this wonderful gentleness and charity which I remember as his great characteristic. Finally he stood up and seemed to be saying, 'You mustn't go over this any more.' His eyes fell on us, and he said to her, 'Emily, look who's here,' and they finished their lunch with us. I can't remember a thing he said, I think we did what is the great resort for people finding themselves in emotional crises near water, we fed some birds with bread. But he was gay and charming, and we all laughed a lot. And then he took her off to her car, her arm in his, jerking her elbow up, telling her to cheer up. I have always remembered this scene with emotion, for later Emily Vanderbilt commited suicide.

On a trip to Paris the end of June, Fitzgerald had met Thomas Wolfe, Scribners' latest prodigy. When they lunched together, Fitzgerald immediately liked the gargantuan Southerner with his extravagant gestures, defiant eyes, and pouting lower lip. They parted at ten that night in the Ritz Bar where, according to Wolfe, Fitzgerald was 'entirely surrounded by Princeton boys all nineteen years old, all drunk and all half-raw'. In July they ran into each other in Switzerland and it appealed to Fitzgerald's sense of the grotesque when Wolfe, striding along and flailing his great arms as he talked, snapped an overhead wire that extinguished the lights in a neighbouring village. By now Wolfe had decided that Fitzgerald was trying to prevent him from working, which was a little like coming between a tiger and his prey. Shortly afterwards, however, Fitzgerald wired Wolfe that he had finished *Look Homeward, Angel* in twenty consecutive hours and was 'enormously moved and grateful'. 'You have a great find in him,' Fitzgerald wrote Perkins, ' – what he'll do is incalculable. He has a deeper culture than Ernest [Hemingway] and more vitality, if he is slightly less of a poet that goes with the immense surface he wants to cover. Also he lacks Ernests quality of a stick hardened in the fire – he is more susceptible to the world.'

Fitzgerald seldom wrote his parents, but since Zelda's breakdown it had been necessary to calm his mother with terse bulletins. Her replies, like everything else about her, annoyed him. When she sent him a moralistic poem, hoping that sorrow might have opened the way for advice, he returned it scornfully, saying the precepts it enjoined were suitable for someone who wanted to be a chief clerk at fifty. But he continued to have a soft spot for his father – that sweet, ineffectual man who had lived in his mother's shadow, taking immense vicarious pleasure in his success. When Edward Fitzgerald died of heart trouble in January, 1931, Scott went home for the funeral.

At all times a side of him struggled towards gaiety, and his voyage on the *S.S. New York* was brightened by a small, vivacious blonde named Bert Barr. She was in the party of Herman Cornell, a Texas oil man who had chartered several suites for his family and friends. All they did was sit in their quarters and play bridge, but the second night out they went on deck, clutching their cards, to see the *Bremen* pass. As the crack new liner coasted by in a blaze of lights, Bert said to Cornell, 'Papa, buy me that,' and Fitzgerald, who had met Cornell in the bar, overheard the *bon mot*.

'Where have you been?' he asked Bert.

'I've been working,' she said in an undertone. 'I'm a card shark and I'm taking this guy for a ride.'

She held out her cards and told Fitzgerald to pick one, which she had no trouble remembering and identifying. He was fascinated, scenting a ready-made story that didn't need to be imagined.

'Aren't you a little young for this?' he said.

'I've been doing it since I was four.'

'Have you been *winning* since you were four?'

He wanted to accompany Bert to her suite, but she said she couldn't waste time on him since he didn't play cards. Fitzgerald went away and the hoax was maintained. Cornell acted the sucker, exclaiming all through dinner that he could hardly wait to start playing again. Fitzgerald kept protesting, 'But it doesn't make sense – this girl gambling for a living!', and dancing her apart from the others, he lectured her about it. Next day, when they let him in on the joke, Fitzgerald was so impressed with Bert's virtuosity that he asked her to be his collaborator. Because of all his worries, he said he was finding it hard to think up comic situations, but if she would feed him the lines, he would write the story.

Fitzgerald stood beside his father's grave in the Rockville cemetery – then visited the Sayres in Montgomery to talk hopefully of Zelda.

Back in Switzerland he kept turning out short stories to meet the expense of the best psychiatric care available. According to Margaret Eglov, who saw a lot of him that spring, he would write a story in four to six days – incarcerating himself in his hotel room and not drinking. Between times, however, he played with the notion of drinking himself to death, for he had always thought it his destiny to die young. He had a collection of photographs, put out by some temperance society, showing the ill effects of alcohol on the kidneys and other organs, and he would mull over them and joke about them in a lugubrious way.

He took refuge from his melancholy in constant clowning. One day Margaret Eglov's aunt invited Margaret and Fitzgerald to lunch with her at her Geneva hotel. Also present was an authority on the League of Nations Opium Conference, a Miss LaMotte, who pointed out the American delegate to the conference at another table and said he lacked backbone. They were eating blue trout from the Swiss lakes, and Fitzgerald solemnly beckoned the waiter and asked for an envelope. Inserting the skeleton of his fish, he addressed it to the spineless delegate and told the waiter to deliver it.

As Margaret was studying with the Jung group, she and Fitzgerald often discussed psychiatry, and once he wrote out a dream he had had, so she could decipher it. Interweaving his embarrassment over his mother with Hemingwayesque fantasies of war and violence, the dream began:

I am in an upstairs appartment where I live with my mother, old, white-haired, clumsy and in mourning, as she is today. On another floor are a group of handsome & rich young men, whom I seem to have known slightly as a child and now want to know better, but they look as me suspiciously. I talk to one who is agreeable and not at all snobbish, but obviously he does not

205

encourage my acquaintance – whether because he considers me poor, unimportant, ill bred, or of ill renown I don't know, or rather don't think about – only I scent the polite indifference and even understand it. During this time I discover that there is a dance downstairs to which I am not invited. I feel that if they knew better how important I was, I should be invited.

Momentarily attention shifts to a magnificent parade going on outside the window – then back to the dance.

I go downstairs again, wander into the doorway of a sort of ballroom, see caterers at work and then am suddenly shamed by realizing this is the party to which I am not invited. Meeting one of the young men in the hall, I lose all poise and stammer something absurd. I leave the house, but as I leave Mother calls something to me in a too audible voice from an upper story. I don't know whether I am angry with her for clinging to me, or because I am ashamed of her for not being young and chic, or for disgracing my conventional sense by calling out, or because she might guess I'd been hurt and pity me, which would have been unendurable, or all those things. Anyhow I call back at her some terse and furious reproach.

The dream now becomes a nightmare. Outside two automobiles collide 'with the dark intended tragedy of an execution'. Everything goes in the direction the parade has gone. Fire engines pass with the first one overturned and drawn along on its side, the others running into it and over it. Scottie appears. When she falls down and has a nosebleed, Fitzgerald hurries her to the first aid station. The Italian wounded arrive in a big charabanc,

sitting like tourists – I can't express the impressive throbbing of the arrival, the terrible dignity, this latter perhaps symbolized by the last row of the great car, filled by three or four officers or princes in rich, dark blues dress uniforms and monocles – and also a young woman in a white evening dress, yet somehow consecrated to the whole scene. This, someone told me, was the Princess Carlotta.

The wounded were lifted on other soldiers' shoulders like football players, and, smiling defiantly and being shaken hands with, were taken into the hospital, I caught a glimpse of some small tents which covered dead men.

The room where I was now began to fill up with Italian soldiers in conventional green, who had evidently had a hell of a bitter fight and were still full of nervous energy. I viewed them with a certain reserve. One of them said to me, 'On the Plain of Orso we killed a hundred Français – only a few know about it.' (His attitude seemed much more vivid and *personal* than any record of war I ever read, as if they had all started off together and then fallen out. Some unguessed at secret hatred.) Then in came a man more savagely wrought up than any and began hating the French aloud and repeating over and over that he was going to kill the next Frenchman he saw.

A French passer-bye in civilian dress stopped, and with a resentful look made as though to hit him. The Italian turned – for a moment there was a brawling confusion and the two disappeared. A moment later the Italian ran back into sight panting, and there were voices: 'He did it – he killed him!'

Several times previously I hadn't seen the end of anything because of obstacles in the way – this time I ran around the corner – and there was the Frenchman on the ground with a bayonet in his stomach and the attached rifle wobbling around in the air as he struggled very feebly.

Here I woke up.

In May came a voice out of the past, a letter from Shane Leslie in London. 'If you could come here and sit with me in the Library and write,' said Leslie,

you would be using more ink than whisky for I live on buttermilk. One has to return to the simplicities of life if one is to continue writing at all after a certain age. I am sorry to learn that poor Zelda was so down in health but I hope she has taken the road to recovery. She was a bright and birdlike thing and I cannot imagine her distraught.

Zelda, happily, was a good deal better. Her eczema, which Fitzgerald likened to an iron maiden in the anguish it caused her, had disappeared – also her fits of wild, inappropriate laughter. In June he took her on a trip to Annecy in southern France, and Zelda remembered that 'it was like the good gone times when we still believed in summer hotels and the philosophies of popular songs ... we danced the Weiner waltz, and just simply swep' around.' By September she was considered well enough to leave the sanatorium and go back to America. The Fitzgeralds planned to winter in Montgomery while Scott finished his novel, which he had barely looked at for a year and a half.

En route they spent a few days in New York, which seemed a ghost town compared to New York of the boom. Fitzgerald's barber, who had retired on a half-million bet in the market, was back at work, and the headwaiters again bowed people to their tables when there were people to be bowed. Climbing the Empire State, Fitzgerald could see where the city faded out into the greens and blues of the country beyond. It made him realize that New York wasn't a universe after all – *it had limits* – and the great metropolis that had been his symbol of power and success in the twenties came crashing to the ground.

Montgomery was unchanged. 'No talk of depression,' Fitzgerald wrote Perkins. 'No thought of it. The boom was never here either. Simply life burning sluggishly on. I like it. We have a nice house & a fine Stutz car (cost $400) & I'm going to do lots of work.' But Zelda's friends were shocked at the change in her. The old vivacity had been replaced by the crumpled, spiritless quality of an invalid, and on the tennis court, when she said she couldn't hit the ball over there because of all that water and there wasn't any water, Scott would be very gentle about taking her home. He never carped at her or complained of her condition, but tried to build her up.

The end of October he went to Hollywood for five weeks' work on MGM's version of *Red-Headed Woman*, a novel by his imitator, Katherine Brush. Insisting on a $1200-a-week contract, he got the money he expected but again the job was a failure; this time he blamed it on director Marcel de Sano, who doctored what he wrote into a bad script that producer Irving Thalberg rejected. The story editor who hired Fitzgerald and acted as Thalberg's liaison man was inclined to blame the nature of the vehicle. The red-headed woman in question had advanced herself by sleeping with every man who crossed her path, and Fitzgerald made the audience laugh *at* her instead of *with* her, as Thalberg had hoped. Fitzgerald was perhaps too much of a romantic to sympathize with such a hard-boiled heroine, though later he regretted he hadn't gone directly to Thalberg (he had been warned against it as bad taste). And so once again he left Hollywood disgusted and disillusioned, vowing never to return.

As an artist he had profited. If only from afar, he had studied Thalberg, the young Napoleon of the films, who would be the model for the hero of *The Last Tycoon*. Moreover a party at Thalberg's had provided the inspiration for a masterly short story, 'Crazy Sunday'. After a few drinks – 'his blood throbbing with the scarlet corpuscles of exhibitionism', like Joel Coles in the story – Fitzgerald had asked to do an act. Thalberg's wife, Norma Shearer, quieted the company and Fitzgerald sang a song about a dog which amused no one. Directly in front of him John Gilbert, the Great Lover of the screen, 'glared at him with an eye as keen as the eye of a potato'. In a doorway at the far end of the room stood the small, slight figure of Thalberg, shoulders hunched, hands plunged deep in pockets, a not unkind smile on his lips. Thalberg was tolerant of artists – 'once a champion, always a champion', he used to say – and next day Fitzgerald received a telegram from Norma Shearer: I THOUGHT YOU WERE ONE OF THE MOST AGREEABLE PERSONS AT OUR TEA. But when it came to evaluating Fitzgerald as an employee, his blunder before Hollywood's élite could hardly have been in his favour. The following week he was dismissed.

'Crazy Sunday' cuts deeper than Fitzgerald's private humiliation. Already in Miles Calman, the director, Fitzgerald had hold of his great theme – the tragedy of the artist and idealist caught in a tough materialistic enterprise. 'Miles Calman, tall, nervous, with a desperate humor and the unhappiest eyes Joel ever saw [shades of Ring Lardner], was an artist from the top of his curiously shaped head to his niggerish feet. Upon these last he stood firmly – he had never made a cheap picture though he had sometimes paid heavily for the luxury of making experimental flops.' When Calman dies in a plane crash, as Fitzgerald intended Monroe Stahr to die at the end of *The Last Tycoon*, one is made to feel that except for its occasional magician Hollywood is a desert.

During Scott's absence Zelda had been troubled. 'I don't think I'm jealous,' she told a friend, 'but it worries me to have Scott out there with all those beautiful women.' She sent him stories to correct, and he was slow about returning them. One of his first concerns on settling in Montgomery had been to find Zelda a ballet teacher, no expenses spared. Zelda was working up a programme which included a Bach fugue with a lot of impossible *pizzicato*, and when her teacher said it was too difficult, Zelda went home in a rage and phoned next day to say she had broken her ankle. She never returned.

In November Judge Sayre died after a long illness. Though Zelda's girlhood had been a constant rebellion against his authority, in the end he was precious to her, his hard-bitten integrity seeming almost the equivalent of moral law. She knew that beneath a proud politeness he had never cared for Scott. Once he had said to her, 'I think you better divorce him – you can't make a life with a fella like that.' (For the judge to speak of his son-in-law as a 'fella' was in itself a sign of disapproval.) Zelda said he was the sweetest person in the world when sober, to which her father replied, 'He's never sober.'

Before going to Hollywood, Scott had knelt beside the judge's bed and pleaded, 'Tell me you believe in me.' 'Scott,' the judge had answered, 'I think you will always pay your bills.'

Shortly after Fitzgerald's return Zelda came down with asthma, and he took her to Florida to recuperate. While there she relapsed into madness. It came as a shock, though Scott was probably exaggerating when he said, 'the nine months before [Zelda's] second breakdown were the happiest of my life, and I think, save for the agonies of her father's death, the happiest of hers.' What he had known in that precarious interim was not so much happiness as relief at her apparent recovery. On 12 February she entered Phipps Clinic, the psychiatric branch of Johns Hopkins in Baltimore, and Fitzgerald, living on in Montgomery, was back on the treadmill of writing pot-boilers, while trying to be what he called 'a nice, thoughtful female mother for Scottie'.

He seldom went out, but once he took his secretary to a dance at the Country Club, and while they were in the bar, a Marine major entered in dress regalia (dark blue uniform with gold epaulets and gold stripes up the side of the pants). He was tall and handsome and well aware of it.

'My God, I've got to talk to that man!' Fitzgerald exclaimed.

Introducing himself, he said, 'I've never seen any one loose on a dance floor in a get-up like this. You've got guts even to appear. Who do you think you are – a member of the fife and drum corps?'

His dignity ruffled, the major protested that it was the regulation dress uniform.

'Well, I don't care,' said Fitzgerald, ' – anyone who's got guts enough to appear in a thing like that I want to know better,' and he ended by inviting the major to lunch.

In retrospect, Fitzgerald was never too clear about his entanglements when drinking. Next day he phoned his secretary to say, 'I understand I invited that big fife and drum number to lunch with us. Well, I'm not lunching with him or you either.'

So far the depression hadn't hurt Fitzgerald's income. Indeed, Zelda's illness had stimulated his production, and with his story price at its zenith of $4,000, he earned a record $37,599 in 1931. He was, however, sacrificing quality to quantity to a point where the *Post* had complained of his recent offerings. Once, when his secretary praised the story she was typing, Fitzgerald said, 'Oh, there's no use lying about it – it's absolute junk and you know it – it's nothing, *nothing*.'

But though he abused his talent, he couldn't suppress it,

and even his watery hack fiction had moments of distinction – an insight here or a descriptive passage there that sang in the memory. As for his superior work, it had new depth and complexity now that life had 'gotten in some hard socks', as he put it. Just as he had written and rewritten the *Gatsby* theme of lost love in stories which preceded it, so now he was foreshadowing *Tender Is the Night* in stories poignant with his own disintegration. Like Bill McChesney, the cocky young producer in 'Two Wrongs', whose marriage, health and career are wrecked by dissipation, Fitzgerald had grown 'a little tired and unconfident – two qualities he could never for a moment tolerate'. 'One Trip Abroad' tells of a couple as full of promise as the young Fitzgeralds who grow hard and destroy each other while drifting around Europe. In 'Babylon Revisited', possibly the most moving story Fitzgerald ever wrote, the widower Charlie Wales, who had gone to pieces during the boom, is trying to reform and regain custody of his child. Like Wales, Fitzgerald would have liked to 'jump back a whole generation and trust in character again as the eternally valuable element'. Everything else wore out.

Fortunately, Zelda's second breakdown seemed less serious than her first. Except at the beginning there had been no hysteria, and her letters to Scottie were gay and spirited. 'I am very glad,' she wrote,

'that you and Daddy have found something to do in the evenings. Chess is such a good game – do learn to play it well. I have never been able to endow it with much of an existence apart from Alice-in-Wonderland and my pieces usually spend most of the game galloping in wild pandemonium before the onslaughts of Daddy. . . . You will soon be an accomplished dame-de-compagnie for him and I shall have to sit cutting paper-dolls and doing my chemical experiments while you two amuse yourselves. . . I expect you to keep the house supplied with soap, flowers, and tap-dancers during my absence. . . . Take care of Daddy. See that there's plenty of spinach and Dinasaurus meat for Sunday. And profit by my absence to be as bad as you can get away with.

Zelda seemed almost to be enjoying her respite at Phipps,

where she found an outlet for her tensions in creative work. She painted, modelled, and sketched, and quickly finished a novel she had begun in Montgomery. It was frankly auto-biographical, including an *exposé* of her quarrels with Scott (in the original version the hero's name was Amory Blaine). Suspecting that Scott might not like it, but also from an old desire to succeed on her own, she sent it to Perkins without Scott's knowledge. Perkins had begun reading it, with admiration for its beauty and vitality, when a telegram from Fitzgerald told him not to consider it until he had seen the revised version. By now Fitzgerald had read it and he was furious.

Professionally he conceded the book a certain virtuosity. Its lack of continuity didn't trouble him, for as he wrote the psychiatrist, Zelda wasn't a natural story teller in the sense he was. 'Unless a story comes to her fully developed & crying to be told she's liable to flounder around rather un-successfully among problems of construction. Anyhow the form of so many modern novels is less a procession than a series of impressions, as you know – rather like the slowly-turned pages of an album.'

What Fitzgerald objected to was the poaching on his territory. Zelda had seen the existing 50,000 words of his novel in progress, whose rhythms, materials, even statements and speeches, she had imitated throughout a section of hers. He also considered the book a personal attack on him.

Turning up in a novel signed by my wife [he said] as a some-what anaemic portrait painter with a few ideas lifted from Clive Bell, Leger, etc. puts me in an absurd & Zelda in a ridiculous position. This mixture of fact & fiction is calculated to ruin us both, or what is left of us, and I can't let it stand. Using the name of a character I invented to put intimate facts in the hands of the friends and enemies we have accumulated *en route* – my God, my books made her a legend and her single intention in this somewhat thin portrait is to make me a non-entity.

Heretofore Fitzgerald had encouraged Zelda in her writ-ing, but now he wrote the psychiatrist that Zelda was an amateur trying to cash in on her lust for self-expression by publishing a book about his private life, with a casual survey of the material upon which he was currently engaged. His anger cooled when she cut the most invidious parts, and on his advice she worked up other parts so as to give the whole a certain artistic cohesion. But Fitzgerald asked Perkins to be measured in praise. He said the doctors didn't want Zelda to feel that acceptance of the book meant immediate fame and money. 'I'm afraid,' he wrote,

all our critical tendencies in the last decade got bullish ... & probably created a lot of spoiled geniuses who might have been good workmen. If Zelda was to have a success, she must associate it with work done in a workmanlike manner for its own sake. ... She is not twenty-one and she is not strong, and she must not try to follow the pattern of my trail which is, of course, blazed distinctly on her mind.'

In April, Fitzgerald moved to Baltimore. Zelda was getting along so well at Phipps – especially after Scribners accepted her novel for fall publication – that he decided to live there and let her slip gradually into domestic routine. In May he found a house that suited him on the estate owned by my father, Bayard Turnbull. 'We have a soft shady place here,' Zelda wrote Perkins,

that's like a paintless playhouse abandoned when the family grew up. It's surrounded by apologetic trees and warning meadows and creaking insects and is gutted of its aura by many comfortable bedrooms which do not have to be floated up to on alcoholic inflation past cupolas and cornices as did the ones at 'Ellerslie'.

Settling into the Maryland countryside, Fitzgerald was better armed for accomplishment than he had been for years. The twenties had taught him something of his limitations, and his novel was at last taking shape. *The World's Fair*, the manuscript begun after *Gatsby*, had been conceived as a novel of sensation; vaguely inspired by the Loeb-Leopold case, he had planned to end it in matricide. He had woven in the Murphys and their life on the Riviera, but the story was too brittle for him. Only with Zelda's breakdown and his own decline had he found a theme worthy of his tragic intent.

And so Fitzgerald entered the sphere of my personal knowledge, and I am able to set down how he affected one family at this turning-point in his life – a time of stock-taking and consolidation, when happiness and success hung in the balance, and he seemed almost pedagogical in his urge to communicate the lessons he had learned.

[13]

'VITALITY,' wrote Fitzgerald in his notebook, 'shows in not only the ability to persist but the ability to start over.' When he rented La Paix, he may have felt that the best was behind him, but he still had plenty of fight and hope.

I remember my father causing a stir at the breakfast table when he announced that a novelist had rented the other house on our property. My mother, the reader of the family, had heard the name Fitzgerald but couldn't recall anything he had written, which was not surprising, for the Jazz Age had roared past almost without our knowing it. Our twenty-eight-acre place on the edge of Baltimore was a cultural pocket whose atmosphere had changed very little since my grandfather built the old house there in 1885. Stolidly Victorian, La Paix had lost whatever charm or style it might have once possessed. It was a ramshackle affair of faded reds, browns, and greys, with the gables and heavy trimmings and discordant bulges of the period, and the whole thing girded round by an open porch. A sign over the door said 'Pax Vobiscum'. Peaceful it certainly was – no one would deny that – but it was also dim, cavernous, and from a child's point of view spooky, and I was glad we weren't living there any more. A few years before Fitzgerald came, my father – an architect – had built us a happier house on a rise overlooking the old one, which now lay half hidden from us in its grove of ancestral oaks.

What odd surroundings for Fitzgerald – this barn of a house and these quietly antiquated acres to which he came trailing sparks from another world! To the once famous but temporarily eclipsed author La Paix must have seemed like the end of the line. Not that it lacked a literary tradition. Here my grandfather had edited a magazine called *The New Eclectic*, and my grandmother, under the spell of Mrs

Humphrey Ward, had written historical romances with titles like *Val-Maria* and *The Royal Pawn of Venice*. In those good days life at La Paix had a graciousness Fitzgerald would have known well how to capture with an image. The velvet lawns were embroidered with flower beds of coleus and geraniums (one of them spelled out 'La Paix'), and each arch of the long porch was hung with a basket of begonias. In summer, my grandfather went out every morning before breakfast and cut a dewy rose for my grandmother's place at table, a gesture that to me has always seemer to typify the era. But by the time Fitzgerald arrived, the sound of carriage wheels had long since faded from the gravel drives, and there were no more flowered patterns on the lawns of rougher cut. The old house, with the red-brown paint bleaching on its Victorian gingerbread, had begun to disintegrate; its trembling windows suggested a massive looseness, and squirrels from the surrounding oaks nested unabashed in its downspouts and mossy eaves. Yet this obsolescence did not daunt Fitzgerald. 'I'll take it,' he said after a brief reconnoitre with my father. 'I never was interested in modern plumbing.'

Fitzgerald came to La Paix as Tom Buchanan came East in *The Great Gatsby* – 'in a fashion that rather took your breath away'. All one morning cars and vans swirled down our quiet lane and out of sight around the bend. Scottie arrived with a French governess who was soon superseded when Fitzgerald hired a secretary. The interviewing of the candidates – in a house cluttered with trunks, furniture, and packing cases full of books – occasioned another deluge of cars, for Fitzgerald's requirements were unique. He wanted someone who was not only competent, attractive, and willing to look after Scottie but with whom it could be constitutionally impossible for him to fall in love.

Fitzgerald at the time seemed both old and young for his thirty-six years. There were moments when he looked a trifle worn and seedy, and yet in his saddle shoes, pink shirt, and black Shaker-knit sweater he had the air of a college athlete home for vacation. I remember his courteous informality, the faint smile on his trenchant, mobile face, and his eyes that were neither hard nor green – as has sometimes been remarked – but grey-blue, faraway, and full of the pathos of burned-out desires. His conversation was taut with emotion, and he seemed always to be analysing or appraising as he talked, in a voice that was normally tender but that rose at times to an abrupt, scornful, 'My God!' Physically he was both delicate and compact, with a fine nervous precision about his movements, and something scrappy, self-contained, and even a little belligerent in the swagger of his walk. Under the impact of this charming, unpredictable man with his gift for intimacy, life on our place began to vibrate to a faster, subtler rhythm than we had ever known.

My friendship with him – I was eleven at the time – grew out of football. I too was a student of the game, though my horizons were limited to my Alma Mater, the Gilman Country School. Fitzgerald opened my eyes to Princeton where a great new coach, Fritz Crisler, and a bumper crop of freshman players foreshadowed the Tiger juggernauts of 1933–5. As it happened, Princeton had just received into its arms one of Gilman's immortals, a fullback named Pepper Constable. I remember running up the hill at top speed to get a Gilman yearbook wherein was an Achilles-like picture of Constable surrounded by his teammates. Fitzgerald took a polite interest in *my* interest, but I couldn't seem to persuade him that here was an authentic hero. Gilman sounded provincial to him; it lacked the authority of Exeter, say, or Kiski, or Lawrenceville. With prep school captains two and three deep in every position on this spectacular freshman squad, Fitzgerald held out little hope that Constable would ever be heard from again.

He bought a football which we tossed around the lawn when he was feeling athletic. Because I was small for my age and not a fast runner, he was going to make a passer out of me. (He was determined to make *something* out of me, for his instinct was always to mould, manipulate, cajole the human material around him – to get it to perform in one way or another.) He gave me a book by Barry Wood called *What*

Price Football? and introduced me to the *Football Annual*, a marvellous publication full of swollen rhetoric and grimacing All-Americans.

That fall, when he took me to Princeton to see the Navy game, I was struck by his uncanny familiarity with the Princeton team. He knew so many details about each player that I suspected him of having memorized the programmes of previous contests. His hopes that day were riding on a sophomore with the pungent name of 'Katz' Kadlic – no ordinary quarterback according to Fitzgerald, but 'a great field general', a kind of Stonewall Jackson with cleats on. Though Kadlic happened to be a pretty fair passer into the bargain, it was his tactical genius that concerned my host, who identified himself in some obscure way with the brains that leavened Princeton's brawn. The best Kadlic could manage that afternoon was a scoreless tie, but the following fall Fitzgerald and I saw him – plus the great freshman team, now sophomores and playing on the varsity – overthrow Columbia 20–0 (the same Columbia team that afterwards defeated Stanford in the Rose Bowl). Unaccountably, my old friend Constable turned up at full back, where he played the smashing brand of ball I had been telling Fitzgerald about. It was only the beginning of a splendid career, for Constable went on to captain Princeton's undefeated team of 1935 and to be mentioned for All-American.

By then Fitzgerald had left La Paix, but he wrote me a letter giving his version of how this Gilman peasant had risen to high estate. 'So far as Constable is concerned,' he said,

– I don't want you to run him down. He's all right – not as good as his substitute Rulon-Miller but *all right*. And I'm glad. In fact I got him elected Captain – I came into the room in a black-beard disguise during the conclave and pled with them. 'See here,' I said, 'A good back hasn't come out of Gilman since Slagle, & they're starving for somebody to admire, them kids are. Pretty soon they'll begin to turn to dolls like "Apples" Fitzpatrick & "Mozart" Hepney –' but I stopped myself at this juncture. I enclose Fritz Crisler's answer.

219

The enclosure, a *bona fide* letter from Crisler, contained a humorous postscript in Fitzgerald's handwriting, which said in part, 'I have had Constable elected captain as a favour to your young friend Turnbull.' Fitzgerald had ceded a point in his fashion, and yet I always thought it typical that on this Princeton team of glory he was excited by the peppery little climax runner, Gary LeVan, rather than the rugged work-horse Constable.

Fitzgerald was a promoter. It was he who prevailed on my father to build the grass court – or rather the rough and homemade approximation that never had all the mole-hills rolled out of it or all the bare spots covered with turf. Lobs had a way of vanishing into overhead boughs and dropping down from unexpected angles, but once you got used to the court's eccentricities you could have a lot of fun on it. Fitzgerald, strong on expertise, imported a bronzed if aging tennis pro, who popped balls at Scottie and me by the hour in an effort to build up our groundstrokes. And sometimes Fitzgerald himself would appear, racket in hand, looking for a doubles match.

He played a cocky, aggressive game with rather more form to it than content. Moving with instinctive grace and poise, he managed to look like a tennis player even when the ball categorically refused to do his bidding. His serve was a short snappy twist with lots of wrist in it and a contortion of the mouth that showed concentration and effort. He sliced his forehand unmercifully, and I do not remember that he had any backhand at all. He was happiest at the net where he could hit the ball hardest and it had the shortest distance to go. I can see him now – a little paunchy in his white flannels and with the first suggestions of baldness behind – swaggering up to his alley and crouching professionally to await the return of service. (His walk was a self-important strut with a slight hunch of the shoulders – the stagy, dramatic walk of a man of action come suddenly on the scene to set things straight.) When playing opposite me he'd threaten me with, 'I'll perforate you, Andrew!' – which he never did, for all the ferocity of his tone. His overheads, when they didn't hit the net, were apt to splatter harmlessly out of the court.

A more direct and satisfactory outlet for his belligerent streak was boxing. He fancied himself a fighter, and the urge coming on him in the middle of dinner, he might insist that a bewildered guest go back to his den with him and put on the gloves. Occasionally he sparred with a lean intellectual who came out from Baltimore to discuss Marxism. The two men squared off in front of La Paix where the road circled a plot of grass to form a natural ring. Watching these contests, one couldn't help feeling apprehensive for Fitzgerald. He had an insubstantial quality made all the more apparent by his gameness – as if one good upper cut might be the end of both his boxing and his writing careers. But Fitzgerald surprised you; he was quite capable of taking care of himself for a short, puffy round or two. Crouching behind the gloves, which fortunately were of a large and squashy make, he kept his head up and his eye on the target as he moved forward with foolhardy resolution. He had a philosophy, no doubt gleaned from Hemingway, that small men – this included me – should get inside their opponents' guard and destroy them at close range. And so, though the gallant Marxist did not press his physical advantage, at least he had a busy time defending himself.

Fitzgerald could never understand my preoccupation with wrestling. At Gilman it was a major sport, which the students were encouraged to learn from the time they entered, and I was starting to be successful at it in a small way. This did not impress Fitzgerald, who refused to see that grovelling around on a mat had either glamour or utility. He would have me know that men of honour settled their differences with their fists, and that if I closed in with a half nelson, I would be accused not only of cowardice but of ill-breeding. To stimulate my interest in boxing he arranged a match between me and Sammy Green, a little tough who lived at the top of our lane. Sammy was a red, stocky, scar-faced lad who was about my age but seemed older because he smoked, drank coffee, swore ruggedly, and worked in a grocery store in his off hours. As we had never liked each other, our collision would have elements of a grudge match, but that was all part of Fitzgerald's plan.

Looking back on it, I doubt whether Sammy was any more eager to fight than I was, yet Fitzgerald put it up to us in such a way that there was no honourable escape, and the bout took place on a summer's evening as the first fireflies were rising off the outdoor ring. Fitzgerald was all polished up for the occasion. He had washed and put on clean clothes, and as he laced my gloves with those tremulous hands of his (rather large, capable-looking hands, the long fingers blunt and squarish at the end and stained with nicotine), he exuded the sharp, spiced reek of tobacco mixed with the bay rum he used as an after-shave lotion. His bearing was serious – even official. When he called us to the centre of the ring, his impartial tone gave no hint of the fact that only an hour before he had been telling me precisely what I should do to defeat Sammy. After several rounds Fitzgerald called a halt to our grunting and sweating and flailing of skinny arms, declaring the match a draw so as not to hurt any feelings.

He was careful about such things. I remember, too, his sympathy for the underdog – the outsider. One balmy afternoon three youths from a Baltimore slum wandered out the single-track railroad that bordered our place, and spying our pond they undressed and jumped in for a swim. The pond was barely two feet deep and a paradise for tadpoles and leeches, but the boys splashed vociferously until my mother came out and ordered them to leave. Fitzgerald must have been watching the drama from his shaded porch, for as the boys straggled off in the direction of the railroad tracks, he called them over to La Paix and asked them to stay for dinner. Part of it, no doubt, was his writer's curiosity – he was starved for life in those days – but also in his gesture there was more than a touch of the good Samaritan. Scottie, my sister Eleanor, and I were pressed into service as co-hosts, and the six of us played games organized by Fitzgerald until dinner time, when an elegant roast was served with Fitzgerald presiding at the head of the table. The boys were invited to come back someday, and Fitzgerald was a little nonplussed when they actually came. 'The poor boys called on me again,' he wrote me at camp. 'I tried to discourage them by making them work, but *I think they liked it!*'

In Fitzgerald's study, a back room where we children were seldom allowed to penetrate, there was a fascinating cupboard that housed a rusted helmet and bayonet which he had picked up on a European battlefield. The helmet had a bullet hole through the crown, and I remember speculating as to whether some of the caked rust on the bayonet might be human gore. Fitzgerald did nothing to discourage this theory. His attitude puzzled me. I had been taught that war was an outmoded barbarism, but here was Fitzgerald predicting another holocaust by 1940 and seeming rather cheerful about it! He owned two lavishly and horribly illustrated French tomes on the World War, and as a toughening exercise he would sit me down before a group of faces that belonged to living men though large sections of them had been chewed away by shrapnel. (Scottie wasn't allowed to look at these, since she was a girl and it might shock her sensibilities.)

The next step was to interest me in firearms. When Fitzgerald offered to buy me a .22, my father hesitated to refuse him, though he made the provision that we shouldn't shoot any of the wildlife on the place. For a few days that bright, oily little weapon was the centre of existence. We practised on bull's-eye targets, and when that palled we improvised a shooting gallery with a set of china dolls that belonged to Scottie. At this point the gardener joined the fun, but while he was relaxing between shots, the gun went off and almost shot him through the leg. It turned out that the .22 was a hair trigger and had to be condemned. So ended Fitzgerald's efforts to bring some of the austerities of war to La Paix.

Remarking my interest in words, he used epithets on me that sent me scurrying to the dictionary, and one day Scottie brought me the following note:

Reputed Bantling,

In deponing and predicating incessantly that you were a

'Shakespearean clown' I did not destinate to signify that you were a wise acre, witling, dizzard, chowder head, Tom Nody, nizy, radoteur, zany, oaf, loon, doodle, dunderpate, lunkhead, sawney, gowk, clod-poll, wiseman of Boeotia, jobbernowl or mooncalf but, subdititiously, that you were intrinsicly a long head, luminary, 'barba tenus sapientes', pundit, wrangler, licentiate learned Theban and sage as are so many of the epigrammatist, wit-worms, droles de corp, sparks, merry-andrews, mimes, posturemasters, pucinellas, scaramouches, pantaloons, pickle-herrings and persifluers that were pullulated by the Transcendent Skald.

Unequivocally,
F. Scott Fitzgerald

Two weeks later came an afterthought:

Dear Andronio,

Upon mature consideration I advise you to go no further with your vocabulary. If you have a lot of words they will become like some muscle you have developed that you are compelled to use, and you must use this one in expressing yourself or in criticizing others. It is hard to say who will punish you the most for this, the dumb people who don't know what you are talking about or the learned ones who do. But wallop you they will and you will be forced to confine yourself to pen and paper.

Then you will be a writer and may God have mercy on your soul.

No! A thousand times no! Far, far better confine yourself to a few simple expressions in life, the ones that served billions upon countless billions of our forefathers and still serve admirably all but a tiny handful of those at present clinging to the earth's crust. Here are the only expressions you need:

'*Yeah*'
'*Naw*'
'*Gimme de meat*'

and you need at least one good *bark* (we all need one good bark) such as:

'*I'll knock your back teeth down your throat!*'

So forget all that has hitherto attracted you in our complicated system of grunts and go back to those fundamental ones that have stood the test of time.

With warm regards to you all,

Scott Fitz –

224

Sometimes, usually after a siege of writing, Fitzgerald would emerge in his bathrobe and we would settle ourselves on the porch corner in the crackly wicker chairs that went back to my grandfather's day and thrash out the moral dilemmas. Fitzgerald was an engaging conversationalist because, as in the case of Dick Diver, 'there was never any doubt at whom he was looking or talking – and this is a flattering attention, for who looks at us? – glances fall upon us, curious or disinterested, nothing more'. Fitzgerald focused on you – even riveted on you – and if there was one thing you were sure of, it was that whatever you happened to be talking about was the most important matter in the world. A further seduction was his smile – quick, tight, and very appealing. It was not so much a smile as a flash of confidence in you and your mortal possibilities. Fitzgerald would be sitting there with a cigarette clenched in the fingers of his gesticulating hand, with the deep inhales oozing out of his fine-cut nostrils (he belonged to that class of smoker that seems to eat the cigarette rather than smoke it) and with a faraway nostalgia in his eyes, and suddenly he would start up and swagger towards a table or some other object as if he were going to tear it apart with the energy of his thought. Then he would lapse into a preoccupied silence, staring at the floor. What held your attention in the final analysis was his keen dramatic sense, for the attitudes and postures he struck were often more profound than his words.

I do not remember much of what he said, but at the heart of his doctrine was a kind of Emersonian self-reliance. He had the idea that I was independent and went my own way, and felt that that was good. He put respect above popularity. 'My God, Andrew!' he would say, facing me with that cocky, shoulder-swinging stance of his. 'Popularity isn't worth a damn and respect is worth everything and what do you care about happiness – and who does except the perpetual children of this world?'

My mother's friendship with Fitzgerald – she was nine years older than he – developed just as spontaneously along different lines. Knowing nothing of his life before she met him may have made it easier for her to come to grips with the quicksilver man behind the garish legend. The first day, when Fitzgerald had drawn up in a taxi like a general in advance of his troops, my mother had been working at La Paix on the heels of the cleaning women and was hastening down the high front steps with a last batch of obsolete china, a basin, and a slop jar. Fitzgerald laughed when he saw her burden. They both laughed, and my mother felt his easiness, his animated interest, and guessed we would see more of him than we usually did of our tenants.

On the fourth of July he invited us to dinner *en famille*. As Father, Mother, my two sisters and I came in sight around a pine tree, Fitzgerald started up the lane to meet us, and my mother called out, 'I've never felt so apologetic for the size of my family before,' to which he replied, 'It's a little late – isn't it? – to do anything about it.' There was still a touch of formality in our relations, but during dinner Fitzgerald grew heated on the subject of Thomas Wolfe and left the table to get his copy of *Look Homeward, Angel*, which he insisted my mother take with her and read at once. For him, all the pride and torment of youth was in that novel, and as he described it, there was no nuance of the small town Southern atmosphere which he did not feel and make my mother feel. Out of such threads their friendship was woven. Each time they met there was a carry-over from the previous meeting – something to discuss that seemed of vital importance.

My mother found Fitzgerald that rare complement to a good talker – a good listener – wonderfully attentive to the other person's point of view, though he could be ruthless in his opposition to it. He had the knack of breaking down your defence, of making you feel there was nothing you couldn't say to him, just as he was quick to open up his own life to you. From the start he wanted to tell my mother about Zelda: her beauty, her brilliance, her daring, her appeal to men – all that he had had and lost, but hadn't given up hope of regaining. He spoke philosophically about his drinking to which he had become reconciled as an exigency of the creative life – the classic vice of authors – though he admitted it was a sign of defeat. Knowing the dryness of our Victorian household, the few times he came to dinner he made mysterious trips to the downstairs lavatory where he had parked a bottle of gin. On shorter visits he would slip into our dining-room and help himself to the homemade currant wine, having discovered the location of the decanter in the sideboard.

Sometimes my mother alluded to her Presbyterian upbringing – she was a minister's daughter – and while Fitzgerald found religion a less congenial topic than some, he approached it with the frontal honesty he reserved for all serious themes. As a writer he was sensitive to the beauty of the Bible, and he could grow eloquent over the majesty of Ecclesiastes or the narrative swiftness of St Mark, but as an intellectual he believed the test of human values should be, as he wrote my mother, 'a conformity to the strictest and most unflinching rationality'. He considered religion primarily the woman's sphere, because women were intellectually less rigorous than men, though he respected, and perhaps envied, all honest believers. His admiration for our gardener – a weather-burned, earth-smelling Irishman, stooped with years of bending over flowerbeds – had, I think, something to do with the man's true Catholic zeal. When the gardener's wife was dying of cancer, Fitzgerald asked after her often, and when she was finally laid out in the neat little 'best parlour' of their cottage, he went to pay his respects. Unshaven, with only a topcoat concealing his habitual pyjamas, he knelt in prayer beside the coffin – not as a Catholic, but out of the kindness of his heart, hoping that it might mean something to the family.

He was constantly lending my mother books: Proust, D. H. Lawrence, Hemingway, Rilke, the diary of Otto Braun (a promising German youth killed in the First World War). Sometimes he would read a passage aloud, and he was a marvellous reader. In his excitement over a page of good prose he seemed almost to caress the words, and his eyes filled easily. Once, seated on the stone coping of our porch, he read my mother his obituary essay on Ring Lardner, which he was about to send off to *The New Republic*. Through the intensity of his feeling he communicated the tragedy of his gifted, lovable friend who, like himself, had lived none too wisely. Fitzgerald had an unfailing eye and heart for the *little* things that make up our existence, the little things that are really of such vast importance – the whole story for most of us.

Aside from books and ideas the chief link between my mother and Fitzgerald was we children. He liked to consider us in terms of our possibilities, and one day he came up to our house to tell her how he had passed Scottie perched high in a tree, with me seated beneath her, my back against the trunk, both of us reading, completely lost, completely at peace. He said it was one of the most beautiful sights he had ever seen. Then he went on to contrast this oblivious child's contentment with the struggle and bitterness that might one day come between us as man and woman. Another time he sent my mother a scrap of paper with 'Frances looks like a trinket' scrawled across it in large letters. Underneath he wrote that he thought it a nice, simple description of my older sister's 'gold quality', and that he would undoubtedly use it in one of his stories. But my younger sister, Eleanor, in whom he saw the makings of an actress, was his pet. He called her Eleanor Duse, and once he and she did the mad scene in *Hamlet*, using as props a couple of faded daffodils and a rusty wastebasket. The image of Ophelia had haunted Fitzgerald since Zelda's collapse.

During the Christmas holidays he spent hours each evening rehearsing a play that he had written for Eleanor with Scottie in the supporting role, a considerable investment of time when one considers the audience: Father, Mother, Frances, and me. He had undertaken, now that I think of it, a systematic campaign to fortify Eleanor's ego. For example, he had brought back from Europe an elaborate collection of lead soldiers and figures and scenery – knights, grenadiers, peasants, farm animals, even Gallic slaves with their hands

228

chained behind their backs, even miniature oases – and one day, having spread these treasures on the dining-room table, he assigned Scottie, Eleanor and me different locales to reconstruct. When we were finished, he strode into the room with that Napoleonic decisiveness of his and pondered the results with folded arms. After a moment he named Eleanor the winner, partly because her subject – a farmyard in Brittany – was the easiest and afforded the least chance for making mistakes, but also, I am sure, because he wanted to impart confidence to the youngest and most fearful contestant. It was the same impulse which, when he thought I was teasing Eleanor too much, made him threaten to terminate his lease if I persevered.

For Eleanor and me (though perhaps not for Scottie, who was too close to him) there was always something of the magician in Fitzgerald. He was the inventor, the creator, the tireless impresario who brightened our days and made other adult company seem dull and profitless. It wasn't so much any particular skill of his as a quality of caring, of believing, of pouring his whole soul and imagination into whatever he did with us. His card tricks were elementary, but he executed them with a special deck – white markings on a black background – and with such an air of mystery that he soon had us thinking the deck was bewitched. He applied the same conviction to helping us build an igloo once when a blizzard was followed by a heavy freeze. Joining us in his hat and galoshes with his overcoat collar turned up, he showed us how to cut the blocks of crusted snow and fit them together. When the structure was completed we could all get inside. Fitzgerald couldn't make it last forever – he wasn't quite enough of a magician for that – but I do recall that when the thaw set in, the igloo was the last patch of snow to disappear from the lawn.

Let me add that about Scottie, Fitzgerald was objective and becomingly modest, though one could see he adored her and was proud of her. She was part of his sense of obligation towards life, and her importance grew as Zelda waned and

229

became a child. Over the years some of his best stories had grown from his paternal affection: 'Babylon Revisited', 'The Baby Party', the slight but charming 'Outside the Cabinet-Maker's', and, most recently, 'Family in the Wind', where the alcoholic doctor's love for the little girl is the spar that keeps him afloat.

Scottie had put up with a great deal during her itinerant girlhood. On the Rivera a wit had remarked that she wasn't a child at all but a little widow of forty, though in the background there had always been a nurse who threw an island of order around her, and since Zelda's breakdown Scott had tried to be a mother and a father as well. It was he who planned the games at Scottie's parties, who worried about her clothes and saw to it that she had the right kind of ballet slippers. He gave her a lot of himself and expected a lot in return. Scottie was under constant pressure to excel – in everything from French to high-diving, from tennis to politeness. Fitzgerald wanted her to be both hard and soft, to be able to make her own way, and yet to appreciate the amenities of those who hadn't had to. His idea of hardness did not include dissipation, and his anxiety about moral questions went to ludicrous extremes.

For example, halfway between our house and La Paix was a forsythia bush where Scottie and Eleanor cached notes to each other, describing the little they knew about sex. (Eleanor claims that on this subject she was the better documented of the two.) The notes were deposited in a soggy shoebox, and one day the box was gone. When Eleanor went to Scottie for an explanation, she was met by Fitzgerald who said he had found the box and that as a punishment Scottie would not be allowed to see Eleanor for a week. He spoke of his terrible disappointment in them both, though he put most of the blame on Scottie, she being the older.

Scottie's natural buoyancy rose above such crises. A round-faced, delicate-featured, golden little girl, she had a gay airiness about her that seemed untouched by family tragedy. She was bright and precocious; when taken to the chambers of the Supreme Court in Washington, she had asked the person she was with, 'Where is the accused?' Every other word was 'Daddy' or 'Daddy says', despite his so-called 'character building', which consisted of promising her things and not coming through with them. They were a winsome duo, this father and daughter, and after an evening at La Paix I can remember the feeling of solidarity they imparted as they waved good-bye from the lighted porch, Fitzgerald singing 'Goodnight, Sweetheart' in a weak, rather tuneless voice, and suddenly breaking into a little foxtrot shuffle.[38]

Fitzgerald's isolation during the La Paix period was spiritual as well as physical. He was learning the sense of Oscar Wilde's epigram that nothing is so dangerous as being too modern, for one is apt to grow old-fashioned quite suddenly. Since 1926, when he published his last book of stories, the whole climate – the air he breathed and condensed into fiction – had changed. The fashionable Byronic despair of the twenties, really an inverted optimism, had given way to the more tangible despair of the worst depression in history.

While recognizing the end of an era, Fitzgerald retained a proprietary affection for 'the Jazz Age' (even the coinage was his). It had '[borne] him up, battered him, and [given] him more money than he had dreamed of, simply for telling people he felt as they did'. 'It is the custom now,' he would write later on in the thirties, 'to look back on the boom days with a disapproval that approaches horror. But it had its virtues, that old boom: Life was a great deal larger and gayer for most people and the stampede to the Spartan virtues in time of war and famine should not make us too dizzy to remember its hilarious glory.' No one had written more gorgeously than he of America's last fling at adolescence. The gay chic of his style, with the wit and tenderness constantly breaking through, had suited a time whose very tawdriness, in a work like Gatsby, he had transformed into lasting beauty.

And yet, even after Gatsby, there lingered doubts as to his ultimate worth. Some thought him slick and superficial, like a many-faceted glass ball revolving in the light which every now and then refracted something quite wonderful. His emphasis on money and success seemed all wrong for a serious artist; it smacked of Booth Tarkington and Robert W. Chambers. And wasn't his great charm, after all, an ephemeral, collegiate thing – an ability to describe girls as flowers, and keep on doing it at an age when most writers had lost the touch if they ever possessed it? The new decade would find him short on ideas – real substance – and taking stock of himself in 1936, Fitzgerald had to admit that he had done very little thinking save within the problems of his craft. For twenty years, he said, Edmund Wilson had been his 'intellectual conscience'.

Between Wilson and Fitzgerald there had occurred not so much a rift as a drift. During the early twenties Wilson had been amused and refreshed by Scott and Zelda and even a little proprietary about them. Thus when he heard of her breakdown in 1930, he wrote Perkins for details – adding that he wished something could be done about the Fitzgeralds, who never saw anyone with any sense. (Wilson had recently had a breakdown himself, which made him conversant with such matters.) In a letter of sympathy to Scott, he said how much he had missed the Fitzgeralds in recent years. He wished they didn't insist on living abroad which he thought unwise for American writers, bad as America could be to live in. The Fitzgeralds' values had always seemed false and childish to Wilson – the more so now that he was going over to Marxism. His new book of reportage on the national crisis ended with a credo. Prosperity, he said, had fooled everyone. 'Our political and economic thinking, like our literature and art, has been mostly mediocre as our world has been mostly middle-class.' The Puritan in Wilson was reacting against the materialistic glut of the twenties. As John Peale Bishop put it, the ghost of Cotton Mather (one of Wilson's ancestors) was burrowing under his conscience like a mole. Wilson's tradition was that of the learned professions. From his forebears – chiefly ministers, doctors, lawyers, and professors – he had inherited a dislike and distrust of American business. It seemed to him that the well-to-do bankers, brokers, bond salesmen, and stockholders, led fatuous lives, and he admitted he wasn't sorry 'to see it all go glimmering'. He now believed that art and science, morals and manners, could only be perfected in a rational (i.e., communist) society, run for the common good.

Fitzgerald was confused by Wilson's new tack. Apropos of it, he wrote Perkins that 'a decision to adopt Communism definitely, no matter how good for the soul, must of necessity be a saddening process for any one who has ever tasted the intellectual pleasures of the world we live in'. Fitzgerald's politics – he seldom read a paper – had remained pretty much the nihilism, cynicism, and indifference of the intelligentsia under Harding. But now it seemed that Marxism might be the wave of the future, and Fitzgerald was eager to move with the times. He read *Das Kapital*, or at least read at it, and discussed it with his Marxist sparring partner. 'The logic of history won't permit us to go backward,' he wrote my mother after one of their talks, and again, 'When a United States Senator *after his election* has to look up the principles of Marxism by which one-sixth of the world is governed, it shows he's a pretty inadequate defender of his own system.' In his Ledger for 1932 he spoke of 'political worries that were almost neurosis'. When a friend took him to call on Maurice Hindus, the well-known writer on Soviet affairs, Hindus had a hard time convincing Fitzgerald of the impossibility of a Communist revolution in America, the richest country in the world.

Marxism, of course, was fundamentally alien to Fitzgerald. Spengler's idealism had come to him more naturally than Marx's materialism, just as Spengler's class society appealed to him more than Marx's classless one. Fitzgerald knew nothing of the poverty out of which Marxism had grown, nor had he studied history in terms of social classes and movements – though occasionally he would show an intuitive grasp of these things, as in Dick Diver's musings on the grown-over battlefield in *Tender Is the Night*. But history for him was chiefly colour, personalities, and romance.

233

It was Jackson's Valley Campaign; it was the Gallant Pelham rapid-firing – one cannon against sixteen – at Fredericksburg. The individual meant everything to Fitzgerald. And so he expounded Marxism to my parents as one seeking to *épater le bourgeois*, the self-made man in him being mildly contemptuous of us as privileged, protected folk who did not know what the real rough-and-tumble was all about.

Despite his claims to 'unflinching rationality', Fitzgerald's political thought, like all his thought, was emotional and impulsive, general ideas being for him little more than a backdrop to his fiction. There might be some facet of Marx and Spengler which he grasped better than anyone else, but he wouldn't see the broad picture. His culture was also deficient in art and classical music – rather surprising when one considers the musical and pictorial qualities of his prose. Nor was he a student of nature. He once told my mother that reading Thoreau made him realize how much he had missed in this respect and yet, rambling on in his nostalgic cadences, he could epitomize in a casual phrase the beauty of our acres – the dark shadows of the pines athwart the moonlit lawns, the scent of honeysuckle and the thorny lemon tree, the winking fireflies, the mist rising from the pond whence came the guttural diatribe of the bull-frogs.

Fitzgerald's gift was narrowly, concentratedly verbal. He performed some alchemy with words that brought out their overtones, 'their most utter value', as he once put it, 'for evocation, persuasion, or charm'. And if his thinking had been restricted to the problems of his craft, that thinking had been authoritative; writers as different from him as Dos Passos and MacLeish have testified to his literary acuity, to the way one always listened to him on technical matters even when he was discussing trifles. He was familiar, too, with the tradition he was working in and what remained to be done. In the field of fiction he had read widely and passionately, and Max Beerbohm's remarks about another Irish writer, George Moore, make one think of Fitzgerald.

'Of learning,' wrote Beerbohm,

[Moore] had no equipment at all; for him everything was discovery; and it was natural that Oscar Wilde should complain as he did once complain to me, 'George Moore is always conducting his education in public.' Also, he had no sense of proportion. But this defect was, in truth, a quality. Whenever he discovered some new old master, that master seemed to him greater than any other: he would hear of no other. And it was just this frantic exclusiveness that made his adorations so fruitful: it was by the completeness of his surrender to one thing at a time that he possessed himself of that thing's very essence. The finest criticism is always passive, not active. Mastery comes only by self-surrender. The critic who justly admires all kinds of things simultaneously cannot love any one of them, any more than a lady can be simultaneously in love with more than one gentleman. That kind of critic is often (if I, who am that kind of critic, may be allowed to say so) very admirable. But it is the Moores who matter.

Among Fitzgerald's contemporaries Hemingway still excited him the most. Without belittling his own talent, Fitzgerald gave the impresion that he thought Hemingway's a talent of a higher order. He was proud of their friendship, too, and once he showed my mother a letter which delighted him because underneath the signature 'Ernest', Hemingway had written in brackets 'Christ, what a name.' Fitzgerald was obsessed by this man of action and prowess, who yet embodied the self-contradictions of the artist. Hemingway was double-edged: on the one hand, warm, gentle, generous, humble, and kind; on the other, arrogant, cruel, rusé. While favouring the underdog, he felt that too much sympathy was soft and weak, and like anyone who lives in his passions he could turn on you brutally, though he might regret it afterwards. He was quite capable of literary vendettas and had a record of quarrelling with writers who had helped him in his ascent. His emotions were of a piece. When he felt something, he was all that way – all-friendly or all-hating – which is perhaps one reason he wrote so intensely well.

By now Fitzgerald realized that the balance of power had shifted. Hemingway's output had been regular and impressive, while rumours continued to spread of Fitzgerald's drinking and domestic chaos. The first time Fitzgerald and Hemingway spent an evening together back in 1925, Fitzgerald had passed out, and this image was firmly rooted in Hemingway's mind. When Fitzgerald went on the wagon in Janury 1933, he wrote Perkins, ' ... but don't tell Ernest because he has long convinced himself that I am an incurable alcoholic, due to the fact that we almost always meet on parties. I am *his* alcoholic just like Ring is mine and do not want to disillusion him, tho even Post stories must be done in a state of sobriety.'

Fitzgerald's impulse to reform had followed a disastrous meeting with Hemingway and Wilson in New York; Fitzgerald, who had been on a bat for several days, afterwards wrote Wilson that he shouldn't have looked up the other two in his mood of impotent desperation. 'I assume full responsibility for all the unpleasantness – with Ernest I seem to have reached a state where when we drink together I half bait, half truckle to him.' 'Ernest – until we began trying to walk over each other with cleats,' he wrote elsewhere.

The result of it all was that Fitzgerald felt very much out of things, and when my mother told him that T. S. Eliot would be staying with us while giving a lecture series at Johns Hopkins, Fitzgerald pricked up his ears. He said Eliot's letter about Gatsby had given him more pleasure than any he had received. Fitzgerald came to a small dinner for Eliot, and my mother remembered the distinction – in appearance and personality – of the poet who was also a philosopher and the novelist who was also a poet. In the intimacy of a fire-lit room Fitzgerald was asked to read some of Eliot's verse, which he did without hesitation in that moving voice that could bring out all the beauty and hint at all the mystery of words.

Afterwards he wrote Wilson of spending an afternoon and evening with Eliot. 'I read him some of his poems and he seemed to think they were pretty good. I liked him fine.'

Zelda all this time had been living at La Paix, with brief

returns to Phipps when she seemed in danger of a relapse. I remember Zelda as a boyish wraith of a woman in sleeveless summer dresses and ballet slippers, with not much expression on her hawk-like face and not very much to say. She is linked in my mind with 'Valencia', a popular song of the twenties which she continually played on a small, wind-up Victrola, increasing her inexplicable air of something lost and left behind. From the tight-wound gramophone would come a high-pitched accelerated man's voice . . .

'Valencia! In my dreams it always seems I hear you softly call to me . . .'

And the answering chorus – 'In all of my *dreams* it *seems* I *hear* your voice when it *calls* to me . . .'

'Valencia!' – the man's voice again – 'Where the orange trees forever scent the breeze beside the sea . . .'

'Forever the *orange trees* the *breeze* is scenting beside the sea . . .'

And sometimes Zelda would dance to this.

I also remember her at the deep, cool quarry in the country where we used to swim. She wore a two-piece maroon bathing suit and her short, tawny hair would be water-slicked and her skin very brown, as she sat on the raft smoking, and glorying in the sun.

During the first months at La Paix she seemed to be improving. She was writing a play and had taken up horseback riding 'as non-committally as possible so as not to annoy the horse. Also very apologetically since we've had so much of communism lately that I'm not sure it isn't the horse who should be riding me.' She wrote John Peale Bishop that Scott was reading Marx while she read the cosmological philosophers, and the brightest moments of their day were when they got the two mixed up. Fitzgerald called their united front 'less a romance than a categorical imperative', but no one who saw them together could doubt that there was real love between them. Fitzgerald lived the phases of Zelda's illness, its ups and downs, the interviews with doctors. My mother thought he would have been more to blame if he had grown a little bored by, or indifferent to, Zelda's tragedy instead of grappling with it daily as he did. His intense concern and fundamental loyalty never wavered, and he probably felt that her condition absolved him from being faithful to her. There were also grievances that had never been forgotten – Zelda's affair with Josanne in 1924 and Scott's to some extent retaliatory interest in Lois Moran in 1927, the terrible resentment which Scott had sensed back of the original version of *Save Me the Waltz* – such wounds as these help to explain why Scott, despite his affection for Zelda and his eagerness to help her, could be cruel to her at times.

There is no other word for his behaviour during a luncheon Zelda gave at La Paix. She had invited my mother, another Baltimore matron who was an old friend from Montgomery, and a relative Scott did not like; he had painted an acid portrait of the latter as Marion in 'Babylon Revisited'. The occasion began auspiciously enough, with gay conversation in the living-room, but soon there intruded sepulchral growls and ejaculations, complete with rattling of chains, from the floor above. Suspecting the origin of these noises, no one paid any attention, and presently the four ladies sat down to lunch. They had begun to eat when they noticed a figure parading back and forth along the porch, which connected with the dining-room through french windows – open wide, for the day was hot. The figure, robed in a trailing sheet with a bath towel around its head and a gold fillet around the towel, was reciting some of the more portentous passages from *Julius Caesar*.

At this moment a new character entered the drama, a *deus ex machina* in the form of a Negro clergyman who visited our place once a year to solicit funds for an orphanage. When he appeared at the front door, Fitzgerald sensed his opportunity and seized it with the audacity of Caesar himself. In a flash, he had ushered the elderly Negro into the dining-room, introducing him as a distinguished visitor from Equatorial Africa, and requesting that he be invited to join the meal. The unbidden guest was polite but terror-stricken and took the first opportunity to escape. Fitzgerald then resumed his solemn march along the porch, this time including the dining-room in his tour, where he circled the table – even pausing to pass a plate of biscuits – until finally he grew tired of his prank and went away. Zelda kept her dignity throughout the performance, pretending to ignore it and making no reference to it afterwards.

She had had other disappointments, such as the reception of her novel. Because it had sold a mere 1,400 copies, she had shifted her hopes to her play, *Scandalabra*, which the Vagabond Players put on the spring of 1933. The opening performance, though fairly well attended, was an embarrassing failure. Afterwards Fitzgerald gathered the cast in the Green Room of the Hotel Belvedere, and sitting in a throne-like chair with a case of beer at his feet – he was 'on beer' at the time – he read the script aloud. Each line had to be justified in relation to the plot or out it came, but after radical surgery, the script was abandoned.

Scott had been trying to assist with Zelda's treatment despite his antipathy for Dr Adolf Meyer, the Phipps' eminent authority on schizophrenia. Meyer considered it a dual case. He wanted Fitzgerald to face his drinking, to be treated for it if necessary, but Fitzgerald balked at psychotherapy – partly from pride (he didn't want to give Zelda's family the satisfaction of being able to say 'You see, it was Scott's fault all these years'), and partly from the artist's instinctive distrust of having his inner workings tampered with. He was afraid that psychiatric treatment might make him a reasoning, analytic person instead of a feeling one, and he instanced several novelists who had been psychoanalysed and had written nothing but trash ever since. He considered alcohol part of his working equipment. 'During the last six days,' he wrote Meyer the spring of 1933, 'I have drunk *altogether* slightly less than a quart and a half of weak gin, at wide intervals. But if there is no essential difference between an over-extended, imaginative, functioning man using alcohol as a stimulus or a temporary *aisment* and a schizophrene, I am naturally alarmed about my ability to collaborate in this cure at all.' He went on to say that if Meyer could interview a series of qualified observers, there would be less doubt in his mind 'as to whence this family derives what mental and moral stamina it possesses. There would be a good percentage who liked Zelda better than me and probably a majority who found her more attractive (as it should be); but on the question of integrity, responsibility, conscience, sense of duty, judgement, will-power, whatever you want to call it' – ninety-five per cent, he said, would pronounce in his favour. Zelda still cherished the illusion that success in her writing would give her some sort of divine irresponsibilty backed by unlimited gold. She was working

under a greenhouse which is my money and my name and my love. ... She is willing to use the greenhouse to protect her in every way, to nourish every sprout of talent and to exhibit it – and at the same time she feels no responsibility about the greenhouse and feels that she can reach up and knock a piece a glass out of the roof any moment, yet she is shrewd to cringe when I open the door of the greenhouse and tell her to behave or go.[39]

Fitzgerald wanted more authority to discipline her. He clung to the notion that part of her trouble was pure selfishness. He wondered if it might not be wise, temporarily, to give her the feeling of being alone, of having exhausted everyone's patience. He was also aware of the history of mental illness on both sides of her family, and when her brother committed suicide in 1933, Fitzgerald came up to our house to tell my mother, 'You see, it's not my fault – it's inherited.' He had taken comfort from the words of the great psychiatrist Bleuler, who had been called in for consultation while Zelda was at Prangins. 'Stop blaming yourself,' Bleuler had said. 'You might have retarded your wife's illness, but you couldn't have prevented it.'

Always complicating and aggravating Zelda's condition was the clash of two artistic personalities, the theme which kept recurring during a transcribed interview between Scott, Zelda, and her psychiatrist, Dr Thomas Rennie, in May 1933. In this interview, a key document, Scott spoke of his battle to become a top-flight professional. He said the difference between a professional and an amateur was hard to define – 'It just simply means the keen equipment; it means a scent, a smell of the future in one line.' Assuming there were ten or twelve first-rate writers in America, he estimated that the chances had been ten million to one against him. He spoke of the integrity that makes one writer better than another.

To have something to say is a question of sleepless nights and worry and endless ratiocination of a subject – of endless trying to dig out the essential truth, the essential justice. As a first premise you have to develop a conscience and if on top of that you have talent so much the better. But if you have the talent without the conscience, you are just one of many thousand journalists.

Fitzgerald spoke of the manuscripts sent him by friends and of his telling them, as politely as possible, 'You can't write, you haven't got a chance – all that has been said and done before.' Then Zelda had come along believing anything was possible. She had written some talented sketches, but she wanted to be a novelist at Scott's expense, for she was using his material. It was as if a good artist came into the room and found something drawn on his canvas by a mischievous little boy. Zelda had no conception of what Fitzgerald had sacrificed to be where he was – of his long, lonely struggle against other finely-gifted authors. A novelist, said Fitzgerald, must reflect the exact shade of opinion of his day, but he must also interpret it, and Zelda could not interpret. If she heard Fitzgerald say something perceptive, she would put it into her writing, unaware of 'the terrible amount of cerebral stuff that comes in – does this relate to human justice? – the enormous moral business that goes on in the mind of anyone who writes anything worth writing.'
Zelda took the position that because of Scott's drinking she needed something to fill her life. She was determined to go on writing, it was part of her make-up, though she agreed to stop work on the new novel she had begun until his was published. Beyond that she made no guarantees. The impasse was so serious that Scott looked into the statutes governing divorce on grounds of insanity. He probably came

nearer the step now than at any other time, for after Zelda's third breakdown his gallantry refused to contemplate it.

The losing battle with Zelda's condition must have had something to do with the change we felt in Fitzgerald his second year at La Paix. We were still friends, of course – we were always that – and our appreciation of him kept growing, but the first year's light-heartedness declined, to be replaced by a haunted sense of hope lost and time run out. Our families alternated driving the children to school, and when it was our week to take Scottie, Fitzgerald didn't appear on the porch so often to stand for a moment in the sunshine and toss some bantering remark across the railing. More and more he withdrew into his study where his light blazed on into the small hours, a point of desperate and mysterious energy in the surrounding dark.

'Drinking increased – things go not so well,' he wrote in his Ledger. In addition to his professional worries he was perplexed by Zelda's attempts at housekeeping. Once Fitzgerald told my mother that there was nothing to eat in the house except five hams. Aquilla, the coloured chauffeur who drove the old blue Stutz, was another responsibility. The orders that one gave him had a way of miscarrying, yet Fitzgerald took a kindly interest in his lackey. Aquilla's nose was so flat that the tip of it almost joined his upper lip, his short stocky frame was packed into purple pin-stripe suits, and his passion for root beer was evidenced by the empty bottles that littered the grass around La Paix. He had a speech defect that made him substitute 's' for 'th' – a challenge to Fitzgerald, who devised a sentence full of 'th's' which he made Aquilla practise over and over.

Money was now such a serious problem that for the first time Fitzgerald complained to Zelda about the expense of her illness. The *Post* was paying him five hundred, a thousand, in some cases fifteen hundred dollars less per story than they had two years before. He had suffered a mild recurrence of the tuberculosis which had first been suspected in his college days, and insomnia was a scourge as it often is with alcoholics. There were nights when he couldn't write and he couldn't sleep either, and he would reach out desperately for human contact.

On such a night Asa Bushnell, Princeton's graduate manager of athletics and a clubmate of Fitzgerald's, was wrenched awake by a phone call at 3 a.m.

'Get a pencil and paper,' said Fitzgerald. 'I have some suggestions for Fritz Crisler.'

Bushnell did not stir but let an appropriate time elapse before telling Fitzgerald to proceed.

'Yale will be laying for us,' Fitzgerald went on. 'They've had a good chance to scout Crisler's system and he's got to cross them up. Here's how he does it. Princeton must have two teams. One will be big – all men over two hundred. This team will be used to batter them down and wear them out. Then the little team, the pony team, will go in and make the touchdowns.'

Before Bushnell had a chance to reply, Fitzgerald had hung up, but half an hour later the phone rang again.

'I forgot to mention,' said Fitzgerald, 'that the big team will be coached on defence and be given only a few power plays. Little team will be coached on offence, great variety of plays. Substitutions to be made as a unit.'

Towards dawn came a final call wrapping it up.

'Incidentally, my system will do away with all the parental and alumni criticism about playing the wrong men in the games because under this system everyone will play.'

Informed of Fitzgerald's brainstorm, Crisler wrote him that the plan had many virtues and would be adopted on one condition – that it be called 'the Fitzgerald system' and that he take full responsibility for its success or failure. Fitzgerald wrote back that he guessed they'd better keep the Fitzgerald system 'in reserve'. The idea, however, was less fantastic than it seemed, and when two-platoon football became universal in the forties, Crisler, as chairman of the NCAA Football Rules Committee, played an important role in its development.

The turning point o fFitzgerald's eighteen months at La Paix was the fire that broke out in June 1933, when Zelda tried to burn something in a long-disused upstairs fireplace. The first we knew of it scarlet engines were hurtling down our lane and smoke was pouring from the second-storey windows. Soon Fitzgerald was seen mixing among the firemen, for he loved to take command of situations. When the flames were finally overcome – the damage had been pretty much confined to the second floor – he passed out drinks to all hands. On the spur of the moment we invited the Fitzgeralds for dinner that evening, and Zelda appeared first, staying only a few minutes. Somewhat later Scott dropped in – his eyes bleary, his lips white and compressed. It was our custom to sing a hymn after dinner, and as he joined us around the piano (we all felt a bit shaky and unreal after the day's excitement), my mother asked for 'Dear Lord and Father of Mankind', an inspired choice in view of its closing lines,

> Speak through the earthquake, wind, and fire,
> O still, small voice of calm.

Next day, Fitzgerald came up to make his formal apologies and to request that repairs on the house be postponed. With his novel nearly finished, he did not want to be disturbed by the din of workmen. And so he laboured on amid the water-stained walls and woodwork in that hulk of a house, whose bleakness matched the colour of his soul.

Though he was reticent about his novel, my mother could see he was excited by it and thought it might be the best thing he had done so far. At the back of his mind, however, lurked an awareness that his star was falling, that the public had ceased to be concerned with the fast, moneyed society which was his material, that interest was shifting to a more grass roots kind of literature – to the works of Farrell, Caldwell, and Dos Passos. It worried him, too, that he had taken so long on the job. 'After all, Max,' he wrote Perkins,

I am a plodder. One time I had a talk with Ernest Hemingway, and I told him, against all the logic that was then current, that I was the tortoise and he was the hare, and that's the truth of the matter, that everything that I have ever attained has been through long and persistent struggle while it is Ernest who has a touch of genius which enables him to bring off extraordinary things with facility. I have no facility. I have a facility for being cheap, if I wanted to indulge that. I can do cheap things. I changed Clark Gable's act at the moving picture theatre [stage show] here the other day. I can do that kind of thing as quickly as anybody but when I decided to be a serious man I tried to struggle over every point until I have made myself into a slow moving Behemoth.

Back of La Paix was a stretch of road where Fitzgerald used to pace hour by hour, refining the last draft of *Tender Is the Night*. There he meditated on the Murphys – their organized sensuousness, their fine gradations of charm – and there he dreamed of the Iles de Lérins, those blessed isles off Antibes where you went in the excursion boats. Returning to his study, he pencilled it all down in his rounded, decorous hand on yellow legal-sized paper. Interrupting him at work, I remember the illumination of his eye, the sensitive pull around the mouth, the wistful liquor-ridden thing about him, the haunting grace of motion and gesture, the looking at you, through you and beyond you – understandingly sweet – with smoke exhaling.

Once the decks had been cleared and he knew where he was going, the book had progressed rapidly, despite his having to turn out *Post* stories to pay the bills. In his Ledger for August, 1932 there is an entry, 'The Novel now plotted & planned, never more to be permanently interrupted.' By late October 1933 he had a complete draft. 'I will appear in person carrying the manuscript and wearing a spiked helmet,' he wrote Perkins. '. . . *Please do not have a band as I do not care for music.*'

When Fitzgerald came to La Paix his period of greatest acclaim was over. He hoped he might regain the lost ground, as he hoped that he might regain Zelda, but he was by no means sure. Two years later, with the mood of 'The Crack-Up' tightening its hold upon him, the hope was dead.

He had come to feel that his mine was exhausted, that other veins were being worked by other writers to whom the public would turn more and more. My mother was grateful she knew Fitzgerald when she did, for he must have been more impressive then than at almost any other time – because more tragic, and therefore more profound. He said to her once with a wry sort of pride, 'It is from the failures of life, and now its successes, that we learn most,' and he was counting himself among the failures. *He* was Dick Diver. My mother became for a brief season a listener to and therefore a sharer of his thoughts, and they blotted out the surface lights and carried her, as the poetry of his books had carried others, down into the depths. And not the depths of weakness and illness alone. They were there, but also the angels.

Tender Is the Night. For the title of his favourite among his books, the one he had wrought most painfully and carefully from his most costly experience, Fitzgerald hit on a phrase from the 'Ode to a Nightingale', evoking that poem's time-less images of flight, dissolution, and the sweetness of death. It was doubly appropriate in that Keats had always been a touchstone of the verbal magic to which Fitzgerald as-pired.

'If you like *The Great Gatsby*,' he inscribed the book for a friend, 'for God's sake read this. Gatsby was a tour de force but this is a confession of faith.' Into *Tender Is the Night* he put his hard-earned beliefs: that work was the only dignity; that it didn't help a serious man to be too much flattered and loved; that money and beauty were treacherous aides; that honour, courtesy, courage – the old-fashioned virtues – were the best guides after all. Beneath the Murphys' façade (for the Divers' way of life, their *style* was that of the Murphys) Fitzgerald had explored his relations with Zelda. He felt she had swallowed him up, or more precisely, that he had al-lowed himself to be swallowed. Zelda, like Nicole, was ill-fated when he met her, but Diver-Fitzgerald had 'chosen Ophelia, chosen the sweet poison and drunk it'. Diver was a clergyman's son – a 'spoiled priest' – and if the worldly side of him was drawn to wealth, his chaste, priestly side mistrusted it and suffered in its toils.

Tender Is the Night was also a confession of faith in the artistic sense; it was Fitzgerald's most ambitious work, his intended masterpiece. In a series of finely-graduated scenes on a broad canvas, he was aiming at something like a con-temporary *Vanity Fair*, and though Perkins questioned the title, he was sure of the text wherein Fitzgerald's prose quiv-ered with a new heartbreak power. During the long ordeal of composition, Perkins had been a bulwark. He was now a well-known figure in American publishing – almost a legend the way he wore his hat around the office and played on his deafness with those he didn't want to listen to. While hoping for a son, he had had five daughters, but some of his authors were like sons to him: Wolfe, the untamed child; Hemingway, the adventurer; Fitzgerald, the prodigal.

It saddened Perkins to see Fitzgerald destroying himself that winter of 1934, though there had never been anything the least moralistic in Perkins' attitude towards Fitzgerald's drinking. Perkins was a compassionate man with a special tolerance for the aberrations of the artistic temperament. Fitzgerald would come into Scribners with liquor on his breath and his speech so thick you couldn't understand him very well, but he worked on his proofs with meticulous care. It was surprising what he could do in a literary way when half seas over. By now he had left La Paix and moved into Baltimore on the grounds that Zelda needed to be near her art school. After a trip to Bermuda, ruined for him by an attack of pleurisy, he had settled at 1307 Park Avenue – a row house with the inevitable white stone steps in a mildly depressing neighbourhood. Here Zelda's sanity had given way and she had gone back to Phipps. After an interim in a New York sanatorium, from which she returned in a catatonic state, she was installed at the Sheppard-Pratt Hospital, whose spacious grounds happened to border La Paix.

Everything now hinged on *Tender Is the Night*. It would be the test of whether Fitzgerald was a big novelist or a flash in the pan. He had *Gatsby* to his credit, but he wasn't sure about *Gatsby*; he was always remarking that it had 'clicked'. *Tender Is the Night* seemed a more solid achievement, yet he was nervous about it on several counts. The man who had begun it in 1925, who had fashioned the beautiful barbarism of its opening sequences, wasn't the same man who completed it in 1933; in between, Zelda's breakdown, the crumbling of American prosperity, and other reverses had changed and darkened his sensibility. Writing the final draft at La Paix, moreover, Fitzgerald had lacked the vitality which sent him dancing over the material of *Gatsby* nine years before. He had found it necessary to stoke himself with gin and feared it might show in the product, which was published 12 April 1934.

The reception of *Tender Is the Night*, though mixed, was not in the main unfavourable. One thinks of Fitzgerald being scored by the critics as Keats was scored in *Blackwood's* after 'Endymion', but this is the exaggeration of legend. The novel received some excellent notices, and even hostile reviewers bowed to the witchery of its prose. There were admiring letters from other writers, yet perhaps no one expressed more aptly what Fitzgerald wanted his readers to feel than Lady Florence Willerts, who had known the Fitzgeralds slightly on the Riviera.

'I have just this minute finished your book,' she wrote.

It is a *living* thing – it is a miracle. It is writing and painting in one, – & instantaneous photography too, transmuted into the highest art. You have somehow got it *all* down – outsides & insides: people & their surroundings to the last fleeting expression of a finger: clothes, houses, rooms & furniture: colour, weather, food – all that makes life and their character. And such an array of people – It is a colossal work – You must have sweated blood to write this 'Gatsby' was good enough a classic now. But this is superlative. And you might be a hundred years old in your wisdom & knowledge of the hearts of men & women!

John Peale Bishop also thought *Tender Is the Night* an advance over *Gatsby*. 'You have shown us,' he wrote Fitzgerald, what we have waited so long and impatiently to see, that you are a true, a beautiful and a tragic novelist.' In a letter to Perkins, Bishop spoke of Fitzgerald's 'inimitable invention, gaiety, tenderness and understanding,' of 'those native talents which for so long were the envy of us all.' James Branch Cabell thought *Tender Is the Night* 'immeasurably [Fitzgerald's] best book,' while Morley Callaghan, after reading it, said Fitzgerald was the only American he knew who had the French classic quality of being able to note a point of character and follow it with a witty generalization that did not break the fabric of the prose. 'Many writers try it,' said Callaghan, 'but you usually get the general observation standing out like a lighthouse on a bleak page.'

Objections to the book centred on the futility of its characters. Left-wingers, especially, were irked by the self-indulgence of this band of neurotic expatriates. Hadn't Fitzgerald heard of the depression? As one reviewer put it, 'Dear Mr Fitzgerald, you can't hide from a hurricane under a beach umbrella.' Some found it hard to believe in Dick Diver as a doctor of medicine or in the ostensible reasons for his downfall. Had Nicole and her money really done him in? Wouldn't this charming weakling have gone to pieces anyway?

Such criticisms, the kind Fitzgerald had foreseen, disturbed him less than Hemingway's reservations about his artistry. In a letter Hemingway said he liked the book and he didn't like it, and went on to advance the theory that when one wrote about real people, he had to stick to what had happened, or what would happen, in their actual lives. By taking liberties with the Murphys, by combining their lives with his own and Zelda's, Fitzgerald had produced not people but damned marvellously faked case histories. Hemingway also said Fitzgerald couldn't think well enough to write a deliberate masterpiece, and paying attention to the highbrow critics had ruined him and made him self-conscious. But most of all Hemingway disliked the novel's suggestions of self-pity.

'Forget your personal tragedy,' he wrote.

We are all bitched from the start and you especially have to be hurt like hell before you can write seriously. But when you get the damned hurt use it – don't cheat with it. Be as faithful to it as a scientist – but don't think anything is of any importance because it happens to you or anyone who belongs to you.

About this time I wouldn't blame you if you gave me a burst. Jesus it's marvellous to tell other people how to write, live, die, etc.

I'd like to see you and talk about things with you sober. You were so damned stinking in N.Y. we didn't get anywhere. You see, Bo, you're not a tragic character. Neither am I. All we are is writers and what we should do is write. Of all people on earth you needed discipline in your work and instead you marry someone who is jealous of your work, wants to compete with you and ruins you. It's not as simple as that and I thought Zelda was crazy the first time I met her and you complicated it even more by being in love with her and, of course, you're a rummy. But you're no more of a rummy than Joyce is and most good writers are. . . . You are twice as good now as you were at the time you think you were so marvellous. You know I never thought so much of Gatsby at the time. You can write twice as well now as you ever could. All you need to do is write truly and not care about what the fate of it is.

Go on and write.

The letter hurt Fitzgerald, especially the remarks about his private life. It didn't help to have these painful truths rubbed in, but he answered without bitterness. Hemingway's 'old, charming frankness', he said, had cleared up the foggy atmosphere through which he felt it was difficult for them to talk any more. Then he went to the mat with Hemingway on the subject of composite characters. 'Think of the case of the Renaissance artists,' he said,

and of the Elizabethan dramatists, the first having to super-impose a medieval conception of science and archeology etc. upon the Bible story; and in the second, of Shakespeare's trying to interpret the results of his own observation of the life around him on the basis of Plutarch's Lives and Holinshed's Chronicles. There you must admit that the feat of building a monument out of three kinds of marble was brought off. You can accuse me justly of not having the power to bring it off, but a theory that it can't be done is highly questionable.

Tender Is the Night had a brief *succès d'estime*, though not the popular success Fitzgerald craved. Its sale of 13,000 was pitiful by his standards. While *Anthony Adverse* and *Goodbye, Mr Chips* swept the country, *Tender Is the Night* hovered for nine weeks in the middle rungs of best-seller-dom, then sank out of sight, taking with it most of its author's self-confidence.

It was a grim year for Fitzgerald. Dazed and wan, he shuffled about the shut-in, unwholesome house in bathrobe and pyjamas, pondering his next move. He rarely went out, caring nothing for society. He wanted Scottie to be a part of it, but his one idea since coming to Baltimore had been to get back on top professionally. His life seemed to be closing in; he had the detachment of a much older man who, having lived hard and fast and run with the best of them, no longer concerned himself with such matters. When he did accept an invitation, there was apt to be unpleasantness. He would lose his temper in arguments about Communism, and once, at a cocktail party, his knees buckled from intoxication and he slid to the floor – no act this time. As he lay on his back, a friend put a calla lily in his hand, giving the aspect of a corpse, and afterwards he laughed and congratulated the friend for saving him from an embarrassing situation.

He was drinking more than ever, but kept a schedule of his drinks and tried to ration himself. He would take one to start writing, and if he didn't stop there, soon he would be drinking not to think but to get lost. Under the circumstances his output was remarkable. During the eight months after he finished the proofs of *Tender* he wrote and sold three stories for the *Post*, wrote another which was refused, wrote two-and-a-half stories for *Redbook*, rewrote three articles of Zelda's for *Esquire* and did an original for them to get emergency cash, collaborated on a 10,000-word movie treatment of *Tender*, wrote an 8,000-word radio script for Gracie Allen (unsold), made five false starts on stories which went from 1,000 to 5,000 words, and wrote a preface to the Modern Library edition of *Gatsby*.

He used the preface to sound off against the critics. During the twenties, he said, H. L. Mencken, with his love of letters and his contempt for what had previously passed as criticism, created a favourable climate for fiction. But now that Mencken had subsided, no one had come along to take his place, and it saddened Fitzgerald to see young talents expiring from sheer lack of any stage to act on. He cited Nathanael West and Vincent McHugh. When McHugh, some ten years younger than Fitzgerald, had published an unsuccessful first novel during the bank holiday of 1933, he received a telegram from Fitzgerald, whom he had never met, assuring him it was good. McHugh was pleased and touched. It seemed to him this was the way an older writer *ought* to behave towards a younger writer he believed in. Reading the preface to *Gatsby*, McHugh was touched again, but this time he smiled a little. Embarked on a new novel, he couldn't see himself in the act of 'expiring', and as for the lack of a stage, that had always been so except for a few years during the twenties. McHugh concluded that Fitzgerald's generation had been spoiled.

In the manner of old pros, whose talent no longer surprises them, Fitzgerald had begun to acquire protégés. Part of it was generosity, his everlasting preoccupation with the promises of youth, and part of it was utilitarian; he was looking for collaborators. He had the idea of making some of Ring Lardner's one-act skits into a Grand Guignol suitable for Broadway, and to help with the continuity he enlisted a youth just out of high school named Garry Morfitt, later Garry Moore of television. One evening Fitzgerald handed Moore a set of coloured pencils and told him to write the dialogue of each character in a different colour. Moore protested. Fitzgerald insisted. Moore changed pencils until he thought Fitzgerald wasn't noticing, but suddenly Fitzgerald was standing over him in rebuke. Moore argued that changing pencils didn't make any difference. 'Are you telling me how to write?' cried Fitzgerald. 'Get out!' He flung his arm dramatically towards the door, ending the evening's efforts.

Meanwhile, two other youths were working on movie treatments of *Tender*. One of the two, aged twenty-one, struck Fitzgerald as having more natural ability than anyone he had met since Hemingway. Fitzgerald staked him to a trip to Hollywood, feeling he deserved the chance to break in and hoping he might sell the script of *Tender*. Fitzgerald was cheered when the young man wrote back, 'Your name is big and hellishly well known in all the studios. You rate out here as a highbrow writer but you rate as a thoroughbred novelist and not a talkie hack and therefore these people look up to you.' The young man's instinct, as Fitzgerald had said in letters of introduction, was for practical showmanship. 'Yes,' wrote the young man, 'I am a dirty skunk – but I want to make money with no delusions about Art for Art's sake.' Soon he was urging Fitzgerald to 'lower your highbrow & help on some trash. They buy trash here – they're quite willing to pay high for it. . . . If you would forget originality and finesse and think in terms of cheap and melo theatrics you would probably have made a howling success of your visits here and would likewise have no financial worries now.'

In the end the young man was unable to sell his script. He said the studios didn't care for *Tender Is the Night* as a book, and because Fitzgerald was considered a millionaire, they thought he would ask too high a price for it.

Weary of struggling, Fitzgerald took refuge in the past. He was writing a series of medieval stories for *Redbook* which he hoped to make into a novel. The hero of his melodrama, a Frankish knight of the ninth century, was modelled on Hemingway. Visitors at 1307 found him poring over a fortress built with Scottie's blocks and rearranging piles of books that signified mountains. He liked the research connected with his project, for military history was a hobby almost on a par with Princeton football.

That fall I went to a game with him, and I remember the tears in his eyes as he stood in the darkening stadium waving his hat and singing 'Old Nassau'. But it wasn't always like that; his bizarre humour hadn't forsaken him. In answer to a questionnaire Fritz Crisler had sent the alumni, Fitzgerald wrote:

Dear Fritz

You write me again demanding advice concerning the coming season. I hasten to answer – *again* I insist that using a member of the Board of Trustees at left tackle to replace Charlie ('Asa') Ceppi and Christian ('Dean') Eisenhart, would be a mistake. My idea is a backfield composed of Kipke, Eddie Mahan, President Lowell, and anybody we can get for the left side – Pepper Einstein in the centre – and then either bring back Light Horse Harry Lee, or else you will fill in yourself for the last place. Or else shift Kadnic to centre and fill in with some member of the 75-lb team.

Failing that, it *is* as you suggest in your round-robbin, a question of using a member of the Board of Trustees. Then who? and where? There is 'Hack' Kalbaugh. There is the late President Witherspoon – but where is he? There is Harkness Hall, but we can't get it unless we pay for the whole expressage *at this end*!

The best suggestion is probably to put Rollo Rulon Roll-on at full, and return to the Haughton system.

Now Fritz, I realize that you and I and Tad know more about this thing than I do – nevertheless I want to make my suggestion: all the end men and backfield men and members of the Board of Trustees start off together – then they all reverse their fields led by some of the most prominent professors and alumni – Albie Booth, Bob Lassiter, etc. and almost before we know it we are up against the Yale goal – let me see, where was I? I meant the Lehigh goal – anyhow some goal, perhaps our own. Anyhow the main thing is that the C.W.A. is either dead, or else just beginning, and to use again that variation of the 'Mexican' shift that I suggested last year will be just *disastrous*. Why? Even I can follow it! Martineau comes out of the huddle – or topples back into it – he passes to some member of past years' teams – (who won't be named here because of the eligibility rules) and then – well, from there on we go on to practically anything.

But not *this* year, Fritz Crisler, if you take my advice!

One way or another Princeton was much in Fitzgerald's thoughts, and when the doctor told him he ought to develop some outside interests, he conceived the plan of giving a lecture series at Princeton on creating fiction. He wrote Dean Gauss that he would do it for nothing, asking merely to use a university lecture hall. He said he had never felt so thoroughly versed in his art, and there was no place he would rather disseminate his knowledge than at Princeton. 'To safeguard you against my elaborate reputation,' he added, 'I would pledge my word to do no drinking . . . save what might be served at your table if you provide me with luncheon before one of these attempts.'

Gauss replied that it was difficult to fit a lecture series into an already complicated programme and suggested that Fitzgerald speak before 'The Club', an undergraduate organization that held monthly meetings at the Nass. Fitzgerald wrote back that he knew about 'The Club' – they had approached him already – but he wanted to lecture under the authoritative aegis of the university. Moreover, what he had in mind was 'pretty serious stuff' which couldn't be developed in a single evening. But he let the matter drop, having guessed what was probably the truth – that because of his reputation Gauss and the English department hesitated to sponsor him before a large audience.[40]

Thrown back on himself, cut off from the adulation which had become a drug to him, he agonized over the past. How he wished he hadn't been drinking so much when writing *Tender Is the Night*! 'A short story,' he told Perkins, 'can be written on a bottle, but for a novel you need the mental speed that enables you to keep the whole pattern in your head and ruthlessly sacrifice the side shows as Ernest did in "A Farewell to Arms."' In his mood of defeat Hemingway seemed invincible. Sometimes Fitzgerald talked as if there weren't any use getting up in the morning with Hemingway off growing a beard and having adventures and writing about them. When an invitation came to go fishing with Hemingway in Florida, Fitzgerald turned it down because, as he told an intermediary, he 'couldn't face Ernest.' There had also been trouble with Edmund Wilson. At their last meeting Fitzgerald had taken the line that he owed Wilson more than Wilson owed him because he, Fitzgerald, was a 'vulgarian' while Wilson was a 'scholar' – a comparison which Wilson found subtly irritating. He wanted to know if, at their advanced age, they couldn't dispense with this 'high school (Princeton University) stuff.' Later Fitzgerald went out of his way to call on Wilson and patch it up.

Altogether he had plenty to occupy him in his nights of insomnia, and that fall he wrote an essay called 'Sleeping and Waking' which foreshadowed the 'Crack-Up' series a year later. Roaming the house in the early morning hours, Fitzgerald goes out on his upstairs porch.

There is a mist over Baltimore; I cannot count a single steeple. Once more to the study, where my eye is caught by a pile of unfinished business letters, proofs, notes etc. I start toward it, but No! this would be fatal . . .

Back again now to the rear porch, and conditioned by intense fatigue of mind and perverse alertness of the nervous system – like a broken-stringed bow upon a throbbing fiddle – I see the real horror develop over the roof-tops, and in the strident horns of night-owl taxis and the shrill monody of revellers' arrival over the way. Horror and waste –

– Waste and horror – what I might have been and done that is lost, spent, gone, dissipated, unrecapturable. I could have acted thus, refrained from this, been bold where I was timid, cautious where I was rash.

I need not have hurt her like that.

Nor said this to him.

Nor broken myself trying to break what was unbreakable.

The horror has come now like a storm – what if this night prefigured the night after death – what if all thereafter was an eternal quivering on the edge of an abyss, with everything base and vicious in oneself urging one forward and the baseness and viciousness of the world just ahead. No choice, no road, no hope – only the endless repetition of the sordid and the semi-tragic. Or to stand forever, perhaps, on the threshold of life unable to pass it and return to it. I am a ghost now as the clock strikes four.'

Father Barron, the priest he had liked in St Paul, was living in Washington and came to see him a few times, but it was sad for them both. 'I'm keeping my eye on Scott,' Barron told a friend, 'but I don't want to say too much. I'm afraid he might turn on me.' Max Perkins tried a different approach. He had introduced Fitzgerald to a charming, intelligent girl named Elizabeth Lemmon, whose family owned an historical mansion near Middleburg, Virginia. (On one of the panes were Jeb Stuart's initials, which the Gallant Pelham had scratched with his diamond ring while waiting for his horse to be brought to the door.) When Fitzgerald felt well enough, he would visit Elizabeth in Middleburg and roam the nearby battlefields. One day they stopped at a roadside stand to buy him a pack of Chesterfields, and when there weren't any he said. 'That's too bad – I've been driving all over the Shenandoah Valley with Mrs Roosevelt here, and I wanted to be photographed with her smoking a Chesterfield.' The joke fell flat; the vendor thought Fitzgerald was crazy. Another time he tiptoed into a delicatessen, cupped his hands, and whispered, 'Have you got a Virginia ham?' The man behind the counter looked at him a moment, then said, 'Down the hall, sir, and the first door on your right.'

Fitzgerald was always fabricating situations that would win him the attention he had won so effortlessly in the past, yet he was shy and self-effacing with people he respected. When Elizabeth introduced him to General Billy Mitchell, the crusader for air power, they discussed some articles Mitchell had been writing for the *Post*, and as they parted Fitzgerald said – as if he were the veriest beginner – 'I write too.' Mitchell was delighted with him and invited him to come around and see his trophies, which Fitzgerald did.

Christmas Eve, Gertrude Stein, visiting America for the first time in thirty years, had tea at the Fitzgeralds'. Miss Stein was now the sententious oracle of her later days, with the close-cropped hair brushed forward that gave her the look of a Roman Emperor. She and Fitzgerald hadn't seen each other more than half-a-dozen times, but they had remained mutually admiring, and Fitzgerald had found comfort in her recent prophecy that he would be read when many of his well-known contemporaries were forgotten.

During the visit, Zelda came in with some of her paintings, and Fitzgerald asked Miss Stein to take any ones she pleased. She chose two which Zelda had promised her doctor.

'But dear,' said Fitzgerald, 'you don't understand. Gertrude will hang them in her salon in Paris and you will be famous. She has been kinder to me than almost anyone and I'd like to give her something.'

'If she has been as kind to you as my doctor has been to me,' said Zelda, 'you should give her everything you own but she can't have those paintings.'

In the end Miss Stein chose two others.

When Scottie appeared, Miss Stein drew from the pocket

of her homespun skirt a handful of hazel nuts which she had gathered on her afternoon walk. She gave one to Scottie, who wanted it autographed.

'That would be appropriate,' said Miss Stein, inscribing it.

The conversation turned to literature and Miss Stein said that sentences must not leak – 'they must not have bad plumbing.'

'My God!' said Fitzgerald. 'If that isn't a woman's point of view! Gertrude, give us a sentence that has good plumbing.'

'Your dedication to *The Great Gatsby* – "Once again to Zelda".' Miss Stein cupped her hands. 'It's complete, it holds together, it doesn't leak.'

Afterwards, Fitzgerald wrote Gertrude Stein that Christmas Eve had been well spent in the company of her handsome face and wise mind and sentences 'that never leak'.

As for Zelda, Fitzgerald had to face the fact that she would never be well enough to live permanently outside an institution. Her illness had been the drama of the past five years. 'I left my capacity for hoping on the little roads that led to Zelda's sanatorium,' he wrote in his notebook.

A New York exhibition of her paintings had been a disappointment. Her art, like her writing, bespoke a powerful, original and lyrical personality with great natural talent, but a psychopathic element was also visible: in her rendering of ballet dancers with the emphasis on their swollen, distorted feet; in the Negro cook picking a chicken – that one was all great black hands. One day when Scott had called for Zelda at the hospital and they were strolling around La Paix, she tried to throw herself in front of the train that ran at rare intervals between our land and that of Sheppard-Pratt, and he barely succeeded in preventing her. From now on he would speak of her as his 'invalid', and in a moment's bitterness he told a friend, 'Can you imagine what it's like being tied to a dead hand?' But he never stopped loving the mem-

ory of what she had been, and that love informed a poem he
wrote near the end of this harrowing year.[41]

Do you remember, before keys turned in the locks,
When life was a close-up, and not an occasional letter,
That I hated to swim naked from the rocks
While you liked absolutely nothing better?

Do you remember many hotel bureaus that had
Only three drawers? But the only bother
Was that each of us got holy, then got mad,
Trying to give the third one to the other.

East, West, the little car turned, right or wrong
Up an erroneous Alp, an unmapped Savoy river.
We blamed each other in cadences acid and strong
And, in an hour, laughed and called it liver.

And, though the end was desolate and unkind:
To turn the calendar at June and find December
On the next leaf; still, stupid-got with grief, I find
These are the only quarrels that I can remember.

[15]

Sick, debt-ridden, and despairing, Fitzgerald went on vacation to Tryon, North Carolina, in February 1935. There he fell in with an unusual couple – the Flynns – who became to some extent an anchorage during the storms of the next two years.

Nora Langhorne Flynn came from a family of famous Virginia belles, of whom the most famous was Lady Astor. A few years older than Fitzgerald, Nora was still glamorous in her white blouses and well-cut suits, but more important, she had the vitality which he sought in others now that his own was fading. Nora's husband, 'Lefty', reminded Fitzgerald of the Leyendecker poster of the halfback. Handsome and rangy, he had been a star athlete at Yale, an actor in the silents, and a naval aviator during the War. After a roving, adventurous life, he and Nora had settled in Tryon where they dominated the scene.

They knew celebrities here and abroad. Nora was a friend of Bernard Shaw and called the Queen of England 'Beth'. Well-known artists, actors, and musicians enlivened their household from time to time, though the Flynns were considerable entertainers in their own right, with a gift for improvisation. They put on skits and sang duets. When one of them launched a joke, the other took it up and they went from star to star till they collapsed with their own merriment. Given the proper training, Nora might have been a professional actress, but she seemed content with her role of a rural duchess. She organized benefits and judged fashion shows, and when she walked down the street in Tryon, people of all ages and descriptions clustered around her.

Despite their advantages, the Flynns remained gypsies at heart – 'not the Hungarian type but the Sigmund Romberg type', a friend recalled. They were the unorthodox rich Fitzgerald enjoyed. (Actually they weren't rich, but behaved as if they were, living beyond their moderate income.) Fitzgerald had a standing invitation with them, and when he said he was coming for a meal, it didn't matter whether or not he appeared, nor did the Flynns expect him to return their hospitality. All they demanded was gaiety. When Fitzgerald came in depressed, Nora would throw her arms around him and kiss him and say she was going to spank him if he didn't snap out of it.

Nora was a Christian Scientist who had made a speciality of salvaging alcoholics, and Fitzgerald seemed to her much too attractive to let go to pieces. She built him up and appreciated him and told him there was nothing he couldn't do if he put his mind to it. During the winter and spring of 1935, much of which he spent in Tryon, he stopped drinking for long periods, but back in Baltimore, faced with Zelda's tragedy, he would begin again. In May, X-rays showed that he was suffering from mild tuberculosis, and closing his house on Park Avenue, he went to the Grove Park Inn in Asheville for rest and rehabilitation. Although the Flynns were now some twenty miles distant, Fitzgerald was just as glad; he thought he might get more work done if he saw them less.

He found it lonely at the cavernous, rock-built Grove Park Inn that catered to the luxury trade, but he didn't want to meet people or be recognized. Attractive young women, vacationing with their families, nudged each other when he passed, and he held the door for them, he was polite, but he didn't get involved. He phoned the Flynns constantly. 'You've had a bad year,' Nora would say, ' — come over and stay with us, we love you,' and Fitzgerald would reply that he was going to be all right — he was just down in the dumps because he couldn't have Scottie with him — he didn't mean to burden Nora with his problems — and she would say, 'Oh no — any time.'

Physically and mentally exhausted, he tried not to think, but instead made endless lists — of cavalry officers, athletes, cities, popular tunes. Later, he realized that he had been witnessing the disintegration of his own personality and likened the sensation to that of a man standing at twilight on a deserted range with an empty rifle in his hands and the targets down. The words of St Matthew seemed to apply: 'Ye are the salt of the earth. But if the salt hath lost its savour, wherewith shall it be salted?'

His tuberculosis subsided, as it always did when he took care of himself, but then he began drinking beer which he could rationalize as not really drinking. One day a total of thirty-two bottles was sent to his room.

'Is someone up there with him?' the switchboard operator asked the bellboy.

'No, ma'am,' said the bellboy, 'he's drinking it himself. And you know something? – that man's a smart man. He's got the biggest sheet of paper and he's writing away. When I bring the beer in he never looks up, he just says set it over there and open me a bottle, and he hands me a dollar without ever taking his eyes off the paper. I don't know when he gets time to drink it but he does.'

The hotel attendants were fond of Fitzgerald, not only because of his largess but because he treated them like human beings and took an interest in their problems.

'Yes, he's a swell man,' the bellboys would say. 'Certainly was too bad about those thirty-two bottles of beer.'

His chief companion that summer was his secretary, Laura Guthrie, whom he summoned at all hours, since he dreaded being alone when he couldn't sleep. He and Laura went to many movies, and sometimes they sat up all night in cabarets. She kept a journal of their talks – a unique record of Fitzgerald's offhand remarks. The conceit running through them, though to some extent an honest self-evaluation, also suggests a defeated man bolstering his crumbling morale.

A graduate of the Columbia School of Journalism, Laura wanted to write and questioned Fitzgerald about his methods.

'State a problem,' he told her, 'don't solve it. Be natural. Above all things be yourself.

'I don't know why I can write stories. I don't know what it

is in me or that comes to me when I start to write. I am half feminine – at least my mind is.'

Laura conceded that he understood women.

I understand everybody, one side of them anyway. I am a romantic and I can't change that – not now. I am mature – in fact, I was mature at thirty but I didn't know it. Now that I'm grown I can only write one way because my ideas won't change. However, there is a new note creeping into literature because of Socialism. It points a moral and a purpose. I belong to an in-between period, between two moralistic periods.

All the small writers look up to me. I am a top-notcher – I am the *maitre*. My stories get truer and truer, I can't keep the truth out of them. I am part of the race consciousness and so have influenced the language of youth and youth itself.

Laura asked if he used models.

'Not any single person but a mélange of the characteristics of several people interpreted through my eyes.' With reference to Jung's psychological types, he said, 'I am an intuitive introvert. I take people to me and change my conception of them and then write them out again. My characters are all Scott Fitzgerald. Even my feminine characters are feminine Scott Fizgeralds.'

Laura asked if drinking helped.

'Drink heightens feeling. When I drink, it heightens my emotions and I put it in a story. But then it becomes hard to keep reason and emotion balanced. My stories written when sober are stupid – like the fortune-telling one. It was all reasoned out, not felt.'

Laura noticed that Fitzgerald wrote his stories three or four times, starting each rewrite with a clean typewritten draft. She asked if he had always taken such pains.

Yes, three drafts are absolutely necessary. First, the high inspirational points. Second, the cold going over. Third, putting both in their proper perspective.

I can be so tender and kind to people in even little things, but once I get a pen in my hand I can do *anything*.

If you want to be a top-notcher, you have to break with everyone. You have to show up your own father. At first they will throw you out for it, but in the end they will take you back on a different footing when the world acclaims you. You've got to go a long, lone path.

I have tried writing when I didn't mean it and it doesn't pay. When anything goes wrong in a story, I go back and see where I left the truth and there I pick up the thread. Of course restrained emotion and understatement are valuable in writing. And never forget to listen to the way people talk.

Fitzgerald was conscious of paying a price for his creativity.

People are divided into two classes. There are those who think, are sensitive and have some fatal flaw. Then there are those who are good and unimaginative – and uninteresting.

Some people think I am a son-of-a-bitch and hate my guts. I can't be one of the herd, I have tried. I get on top as I did in St Paul when Zelda and I went out there to live, and then something happens and I come out at the bottom. But I make the curve again every time to the top.

I had to excel in everything I undertook so they would seek me out. I am really a lone wolf, and though I wanted to be one of the gang, I wasn't permitted to be until I proved myself. When I was twelve, I was at camp, and once in a baseball game I was catcher and played without a mask. A ball hit my forehead and cut it terribly. Then I became a hero, but I was so puffed up about it I became insufferable and lost prestige again.

I'm so bad, such a lousy son-of-a-bitch that I've got to do something good – so good in my work – that it counterbalances the bad. I've *got* to be good and I *can* be in my work.

'I must be loved,' he often mused. 'I tip heavily to be loved. I have so many faults that I must be approved of in other ways.'

Of his friends Fitzgerald said,

They have always been strong and have usually excelled in some line. I pick out a person here and there – not many – to be interested in. I can't dismiss a servant and it is the same way with friends. I pick them out carefully and then they are part of my life and I can't cut them off.

Every one is lonely – the artist especially, it goes with creation. I create a world for others. Because of this women want to go away with me, they think the world of delight I make for them will last forever. I make them seem brilliant to themselves and most important.

But no woman could take Zelda's place.

Our love was one in a century. Life ended for me when Zelda and I crashed. If she would get well, I would be happy again and my soul would be released. Otherwise, never.

Zelda and I were everything to each other – all human relationships. We were sister and brother, mother and son, father and daughter, husband and wife.

A strange thing was I could never convince her that I was a first-rate writer. She knew I wrote well but she didn't recognize how well. When I was making myself from a popular writer into a serious writer, a big-shot, she didn't understand or try to help me.

Women are so weak really – emotionally unstable – and their nerves, when strained, break. They can endure more physical pain than men, and also more boredom. The boredom they endure is incredible, but they can't take nerve or emotional strain. The greatest women of all time are those of conquered passion or no passion. Women like Florence Nightingale, Jane Addams, Julia Ward Howe. Theirs has been a sublimated and useful work. They had no conflicts as Zelda had.

'This is a man's world,' he often said. 'All wise women conform to the man's lead.'

And yet, despite his emphasis on male superiority, Fitzgerald was essentially a woman's man. Perhaps one needed to be a woman to catch the feelings, rising and dying like the wind, that flitted across his mobile face. (Men would be more on guard against the vein of weakness in him.) His conversation, too, was the sort that women delight in; it was emotional analysis, people, their nuances, the sparks between them. Fitzgerald, who could beat a woman at her own game of intuition, would tell her maddening things about herself, and just as she was about to lose her temper he would say, 'Has any one ever told you you have a most expressive mouth?'

As with Rilke or D. H. Lawrence the feminine strain in

Fitzgerald, the extreme delicate sensitivity, went a long way towards explaining his artistic power, yet he was in no way effeminate. He was normally but not overly sexed. Perhaps one could say that with him a strong sex drive had been geared to beauty and creation, while the destructive side of his nature found an outlet in drink. For someone who had been instrumental in relaxing censorship his writing was remarkably chaste. A book like *Gatsby*, though electric with passion, is almost devoid of sex, even Tom Buchanan's commerce with his earthy mistress being suggested rather than shown. The line Fitzgerald most regretted in *Tender Is the Night* was Dick Diver's comparatively mild jibe at Nicole, 'I never did go in for making love to dry loins.'[42]

Since Zelda's breakdown Fitzgerald had drifted into affairs here and there – not many, considering the opportunities. In July a young married woman from Memphis, visiting Asheville, fell in love with him on sight. She was already enamoured of his writings, and when she pursued him, they became lovers despite misgivings on his part. She was pretty and wealthy but not otherwise remarkable, and he resented wasting time on her – that is, until her husband joined her. Then Fitzgerald decided he really did love her and was plunged into a misery which he prolonged and dramatized, continuing to meet her at grave risk of being found out. After the woman had gone, she wrote Fitzgerald heartbreaking letters which he was reluctant to answer, for by now he saw the affair for what it was – an evasion like his drinking. Finally he wrote her a sermon which, though he never sent it, showed the skeleton of character beneath his flabby weakness.[43]

Gloria [so we shall call her]

This is going to be as tough a letter to read as it is to write. When I was young I found a line in Samuel Butler's Note Books – the worst thing that can happen to a man is the loss of his health, the second worst the loss of his money. All other things are of minor importance.

This is only a half truth but there are many times in life when most of us, and especially women, must live on half truths. The utter synthesis between what we want and what we can have is so rare that I look back with a sort of wonder on those days of my youth when I had it, or thought I did.

The point of the Butler quotation is that in times of unhappiness and emotional stress that seemed beyond endurance, I used it as a structure, upon which to build up a hierarchy of comparative values:

– This comes first.

– This comes second.

This is what you, Gloria, are not doing!

Your charm and the heightened womanness that makes you attractive to men depends on what Ernest Hemingway once called (in an entirely different connection) 'grace under pressure'. The luxuriance of your emotions under the strict discipline which you habitually impose on them, makes that tensity in you that is the secret of all charm – when you let that balance become disturbed, don't you become just another victim of self-indulgence – breaking down the solid things around you and, moreover, making *yourself* terribly vulnerable? – imagine having to have had call in Doctor Cole in this matter! The *indignity*! I have plenty [of] cause to be cynical about women's nervous resistance, but frankly I am concerned with my misjudgement in thinking you were one of the strong – and I can't believe I was mistaken.

The tough part of the letter is to send you this enclosure – which you should read now [a loving, dependent letter from Zelda] –

– now you've read it?

There are emotions just as important as ours running concurrently with them – and there is literally no standard in life other than a sense of duty. When people get mixed up they try to throw out a sort of obscuring mist, and then the sharp shock of a *fact* – a collision seems to be the only thing to make them soberminded again. You once said, 'Zelda is your *love!*' (only you said 'lu-uv'). And I gave her all the youth and freshness that was in me. And it's a sort of investment that is as tangible as my talent, my child, my money. That you had the same sort of appeal to me, deep down in the gut, doesn't change the other.

The harshness of this letter will have served its purpose if on reading it over you see that I have an existence outside you – and in doing so remind you that you have an existence outside of me. I don't belittle your fine intelligence by supposing that anything written here *need* be said, but I thought maybe the manner of saying it might emphasize those old dull truths by which we live. We can't just let our worlds crash around us like a lot of dropped trays.

– *You have got to be good.*

– Your sense of superiority depends upon the picture of yourself as being *good*, of being large and generous and all-comprehending, and just and brave and all-forgiving. But if you are not *good*, if you don't preserve a sense of comparative values those qualities turn against you – and your love is a mess and your courage is a slaughter.

Scott

From the point of view of work the summer had been wasted. Drifting about in a fog of beer, Fitzgerald had put in the hours without being able to complete anything. Physically he was wretched. He needed sedatives to sleep and had switched from luminal to amytal because the former made him itch. Devoid of appetite, he wolfed a little food now and then as if it were medicine. In September, to help him finish the story he was stuck in, he went back to gin.

'Do I seem different now that I'm on hard liquor?' he asked Laura. 'Do I seem more depraved?'

One day they went sight-seeing to Chimney Rock, which offered a panorama of far-off ranges with Lake Lure glistening a thousand feet below them.

'This place speaks to me of death,' Fitzgerald said. 'Nothing else, just death. These huge rocks, these distant mountains will be here a million years from now when we'll be *dead* – resolved back into the elements from which we came.'

As they started down, he said, 'To be with me is like reading a book. You learn something all the time. I am a weak character, self-indulgent, but with a powerful will. I have no patience and when I want something I *want* it. I break people. I am part of the break-up of the times.' (He was always of talking of breaking and being broken.)

Drink is an escape. That is why so many people do it now. There is *Weltschmerz* – the uncertainty of the world today. All sensitive minds feel it. There is a passing away of the old order and we wonder what there will be for us in the new – if anything.

Life is not happy. All I ask is that it be endurable. I used to like being with my own thoughts, but for a year and a half I haven't been able to enjoy myself. I would like a blank period. I have suffered too much and too long. I would like not to feel for a while.

A few days later, when Ted Coy's death was announced in the papers, Fitzgerald said,

Ted Coy was my idol. I worshipped him and put him in some of my stories. He *was* a back! What a football man! And he died a drunk. All drunks die between thirty-eight and forty-eight. He was forty-seven.

People [he went on] aren't going to let F. Scott Fitzgerald act as he chooses now. Four years ago the publisher would have said, 'Oh, that's just Fitzgerald's way and as long as he produces good stuff it doesn't matter.' Today they wouldn't be so lenient if I told the real story of this wasted summer.

'What about four years hence?' said Laura, meaning that she hoped for an improvement.

'I won't be here then,' said Fitzgerald. 'I'll be where Ted Coy has gone.'

He was anxious to return to Baltimore and be with Scottie and Zelda, but first he was determined to finish his story. The chef of the Grove Park Inn, eager to help, sent up the kind of gravy he could sometimes eat with bread or mashed potatoes. That and soup was all he would touch.

He railed at Laura, typing his story, for being unable to make out what he had written. Some of the pages contradicted each other. There were two farewell scenes between the hero and his mother, and people were going upstairs when they should have been going down.

One day Laura came in to find Fitzgerald wearing a thick wool jersey over his pyjamas. He was trying to sweat the gin out of his system while continuing to drink more. His eyes were bloodshot and his lips were thin lines.

270

'Look,' he said, 'my leg muscles are twitching. This morning I spat blood.'

When Laura said she would call the doctor, Fitzgerald protested, but finally the doctor came and ordered him to the hospital. During the five days he was there – white, pitiful, and shaking – he finished his story.

Laura got a cheerful letter from him on his return to Baltimore. Scottie had arrived like 'a sun Goddess . . . all radiant and glowing' and they had spent a happy evening walking the dark streets. Zelda was fine –

almost herself. It was wonderful to sit with her head on my shoulder for hours and feel as I always have, even now, closer to her than to any other human being . . .

I love [Baltimore] more than I thought – it is so rich with memories – it is nice to look up the street and see the statue of my great uncle [an approximate description of Francis Scott Key] & to know that Poe is buried here and that many ancestors of mine have walked in the old town by the bay. I belong here, where everything is civilized and gay and rotted and polite. And I wouldn't mind a bit if in a few years Zelda & I could snuggle up together under a stone in some old graveyard here. That is really a happy thought and not melancholy at all.

The happiness was momentary. Zelda grew worse and Fitzgerald continued to flounder in his work. His agent, Harold Ober, was having trouble marketing his stories at any price.

Ober had been a mainstay since 1919, when as Paul R. Reynolds' assistant he had begun handling Fitzgerald (during the next twelve years Fitzgerald's story price had jumped eight-fold), and in 1928, when Ober left Reynolds to start his own firm, Fitzgerald had wired him from abroad, UNRESERVEDLY YOURS. Fitzgerald had come to admire this gentleman of the old school with the mild, clear blue eyes, the shy smile, the hesitant speech. Ober understood a great deal more about human and literary problems than he was able to express, and when bargaining was in process, one rejoiced to be on the side of this shrewd New Hampshire man.

The stiff Yankee in Ober and the mercurial Irishman in Fitzgerald made an amusing contrast. Once when Ober met Fitzgerald at the boat on his return from Europe, Fitzgerald said he had a friend he knew Ober would be proud to handle. He then produced the largest mortal Ober had ever seen – a giant who had come over to join the Ringling Circus. Being Fitzgerald's agent was not without embarrassments, though Ober would remember him as one of the most courteous and thoughtful authors he had ever dealt with. Ober was grateful to him besides, for it had meant a good deal to Ober when he was starting his business on borrowed capital to have such a lucrative author as Fitzgerald in his stable.

Lately Fitzgerald had been a headache. He had grown unreliable about sending in stories when he said he was going to, and he asked for huge loans which Ober had to borrow at six per cent, knowing all too well how Fitzgerald would spend it. One day Fitzgerald took Ober and Charlie MacArthur to Twenty-One, where Ober – who didn't drink because of a tendency towards ulcers brought on, in part, by worrying over Fitzgerald – had to sit and watch the others drink up the money he had just lent. As they went out, Fitzgerald handed the waiter a tip the size of the bill.

But Ober went on backing Fitzgerald – out of sympathy as well as loyalty. About this time Philip Wylie came into Ober's office unannounced to find him standing beside his desk with a manuscript in his hand and tears running down his cheeks. When Wylie started to withdraw, Ober called him back.

'Look,' he said, handing over the blotted manuscript with illegible interlinings, 'I was always the one who could read Scott's corrections and these pages are the ending of a story that I can read – up to here. These last six pages I can't make anything of. Scott was drinking, but he never before sent me something I couldn't decipher. I'm afraid that Scott . . .'

He dropped it there.

Fitzgerald had always been a perfectionist, even in his routine work, and Ober had respected him when he wrote,

There is no use of me trying to rush things. Even in years like '24, '28, '29, '30, all devoted to short stories I couldn't turn out more than 8–9 top price stories in a year. It simply is impossible – all my stories are concieved like novels, require a special emotion, a special experience – so that my readers, if such there be, knowing that each time it'll be something new, not in form but in substance (it'd be far better for me if I could do pattern stories but the pencil just goes dead on me).[44]

The past few months, however, Fitzgerald had been playing roulette with his talent, spinning it recklessly in the hope that something would score, and as his stories became more slapdash, Ober was obliged to hold them up for revision. When a sale was made, Fitzgerald's confidence soared. Instead of using some of the proceeds to liquidate his debt he would ask for all of it, saying he had tried life on a subsistence level and it didn't pay. Once, in his desperation for funds, he bypassed Ober and sent a story direct to the *Post*. When they refused it, Ober took it mildly enough, merely remarking that he hoped that Fitzgerald wouldn't do it again.

Part of the trouble was the discrepancy between what Fitzgerald actually felt and what the magazine editors expected him to write. How, in his present mood, could he put his heart into tales of young love? Since the early twenties, when they had come to him naturally, he had undergone a profound change. He needed to face this new self and burst the wall that was blocking his emotions. One night in November 1935, he packed a briefcase and fled to Hendersonville – a little town between Asheville and Tryon – to think out why 'I had developed a sad attitude towards sadness, a melancholy attitude towards melancholy and a tragic attitude towards tragedy – *why I had become identified with the objects of my horror or compassion*'. Eating twenty-cent meals and washing his own clothes in a two-dollar room at the Skylands Hotel, he wrote an essay called 'The Crack-Up', and returning to Baltimore 'for what Xmas [was] to be found there,' he wrote two more in the same vein.

Taken together these pieces were a post-mortem on his

nervous and psychological breakdown. What had become of his early conviction that 'life was something you dominated if you were any good'? He realized that for some time he had been drawing on resources, spiritual as well as material, which he did not possess. He realized, too, his dependence on others: on Wilson as an 'intellectual conscience'; on Hemingway as an 'artistic conscience'; on Gerald Murphy as a social arbiter. He had let himself become too involved in other people's lives. From now on, he would outlaw as waste the ceaseless giving of himself which was so much a part of his charm and indeed of his talent, for in giving himself to others he had come to understand them. From now on he would be a writer only, hard-boiled – as if such a resolve were possible for one of his temperament.

In its casual nakedness and candour 'The Crack-Up' was reminiscent of certain European authors: Dostoevsky, Kierkegaard, Strindberg. Fitzgerald had *lived* the Jazz Age and paraded it in his writings, and now he was living its aftermath, the wave of despair which followed. But 'The Crack-Up' was also the work of a lapsed Catholic, for whom confession was a rhythm of the soul. The Church had a stronger hold on Fitzgerald than he perhaps realized or would have admitted. He had broken with it intellectually but not emotionally. If, on the one hand, he railed against the 'mumbo-jumbo' of Catholicism, saying he didn't see how civilized people could put up with it, on the other he would talk nostalgically of going to mass and admiringly of the great saints like Augustine and Ignatius. His writing, though blasphemous at times (Nicole Diver crossing herself with Chanel No. 5), was also deeply religious in its spiritual yearning, its haunting sense of loss.[45]

'Scott played hide and seek with the angels,' Nora Flynn used to say. 'He was fundamentally a moralist and a very religious person. He kept his soul.'

Since October Fitzgerald had been living with Scottie at the Cambridge Arms, across Charles Street from the campus of Johns Hopkins University. In his seventh-floor apartment, he was trying to write his way out of debt, but with his world contracting he found less and less to say. One of his best pieces that year was simply a description of a typical day in his now uneventful life.

Waking on a bright April morning, he feels better than he has for some weeks, but after breakfast he lies down for fifteen minutes before beginning the day's work. 'The problem was a magazine story that had become so thin in the middle that it was about to blow away. The plot was like climbing endless stairs, he had no element of surprise in reserve, and the characters who had started so bravely day-before-yesterday couldn't have qualified for a newspaper serial.'

His mind wandered to trips he would like to take, but they required time and energy and he hadn't much of either; what there was must be conserved for his work. Going through the manuscript, he underlined the best phrases in red crayon. When his secretary had copied these, the 'stripped' story would be thrown away.

Pacing the room and smoking, he talked to himself.

'Wee-l, let's see – ' (Fitzgerald, musing, had this way of drawling his expletives.)

'Nau-ow, the next thing – would be . . .'

He felt stale and decided to go downtown for an airing. With a tube of shampoo ointment in his pocket, he set out for a hotel barber shop where he liked the barber. He stood carefully on the corner waiting for the light to change while young people hurried by with what seemed to him a fine disregard of traffic. In matters of self-preservation he was as cautious as he had once been reckless.

From the upper deck of the bus with the green branches ticking against the window, he saw men rolling the college football field and a story idea came to him, ' "Turfkeeper" or else "The Grass Grows", something about a man working on turf for years and bringing up his son to go to college and play football there. Then the son dying in youth and the man's going to work in the cemetery and putting turf over his son instead of under his feet. It would be the kind of piece that is often placed in anthologies, but not his sort of thing – it was sheer swollen antithesis, as formalized as a popular magazine story and easier to write. Many people, however, would consider it excellent because it was melancholy, had digging in it and was simple to understand.'

Downtown the sight of the brightly-dressed young women made him love life terribly for a moment – made him not want to give it up at all. He got off the bus, holding carefully to the railings. In the barber shop he sat rather happy and sensually content under the strong fingers on his scalp.

The shampoo over, he came out into the hall and listened to the orchestra which had begun to play in the cocktail room across the way. He thought how long it had been since he danced –

perhaps two evenings in five years, yet a review of his last book had mentioned him as being fond of night clubs; the same review had spoken of him as being indefatigable. Something in the sound of the word in his mind broke him momentarily and feeling tears of weakness behind his eyes he turned away. It was like in the beginning fifteen years ago when they said he had 'fatal facility', and he laboured like a slave over every sentence so as not to be like that.

Going home on the bus, he noticed a boy and a girl sitting on the high pedestal of the Lafayette statue. 'Their isolation moved him and he knew he would get something out of it professionally, if only in contrast to the growing seclusion of his life and the increasing necessity of picking over an already well-picked past. He needed reforestation . . .'

Back at the apartment house he glanced up at his windows before going in.

'The residence of the successful writer,' he said to himself. 'I wonder what marvellous book he's tearing off up there. It must be great to have a gift like that – just sit down with pencil and paper. Work when you want – go where you please.'

Scottie wasn't home yet, but the maid came out of the kitchen and asked him if he'd had a nice time.

'Perfect,' he said. 'I went roller skating and bowled and played around with Man Mountain Dean and finished up in a Turkish bath.'

Quite tired, he thought he would lie down for ten minutes – then see if he could get started on an idea in the two hours before dinner.

The happiest thing in his life was Scottie. She exasperated him by her impulsiveness and the habitual messiness of her room, but he gave her credit for 'conscientiously wrestling with her ebullient temperament'. He was writing some stories about her – the 'Gwen' series – four of which he completed, though only two were published. Like Gwen, Scottie was under the spell of Ginger Rogers and Fred Astaire; her favourite song was 'Cheek to Cheek', which Fitzgerald referred to maliciously as 'Cheek by Jowl'.

Out of love for her and out of concern because she had no mother to look after her, Fitzgerald was excessively strict. When he went to Asheville for a few weeks in April, he left the following instructions with Scottie's supervisor:

Not more than half an hours radio or phonograph on school nights.

No long telephone gossiping on school nights.

No *night dates* with boys except here in the apartment on *any* night. I don't want some sixteen yr. old to crash her into a telephone pole. Anyhow it isn't done here in Baltimore under sixteen. I don't object to parties of six, however, even without a chaperone if they're all together, have a destination & are in by 10:30. This is of course on free nights only.

[Scottie's] French is getting rusty – none for a year almost except a little reading. I wish you could find a *native* French woman – I had a fine woman for three years but she left town. It would absolutely have to be a native & of good education. . . . I've never let her take school French, which is simply ruinous & demoralizing. Anyhow she'd take senior college work in it.

No *lip rouge* & no half-hours work with tin curlers on school nights. The general opinion is here that Scottys getting way ahead of her age.

Now that she was beginning to have callers her father's

drinking was doubly embarrassing, for he no longer pretended even to himself that he wasn't an alcholic. He had tried everything – stopping abruptly, tapering off, smoking or eating candy when he felt the craving – but nothing prevailed against it. In July 1936, having sent Scottie to camp, he moved to Asheville to be near Zelda who had recently been transferred to the Highland Sanatorium. He was trying to be hard-boiled about her condition, but as he wrote Oscar Kalman, caring for her was 'a life-long consecration & all the friends I ever had couldn't argue me out of the idea that that's where my first duty lies'. Zelda's illness had taken a religious turn; she often had a Bible with her and knelt in public places to say her prayers. She wore her hair shoulder-length and dressed like a young girl in the forgotten robes of the twenties. When she came to the Grove Park Inn for a meal, she and Scott wouldn't have much to say to each other, though he was patient with her and very attentive about ordering the dishes she liked.

When they called on the writer Margaret Culkin Banning, Zelda came in, Ophelia-like, with a bunch of water lilies she had gathered on the way. On the Bannings' terrace Fitzgerald led her to a stone wall against a background of mountains and said to her, 'You're the Fairy Princess and I'm the Prince,' and for several minutes they tossed this back and forth in a terrible and touching way. Another time they went to see the Flynns, and Zelda, after walking around just putting her hands on things, suddenly began to dance. Fitzgerald sat watching her, his chin resting on his palm, a look of unutterable sadness on his face. They had loved each other and though it was over, he loved that love and hated to relinquish it.

From the hospital Zelda sent him strained, beautiful letters, for even in her reduced state she wrote a better letter than most people are capable of in their right minds. Some were as lucid as the following which Fitzgerald sent Harold Ober so he might gauge 'the awful strangling heart-rending quality of the tragedy that has gone on now more than six years, with two brief intervals of hope. ... With things so black I hang on to every scrap that is like things used to be.'

Dearest and always Dearest Scott:
I am sorry too that there should be nothing to greet you but an empty shell. The thought of the effort you have made over me, the suffering this *nothing* has cost would be unendurable to any save a complete vacuous mechanism. Had I any feelings they would all be bent in gratitude to you and in sorrow that of all my life there should not even be the smallest relic of the love and beauty that we started with to offer you at the end.

You have been so good to me – and all I can say is that there was always that deeper current running through my heart: my life, you.

You remember the roses in Kenney's yard – you were so gracious and I thought – he is the sweetest person in the world – and you said 'darling'. You still are. The wall was damp and mossy when we crossed the street and said we loved the south. I thought of the south and a happy past I'd never had and I thought I was part of the south. You said you loved this lovely land. The wisteria along the fence was green and the shade was cool and life was old.

I wish I had thought something else – but it was a confederate, a romantic and nostalgic thought. My hair was damp when I took off my hat and I was safe and home and you were glad that I felt that way and you were reverent. We were glad and happy all the way home.

Now that there isn't any more happiness and home is gone and there isn't even any past and no emotions but those that were yours where there could be my comfort – it is a shame that we should have met in harshness and coldness where there was once so much tenderness and so many dreams. Your song.

I wish you had a little house with hollyhocks and a sycamore tree and the afternoon sun imbedding itself in a silver tea-pot. Scottie would be running about somewhere in white, in Renoir, and you will be writing books in dozens of volumes. And there will be honey for tea, though the house should not be in Granchester.

I want you to be happy – if there were justice you would be happy – maybe you will be anyway.
Oh Do-Do, Do Do

I love you anyway – even if there isn't any me or any love or even any life –

I love you.

In periods of depression Fitzgerald was used to hiring a registered nurse to keep him company and help control his drinking. Not long after he came to Asheville he went swimming with one such nurse, who happened to be young and pretty, and trying to impress her with a swan dive, he fractured his shoulder and ended up in a plaster cast with his right arm high above his head in a Nazi salute. The cast itched unbearably in the hot weather, but the fracture was healing when late one night he tripped and fell in the bathroom. Lying helpless on the tile floor, he developed a form of arthritis which set him back another five weeks.

All this time he was trying to write, or rather, dictate. The response to his 'Crack-Up' pieces had at least given him the feeling of being read again. Two publishers, hoping for a more complete *exposé*, had sounded him out on the possibility of a book, but his literary friends felt he had made a mistake to let down his guard as much as he had. 'Christ, man,' wrote John Dos Passos, 'how do you find time in the middle of the general conflagration to write about all that stuff. ... We're living in one of the damnedest tragic moments in history – if you want to go to pieces I think it's absolutely O.K. but I think you ought to write a first rate novel about it (and you probably will) instead of spilling it in little pieces ...'

This was fair enough. It was only Hemingway's reaction that caught Fitzgerald off guard.

Since the exchange over *Tender Is the Night* their relations had continued strained, though Hemingway conceded that the novel got better in retrospect. Fitzgerald told Perkins he would always consider his friendship with Hemingway 'one of the high spots of life. But I still believe that such things have a mortality, perhaps in reaction to their very excessive life, and that we will never again see very much of each other.' Fitzgerald thought Hemingway's latest book, *Green Hills of Africa*, his weakest. When he wrote

Hemingway to that effect, the latter replied that he was glad to see by Fitzgerald's comments that he did not know any more about when a book was good and what made it bad than ever. Then Hemingway slipped into the old kidding vein. He was living in Key West and wanted Fitzgerald to go to Cuba with him and see the next revolution. He told Fitzgerald to come down any time and they'd go over in Hemingway's boat and get a good story out of it.

If you really feel blue enough get yourself heavily insured and I'll see you can get killed. . . . I'll write a fine obituary that Malcolm Cowley will cut the best parts out of for the new republic and we can take your liver out and give it to the Princeton Museum, your heart to the Plaza Hotel, one lung to Max Perkins and the other to George Horace Lorimer [editor of the *Post*]. . . . We will get MacLeish to write a Mystic Poem to be read at that Catholic School (Newman?) you went to. Would you like me to write a mystic poem now? Let's see . . .

Fitzgerald's attitude towards Hemingway was resignation tinged with jealousy. They had been in a race, and it seemed that Hemingway had won. If Fitzgerald had carried more sail, Hemingway had more keel to him, more ballast. Remembering the early days, Fitzgerald thought Hemingway a little lean on gratitude, but he half expected it in a man of Hemingway's pride and independence. The previous summer, when Laura Guthrie had asked Fitzgerald why he never heard from his friend Hemingway, Fitzgerald replied, 'I thought the world was one way, and he said it was another, so we split.'[46]

Hemingway's attitude towards Fitzgerald was a mixture of condescension and scorn. People who knew him at this time remember him saying that Fitzgerald was 'a rummy', that he was washed up, that he had 'gone social' and hung around the rich. 'The Crack-Up' merely confirmed this view. On reading the first instalment, Hemingway wrote Perkins that it was so miserable – this whining in public. A writer could be a coward but at least he should be a writer. Fitzgerald had gone from youth to senility without manhood in between.

Nevertheless, it made Hemingway feel badly and he wished he could help.

His method of doing so, after two more instalments of 'The Crack-Up', was curious indeed. In his short story 'The Snows of Kilimanjaro', published in August 1936, he had the hero musing

The rich were dull and they drank too much, or they played too much backgammon. They were dull and they were repetitious. He remembered poor Scott Fitzgerald and his romantic awe of them and how he had started a story once that began, 'The very rich are different from you and me.' And how someone had said to Scott, Yes, they have more money. But that was not humour to Scott. He thought they were a special glamorous race and when he found they weren't it wrecked him just as much as any other thing that wrecked him.

Fitzgerald was stunned by this public laying of a wreath on his career – gratuitous also, for there was no need to bring real names into fiction. There was, of course, the traditional right of authors, older than the Elizabethan pamphlet war, to tear each other to pieces, but Fitzgerald's printed references to Hemingway had been nothing but praise. According to James Fain, a young newspaper man who was seeing Fitzgerald at the time, 'Hemingway would have done better to hit him over the head with a bat – you have no idea how that man could be hurt.'

Fitzgerald described the sequel in a letter to Perkins.

I wrote Ernest about that story of his asking him in the most measured terms not to use my name in future pieces of fiction. He wrote me back a crazy letter, telling me about what a great Writer he was and how much he loved his children, but yielding the point – 'If I should outlive him' – which he doubted. To have answered it would have been like fooling with a lit firecracker. Somehow I love that man, no matter what he says or does, but just one more crack and I think I would have to throw my weight with the gang and lay him. No one could ever hurt him in his first books, but he has completely lost his head and the duller he gets about it, the more he is like a punch-drunk pug fighting himself in the movies.

In subsequent printings of 'The Snows of Kilimanjaro', 'Scott Fitzgerald' became 'Julian'. Perkins sided with Fitzgerald, he said he resented what Hemingway had done, but some months later he wrote Fitzgerald that Hemingway's intentions had perhaps been kinder than Fitzgerald realized. Hemingway had wanted to give Fitzgerald a 'jolt' that would be good for him. 'Thanks for the word about Ernest,' Fitzgerald replied. 'Methinks he does protest too much.'

By then Fitzgerald had suffered a worse humiliation, for weakness invites betrayal. The editor of the *New York Post*, having read 'The Crack-Up', thought a sensational story might be written about Fitzgerald's fortieth birthday. Was he really a 'cracked plate' beyond repair? Would he soon be jumping out the window? These were the questions a reporter named Michael Mok was sent to answer.

After preliminary scouting around Baltimore, Mok trailed Fitzgerald to Asheville. Fitzgerald's drinking had grown steadily worse during his confinement in the plaster cast, and he was in no condition to be interviewed, but Mok said he had come all the way from New York and expressed admiration for Fitzgerald's writing. Inviting Mok to his room, Fitzgerald received him wearing a tan suit and a soft green tie. He was boyish, keen, polite, but pale and unwell, and the nurse was giving him injections. Mok stayed several hours, and Fitzgerald thought the occasion had gone pleasantly enough until he read the results in the *New York Post*.

'The poet-prophet of the post-war neurotics,' said the front-page article,

observed his fortieth birthday yesterday in his bedroom in the Grove Park Inn here. He spent the day as he spends all his days – trying to come back from the other side of Paradise, the hell of despondency in which he has writhed for the last couple of years . . .

Physically he was suffering the aftermath of an accident eight weeks ago when he broke his right shoulder in a dive from a fifteen-foot springboard. But whatever pain the fracture might still cause him, it did not account for his jittery jumping off and onto his bed, his restless pacing, his trembling hands, his twitching face with its pitiful expression of a cruelly beaten child. Nor could it be held responsible for his frequent trips to a highboy, in a drawer of which lay a bottle. Each time he poured a drink into the measuring glass beside his table, he would look appealingly at the nurse and ask, 'Just one ounce?'

The lengthy article concluded with Fitzgerald's *résumé of* his own generation.

' "Some became brokers and threw themselves out of windows. Others became bankers and shot themselves. Still others became newspaper reporters. And a few became successful authors." His face twitched. "Successful authors!" he cried. "Oh, my God, successful authors!" '

After reading the story, Fitzgerald attempted suicide. He swallowed the contents of a phial of morphine, but the overdose made him vomit, and later he felt like a fool when the nurse came in and discovered what he had done. Gradually anger and despair gave way to shame. He had touched bottom. Mok's article rallied his self-respect and laid the foundation for a comeback of sorts.

Meanwhile his finances were at a low ebb. Ill and depressed, he was only capable of the sketches and slight stories which *Esquire* – then a young, struggling magazine – bought for $250–$350 apiece. He owed thousands each to Ober and Scribners and had borrowed to the limit on his life insurance. Early in September his mother had died, leaving an estate of $42,000 to be divided between him and his sister, though after Fitzgerald had repaid the sums his mother had lent him, his share was only $17,000. During the six months it took to settle the estate, Oscar Kalman came to his rescue with a sizeable loan.

His adolescent revolt against his mother had softened a little towards the end. He still spoke of her as an 'old peasant', and described her 'majestically dipping her sleeves in the coffee', but she had a dignity withal – 'a shabby grandom', as one of her husband's relatives put it – and perhaps Fitzgerald realized that his vitality came from her. There was something of the soil about her, something unconscious and intuitive that had a good deal more to do with his creativity than his father's tired refinement. All the time Fitzgerald had been living in Baltimore, his mother was in Washington, and in June, when she had a stroke and he transferred her to the hospital, the tragedy of her life came over him in a rush.

'It was sad,' he wrote his sister,

taking [Mother] from the Hotel, the only home she knew for fifteen years, to die – and to go thru her things, the slippers and corset she was married in, Louisa's dolls in tissue paper [Louisa was one of the two daughters who had died before Fitzgerald was born], old letters and souvenirs, and collected scrap paper, and diaries that began and got nowhere, all her prides and sorrows and disappointments come to nothing and her lugged away like so much useless flesh the world had got thru with.

Mother and I never had anything in common except a relentless stubborn quality, but when I saw all this it turned me inside out realizing how unhappy her temperament made her and how she clung to the end to all things that would remind her of moments of snatched happiness. So I couldn't bear to throw out anything, even that rug, and it all goes to storage.

Fitzgerald's secretary that summer of 1936 remembered his frenzied efforts to write amid fears his talent had deserted him. She remembered the trouble the nurse had getting him to eat, and she remembered coming into his darkened room when he was lying on the bed and saying, 'Scott, what is going to become of you?' Staring at the ceiling, he answered quietly, 'God knows.' He wasn't devoid of self-pity, yet he viewed his life with detachment and blamed himself for his plight.

Thinking it might cheer him to meet an admirer, Perkins asked Marjorie Kinnan Rawlings, then in Fitzgerald's vicinity working on *The Yearling*, to look him up. When she lunched with him in his room the end of October, he was still in bed, plagued with arthritis, but she was able to send Perkins an optimistic report.

Max, we had a perfectly delightful time. Far from being depressing, I enjoyed him thoroughly, and I'm sure he enjoyed it as much. He was nervous as a cat, but had not been drinking – had had his nurse put his liquor away. We had only sherry and a table wine, and talked our heads off. His reaction to the NY Post story had been to go to New York and kill ... Mok, until he decided that would be a silly gesture with one arm disabled. He was terribly hurt about it, of course, for he had listened to a sob story from Mok, to let him in at all, and had responded to a lot of things the man had told him – possibly spurious – about his own maladjusted wife, by talking more freely than he should have done. But he has taken the thing very gracefully and is not unduly bitter or upset about it. He was also more forgiving and reasonable than I think I should have been, about Hemingway's unnecessary crack at him in the Snows of Kilimanjaro. We agreed that it was part of Hemingway's own sadistic maladjustment, which makes him go around knocking people down. Scott said that Hemingway had written him very violently damning him for his revealing self-searchings in Esquire, and Scott expressed the idea that it was just as legitimate to get one's grievances off one's chest that way, as by giving an upper-cut to some harmless weakling. He resented Hemingway's calling him 'ruined', and from other things he said, it was plain to me that he does not consider himself 'ruined' by a long shot ...

His point of view lets him in for much desperate unhappiness and disillusion, because he simply cannot expect the consistent perfection and magnificence of life that he does, frankly, expect. But as a writer, except for the times such as this one has been, when his misery holds him up too long, his masochisms will not interfere with his work. ... I do not think you need to worry about him, physically or psychologically. He has thrown himself on the floor and shrieked himself black in the face and pounded his heels – as lots of us do in one way or another – but when it's over he'll go back to his building blocks again.

Through it all Scottie had been a reason to keep struggling. 'Seeing her,' Fitzgerald wrote Oscar Kalman, 'you will see how much I still have to live for.' Now in her first year at Ethel Walker's, she was showing a literary bent which Fitzgerald tried to discourage by stressing the scientific subjects which were hard for her. If she became a writer – which he hoped she wouldn't – he wanted it to happen against the grain, rather than as the result of a fundamentally literary training.

During the Christmas holidays he gave her a dance in Baltimore. It was an afternoon affair at the Belvedere Hotel, and Fitzgerald had been terribly earnest about working out the plans with my mother and two other hostesses, though he teased Scottie in a letter,

I am determined to have a hurdy gurdy for the orchestra – you know, an Italian with a monkey, and I think the children will be very content with that. They don't want much, children of sixteen or seventeen, and they will be amused by the antics of the monkey. Your idea of a swing orchestra seems zero to me. However, in the next room I will have some of the older people with a swing orchestra I have engaged, and from time to time you may bring some of your choice friends in there to dance.

Fitzgerald was sober when the occasion began, but soon he was making trips to the bar, and those who realized what was happening tried to pretend he wasn't there. Not that he grew loud or angry; he was just bleary-eyed, tottering and silly, and to make matters worse he insisted on dancing with some of the girls, who looked scared or embarrassed, while the others giggled behind his back.

Before the holidays ended, he was in the hospital where he finally came to his senses. He must have hated himself for humiliating Scottie before her friends, and the past year had been his least productive since 1926 when he was squandering the proceeds of the *Gatsby* movie rights on the Riviera. He was tired of slinking through life and wanted to face the world again, but to get a job in Hollywood, which now seemed the only way of paying his steadily accumulating debts, he would have to stay sober. With the help of a doctor in Tryon, where he spent the winter and spring of 1937, he made a supreme effort and managed to stop drinking altogether.

Treading water until Ober could negotiate a Hollywood contract, he lived quietly in a top-floor room at the Oak Hall Hotel. Once more he was seeing a good deal of the Flynns, who had recently built a house in the hunting country north of Tryon. There was honeysuckle along the drive where they strolled after dinner, and dogwood, lilac, jasmine, and wisteria all about, and an awesome view of the Smokies through the picture window. At the Flynns' parties Fitzgerald was polite but withdrawn. He was more his old self in Misseldine's drug store down the hill from his hotel, where he and the Flynns and a few others often gossiped over milkshakes and cups of coffee. One day Fitzgerald dashed off a lyric on a paper napkin, which became thereafter a kind of theme song that they harmonized to the melody of 'O Tannenbaum'.

> Oh Misseldines, dear Misseldines,
> A dive we'll ne'er forget,
> The taste of its banana splits
> Is on our tonsils yet.
>
> It's chocolate fudge makes livers budge,
> It's really too divine,
> And as we reel, we'll give one squeal
> For dear old Misseldines.

Struthers Burt, whom Fitzgerald had presented with the first copy of *This Side of Paradise*, remembered a glimpse of him that spring.

My wife and I were having supper on the terrace . . . and Scott, totally unexpected, came in through the twilight as quiet as a moth. We sat late on the terrace talking, and a moon came up, and the dogwoods were like white cascading water, and there were even whippoorwills. . . . My wife and I were astonished. Scott wasn't drinking and he was sweet, and reasonable, and earnest, although still amusing.

Fitzgerald had begun to see his crack-up in perspective. He had gone into the romantic sickness anatomized in *Tender Is the Night* and come out the other side. 'My life looked like a hopeless mess there for awhile,' he wrote Oscar Kalman, 'and the point was I didn't *want* it to be better. I had completely ceased to give a good God damn.' He put on seventeen pounds and felt his strength returning, yet he seemed unable to write a saleable story and had begun to fear that his drinking had ruined his chances in Hollywood, when Ober got him a six-month contract with MGM at $1,000 a week, and the future opened out again.

[16]

THE MGM story editor who hired Fitzgerald in New York was surprised at the change in him. Instead of the fiery youth remembered from the twenties, here was this shy, evasive man with a limp handshake. The light had gone out of him, he seemed depolarized, but the story editor felt that what an author had once done he could do again in the right circumstances, and that if Fitzgerald came through, the results would more than justify the risk of hiring him. For Fitzgerald, the contract was the lifting of a great weight. A few months earlier his debts had totalled $40,000 – some of it cancelled by his mother's legacy – but he still owed Ober $12,500 and almost as much again to Scribners, if one included his private debt to Perkins. Keeping $400 a week for his, Scottie's, and Zelda's expenses, he arranged to have the remaining $600 sent to Ober towards discharging his various obligations.

No one took more delight than Fitzgerald in planning, in contemplating new possibilities, and though his dislike of Hollywood on two previous visits had made him swear never to return, he approached it now with a certain *élan*. In 'The Crack-Up' he had mourned that 'the novel, which at my maturity was the strongest and supplest medium for conveying thought and emotion from one human being to another,' was becoming subordinated to the mechanical and communal art of the movies, but rolling west on the train early in July, he plotted how he would conquer this insurgent technique. Tactful but resolute, he would win the confidence of the key man among the bosses and ask for the most malleable of the collaborators so that, in effect, he would be alone on the picture – the condition for doing his best work. He also planned to rise early and devote his freshest hours to his own writing, but this turned out to be a pipe dream. Despite six months on the wagon, his health and energy hadn't fully returned, and to get through a day at the studio he needed the stimulus of innumerable cokes.

He settled in at the Garden of Allah Hotel on Sunset Boulevard, then a favourite haunt of screen writers. Once the residence of the actress Alla Nazimova, it had a swimming pool built in the shape of the Black Sea to remind her of her native Yalta. Taking an apartment in one of the two-storey bungalows out back, Fitzgerald tackled his job with a conscientiousness he hadn't shown for a long while. He kept a file of the plot-lines of pictures, just as he had once diagrammed scores of *Post* stories when he was learning to write for them. He read 'How-to-do-it' books and grilled his colleagues at Metro. 'Don't worry about a fade-in, a wipe, a dissolve,' they told him. 'The cutters and directors will take care of that. Go ahead and write your story. Write what's in your guts.'

But Fitzgerald had to know. He approached the medium with refreshing humility. He was sober, reliable, 'grown-up' at last – though one couldn't help regretting certain aspects of the man he had been. Dropping into the office of a fellow writer, he would say after a few minutes, 'You don't want to talk to me, do you? I'm boring you, aren't I? Hadn't I better leave?' The old confidence and dynamism were gone. Fitzgerald seemed like some mild-mannered clerk – sweet, gentle, amiable, but devoid of temperament or bite, as if he had been erased.

The playwright Edwin Justus Mayer, who shared his bungalow at the Garden of Allah, thought how different it had been when they met in 1923. Mayer, whose first book had failed ignominiously, was sitting in the office of his publisher, Horace Liveright, when a blond, spruce young man brushed past the receptionist and entered the room talking volubly. With his boater perched on the back of his head, he had the assurance of someone who is welcome anywhere. He was light, airy, golden with talent, and as Mayer said later, 'so successful he made me feel dirty'.

Fitzgerald had been in Hollywood less than a week when he met the girl who would sustain him for the rest of his life. An attractive blonde, Sheilah Graham had spent most of her twenty-eight years getting away from the pinch and poverty of her childhood. She had been born Lily Sheil in a London tenement. Her father died when she was a baby, and she and her mother had shared a basement room with a woman who took in washing. Her earliest memory was the stinging smell of laundry soap, blended with that of boiled potatoes on which they largely subsisted. At six she was sent to an orphanage, returning at fourteen to care for her mother who had been operated on for cancer and who died a few years later. Sheilah worked as a maid and a salesgirl, and when she was seventeen married an unsuccessful business man of forty-two who let her do as she pleased. She became one of Charles Cochran's Young Ladies – the equivalent of a Ziegfeld Girl – but restless and searching, she drifted into journalism and went to America, where she got the job of Hollywood columnist for the North American Newspaper Alliance. By now a divorcée, she was engaged to the Marquis of Donegall who wrote a society column for a London daily. The engagement lapsed soon after she met Fitzgerald.

They were a curious pair – the broken novelist and the ambitious girl from the slums. Sheilah was fickle, and in a sense Fitzgerald was fortunate to have been loved by anyone so vital and alluring. In his present state of frailty and eclipse, his choice was not unlimited, but he held her absolutely with a charm, a tenderness, and an understanding that she hadn't known to exist. She had invented a story about her origins that included a family background in Chelsea, a finishing school in Paris, and presentation at court by a rich aunt. When the story broke down under Fitzgerald's relentless questioning, she feared she had lost him, but instead he was touched. He said he wished he had known her in her early days so he could have taken care of her.

Their liaison soon had a settled, comfortable air. They kept to themselves, and when they went to parties Fitzgerald stayed in the background, quietly observing. Sheilah wasn't an intellectual, her tempo was quite different from that of the wits and writers he was used to consorting with, but he was tired and glad not to make an effort. He sparkled one evening when Thomas Mann was in the company; Fitzgerald talked delightfully, lifting the whole room, and gave the impression of knowing more about Mann's writing than Mann did. But mostly he stood apart, the fact that he no longer drank having something to do with it. Sheilah didn't drink either, and when Fitzgerald went on a binge after they had been together several months, she was horrified but made up her mind to fight his alcoholism. Her influence in this regard may well have prolonged his life.

By October the first excitement of the studio had worn off, and Fitzgerald was telling Ober he wished he could do an original script to 'exercise the intellectual muscles in a more amplified manner'. After working several weeks on *A Yank at Oxford*, he had been switched to a Remarque war novel, *Three Comrades*. He liked the material but disliked the interminable story conferences where, as he once said, 'personality was worn down to the inevitable low gear of collaboration'. His co-writer, Ted Paramore, was another frustration. According to Fitzgerald Paramore was still turning out 'Owen Wister dialogue' – putting such expressions as 'Consarn it!' in the mouth of a German sergeant.

But when Fitzgerald heard that the job would earn him a screen credit, his morale picked up and just before Christmas he wrote Mrs Harold Ober,

I love it here. It's nice work if you can get it and you can get it if you try about three years. The point is once you've got it – Screen Credit 1st, a Hit 2nd, and the Academy Award 3rd – you can count on it forever . . . and know there's one place you'll be fed without being asked to even wash the dishes. But till we get those three accolades we Hollywood boys keep trying. That's cynical but I'm not a bit cynical. I'm delighted with screen credit and really hopeful of a hit.

The future looked even brighter when Metro took up his option for a year's renewal of contract at $1,250 a week, but in January producer Joe Manckiewicz rewrote the script of *Three Comrades* so that very few of Fitzgerald's words remained. Though Manckiewicz liked the way Fitzgerald had brought the characters to life against their background, he found Fitzgerald's dialogue too flowery and redundant – the work of a novelist rather than a scenarist. Fitzgerald's touches of magic also seemed irrelevant. For example, when one of the three comrades phoned his sweetheart, an angel was supposed to plug in the connection at the hotel switchboard. 'How do you film *that*?' someone asked drily.

Fitzgerald was crushed by what he considered the mutilation of an honest and delicate script, for it wasn't his nature to write tongue in cheek. '37 pages mine,' he scrawled on Manckiewicz's version, 'about ⅓, but all shadows and rhythm removed.' 'To say I'm disillusioned,' he wrote Manckiewicz,

is putting it mildly. For nineteen years I've written best selling entertainment, and my dialogue is supposedly right up at the top. ... You *had* something and you have arbitrarily and carelessly torn it to pieces. ... I am utterly miserable at seeing months of work and thought negated in one hasty week. I hope you're big enough to take this letter as it's meant – a desperate plea to put back the flower cart, the piano-moving, the balcony, the manicure girl – all those touches that were both natural and new. Oh Joe, can't producers ever be wrong? I'm a good writer – honest. I thought you were going to play fair.

Separated from Zelda by a continent, as well as a life she couldn't share, Fitzgerald went East periodically to take her on vacations – to Charleston in September, to Miami at Christmas. Her condition had stabilized to the point where it was thought she could visit her mother in Montgomery from time to time, and Fitzgerald almost dared to hope for the miracle of her being able to get along without him. 'Certainly,' he wrote her doctor,

the outworn pretence that we can ever come together again is better for being shed. There is simply too much of the past between us. When that mist falls – at a dinner table, or between two pillows – no knight errant can traverse its immense distance. The mainsprings are gone.

And if the aforesaid miracle should take place, I might again try to find a life of my own, as opposed to this casual existence of many rooms and many doors that are not mine. So long as she is helpless, I'd never leave her or ever let her sense that she was deserted.

The end of March Fitzgerald joined Scottie and Zelda at Virginia Beach. Under the strain he got drunk, and Zelda went up and down the hotel corridors convincing everyone he was a dangerous maniac. After this fiasco he decided his usefulness in the case was over. He wrote Zelda's doctor that he had

no desire ever again to personally undertake her supervision. That period has gone, and each time that I see her something happens to me that makes me the worst person for her rather than the best, but a part of me will always pity her with a sort of deep ache that is never absent from my mind for more than a few hours: an ache for the beautiful child that I loved and with whom I was happy as I never shall be again.

Back in Hollywood, Sheilah prevailed on Fitzgerald to take a house at Malibu Beach. For $200 a month – half of what he was paying at the Garden of Allah – he rented a green-shuttered 'cottage' with four bedrooms, a sunroom, a dining room, a captain's walk, and a small garden. He hired a coloured woman to keep house, and Sheilah spent as much time with him as her work permitted. She found to her dismay that he never went swimming and stayed out of the sun on principle, though in the late afternoons he might stroll up the beach, and he played a little ping-pong. In any case, the home life was good for him. He and Sheilah amused themselves by concocting rare dishes – say a crab soup and a chocolate soufflé – which Fitzgerald would eat in reverse order, for his appetite was finicky and exotic.

The crisis of the summer was a scrape Scottie got into at Ethel Walker's. She was constantly on her father's mind, and as her horizons enlarged, his advice had become more portentous. 'For premature adventure,' he had written her,

one pays an attrocious price. ... The girls who were what we
called 'Speeds' (in our stone-age slang) at sixteen were reduced to
anything they could get at the marrying time. It's in the logic of
life that no young person ever 'gets away with anything'. They
fool their parents but not their contemporaries. It was in the
cards that Ginevra King should get fired from Westover – also
that your mother should wear out young.

After graduation, when Scottie was staying on at Walker's
to prepare for college boards, she and another girl hitchiked
to New Haven to have dinner with two Yale students. They
were caught and asked to leave school, thus imperilling
Scottie's chances of getting into Vassar. Her father was beside himself. He wrote her a tirade, citing her mother who
had idled through life until she realized 'that work was dignity and the only dignity and tried to atone for it by working
herself but it was too late and she broke and is broken forever'. Fitzgerald said his job in Hollywood was the last tired
effort of a man who had once done something finer and better; there wasn't enough money, or call it energy, to carry
someone who was a dead weight. As punishment, he thought
of cancelling Scottie's summer abroad but decided in the end
to let her go.

When Vassar accepted her in July, Fitzgerald contained
his joy. He wrote Scottie that she might as well have a try at
it – at least till Christmas – to see whether she was honestly
interested in higher education. He wanted her to be a
scholar. He *didn't* want her dyeing her hair – 'You will
coarsen it and look like a full-fledged "lady buyer" before
you're 19.' If he heard of her taking a drink before she was
twenty, he would feel entitled to begin his last and greatest
non-stop binge. 'Thank God,' he wrote her, 'there are no
snobbish time-wasting clubs [at Vassar] – you will stand for
what you are.' He didn't mention the fact that Scottie would
be entering at sixteen. He took precocity for granted.

During Fitzgerald's second year in Hollywood his hopeful ambition turned to discontent. For someone who came there as he had, out of need, there was depression in the flat, drugstore sprawl of Los Angeles with its unnatural glaring sun. Around the studio the older writers treated him with respect, though some of the brash younger ones, who had mastered a technique comparable to making Panama hats under water, made him feel his unimportance. Hollywood was such an industrial town that not to be a power in the movies was to be unknown.

Running into a college classmate, Gordon McCormick, Fitzgerald said, 'I'm trying a great experiment – I'm trying to break into Hollywood.'

McCormick said he thought Fitzgerald would be in automatically with all he had done.

'No, it doesn't work that way,' said Fitzgerald. 'Sometimes I get it over to them, but sometimes it's mislaid. With all the red tape I don't know who has it. Other times I can't get going. I thought it would be so easy, but it's been a disappointment. It's so barren out here. I don't *feel* anything out here.'

In a letter to Perkins, Fitzgerald spoke of

this amazing business which has a way of whizzing you along at terrific speed and then letting you wait in a dispirited, half-cocked mood when you don't feel like undertaking anything else, while it makes up its mind. It is a strange conglomeration of a few excellent overtired men making the pictures, and as dismal a crowd of fakes and hacks at the bottom as you can imagine.

After *Three Comrades* Fitzgerald had worked on *Infidelity*, starring Joan Crawford (the title was changed to *Fidelity* in the hope of getting it past the censor). On hearing that Fitzgerald would be doing her next picture. Miss Crawford fixed him with her burning eyes and said, 'Write hard!' It wasn't easy, for as he explained to Gerald Murphy,

[Crawford] can't change her emotions in the middle of a scene without going through a sort of Jekyll and Hyde contortion of the face, so that when one wants to indicate that she is going from joy to sorrow, one must cut away and then cut back. Also, you can never give her such a stage direction as 'telling a lie', because if you did, she would practically give a representation of Benedict Arnold selling West Point to the British.

At the end of three months the picture was abandoned because of censorship difficulties.

Fitzgerald was transferred to *The Women*, then to *Madame Curie*, only to be taken off the latter when he disagreed with everyone on how it should be done. His final job at Metro was revision on *Gone With the Wind*. After reading the novel he declared it 'good' but 'not very original, in fact leaning heavily on the Old Wives' Tale, Vanity Fair, and all that has been written on the Civil War. There are no new characters, new techniques, new observations – none of the elements that make literature – especially no new examination into human emotions. But on the other hand it is interesting, surprisingly honest, consistent and workmanlike throughout, and I felt no contempt for it but only a certain pity for those who considered it the supreme achievement of the human mind.' In writing the script Fitzgerald was told to use Margaret Mitchell's own words, and it angered him to have to thumb through the book as though it were Scripture, checking the phrases that suited his purpose.

He had worked hard all year and was deeply hurt when Metro failed to renew his contract, though in a letter to Ober he sounded relieved. 'Baby, am I glad to get out!' he said. 'I've hated the place ever since [Manckiewicz] rewrote 3 Comrades.' He told Perkins that it was morally destructive to work on a factory basis, faced with the paradox 'We brought you here for your individuality but while you're here we insist that you do everything to conceal it.' Though the conception of a novel was stirring in him, he would have to freelance in pictures until he had laid by sufficient funds. Meanwhile, he hoped to improve his position with another screen credit, not having gotten one since *Three Comrades*.

He found a job almost at once. Early in February 1939,

Walter Wanger hired him to collaborate with Budd Schulberg on a screen play to be set against the background of the Dartmouth Winter Carnival. Several years out of Dartmouth, Schulberg was to supply the local colour while Fitzgerald was counted on for the mature love story Wanger had in mind. After preliminary conferences, during which the collaborators got to know each other at the expense of their script, Wanger ordered them to the Winter Carnival where a camera crew was shooting background material.

In recent weeks Fitzgerald had been sweating and running a temperature. He feared a recurrence of TB and tried to get out of the trip but Wanger insisted. Sheilah Graham was so apprehensive that she flew East with him and waited in New York while he went on to Dartmouth. During the plane ride he sat with Schulberg, whose father had presented them with two bottles of champagne at the airport, and as soon as they were airborne, Schulberg persuaded Fitzgerald to join him in a toast – the start of a binge that would land Fitzgerald in the hospital a week later.

Fitzgerald's colleagues on the film at Dartmouth remembered his haggard illness more than his misconduct. They felt sorry for him and looked after him as best they could. He was incoherent at a faculty reception and made a spectacle of himself falling down in the snow, but he also had a dignity that wasn't to be tampered with. One of the crew members gave a small party at which some of the professors undertook to criticize the script. Knowing it was weak, the movie team welcomed advice, but the professors dissected it with a pettiness that showed their limitations. Sunk in his chair, Fitzgerald waved his hand now and then, mumbling, 'Lotta nonsense'. Finally he rose and said, 'You know, I'd love to be a professor in a university like this with all the security and the smug niceties, instead of having to put up with the things we have to put up with out there in the world. I bid you good night, gentlemen.'

Then the professors said wasn't it too bad that after such a brilliant start Fitzgerald should turn into a stumbling drunk, wasting his time on trash. 'He walked out of here on his own feet, didn't he?' said one of the cameramen. 'He knows more than any of you will ever know.'

Because someone had neglected to make reservations, Schulberg and Fitzgerald shared a servant's room in the attic of the Hanover Inn. (Fitzgerald thought it symbolic of the writer's rôle in Hollywood.) The only piece of furniture was a double-decker bed and lying in the lower berth Fitzgerald thought aloud:

You know, I used to have a beautiful talent once, Baby. It used to be a wonderful feeling to know it was there, and it isn't all gone yet. I think I have enough left to stretch out over two more novels. I may have to stretch it a little thin, so maybe they won't be as good as the best things I've done. But they won't be completely bad either, because nothing I ever write can be completely bad.

Publicly Fitzgerald was polite to Wanger, though in private he poured a year and a half's indignation with the movie industry into Schulberg's receptive ear. When Schulberg and Fitzgerald, at the end of a rowdy evening, ran into Wanger on the steps of the Hanover Inn, the producer lost patience and fired them. Schulberg accompanied Fitzgerald to New York where Sheilah Graham took over, and then, having made peace with Wanger, Schulberg went back to Dartmouth to complete the film.

Schulberg's brief association with Fitzgerald was complex and ambivalent. A husky, heavy-featured young man with a soft stammer that enlisted your sympathy, Budd was likeable and seemed usually in some agreement as he listened to you with his head down, toeing imaginary sand. Son of producer B. P. Schulberg, he was celebrity-conscious. He had been used to first-naming movie stars since he was a child, but it was literary celebrities he really looked up to and wanted to be in with. He was therefore flattered to be collaborating with Fitzgerald, the glamorous success of the twenties, whom he would like to have emulated and whom he had supposed dead.

But there was another side to it. Schulberg was an ambitious junior script writer hungry for credits that would push him up the Hollywood ladder. Since Fitzgerald had been assigned to *Winter Carnival* because Schulberg wasn't making a go of it alone, there was bound to be a touch of resentment on the part of the younger man. That resentment increased when Schulberg – albeit pained by Fitzgerald's drinking and impatient as it got more and more out of hand – found himself thrust into the rôle of Fitzgerald's chaperon and nurse. At bottom Schulberg couldn't help feeling a little superior to this derelict 'genius', who was not only making a fool of himself but compromising Schulberg's first big assignment.

Schulberg had already published stories in the national magazines, he was serious about writing, and this appealed to Fitzgerald, who also viewed him as a specimen of the young Marxist intellectual then very much in vogue. Schulberg had spent a summer in Russia, and while editing *The Dartmouth Daily* had caused a furore by championing a nearby quarry strike. He was thus a window on a generation which, in Fitzgerald's opinion, confused art with social consciousness. Another interesting thing about Schulberg was his inside knowledge of Hollywood, the setting of the new novel Fitzgerald had in mind. Sensing these *arrières pensées*, Schulberg could never be sure how much Fitzgerald liked him and how much he was simply using him as a source and a sounding board. It wasn't a clear friendship.

Now was the time of hospitals, nurses, night sweats, sedatives, and despair. Fitzgerald seemed to be slipping back into the morass of 1935–6. Half-crazed with worry and isolation, he was also blocked in his work, and 'a writer not writing,' he once remarked, 'is practically a maniac within himself.'

The previous autumn, when Malibu turned chilly, he had moved to Encino in the milder San Fernando Valley where, at a nominal $200 a month, he had rented a house on the Edward Everett Horton estate. There was a rolling lawn, a picket fence, a rose garden, magnolias, a swimming pool, but surroundings had ceased to mean much to Fitzgerald, who lived in the palace or the prison of his moods and thoughts. He had rightly guessed that after his performance at Dartmouth screen jobs would be more difficult to come by; nevertheless, in March and April he spent several weeks on a Madeleine Carroll–Fred MacMurray vehicle. Of this period he later wrote, 'I was going to sleep every night with a gradually increasing dose of chloral – three teaspoonfulls and two pills of nembutol every night and 45 drops of Digitalin to keep the heart working to the next day. Eventually one begins to feel like a character out of "Wizard of Oz".' At the same time he was trying to make gin a substitute for energy, and each week his secretary collected the bottles and disposed of them lest they be noticed in the rubbish.

The end of April, against his better judgement, he took Zelda to Cuba where he wandered into a cockfight and got beaten up for trying to stop it. From Cuba he went to New York where he was hospitalized, and returning to Encino, he spent the next two months in bed, x-rays having shown a lesion on one of his lungs. He was running a fever, which he dramatized in his letters when he wanted something, but his chief trouble was drink. He drank vindictively, as if he were trying to punish someone – himself, his mother, Zelda, Sheilah, the world – who knows? But still he kept writing, though what he composed might be little more than gibberish. In his worst periods there was always a slim thread pulling him back.

One night his damp pyjamas got twisted around him so he couldn't move his arms, and the doctor, hoping to scare him, pronounced it alcoholic paralysis. After that he took hold, his need for funds being an added spur. Though he had cancelled his debt to Ober, he still owed Scribners $7,000, and his medical expenses had been heavy. Pictures being out of the question because of his health, he began considering the high-priced magazine field where he had once been enthroned. After a two-year layoff he felt he should have some good short stories in him.

The middle of June he wired Ober for a $500 advance against a story he would shortly be mailing. Ober complied but said it would be hard on him and bad for Fitzgerald if they slipped back into the previous indebtedness. A month later, having sent Ober two stories that hadn't sold, Fitzgerald asked for another advance and Ober refused. Fitzgerald was stunned. It had been Ober's policy to lend him up to the probable yield of a completed story, and Fitzgerald couldn't bear the thought that after long association Ober should lose faith in him. 'I have been all too hauntingly aware during these months,' he wrote Ober,

of what you did from 1934 to 1937 to keep my head above water after the failure of *Tender*, Zelda's third collapse and the long illness. But you have made me sting none the less. ... If it is of any interest to you, I haven't had a drink in two months, but if I was full of champagne I couldn't be more confused about you than I am now.

Ober's affectionate concern for Scottie – he and his wife, Anne, were practically her adopted parents – made a rupture embarrassing, yet it seemed to Fitzgerald that Ober had turned disciplinarian. He wrote Perkins, who tried to heal the breach, that Ober was a single-tracked man and the feeling that he once had of definite interest combined with forgiveness of my sins, has changed to a sort of general disapproval and a vague sense that I am through – this in spite of the fact that I paid him over ten thousand dollars in commissions in the last year-and-a-half and returned the whole thirteen thousand that I owed him.

From now on Fitzgerald would be his own literary agent, dealing directly and none too successfully with the magazines. The truth was he had lost his touch for the commercial love story. 'I can't write them convincingly,' he said. 'It requires a certain ebullience about inessential and specious matters which I no longer possess. In August, and again in September, he picked up movie jobs that lasted only a week. 'I have been playing the grocer with short pieces for Esquire,' he wrote Zelda,

meanwhile trying to get the detachment from physical and mental worries which is necessary for a good short story. . . . I have many times wished that my work was of a mechanical sort that could be done or delegated irrespective of morale, for I don't want or expect happiness for myself – only enough peace to keep us all going.

It made him wistful to think of his contemporaries moving ahead in various fields. He had recently exchanged letters with John Biggs, now a federal judge. Biggs described his family life, his travels, his satisfaction with his work: in two years on the Third Circuit bench he had written 113 opinions, none of them reversed by the Supreme Court. 'I hope you'll be a better judge than I've been a man of letters,' Fitzgerald had replied, conscious that his own reputation had never been lower. It was fashionable now to consider him *passé*, buried with the foolishness of the twenties. Of his last volume of stories – his best – one reviewer had said, 'The children of all ages – from thirteen to thirty – who decorate Fitzgerald's pages seem as remote today as the Neanderthal man.' Nine of his books were in print, but no one was buying them (his total royalties for 1939 came to a little over $33), and the Modern Library edition of Gatsby would presently be dropped because it didn't sell. Thinking his name might even be a handicap, he published a piece in *Esquire* under a pseudonym to see if it improved the reception.

Two years before, when he had noticed in the paper that the Pasadena Playhouse was staging an adaptation of 'The Diamond as Big as the Ritz', he had decided to take Sheilah to the opening and make a celebration of it. He phoned the theatre, saying he was the author and asking them to reserve two seats. He rented a chauffeur-driven limousine which seemed more in keeping with the occasion than his second-hand Ford, and he and Sheilah, in evening clothes, dined at the Trocadero beforehand. When they reached the theatre, they were surprised to see no one entering. The lobby was deserted, and Fitzgerald thought he might have mistaken the date. He went off to inquire, coming back with the news that the students were giving the play in the upstairs hall. Though dashed, he was trying to be casual.

Upstairs the little hall with fifteen rows of wooden benches was empty too, but just before curtain time a few students came in – then a few women and girls in slacks and skirts. There were perhaps a dozen in the audience. After the performance, which Fitzgerald followed closely and stoutly applauded, he said, 'I'm going backstage – it might encourage them to know the author came to see them.' Rejoining Sheilah, he said they were 'nice kids – I told them they'd done a good job,' but driving back to Hollywood he was silent and depressed.

Such bitter experience lay back of the games he played with the occasional fan letter that trickled in. He wrote a Chicago dentist who asked for his photograph, 'I'm terribly sorry but I haven't had a picture taken for about twelve years. I think now that I shall wait until it's time for a death mask because I am in that unattractive middle-aged phase that doesn't seem safe to record for prosperity. (This is not a misprint).'

A lady who said she was making a study of his life and works got the following reply:

My dear Miss Feuerherm:

In regard to your letter about F. Scott Fitzgerald we refer you to the following:

'F. Scott Fitzgerald His Youth and Parentage' – C. B. Ansbrucher, Berlin. Privately printed.

'F. Scott Fitzgerald: The Image and the Man' – by Irene Kammer Thurston, Brentanos, 1937.

'Fitzgerald As I knew Him' – J. B. Carstairs. Scribners, 1928.

'F. Scott Fitzgerald and the Rise of Islam'. Harcourt, Brace and Howe, 1922.

'The Women Who Knew F. Scott Fitzgerald' – by Marie Comtesse de Segours. Editions Galentière, Paris.

I hope that these books will serve your purpose.

Sincerely yours,
J. P. Carms
Secretary

His pique showed through, however, when Arnold Gingrich's secretary asked for personalia to accompany a story in *Esquire*. 'Attached is some biographical data,' Fitzgerald replied.

Sorry I have no picture but I may say that out here I am known as the old 'oomph man'. So any haberdasher's advertisement will do as a portrait. Will you tell that so-called Mr Gingrich that I am accustomed, in my haughty way, to some word of approbation if not ecstasy about my contributions. Bland and chaste as your check was it somehow lacked emotion. However, we are accepting it.

Fitzgerald felt his rejection keenly. '... to die so completely and unjustly,' he wrote Perkins, 'after having given so much. Even now there is little published in American fiction that doesn't slightly bare my stamp – in a *small* way I was an original.' He had been pressing Scribners to bring out an omnibus volume of *Paradise, Gatsby,* and *Tender,* but Perkins thought they should wait until the past described in those books had acquired a romantic glamour. Meanwhile Fitzgerald's consolation was his new novel. By October 1939 he had done what he called 'the thinking according to my conscience' and accumulated sixty pages of outline and notes. 'Look!' he wrote Scottie. 'I have begun to write something that is maybe great, and I'm going to be absorbed in it four to six months. It may not make us a cent, but will pay expenses and it is the first labour of love I've undertaken since the first part of "Infidelity" ... Anyhow I am alive again.'[48]

Colliers had thought of serializing it. If they liked the first 15,000 words, they would pay Fitzgerald $30,000, in instalments, thus sparing him the necessity of doing hackwork. By the end of November he was so pinched that he sent *Colliers* the first 6,000 words, hoping for a small advance. When they asked to defer judgement until they had seen more, Fitzgerald sent the manuscript to the *Post*, 'THE COLLIERS BUSINESS WAS WISH FULFILLMENT ANYHOW,' he wired Perkins, 'AS I HAVEN'T SEEN A PIECE OF FICTION IN THERE FOR SEVERAL YEARS THAT WOULD SERVE THE PURPOSE OF A SEARS ROEBUCK CATALOGUE.' But the *Post* wouldn't commit themselves either. Meanwhile Perkins read it and said it was 'a beautiful start – stirring and new'. He sent Fitzgerald $250 out of his own pocket, adding that he would be able to spare $1,000 by 1 January. Fitzgerald immediately showered Perkins with drafts against the $1,000, until Perkins was obliged to remind him that he had helped all he could for the present.

Perkins' support had been crucial. Fitzgerald wrote him that he and one other man – Gerald Murphy – had been friends through every dark moment of the past five years (it was Murphy who had lent Fitzgerald the money to send Scottie back to Vassar). Though Fitzgerald had seen the Murphys only a few times since their return to America in 1931, tragedy had deepened their intimacy. The Murphys' two sons had died, one of spinal meningitis and the other of tuberculosis, and Gerald told Scott that of all their acquaintance he alone seemed to understand what they had been through. 'You are the only friend to whom I can tell the blank truth of what I feel ...' wrote Murphy. 'I know now that what you said in *Tender Is the Night* is true. Only the invented part of our life – the unreal part – has had any scheme, any beauty. Life itself has stepped in now and blundered, scarred, and destroyed.'

The Murphys could also appreciate what Scott had been through with Zelda. 'I think of her face so often,' Sara wrote,

& so wish it had been *drawn* (not painted, drawn). It is rather like a young Indian's face, except for the smouldering eyes. At night, I remember if she was excited, they turned black – & impenetrable – but always full of impatience at – *something*, the world I think. She wasn't of it anyhow – not really. I loved her & felt a sympathetic vibration to her violence. But she *wasn't throttled* – you mustn't ever think she was – except by herself. She had an inward life & feelings that I don't suppose any one ever touched – not even you.

Meanwhile Sheilah was having a time of it. Her base was her Hollywood apartment, but she went to Encino several days a week to be with Fitzgerald. He depended on her, was jealous and possessive, while antagonizing her with his drinking. Once they tussled over a loaded gun, which Fitzgerald kept against prowlers and which she felt he shouldn't have. When her work took her away from Hollywood, his drinking increased with his loneliness. One night, unable to sleep, he sent for Gay Lloyd Smith, the coloured man who worked for him, and he and Gay stayed up till dawn, talking and putting golf balls on the rug.

The drinking grew worse in December after *Colliers* and the *Post* declined his manuscript. One evening Sheilah came in to find him entertaining two hobos, whom he had picked up when they were thumbing a ride on Ventura Boulevard. He had asked them to stay for dinner and was offering them some of his clothes, but Sheilah ordered them out of the house. As soon as they were gone, Fitzgerald flew into a rage. He threw a bowl of soup at the wall, he struck Sheilah, he kicked the nurse when she tried to interfere, he danced around the room chanting the name Sheilah was ashamed of, 'Lily Sheil! Lily Sheil! Lily Sheil!' He threatened to kill her, but while he was looking for the gun which she had hidden, she called the police.

Sheilah now made up her mind to break with him. When she wouldn't speak to him on the phone, he sent her threatening notes. 'Get out of town, Lily Sheil, or you'll be dead in 24 hours' – 'Leave town or your body will be found in Coldwater Canyon.' One day he slipped into her apartment and took back a silver fox jacket he had given her. It hardened her against him until letters began to arrive in a softer key – then a bouquet of roses – finally a phone call which she answered. When she saw him, he told her he was determined to stop drinking whether she went back to him or not. She went back to him.

'I am not a great man,' Fitzgerald wrote Scottie the spring of 1940, 'but sometimes I think the impersonal and objective quality of my talent and the sacrifices of it, in pieces, to preserve its essential value has some sort of epic grandeur.' His talent was his lifeline. He would speak of it with tears in his eyes, and when his sister Annabel had criticized some of his recent work, he had said, 'Don't tell me I can't write – it's like telling Cliff he can't fly.' (Annabel had married a naval aviator, Clifton Sprague, who later commanded the escort carrier group that turned back the Japanese Fleet in the Battle of the Philippine Sea.)

Part of Fitzgerald's difficulty had been finding a theme, for he was still a romantic at heart, albeit the ash end of one, and he needed a romantic hero. As he said in his notes, 'Show me a hero and I'll write you a tragedy.' At last he had found his hero in the legendary producer, Irving Thalberg – the frail, sickly son of an Alsatian-Jewish lace importer who had come to Hollywood in 1919 as the personal secretary of Carl Laemmle, president of Universal Pictures. When Laemmle went East, he left Thalberg behind as his liaison man, so that at the age of twenty Thalberg was assigning actors and directors and giving orders for the making of films as if he were head of a studio. When Fitzgerald met him eight years later, he had rocketed to production chief of MGM with a salary of $400,000. He was small, slender, and finely-made, with long-fingered sensitive hands of which he was proud.

With his hair combed in a pompadour and his dark, magnetic eyes and considerate mien, he seemed like some French youth *bien élevé*, though he was tough underneath. He ruthlessly pursued his goal of making pictures a little better than they had ever been made before, and his passion for creation was wedded to a romantic belief that money would buy anything. A perfectionist, he shot his films over and over, meanwhile taking a hand in every facet of their production. He was a benevolent autocrat who, with few exceptions, deferred to talent and encouraged differences of opinion, thereby winning the loyalty and affection of his subordinates.

Thalberg had dazzled Fitzgerald with 'his peculiar charm, his extraordinary good looks, his bountiful success, the tragic end of his great adventure.' Fitzgerald conceded it was Thalberg who 'inspired the best part of the character of Monroe Stahr [hero of *The Last Tycoon*] – though I have put in some things drawn from other men and inevitably much of myself'. Like Fitzgerald, Thalberg had been the gifted child; he was Christ in the Temple, with a scorn for what had been done before and a sure knowledge of how it should be done in the future. He was, moreover, the master of a medium with unprecedented power over men's minds; Napoleonic in his vigour, he had flourished like Napoleon at a time when it was still possible for one man to keep his hand on all the controls. Fitzgerald saw the struggle at MGM between Thalberg and Louis B. Mayer (the struggle between Stahr and Brady in *The Last Tycoon*) in terms of art versus money, quality versus quantity, the individualist versus the industrialist. In 1936, when Thalberg died at the age of thirty-seven, he left behind him a void such as Stahr was intended to leave at the end of *The Last Tycoon*. With Thalberg gone, a wag had said, working at MGM was like going to the Automat.

The novel Fitzgerald hoped to fashion from this material would be concentrated like *Gatsby*. On his way to Hollywood the summer of 1937 he had written a friend that his novels had alternated between being selective (*Paradise* and *Gatsby*) and blown up (*The Beautiful and Damned* and *Tender*). The latter two, he said, might profitably have been cut by one-fourth –

(of course they were cut that much but not enough.) In *This Side of Paradise* (in a crude way) & in *Gatsby* I selected the stuff to fit a given planned mood or 'hauntedness' or whatever you might call it, rejecting in advance in *Gatsby*, for instance, all the ordinary material for Long Island, big crooks, adultry theme, and always starting from the *small* focal point that impressed me – my own meeting with Arnold Rothstien for instance.

The novel Fitzgerald had in mind would be tragic. As far back as 1920, when he was giddy with success, he had written the president of Princeton that 'my view of life, President Hibben, is the view of [the] Theodore Driesers and the Joseph Conrads – that life is too strong and remorseless for the sons of men.' He was being a little dramatic perhaps, but experience had confirmed this opinion, so that in 1940 he would tell Scottie of

the thing that lies behind all great careers, from Shakespeare's to Abraham Lincoln's, and as far back as there are books to read – the sense that life is essentially a cheat and its conditions are those of defeat, and that the redeeming things are not 'happiness and pleasure' but the deeper satisfactions that come out of struggle.

Finally, his novel would say something fundamental about America, that fairy tale among nations. Fitzgerald saw our history as a great pageant and romance. 'I look out at it,' he said,

– and I think it is the most beautiful history in the world. It is the history of me and my people. And if I came here yesterday like Sheilah I should still think so. It is the history of all aspiration – not just the American dream but the human dream and if I came at the end of it that too is a place in the line of the pioneers.[49]

Monroe Stahr is the end product of this race of pioneers. 'Is this all America amounts to?' he seemed to be saying, and though the answer is 'Yes', he views his world with compassion.

For a long time Fitzgerald had looked younger than his years, but lately he had looked older. He seemed washed out, drained of vital energy, and his fine face, paling and losing some of its definition, had taken on an ascetic cast. There was a greyness about him, a dust of the attic, and a woman who met him now for the first time remarked that she had never seen a man with such dead hair. But his eyes were still alight in the tired body – whether soft and pliant with sympathy or summing you up with a hard, objectifying stare. Fitzgerald had lost little of his quick, absorptive interest in people and their doings.

He was just as courteous, too, in his attractively old-fashioned way, and he dressed with the same Brooks Brothers propriety, with even a touch of elegance; 'I have an idea he was careful about ties,' a friend of this period recalls. Yet he seemed transplanted, immaterial, archaic. He would ask questions about celebrities of the twenties as if they were still in the news, and much of the time he was cold and huddling – a psychic as well as a physical state. One evening at Encino, when he and Edwin Justus Mayer wandered out in the garden after dinner, Fitzgerald excused himself – to get a drink, Mayer thought – but he reappeared wearing a hat and coat, although there wasn't a trace of chill in the air. The gesture sent a chill through Mayer.

Fitzgerald played on his failure a little. One felt it in a gentle condescension he had, an exquisite consideration of others. Around Hollywood most people didn't know who he was, though if he were pointed out, there might be a flicker of interest at his once illustrious name. He was still someone in his own eyes, however. He had an essential dignity that wouldn't let you patronize or intrude. If you asked him whether he needed money, or if you sympathized about Zelda when he hadn't brought the subject up, he put you in your place.

Having learned the lessons of success and the deeper ones

of failure, he spoke with new authority. Whatever he may have been at the start, he was now the least superficial of men. He had not only grown up, he had grown way beyond the 'maturity' most people achieve in a safe, conventional existence, as any reader of his last letters to Scottie cannot fail to notice. Schooled by suffering – some self-inflicted, some not – he had attained a knowledge of himself and of the human condition that may truly be described as tragic.

Since *Tender Is the Night* he had pondered the art of the novel, while following the work of his contemporaries, and though he admired Faulkner, Thornton Wilder, and Erskine Caldwell, he still considered Wolfe and Hemingway the foremost contenders, their connexion with Max Perkins perhaps having something to do with it. Enthusiastic as he had been about Wolfe's first novel, he was critical of 'the gawky and profuse way' Wolfe handled his material in the second one. 'Tom's genius is gigantic, tremendous, immense in its prolific scope,' he had told Laura Guthrie, 'but he'll have to learn to cut down, choose, condense.' Fitzgerald wrote Perkins that Wolfe with his 'infinite power of delicacy and suggestion' had no right to 'glut people on whole meals of caviar.' A further shortcoming was a self-absorption which stood in the way of his understanding others. '. . . the lyrical value of Eugene Gant's love affair with the universe – is that going to last through a whole saga?' Fitzgerald asked Perkins, 'God, I wish he could discipline himself and really plan a novel.'

Such had been Fitzgerald's 'case' when he wrote Wolfe the summer of 1937. Fitzgerald told Wolfe he should cultivate the alter ego of a more conscious artist; the higher one's emotional pitch, the more it needed to be rarefied and controlled and thrown into relief. Flaubert in a novel of selected incident had left out the things which Zola presently came along and said, with the result that *Madame Bovary* was eternal while Zola already rocked with age. Wolfe fired back that *Tristram Shandy* was a great novel for an entirely different reason, 'because it *boils* and *pours* – for the *unselected* quality of its selection.' Great writers, he said, were 'putter-inners' as well as 'leaver-outers', and Shakespeare, Cervantes and Dostoevsky would be remembered for what they put in as long as Flaubert would be remembered for what he left out.

It was a temperamental difference that nothing could bridge, just as the crystalline destiny of Fitzgerald's best work lies at the opposite pole from Wolfe's loose, shambling eloquence. Nevertheless, Fitzgerald respected Wolfe's 'rich mind', his verbal felicity, his strength of emotion ('though a lot of it is maudlin and inaccurate'), and the few times he had criticized Wolfe in conversation he had felt badly afterwards 'for putting sharp weapons in the hands of his inferiors'. When Wolfe sickened and died in the fall of 1938, Fitzgerald wrote Perkins of

that great, pulsing, vital frame quiet at last. There is a great hush after him – perhaps even more than after the death of Ring who had been moribund so long. . . . The more valuable parts of Tom were the more lyrical parts or rather those moments when his lyricism was best combined with his powers of observation – those fine blends such as the trip up the Hudson in *Of Time and the River*.

As for the other master – Hemingway – Fitzgerald had caught a glimpse of him shortly after reaching Hollywood the summer of 1937. Hemingway had come out with a documentary of the Spanish Civil War for which he had written the narration, and Fitzgerald accompanied Lillian Hellman to a private showing at the home of Frederic March. Driving her there in his 1934 Ford coupé (he drove so slowly nowadays that people honked at him), Fitzgerald poured out the story of his break with Hemingway. With the air of a small boy put upon by an older one, he said he didn't want to see Ernest or speak to him.

He needn't have worried. That evening Hemingway was engrossed in his own affairs. Vigorously expansive, he grew angry at one point and dashed his glass in the fireplace. When he passed the hat for the Loyalist cause, movie stars began making out thousand-dollar cheques, and Fitzgerald felt very much excluded. Later, he wrote Perkins that Hemingway had come through 'like a whirlwind' and put Lubitsch, the great director, in his place by refusing to have his picture remade à la Hollywood. 'I feel he was in a state of nervous tensity,' said Fitzgerald, 'that there was something almost religious about it.' When Perkins wrote back describing some bad publicity Hemingway had gotten as the result of a scrap with Max Eastman in the Scribners office, Fitzgerald replied,

He [Hemingway] is living at present in a world so entirely his own that it is impossible to help him even if I felt close to him at the moment which I don't. I like him so much, though, that I wince when anything happens to him, and I feel rather personally ashamed that it has been possible for imbeciles to dig at him and hurt him.

Nevertheless, Fitzgerald had begun to notice cracks in the once impregnable façade. After 'The Snows of Kilimanjaro' incident he had said that Hemingway 'is quite as nervously broken down as I am but it manifests itself in different ways. His inclination is towards megalomania and mine towards melancholy.' In Fitzgerald's opinion, Hemingway was still rebelling against having been made to take cello lessons when growing up in Oak Park, Illinois. Fitzgerald also doubted whether one could write artistically about experience sought for the sake of writing about it, which Hemingway's experience had tended more and more to be. *For Whom the Bell Tolls* seemed to Fitzgerald a cut below Hemingway's best. He called it 'Ernest's *Tale of Two Cities* though the comparison isn't apt. I mean it is a thoroughly superficial book which has all the profundity of *Rebecca*.' It hadn't the

tensity or the freshness [or] the inspired poetic moments [of *A Farewell to Arms*]. But I imagine it would please the average type of reader, the mind who used to enjoy Sinclair Lewis, more than anything he has written. It is full of a lot of rounded adventures on the Huckleberry Finn order and of course it is highly intelligent and literate like everything he does.

Of the book's commercial success, Fitzgerald was patently jealous and said so in a letter to Hemingway. A Book-of-the-Month-Club selection, it had been sold to the movies for upwards of $100,000. 'Rather a long cry from his poor rooms over the saw mill in Paris,' Fitzgerald wrote Zelda. '. . . Do you remember how superior he used to be about mere sales?'

And yet, in the last analysis, Fitzgerald hesitated to stand in judgement on Hemingway who, like some force of nature, was a law unto himself. Familiar with his background, Fitzgerald understood how certain of his quirks and demons had been the result of circumstances, and Hemingway, the Byronic hero, would always magnetize Fitzgerald, who alluded to him far more than any other contemporary. 'People like Ernest and me were very sensitive once,' he wrote at this time, 'and saw so much that it agonized us to give pain. People like Ernest and me loved to make people very happy, caring desperately about their happiness. And then people like Ernest and me had reactions and punished people for being stupid, etc. etc. People like Ernest and me – '

Right up to the end Fitzgerald peppered his letters to Perkins with questions about Ernest: where was he? – what was he doing? – how did he feel about the war? And Hemingway, for all his condescension, sent Fitzgerald a copy of *For Whom the Bell Tolls* inscribed, 'To Scott with affection and esteem'. 'It's a fine novel, better than anybody else writing could do,' Fitzgerald wrote back, and signed himself 'With Old Affection'.

Among the notes for *The Last Tycoon* there is the following: 'This novel is for two people – S.F. [Scottie] at seventeen and E.W. [Edmund Wilson] at forty-five. It must please them both.' If there had been a coolness between Wilson and Fitzgerald, they were drawing closer at the end. For one thing Wilson, disillusioned with Stalinism, was emerging from his Marxist political phase and addressing himself once more to contemporary fiction, and for another, the new Fitzgerald, humbled and sobered, was somewhat easier for Wilson to take than the high-riding irresponsible of the twenties. The fall of 1938 Fitzgerald and Sheilah had spent a night at Wilson's home in Stamford, Connecticut, where he was living with his recent bride, Mary McCarthy. Wilson, with middle age, had taken on a brisk corpulence, a burgher-like solidity, and the domed forehead beneath his thinning auburn hair gave him somewhat the aspect of a judge. Rather like a sixth-former at the feet of his headmaster, Fitzgerald had listened while Wilson – with a brown, weigh-ing seriousness of the eye, an occasional challenging glare – held forth on Kafka and other topics that interested him. In conversation he didn't skip about like Fitzgerald but pursued one theme until he had exhausted it. Afterwards, Fitzgerald wrote Wilson that the evening 'meant more to me than it could possibly have meant to you', and Wilson replied that Fitzgerald mustn't spend the rest of his life in Hollywood – 'Everybody is waiting for your later period to begin.'

The ties between them had remained, as they were in the beginning, primarily literary. The man who blue-pencilled Fitzgerald's first efforts for the *Nassau Lit* was still a mentor. Fitzgerald equated Wilson's approval with literary immor-tality, for Wilson was a critic in the great tradition of a soul adventuring among masterpieces, and his judgements were backed by a wide, humane, negotiable learning. Wilson, on his side, had been interested in Fitzgerald as a writer whom he had helped to launch and in a way develop, by urging him towards hardness, objectivity, and a classic sense of form. Wilson had been impressed with Fitzgerald's growth, but if his pronouncements showed a sense of Fitzgerald's importance as an artist, they scarcely concealed an annoy-ance, a kind of superciliousness towards the man and his ro-mantic legend.

Indeed Wilson and Fitzgerald were so different that it is surprising they got along as well as they did. Wilson had found his vocation at fifteen, when he happened on Taine's *History of English Literature* in his father's library and be-came absorbed in the chapters on the poets and novelists he was then reading. His approach had remained to a large extent Tainean: tell me a man's background and origins and I'll tell you what he is and can do: *tel arbre, tel fruit*. Wilson's strength lay in logical analysis, in his ability to reason a problem through to plausible conclusions. He was a master of the literary case or argument, marshalling his evidence with the cogency of a legal brief and pushing his point across in persuasive, common-sense prose. Fitzgerald's mind and sensibility ran counter – towards the imaginative, the intuitive, the evocative, the inconsistent, the magical, even the mystical. He was a natural poet as Wilson was a natural critic.[50]

And yet in each there was a grain of the other which went a long way towards explaining their compatibility. While basically not a student or an intellectual Fitzgerald had been growing in that direction, and he envied Wilson the superb assurance of a mind that had always done its homework, so to speak. In a different way Fitzgerald had gotten under Wilson's skin, for Wilson had a wistful romantic side – his impulse to satirize Fitzgerald's romanticism springing from a disposition towards it. As a young man Wilson used to speak of his own Byronic trait, which no one seemed aware of, and he had been in love with Edna St Vincent Millay – one romantic lead on the stage of the twenties as Fitzgerald was the other. Wilson, in the beginning, had wanted to be a poet or a novelist or a dramatist, but while Fitzgerald was gallivanting around Princeton sopping up impressions and atmosphere, Wilson had been closeted with his books. The living scene had never been quite as real to him as the printed page on which he could bring his full intelligence to bear. Compared to Fitzgerald, he saw life a little coldly on the one hand and on the other a little indirectly through the veil of what he had read.[51, 52]

He was withal an admirable and in some ways an affecting character. His lofty impatience, the snappish Dr Johnson side he showed the world, covered a vein of kindness, loyalty, sympathy, and chivalry. As a lonely little boy he had learned conjuring tricks, and he was almost his best when putting on a performance for the neighbourhood children. His integrity, his refusal to be swayed by mere popular opinion, had been an object lesson to Fitzgerald. The sensitive, diffident youth, who had bucked Philistinism at Princeton, had remained true to something in himself through the intellectual cross-currents of two decades. If he had achieved less than he hoped, he had aimed high, trying his hand at every sort of literary production like a good eighteenth-century man of letters. He had a conscience, too, and when Fitzgerald died – when the difficult personality fell away from the monument of his work – Wilson immediately felt that Fitzgerald's contemporaries had done him less than justice. For all their divergences, Wilson and Fitzgerald had been born under the same star, they had blossomed in the same spring. 'I have felt Scott's death very much,' Wilson wrote Bishop, ' – the men who start out writing together write for one another more than they realize till somebody dies.'

Of the Princeton group, it was Bishop who understood Fitzgerald best and responded most deeply to his tragedy. When Fitzgerald was writing *Tender Is the Night* at La Paix, he had named Bishop his literary executor, should anything happen to him before the novel was finished. In a sense Bishop, too, had fallen short of his early promise. He had spent long periods rusticating abroad and his life now had a pastel quality. Recently he had offended Fitzgerald with an essay in *The Virginia Quarterly*. '[Bishop] reproached me with being a suck around the rich,' Fitzgerald wrote Wilson. 'I've had this before but nobody seems able to name these rich. I always thought my progress had been in the other direction – Tommy Hitchcock and the two Murphys are not a long list of rich friends for one who, unlike John, grew up among nothing else . . .'[53, 54]

But Bishop had seen into Fitzgerald's heart and anguish, and in his requiem for Fitzgerald he wrote:

> I have lived with you the hour of your humiliation.
> I have seen you turn upon the others in the night
> And of sad self-loathing
> Concealing nothing
> Heard you cry: *I am lost. But you are lower!*

And you had the right.
The damned do not so own to their damnation.

Because of the summer heat in Encino – also to economize and be near Sheilah on whom he depended more and more – Fitzgerald moved to Hollywood in May 1940. At $110 a month he rented an apartment a block from hers, and they shared the same maid and dined at each other's places on alternate nights. His only regular income came from *Esquire* for which he was doing the Pat Hobby stories – Hobby being a studio hack and a heel, about whom it was a consolation to write since his plight was always a little worse than Fitzgerald's. Luckily, an independent producer named Lester Cowan, having bought the rights to 'Babylon Revisited', now paid Fitzgerald $5,000 to do a script. Fitzgerald exulted in the work. Not only was 'Babylon Revisited' a favourite among his stories, it was about a man who gets a second chance. It was also about Scottie, one place where he felt he hadn't failed.

He wrote Zelda that Scottie was 'an awfully good girl in the broad fundamentals'. True, they squabbled when they were together for any length of time, as during her visits to Hollywood the past two summers, and he had to keep reminding her of their meagre finances ('Have paid Peck & Peck & Peck & Peck & Peck'). But for years she had been the lift in his life as he dragged himself towards uncongenial tasks, and through her career at Vassar he was reliving Princeton. Like him, she had enjoyed her first term so much that she went on probation. Like him, she wanted to write, and he was advising her as best he could in some of the most profound and moving letters he ever wrote. When she sold an essay to *Mademoiselle* in June 1939 he was jubilant until he read it. Scottie had criticized his generation for its lack of character and responsibility, and he rebuked her for 'riding on my shoulder and beating me over the head with a wooden spoon'. A few months later she redeemed herself by selling a sketch to *The New Yorker*. She also wrote and produced a musical comedy and founded a club called the OMGIM (Oh My God Its Monday) to perpetuate the idea – 'almost the same thing that Tarkington did in 1893 when he founded the Triangle at Princeton', crowed Fitzgerald. But immediately he was cautioning her not to waste her energies on amateur theatricals as he had. He was more concerned that she develop a literary style and hammered home the importance of poetry, 'the most concentrated form of style. . . . Anybody that can't read modern English prose by themselves is subnormal – and you know it. . . . The only sensible course for you at this moment is the one on *English Poetry – Blake to Keats* (English 241).'

Fitzgerald had been eager for Scottie to make her Baltimore debut 'just in case' – he never said in case of what – and he continually fretted over her summer plans. When she suggested New England summer stock, he wrote her, 'Honey, I might as well turn you over to the white slavers and do a thorough job of it.' The Vassar Employment Bureau was no solution either.

It would mean (quite selfishly) a worry for me, for I would have to come East and investigate the job. And though I appreciate the remorse and the intensity of purpose that inspired your five-and-dime suggestion, I assure you that Barbara Hutton is not going to let a rival in there. She kind of feels she owns it you know.

He was adamant that Scottie finish college before getting married, and then – while business seemed to absorb most of the attractive and energetic boys – he hoped life would throw her among lawyers or those going into politics or big-time journalism, as they led rather larger lives. But fundamentally all he cared was that she shouldn't marry someone who was 'too much a part of the crowd'.

The 'Babylon Revisited' script, though it wasn't produced, helped Fitzgerald's standing with the studios, and in September he successfully adapted an Emlyn Williams play for Darryl Zanuck. He knew in his heart, however, that he would never belong in Hollywood. The movies in their present state seemed to him 'nothing more nor less than an industry to manufacture children's wet goods', and he was constantly fighting producers about the way pictures ought to be done. As for Hollywood itself, he called it 'a dump ... A hideous town, pointed up by the insulting gardens of its rich, full of the human spirit at a new low of debasement.' 'It is,' he wrote Gerald Murphy,

... such a slack *soft* place – even its pleasures lacking the fierceness and excitement of Provence – that withdrawal is practically a condition of safety. ... Except for the stage-struck young girls people come here for negative reasons – all gold rushes are essentially negative – and the young girls soon join the vicious circle. ... Everywhere there is, after a moment, either corruption or indifference.[55]

But if Fitzgerald had failed in his ambition to conquer Hollywood, he wasn't going to let Hollywood drag him down. Engrossed in his novel, he wrote Scottie that he wished he had never relaxed or looked back but had said to himself after *Gatsby*: 'I've found my line – from now on this comes first. This is my immediate duty – without this I am nothing.' He and Sheila were each living in quiet seclusion. They shopped together in the supermarkets along Sunset Boulevard and lingered in Schwab's drugstore over magazines and malted milks. Sometimes they went to a preview in the evening, but mostly they stayed at home, reading and listening to music. Fitzgerald was helping her with a series of liberal arts courses he had mapped out for her – his version of what a college education should be. The war was an excitement; far from making everything seem unimportant Fitzgerald said it had created in him 'a rebirth of kinetic impulses'. He had prophesied the quick extinction of Britain, followed by Americans fighting Germans in the swamps of Brazil, but Sheilah said he didn't know the British, and he had to agree with her after the evacuation of Dunkirk. He had flashes of his old gaiety; inside the man there was still a boy who talked in football metaphor and danced an occasional jig. He and Sheilah were happier than they had ever been together, though sometimes, when she came on him unwares, she couldn't help noticing his lines of sadness and oppression.

His life was a fragmented thing: the novel; the paid labour for the movies and *Esquire*; Sheilah; the old sunken Eastern ties; Scottie and Zelda, with always the shadow of Zelda's illness. Fitzgerald had written of 'the voices fainter and fainter – How is Zelda, how is Zelda – tell us – how is Zelda.' She was well enough to visit her mother in Montgomery without a nurse, and he corresponded with her more than he ever had. But reading her letters to Sheilah, he would pause and say, 'You see, they don't quite add up – they're a little out of focus.' 'How strange,' he wrote Scottie, 'to have failed as a social creature – even criminals do not fail that way – they are the law's "Loyal Opposition", so to speak. But the insane are always mere guests on earth, eternal strangers carrying around broken decalogues that they cannot read.'

Ashen and frail, subject to recurring coughs and fevers, Fitzgerald was best off in his apartment where the wall was covered with charts, as it had been for *Tender Is the Night*, showing the movements of his characters and their histories. He wrote Zelda that it would be 'a *constructed* novel like *Gatsby*, with passages of poetic prose when it fits the action, but no ruminations or sideshows like *Tender*. Everything must contribute to the dramatic movement.' He remarked how odd it was that his talent for the short story should have vanished. 'It was partly that times changed, editors changed, but part of it was tied up somehow with you and me – the happy ending.' On 2 November he wrote that the novel was 'hard as pulling teeth but that is because it is in its early character-planting phase. I feel people so less intently than I did once that this is harder. It means welding together hundreds of stray impressions and incidents to form the fabric of entire personalities.' He spoke of 'digging it out of myself like uranium – one ounce to the cubic ton of rejected ideas. It is a novel *à la Flaubert* without "ideas" but only people moved singly and in mass through what I hope are authentic moods.'

Since Dartmouth, Fitzgerald had been slightly in touch

with Budd Schulberg who by now had finished a first novel, *What Makes Sammy Run?* Fitzgerald was never one to underrate competition. When he heard that Schulberg was also writing about Hollywood, he was concerned – though in another way he wished Schulberg well and hoped his book would be good. When he read it, however, he laid it aside with a little half-smile, saying the novel on Hollywood had yet to be written. It wasn't the exaltation he got from a piece of writing he really admired. 'Bud Schulberg, a very nice, clever kid out here is publishing a Hollywood novel with Random House in January,' Fitzgerald wrote Perkins. 'It's not bad but it doesn't cut into my material at all.' Ever generous and encouraging to tyros, he was only too glad to send Schulberg's publisher a complimentary letter to be used as a blurb. But in his notebook he put, 'Bud, the untalented'.[56]

The French have a saying that the sword wears out its sheath. There are spirits whose intensity erodes the flesh. Fitzgerald's first prophetic title for *The Beautiful and Damned* had been *The Flight of the Rocket*, and the rocket was coming to earth. He was a more delicate, complex transmitter than he had ever been, but the signal was growing faint. Whether *The Last Tycoon* would have been his best novel we cannot know, but does it matter? The important thing was Fitzgerald's belief in his work and in himself ... against great odds ... and after long apostasy. The quality of a life can be more impressive than art.

One afternoon towards the end of November he went out to the drugstore and came back trembling. Easing himself into a chair, he lit a cigarette carefully before answering Sheilah's question. 'I almost fainted in Schwab's,' he said. 'Everything started to fade.' Sheilah thought it was probably hypochondria, but next day a cardiogram showed he had had a heart attack. The doctor told him he must stay in bed six weeks, and to avoid climbing stairs he moved into Sheilah's ground-floor apartment. Writing Proust-like on a desk fitted to his bed, he seemed in good spirits. 'Françoise,' he would joke about his devoted secretary, Frances Kroll, 'is asking for

324

the day off to atone for my sins.' If he felt the end was near, he didn't show it, though it may have been now that he scribbled the lines

There was a flutter from the wings of God and you lay dead.
Your books were in your desk
I guess & some unfinished chaos in your head
Was dumped to nothing by the great janitress of destinies.

The evening of 20 December, after conquering a difficult scene, he decided to celebrate by accompanying Sheilah to a preview. When they rose to leave the theatre, she saw him stumble and grip the arm of his seat. In a low, strained voice he told her everything had started to go. It was the same sensation he had had in the drugstore a few weeks earlier, and when she gave him her arm, he didn't push it away as he had on previous occasions.

The outside air revived him, and next day he was cheerful, talking with satisfaction of Scottie and of his progress on the book, which was more than half done. The doctor was coming to see him that afternoon. Sitting in an armchair after lunch, he was eating a chocolate bar and making notes on next year's football team in a *Princeton Alumni Weekly,* when suddenly he stood up as if jerked by a wire, clutched the mantelpiece, and fell down with his eyes closed, gasping for breath. It was over in a moment.

Fitzgerald had wanted to be buried with his family in the Catholic cemetery in Rockville, but since he had died a non-believer the Bishop raised objections, and he was buried in the Union Cemetery not far away. The simple service specified in his will was held 27 December. It was a meaningless occasion, having no apparent connexion with the man, save as one of life's grim jokes designed to make us think. It was the sort of *envoi* a great dramatist might attach to the end of a play. In the airless hall and communicating rooms of the funeral parlour were a few spindly poinsettias, while here and there a cheap print of a winter scene or an autumnal forest decorated the walls. The casket was open, and the suave funeral director ushered us up to it. All the lines of living had gone from Fitzgerald's face. It was smooth, rouged, almost pretty – more like a mannequin's than a man's. His clothes suggested a shop window. The waxen hands were crossed.

We sat on stiff chairs in the overlit room as friends and relations arrived in twos and threes – the Murphys, the Perkinses, the Obers, Cousin Ceci and her daughters, Ludlow Fowler, John Biggs, Zelda's brother-in-law Newman Smith – twenty or thirty in all. At the last, there was a flurry of boys and girls – Scottie's friends on their way to or from some party – who seemed to have dropped their gaiety on the other side of the door. The coffin was closed. The roll of a carpet sweeper was heard gathering stray leaves and petals, and then the voice of the clergyman droning the Protestant burial. It was as if nothing were being said *of* him or *to* him that the heart could hear.

Afterwards, we drove to the cemetery in the rain, and when the casket had been covered, my mother laid some pine branches from La Paix over the red earth.

*

'He was,' wrote Zelda after Scott's death,

as spiritually generous a soul as ever was. . . . In retrospect it seems as if he was always planning happiness for Scottie and me. Books to read – places to go. Life seemed so promising always when he was around. . . . Although we weren't close any more, Scott was the best friend a person could have to me . . .

Maybe he wanted his rest: came unto me all ye that labour and are heavy laden and I will give you rest.

When *The Last Tycoon* appeared, Zelda said it made her want to live again; it differed from so much contemporary literature that revelled in the futility of human destiny till there seemed nothing worth doing 'save the publishing of volumes establishing the uselessness of having written them.' Zelda rejoiced over Scottie's marriage in 1943 and the birth of her first grandchild. Living most of the time

326

with her mother in Montgomery, she tried courageously to find a little happiness between the attacks of her incurable malady. She painted and tended her flowers. 'Down here,' she wrote a friend, 'the little garden blows remotely poetic under the *voluptés* of late spring skies. I have a cage of doves who sing & woo the elements and die.' Sometimes she walked the streets in a long black dress and a floppy back hat with an open Bible before her and her lips moving, and once she told an acquaintance that she was riding the streetcar to the end of the line just for something to do.[57]

The fall of 1947 she wrote her sister, 'I have not been well. I have tried so hard and prayed so earnestly and faithfully asking God to help me, I cannot understand why He leaves me in suffering.' As she always did when she felt herself slipping, she went back to Asheville. She had grown to love the mountain country and the régimes of the sanatorium restored her. Early in March the doctor said she was well enough to go home, but she decided to stay on a little longer to make sure. The night of 11 March, the main building of the Highland Hospital caught fire, and Zelda was one of seven patients trapped on the top floor. In those flames she died her second death and was buried in Rockville beside Scott, where she belonged.

Method and Sources

WHEN I began the research for this book in the spring of 1957, I knew my focus would be Fitzgerald's personality. Since the revival of interest in him, there had been extensive criticism and exegesis of his work, but the man remained elusive, as he had been in life. My desire was to get back to the sources, to ponder the written evidence and probe the memories of those who had known him.

My interest in his drama had been increased by my having met some of the other participants. At Fitzgerald's funeral I had shaken hands with Max Perkins, later exchanging letters with him about a sketch of Fitzgerald I wrote just after he died. While heeling for the *Princetonian*, I had interviewed H. L. Mencken, and I had sat under Dean Gauss in his celebrated course on the French Romantics. I remembered T. S. Eliot's eagle countenance from his visit with us, as well as his remark to my mother when she told him enthusiastically that his essay on Dante had made her want to read *The Divine Comedy*. ('You mean,' said Mr Eliot, '*begin* to read it.')

I set about exploring all the places Fitzgerald had lived for any length of time: Buffalo, St Paul, Princeton, Montgomery, Westport, Great Neck, Paris, the Riviera, Wilmington, Baltimore, Asheville, Tryon, Los Angeles, and of course the Plaza Hotel where he survived in the memory of a single bellboy. Along the way, I interviewed everyone I could find who had known him, and their testimony is part of the fabric of this book, though the interpretation of people and events is strictly my own.

I am particularly indebted to the following for information on Fitzgerald's parents and their early years in St Paul: Mrs Blair Flandrau, Miss Constance Goodrich, Mrs A. M. Hennessy, Mrs Victor Robertson, Mrs Edwin R. Sanford.

On the Fitzgeralds in Buffalo: Helen Powell Collard, Kiddy Williams Frederick, Theodore Keating, John Kimberley, Mrs George Manning, Marie Lautz Rose, William D. Van Arnam, Hamilton Wende.

On Fitzgerald growing up in St Paul (a number of these went

on seeing him in later life): Henry Adams, Theodore Ames, Paul Baillon, Donald Bigelow, Ralph Boalt, Mrs Laurance Boardman, John deQ. Briggs, Gordon Bryant, Alida Bigelow Butler, Francis Butler, James Cathcart, Miss Caroline Clark, Dean Clark, Robert Clark, Mrs Robert Clark, Sr, Worrell Clarkson, Mrs C. J. Claude, Mrs Stanislas Czertvertinski, Margaret Armstrong Dean, Egbert Driscoll, Mrs Edward K. Dunn, Robert R. Dunn, Jr, Elizabeth Konantz Ellis, Katharine Tighe Fessenden, Philip Fitzpatrick, Dr Fred Foley, Dr John Fulton, Ben Griggs, Marie Hersey Hamm, Jay Hevener, Mrs Florence Hubbell, Frank Hurley, Archie Jackson, Mr and Mrs Norris Jackson, Mrs Crawford Johnson, Mrs Oscar Kalman, Mrs R. S. Kinkead, Mrs Leonard Lampert, Frank Leslie, Mrs Herbert Lewis, Miss Katherine Ordway, Lucius Ordway, David McQuillan, Mrs A. T. Miller, Mrs Mary Morrissey, Archie Mudge, Dudley Mudge, Grace Warner Mudge, Miss Alice O'Brien, Mrs Willem Panman, Cecil Read, Clifton Read, Gustave B. Schurmeier, Mrs Alfred Schweppe, McNeil Seymour, Frank Shepard, Wharton Smith, Mrs Lucian Strong, Sidney Strong, General Samuel Sturgis, Mrs J. J. Summersby, Mother Theresa and Sister Frances de Sales of the Visitation Convent, Miss Lynne Thompson, Mrs James Towle, Mrs Vlacau Vytlacil, Reuben Warner, Richard Washington, William Webster, Ardita Ford Wood.

On Fitzgerald at Newman: Herbert Agar, William Agar, Martin Amorous, Frank Brophy, Thornton Delehanty, Charles W. Donahoe, Richard Farrelly, Howard M. Hart, Augustine Healy, Cyril Hume, John L. Kuser, Paul Nelson, Joseph B. Pearman, Bernard Shanley, Joseph Shanley, Walter Tracey.

On Fitzgerald at Princeton: James F. Adams, T. Hart Anderson, Hamilton Fish Armstrong, Charles Arrott, A. C. M. Azoy, Howard Ballantyne, Robert F. Barnett, Newton Bevin, Paul Bigler, J. F. Bohmfalk, A. L. Booth, William Bowman, J. Clement Boyd, W. Rex Brashear, Percy Buchanan, Asa Bushnell, C. Lawton Campbell, H. Ranald Chambers, Henry Chapin, William R. Compton, Francis Comstock, Samuel Conant, Robert Crawford, James Creese, Jarvis Cromwell, Arthur P. Davis, Stanley Dell, Paul Dickey, Gregg Dougherty, Henry Doyle, Wells Drorbaugh, Richard Dunn, Rudolph Eberstadt, Herbert Eldridge, Gerald English, John F. Fennelly, Bernard Feustman, Eben Finney, Charles Folwell, James R. Forgan, Porter Gillespie, Prof Walter P. Hall, Erdman Harris, Gardiner Hawkins, Ashley Hewitt, Lambert Heyniger, Paul Hills, Raymond Holden, Harry Hoyt, Alan Jackman, F. Winston Johns, Walter Johnson, Graham Johnston, E. Winslow Kane, Samuel Kauffman, W. Boulton Kelly, A. D. Kimball, John R. Kimbark, S. Whitney Landon, Lewis Lukens, Edward MacNichol, Gordon McCormick, Edward D. McDougal, John D. McMaster, Allyn Marsh, Robert L. Nourse, Norman Pearson, Landon Raymond, George Rentschler, Oliver Rodgers, John R. T. Ryan, Charles M. Scott, Sidney Shea, Eugene W. Sloan, Harvey Smith, George R. Stewart, Edward L. Strater, Henry Strater, William E. Studdiford, Perry Sturges, David Tibbott, Reginald Tickner, David Williamson, Frederick Yeiser, Joseph S. Young, Richard Ziesing. Also Ruth Sturtevant Brown, Catherine Crapo Bullard, Marjorie Muir Hotchkiss, Fluff Beckwith Mackey, Ginevra King Pirie, Helen Walcott Younger. Also Monsignor William Hemmick and Sir Shane Leslie.

On Fitzgerald in the army: Richardson Bronson, Louis Cardinal, Harold A. Conrad, Elwood C. Cornog, Ernest Hoftyzer, David H. Jones, Devereux Josephs, Edward G. Knowles, C. J. Malone, Alonzo F. Myers, Raymond J. Poirier, James O. Tarbox. Also Mrs Henry Flower.

On Fitzgerald at the Barron Collier advertising agency: C. F. Chatfield and T. B. Hilton.

On Zelda growing up in Montgomery (a number of these also knew Scott): Eleanor Browder Addison, Mrs Harry Allen, Warren Andrews, Mrs Frederick Atterbury, Ed Auerbach, Fred Ball, Mrs Lloyd Barnett, Lewis Clark, Dan Cody, May Steiner Coleman, Mrs W. R. J. Dunn, Mrs John Durr, Mrs Laura Fuller, Mrs Carter Gannon, Miss Lucy Goldthwaite, Mrs Frederick Gunster, Mrs Paxton Hibben, Lloyd Hooper, Mrs W. H. Hooper, Mrs H. C. Hutchings, Irby Jones, Mr and Mrs Paul LeGrand, Mrs Fendall Marbury, Mrs Joseph Matthews, Mrs R. S. Minier, Mrs Frank Morgan, Mrs Isabelle Nunnally, Clotilde Sayre Palmer, Mrs Nash Read, Mrs Harry Ridgeway, Miss Adelaide Rogers, Emmett Ruth, Leon Ruth, Mrs Mildred Saffold, Mrs E. Saffold-Holt, J. J. Steiner, Mrs William Brock Taber, John Tilley, Mrs H. L. Weatherby, Louis Whitfield, Mrs Ellen Wiley.

On the Fitzgeralds when they returned to Montgomery in 1931: Mrs Edward Breslin, Mrs Joseph Garland, Mrs Frances Nix, Amalia Harper Rosenberg, Mrs Frances Stevenson.

On Fitzgerald in Baltimore: Louis Azrael, Dr Benjamin Baker, Curtis Carroll Davis, Edmund Duffy, Mrs Gaylord Estabrook, Dr Lindol French, Dr Horsley Gantt, Mrs Henriette M. Hill, Mrs Sidney Lanier, Miss Elizabeth Lemmon, William Leonard, Garry Moore, Dr Charles O'Donovan, John Ostermaier, Mrs Allein Owens, Edgar Poe, Alice Wooten Richardson, Mrs Don Swann, Francis Swann, Gordon Van Ness, Charles Warren, Zack Waters.

On Fitzgerald in Asheville and Tryon: Margaret Culkin Banning, Mrs Albert Barnett, Hamilton Basso, Frederick Bowes, Mr and Mrs Carter Brown, James Fain, Maurice Flynn, Laura Guthrie Hearne, Mrs Walter Hill, James Hurley, Mrs Julia Lytle, Michael Mok, Mrs W. W. Orr, Edwin Peeples, Thomas Phipps, Dr and Mrs John Preston, Miss Marie Shank, Mrs John L. Washburn.

On Fitzgerald's last years in Hollywood: Lester Cowan, George Cukor, Corey Ford, Mrs Richard Gordon, Mr and Mrs Albert Hackett, Colleen Moore Hargrove, Lilian Hellman, Mrs Earleen Henderson, Nunnally Johnson, Albert Lewin, John Lee Mahin, Joseph Manckiewicz, Dr Clarence Nelson, Edwin Knopf, Morton Kroll, Kenneth Littauer, Otho Lovering, S. J. Perelman, Maurice Rapf, Frances Kroll Ring, Cameron Rogers, Budd Schulberg, Lawrence Stallings, Gay Lloyd Smith, Mr and Mrs Harlan Thompson, Walter Wanger, Max Wilkinson, Edwin Justus Mayer.

On Scott and Zelda at various times during the twenties and thirties (in a few cases these people did not know the Fitzgeralds but someone else in the story): Mrs Charles Abeles, Mrs John Amen, Charles Angoff, Mrs Chester Arthur, Carlos Baker, Miss Jeanne Ballot, Miss Natalie Barney, the Misses Grace and Irene Barron, Mrs A. W. Barrow, Mrs Philip Barry, Richard Barthlemess, Monsignor Gerald Baskfield, Clive Bell, Nathanael Benchley, Mrs Robert Benchley, Mrs Stephen Vincent Benét, Konrad Bercovici, Louise Bogan, Mr and Mrs Ian Boissevin, Madeleine Boyd, Catherine Drinker Bowen, Charles Brackett, Mme Jenny Bradley, Mario Bragiotti, Stiano Bragiotti, Van Wyck Brooks, Mrs Richardson Bronson, Arthur William Brown, Slater Brown, Robert Buechner, Roger Burlingame, Alan Campbell, Mrs James Campbell, André Chamson, Theodore Chanler, Morrill Cody, Padriac Colum, Marc Connolly, T. B Costain, Malcom Cowley, Caresse Crosby, Whitney Darrow, Marcia Davenport, John Dos Passos, J. Hyatt Downing, Mrs Ruth Dubonnet, John Stuart Dudley, Gstavo Duràn, Egarova, Dr Helen Evarts, John Farrar, Mlle Françoise Féret, Ben Finney, Michael Fisher, W. H. G. Fitzgerald, James Montgomery Flagg,

Dr Louis B. Flinn, Miss Mary French, Lewis Galantière, Arnold Gingrich, Dr Margaret Gildea, Dorothy Gish, Lillian Gish, Rube Goldberg, Mrs Louis Goldstein, Caroline Gordon, Mrs Elizabeth Gorsline, Mr and Mrs James Gray, Ramon Guthrie, Margaret Case Harriman, John Held, Josephine Herbst, Maurice Hindus, Gerald Hirsch, Mrs Thomas Hitchcock, Miss Elizabeth Huling, Matthew Josephson, Mrs Frank Ketcham, Miss Thelma Laird, John Lardner, Ring Lardner, Jr, Mrs Ring Lardner, Sr, Lawrence Lee, Mrs Thomas Lineaweaver, Mrs Conrad Little, Harold Loeb, Anita Loos, Holger Lundberg, Dorothy MacKail, Archibald MacLeish, Mary McCarthy, Robert McClure, Vincent McHugh, Marya Mannes, Sam Marx, Wallace Meyer, Robert Montgomery, Arthur Moss, Mrs Allen Myers, Carmel Myers, Mr and Mrs Richard Myers, Whitney Oates, Mrs Harold Ober, John O'Hara, Mrs Victor Onet, Dorothy Parker, Stephen Parrott, Mrs Maxwell Perkins, Mrs Keith Pevear, Mrs Burton Rascoe, James Rennie, Mike Romanoff, Gilbert Seldes, Mr and Mrs David Silvette, George Slocombe, Col Newman Smith, T. P. Smith, William B. Smith, Y. K. Smith, Donald Ogden Stewart, Julian Street, H. N. Swanson, Herbert Bayard Swope, Allen Tate, Dwight Taylor, Miss Virginia Taylor, Alice B. Toklas, Ralph Tompkins, Ernest Truex, Carl Van Vechten, King Vidor, Orville Wales, William Weber, Glenway Wescott, Rebecca West, Jerome Weidman, John N. Wheeler, John Hall Wheelock, Otis Wiese, Thornton Wilder, Mrs Stephens Wiman, Lois Moran Young.

Among numerous librarians who helped me I am specially indebted to Alexander P. Clark and Mrs Alden Randall of the Princeton University Library, to James Taylor Dunn of the Minnesota Historical Society, and to Miss Myra Champion and Miss Ida Padelford of the Pack Memorial Library in Asheville. Mrs Norris Harris gave me expert assistance with genealogy. Dr John O. Neustadt, for a while the Fitzgeralds' neighbour in Baltimore, advised me on the psychiatric aspects of my story, as did Dr William T. Dixon. I am grateful to Lynwood Bryant, Richard L. Schowenwald and Francis D. Murnaghan for help and advice.

Fitzgerald, though he never managed to save any money, was a great hoarder of the written word. His papers in the Princeton Library are one of the finest collections of their kind to come out of the period. They include a large and representative group of his manuscripts. The files of received correspondence are enriched by carbons of many of his letters for the period 1932–40. Outside the Princeton collection, Fitzgerald's complete and voluminous correspondences with Max Perkins and Harold Ober were of primary importance, while Scribners' correspondence with other authors who knew Fitzgerald yielded interesting sidelights.

My starting point was Fitzgerald's 'Ledger', which he began keeping in the summer of 1922. This legal-sized record book of two hundred lined pages contains an 'Outline Chart' of his life – a rough précis by months, telling what he did, where he went and the people he saw. There is a page for each year, and at the top of the page, beginning with his fourteenth year, there are summary remarks (i.e. Twenty-two Years Old – 'The most important year of my life. Every emotion and my life work decided. Miserable and exstatic but a great success'; Twenty-six Years Old – 'A comfortable but dangerous and deteriorating year at Great Neck. No ground under our feet'). The outline chart ends in March 1935, and there are supplementary notes for it among Fitzgerald's papers.

The Ledger also contains a statement of Fitzgerald's annual earnings from 1919 through 1936 and of Zelda's from 1922 through 1930, as well as a record of his published fiction through June 1937, when he went to Hollywood for the last time. For each story Fitzgerald tells when it was written, the magazine where it appeared, whether it was published abroad, whether it was made into a movie or a broadcast, whether it got into a short story collection or received any prizes, whether it was published in a volume of his own short stories, or whether it was 'stripped' of its best phrases and 'permanently buried'.

From childhood Scott and Zelda each kept a personal scrapbook. Scott discontinued his after he left the army, but Zelda's goes on till the end of 1924. Their joint history runs through five scrapbooks devoted to Fitzgerald's work (I – *This Side of Paradise*; II – *The Beautiful and Damned*; III – *Tales of the Jazz Age*, *The Vegetable*, and *All the Sad Young Men*; IV – *The Great Gatsby*; V – *Tender Is the Night* and *Taps at Reveille*). Besides a great many reviews, these scrapbooks contain letters, newspaper gossip, photographs and other memorabilia. Fitzgerald's 'Baby Book', kept by his mother during his boyhood, as well as scrapbooks, letters and other genealogical materials relating to the Fitzgerald and McQuillan families have also been preserved.

There is a wealth of published reminiscence about Fitzgerald.

I also drew on unpublished memoirs by C. Lawton Campbell, Edwin Justus Mayer, Alonzo F. Myers, James Rennie, and Alice Wooten Richardson, as well as on Laura Guthrie Hearne's diary of several hundred typewritten pages, describing her association with Fitzgerald in 1935–6.

Among previous books on Fitzgerald, the most useful for my purposes were Sheilah Graham's memoir, *Beloved Infidel*, and Arthur Mizener's pioneering biography, *The Far Side of Paradise*.

Notes

1. Struthers Burt wrote a little known, perceptive essay on Fitzgerald's novels as the work of an unreconciled poet (*New York Herald Tribune Book Review*, 8 July 1951). Yet Fitzgerald left behind no significant body of verse – only passages of great prose poetry which he knew by heart. Words came to him rhythmically charged with feeling. Driving with a friend one night in 1934, he had been dozing and woke up suddenly to mumble something about a bus that hurtled past. 'Write that down,' he told the friend, 'that's my rhythm.' Later the remark went into his notebook as 'The nineteen wild green eyes of a bus were coming up to them through the dark.' (*The Crack-Up*, p. 109).

2. Through his mother Edward Fitzgerald was related to the Scotts, the Keys, the Dorseys, the Ridgeleys, the Tildens and the Warfields. Save for the Keys, who immigrated in 1720, these families had been in Maryland since the first half of the sixteen hundreds. Cecilia Ashton Scott's lineage can be traced back twenty-eight generations to Roger Bigod, a surety for Magna Carta, Earl of Norfolk and Suffolk and 15th in descent from Sveid, the Viking. Born about 1150 Bigod died in 1221, having married Isabelle, daughter of Hameline Plantaganet.

3. Much has been made of Fitzgerald's bad spelling, partly the result of a keen ear which led him to spell words phonetically. Yet he was also capable of such fanciful misspellings as 'knaw' for 'gnaw'.

4. The figure of $125,000 was supplied by Scott Fitzgerald's sister, Mrs Clifton Sprague.

5. For my understanding of the social structure of St Paul I am specially indebted to Mrs Blair Flandrau (the author, Grace Flandrau). The St Paul families referred to by name in *The Great Gatsby* ('Are you going to the Ordways? the Herseys– the Schultzes?') were not old Eastern aristocrats but the newly rich.

6. Fitzgerald's attitude towards his family parallels James Joyce's attitude towards his. At home Joyce felt 'his own futile isolation'. He felt that he was scarcely the same blood as his mother and brother and sister, but stood to them 'rather in the mystical kinship of fosterage, foster child and foster brother'. (*Portrait of the Artist*)

7. Fitzgerald's sister told me that Aunt Annabel McQuillan sent her to boarding school but did *not* pay Fitzgerald's way at Newman, as was previously thought. Aunt Annabel did, however, offer to pay

Fitzgerald's way at college if he would go to Catholic Georgeton University where his father had gone.

8. Alfred Noyes is thought to have been the target of 'Inside the Lecture Room', Fitzgerald's satirical poem in *This Side of Paradise,* which begins 'Good morning, fool . . .'

9. The remark about Frank Harris' memoirs was made in the mid-twenties to Gerald Murphy's sister, Mrs Chester Arthur.

10. John Biggs said he thought he would never hear the end of 'Tarquin at Cheapside'. Herbert Eldridge, who roomed near Fitzgerald in Little Hall, remembers him coming in to read parts of it aloud.

11. James Creese, an editor on the *Nassau Lit,* recalled a young professor who talked with Fitzgerald about his religion and came away with the impression that he was undergoing some sort of spiritual crisis.

12. On her father's side Zelda was also related to General John Hunt ('Raider') Morgan, the famed Confederate guerilla. Fitzgerald doubtless knew the standard biography of him by Basil Duke, which may account for the name Basil Duke Lee (hero of the Basil stories).

13. Eighteen years later Fitzgerald used the barge episode in his story 'I Didn't Get Over'.

14. In 1930 Fitzgerald would describe his feelings about getting into the war as follows: 'I can't remember in life being afraid to go to war. I was firstly then a Roman Catholic, which meant heaven; secondly I thought I'd finished a great novel; thirdly, at the port of embarkation where my progress ended I was so in love with Zelda that I could think of nothing else. I wasn't even afraid of not doing my stuff, yet I was sure all infantry officers were killed – which was why I'd written my novel in camp.' (Quoted from the dream he wrote out for Margaret Eglov.)

15. It has been falsely supposed that one of Fitzgerald's principal rivals was the golfer Bobby Jones. Mr Jones wrote me that though he may have met Zelda, he was several years her junior and is certain he never had a date with her.

16. Zelda's description of the graveyard was copied almost verbatim into *This Side of Paradise.*

17. Fitzgerald may well have felt that his religion stood in the way of his literary success. Before his time the only Irish Catholic writer of national reputation was Peter Finley Dunne. (See Malcolm Cowley, *The Literary Situation*).

18. One incident connected with the book's reception must have delighted Fitzgerald when he heard it. Mrs James J. Hill, wife of the railroad king, told the manager of a St Paul bookstore, 'I've been looking for some one to write the life of Archbishop Ireland and now I think I've found him. They tell me there is a fine young Catholic writer who has just published a religious book, *This Side of Paradise.*'

338

19. Subsequently Broun shifted to grudging praise of Fitzgerald's first volume of short stories, and after joining the *New York World* in 1921, he even tried to enlist Fitzgerald as a feature writer.

20. A year and a half later Fitzgerald wrote Max Perkins, 'I've always hated & been ashamed of that damn story *The Four Fists*. Not that it is any cheaper than *The Offshore Pirate* because it isn't but simply because its a mere plant, a moral tale & *utterly* lacks vitality.'

21. For the excerpts from Alexander McKaig's diary I am indebted to his nephew, Robert Taft.

22. Fitzgerald's attitude towards the *Post* could not help being coloured by the opinion of some one like Charles G. Norris, whose novel *Salt* had made a deep impression on him. In November 1920, Norris wrote Fitzgerald, 'I am delighted to hear you are novel-writing. I make it a point *not* to see the Post, so I don't know whether you've been slipping or not. You can rechristen that worthy periodical "The Grave-yard of the Genius of F. Scott Fitzgerald" if you like and go on contributing to it until Lorimer sucks you dry and tosses you into the discard where nobody will care to look to find you! I've never aspired to be a contributor to the "Post" so I'm not speaking from personally hurt feelings.'

23. In the copy of *Flappers and Philosophers* which he sent H. L. Menken Fitzgerald classified its contents as follows: *Worth reading* – 'The Ice Palace', 'The Cut-Glass Bowl', 'Benediction', 'Dalyrimple Goes Wrong'; *Amusing* – 'The Offshore Pirate'; *Trash* – 'Head and Shoulders', 'The Four Fists', 'Bernice Bobs her Hair'.

24. Thomas Boyd's letter to Fitzgerald, on hearing that Scribners had accepted *Through the Wheat*, shows the sort of appreciation Fitzgerald's generosity inspired. 'Dear Scott: To attempt to tell you of my honest gratitude would only show up my inability fully to express myself. When Scribner's turned down Through the Wheat I cried on reading the letter of rejection – as I also did when I wrote certain parts of the book. And besides, I felt that so long as it remained unpublished I could never write anything else: the best of which I am capable is in Through the Wheat, and to damn that would be damn all subsequent transcriptions of thoughts and experiences. I feel quite aware that it is only through you and your inexhaustible exuberance that Scribners took the book. I hope for all of your sakes that it exhausts one edition. Strange, but I doubted that you would like it; why, I don't know. And when I sent it I did not believe that you intended doing with it [what you did]. I thought you wanted only to read it. Well, it was a surprise. The wire came early in the morning over the telephone and getting me angrily out of bed at seven – I had not planned to do anything with it for five or six more years. But while the M S was sunk my ambition was sunk also. You know how much I appreciate what you have done, don't you? . . .'

25. In 1958 the critic, Granville Hicks, reviewing recent college novels

by Richard Frede and Robert Gutwillig, harked back to *This Side of Paradise*: 'How naïve and yet how fresh and vital it is! Page after page would make Frede and Gutwillig blush if they had written them, and probably Fitzgerald blushed over some of them in his later years. But there never was another novel of college life like *This Side of Paradise*. There had been Owen Johnson's *Stover at Yale*, to which Fitzgerald admitted a debt, but Johnson had observed the proprieties whereas Fitzgerald was a pioneer of emancipation. He was out to tell all, and for him college had been many kinds of experience. The sentimentality of the loyal undergraduate, the desire to be a big man on campus, the quest for sophistication, his loves, his discussions, his rebellions – he poured them all into his book.'

26. In May Edmund Wilson had written Fitzgerald: 'As I say, I think that the play as a whole is marvellous – no doubt, the best American comedy ever written. I think you have a much better grasp of your subject than you usually have – you know what end and point you are working for as isn't always the case with you. If I were writing my Bookman article now I'd have to do parts of it in a different strain. I think you have a great gift for comic dialogue – even though you never can resist a stupid gag – and should go on writing plays.'

Wilson assisted Fitzgerald in trying to get the play produced.

27. 'Queel' was a nonsense word Lardner had invented. Edmund Wilson remembered an occasion when Lardner said he had just seen a queel looking in through the window and another occasion when he claimed to have brushed some off his coat (*Ring Lardner* by Donald Elder).

28. In his correspondence with Zelda's psychiatrists Fitzgerald identified her lover as Edouard Josanne. The name also appears in his Ledger for June 1924.

29. Other titles contemplated by Fitzgerald were *Among Ash Heaps and Millionaires*, *Trimalchio*, *Trimalchio at West Egg*, *Gold Hatter Gatsby*, *High Bouncing Lover*, and *On the Road to West Egg*.

30. Earlier, Fitzgerald had personified the sinister corruption of the rich in Braddock Washington, the homicidal tycoon of 'The Diamond as Big as the Ritz'.

31. In 'The Crack-Up' Fitzgerald would also tell of his distrustful animosity towards the leisure class – 'not the conviction of a revolutionist but the smouldering hatred of a peasant.' In the years since Zelda had turned him down because he couldn't support her, he had never been able to stop wondering where his friends' money came from, 'nor to stop thinking that at one time a sort of *droit de seigneur* might have been exercised to give one of them my girl.'

32. In 1925 Fitzgerald wrote Mencken that 'the influence on [*Gatsby*] has been the masculine one of The Brothers Karamazov, a thing of incomparable form, rather than of the feminine one of the Portrait

of a Lady.' The same year, with reference to *Gatsby*, he wrote Mencken, 'God! I've learned a lot from [Conrad].'

33. A letter from Fitzgerald to Ludlow Fowler the summer of 1924 throws light on this change of sensibility. 'I remember our last conversation,' wrote Fitzgerald, 'and it makes me sad. I feel old too, this summer – I have ever since the failure of my play a year ago. Thats the whole burden of this novel – the loss of those illusions that give such colour to the world so that you don't care whether things are true or false as long as they partake of the magical glory.'

34. The following statement from Jean Cocteau to the French translator of *The Great Gatsby* is eloquent testimony of the book's magic: 'Voulez-vous faire savoir à F. Scott Fitzgerald que son livre m'a permis de passer des heures très dures (je suis dans une clinique) C'est un livre *celeste*: chose la plus rare du monde. Vous lui demanderez qu'il vous félicite d'en être le traducteur – car il faut une plume mystérieuse pour ne pas tuer l'oiseau bleu, pour ne pas le changer en langue morte.'

35. I have described the encounter between Fitzgerald and Edith Wharton as it was told me by Theodore Chanler, who was there.

36. During his last spring at Princeton, Fitzgerald was driving home after a gay evening in Lawrenceville, when the car ahead of him skidded and one of the boys in it was hurled out, smashing his head on the curb. It was Fitzgerald's first encounter with violent death and he never got over it. It gave him a dramatic scene in *This Side of Paradise* and doubtless coloured the automobile slaying of Tom Buchanan's mistress in *The Great Gatsby*.

37. Rebecca West had an inkling of Zelda's condition even earlier. Of her acquaintance with Fitzgerald at Great Neck in 1923, Miss West wrote, 'I was terrified not exactly of, but for, his wife. I knew Zelda was very clever but from the first moment I saw her I knew she was mad. There was this smooth, shining hair and the carefully chosen wild-twenties dress, which would suggest a conforming personality because it was conformity even then to be a non-conformist. There was this large, craggy face – a handsome face – but when one got the after-image it always showed a desolate country without frontiers. It is not quite easy to get on good terms with a man if you think his wife whom he is very fond of is mad as a hatter. And I remember once Scott Fitzgerald saying something about Zelda having done something odd, and I had to check the words on my lips, "But surely you realize she's insane?" I haven't invented this. I think two friends of mine could confirm that I told them my uneasy feeling about her.'

38. When friends reproved Fitzgerald for his sternness with Scottie, he would answer that there was always a 'whipped and an unwhipped generation'. Connecting his own faults with his parents' leniency, he intended to reverse the process.

39. Fitzgerald was also wary of mixing psychiatry with his art. Though writing on a psychiatric theme in *Tender Is the Night,* he reminded himself that he 'must avoid Faulkner attitude and not end with a novelized Kraft-Ebing – better Ophelia and her flowers.' The same point of view colours his note on Hemingway, 'Some day when the psycho-an[alysts] are forgotten E. H. will be read for his great studies into fear.'

40. Fitzgerald's concern with Princeton was also shown by a plan for enlarging the library which he sent Asa Bushnell in response to a *Princeton Alumni Weekly* editorial. The books were to be housed in subterranean galleries covered with glass brick, each gallery extending towards a convenient hall. Thus the gallery that housed the scientific books would lead towards the laboratories, the gallery that housed the religious books towards the chapel reading room. In the letter covering his diagrams Fitzgerald wrote, 'The idea of a sort of subway, served (as I should envisage it) by electric trucks, and passing a series of alcoves, lit overhead by skylights paralleling the present walks, or by the aforementioned glass brick, is certainly revolutionary. But it would keep the library in the centre of the campus. It would solve so many problems and without violating any of the strategical plan for future Princeton architectural development.'

41. *Time* described Zelda's exhibit as follows: 'Last week in Cary Ross's Manhattan studio, Zelda Fitzgerald showed her pictures, made her latest bid for fame. The work of a brilliant introvert, they were vividly painted, intensely rhythmic. A pinkish reminiscence of her ballet days showed figures with enlarged legs and feet – a trick she may have learned from Picasso. An impression of a Dartmouth football game made the stadium look like the portals of a theatre, the players like dancers. *Chinese Theatre* was a gnarled mass of acrobats with an indicated audience for background. There were two impressionistic portraits of her husband, a verdant *Spring in the Country* geometrically laced with telephone wires.'

42. In 1923, when the editor of *The Literary Digest* had asked Fitzgerald for his opinion on censorship, he replied, 'The clean book bill will be one of the most immoral measures ever adopted. It will throw American art back into the junk heap where it rested comfortably between the Civil War and the World War. The really immoral books like *Simon Called Peter* and *Mumbo Jumbo* won't be touched – they'll attack Hergeshiemer, Drieser, Anderson and Cabell whom they detest because they can't understand. George Moore, Hardy, and Anatole France who are unintelligible to children and idiots will be suppressed at once for debauching the morals of village clergymen.'

43. He was apparently planning to use some of his emotions in this love affair in *The Last Tycoon.* In his outline for the unwritten part of the novel there is a point where '[Stahr] and Kathleen have been

342

"taking breathless chances". They have succeeded in having "one last fling", which has taken place during an overpowering heat wave in the early part of September. But their meetings have proved unsatisfactory.'

44. One cannot fail to notice how much of himself Fitzgerald put into *all* his work, even the most ephemeral. Thus he spoke of writing as being a 'sheer paring away of oneself', and of his inferior stories as 'sections, debased, over-simplified, if you like, of my soul'. During his crack-up he wrote, 'I have asked a lot of my emotions – one hundred and twenty stories. The price was high, right up with Kipling, because there was one little drop of something – not blood, not a tear, not my seed, but me more intimately than these, in every story, it was the extra I had. Now it has gone and I am just like you now.'

45. Though Fitzgerald did not know Kierkegaard, who was little read in this country before the Second World War, I can think of few books more descriptive of Fitzgerald's despair than Kierkegaard's *Sickness Unto Death*.

46. Fitzgerald had come to feel an opportunistic strain in Hemingway. 'Ernest,' he presently wrote, 'would always give a helping hand to a man on a ledge a little higher up.'

47. The change which Fitzgerald's friends felt in him during his last years is illuminated by the following note for *The Last Tycoon*: 'When you once get to the point where you don't care whether you live or die – as I did – it's hard to come back to life. . . . It's hard to believe in yourself again – you have slain part of yourself.'

48. In the proposed omnibus, *This Side of Paradise* would appear with a glossary of its inaccuracies and absurdities, *The Great Gatsby* would be unchanged except for minor corrections in the text, but Fitzgerald had come to feel that *Tender Is the Night* had failed through faulty construction, that its true beginning – the young psychiatrist in Switzerland – was tucked away in the middle of the book. He therefore planned to revise it (see *Tender Is the Night*, with the Author's Final Revisions, Preface by Malcolm Cowley, Scribners, 1951).

49. Fitzgerald would have agreed with Gernard de Voto's view of American history, as expressed in a letter to Catherine Drinker Bowen: 'Sure you're romantic about American history. What your detractor left out of account was the fact that it is the most romantic of all histories. It began in myth and has developed through centuries of fairy stories. Whatever the time is in America it is always, at every moment, the mad and wayward hour when the prince is finding the little foot that alone fits into the slipper of glass. It is a little hard to know what romantic means to those who use the word umbrageously. But if the mad, impossible voyage of Columbus or Cartier or La Salle or Coronado or John Ledyard is not romantic, if the stars did not dance in the sky when our Constitutional Convention

met, if Atlantis has any landscapes stranger on the other side of the moon any lights or colours or shapes more unearthly than the customary homespun of Lincoln and the morning coat of Jackson, well, I don't know what romance is. Ours is a story mad with the impossible, it is by chaos out of dream, it began as dream and it has continued as dream down to the last headlines you read in a newspaper. And of our dream there are two things above all others to be said, that only madmen could have dreamed them or would have dared to – and that we have shown a considerable faculty for making them come true. The simplest truth you can ever write about our history will be charged and surcharged with romanticism, and if you are afraid of the word you better start practising seriously on your fiddle.'

50. As a critic Wilson is often compared to Sainte-Beauve – an apt comparison in many ways, although Wilson has been kinder and juster to his contemporaries than was Sainte-Beauve.

51. A few years previous Fitzgerald had judged his own formal learning as follows, 'How I would Grade My Knowledge at 40 – Literature & Attendant Arts, B+; History & Biography, B+; Philosophy, B+; Psychiatry, C; Military Tactics and Strategy, D+; Languages, D; Architecture, D; Art, D; Marxian Economics, D. Everything else way below educated average including all science, natural history, ect. ect., music, politics, business, handicrafts – save for some specialized sport knowledge – boxing, football, women, etc.'

52. Concerning Wilson's novel, I Thought of Daisy, which Scribners had published in 1929, Fitzgerald wrote Perkins, 'Sorry Bunny's book didn't go – I thought it was fine, & more interesting than better or at least more achieved novels.'

53. In 1957 Edmund Wilson wrote me of his relationship with Fitzgerald, 'In a sense, we were not very close. I was ahead of him at college, and from the time he went to live in Europe, I hardly ever saw him.' At John Peale Bishop's funeral Wilson remarked to Bishop's sister, 'John was Scott's great friend – I wasn't.'

54. Beneath Fitzgerald's rivalries and differences with the writers of his generation was a fundamental loyalty, a sense of common struggle, and no doubt he was thinking primarily of them when he rounded off an essay the summer of 1940: 'Well – many are dead, and some I have quarrelled with and shall never see again. But I never loved any men as well as these who felt the first springs when I did, and saw death ahead, and were reprieved – and who now walk the long stormy summer step in step with me. If my generation was ever lost it certainly found itself. It is staunch by nature, sophisticated by fact – and rather deeply wise. And this tragic year, so like another year, I keep thinking of a line of Willa Cather's – "We possessed together the precious, the incommunicable past." ' ('My Generation', unpublished)

55. Fitzgerald's inability to get along with producers is made still

clearer by an anecdote which a Hollywood columnist printed the summer of 1938. Fitzgerald was dining at a producer's house and the conversation had been restricted to motion pictures. Finally the producer said, 'But I'm talking too much shop and you aren't interested in my opinions on the movies.' 'On the contrary,' Fitzgerald replied, 'I'm not interested in your opinions on anything else.'

56. Sheilah Graham and Fitzgerald's secretary, Frances Kroll, gave me almost identical accounts of his reaction to *What Makes Sammy Run?*

57. I had a last glimpse of Zelda the winter of 1943 when she was visiting Scottie in New York and the three of us went to see *Oklahoma!*

Documentation

The references hereafter are keyed to the text by page number, line number, and catch phrase. The following abbreviations have been used:

AA *Afternoon of an Author*, edited by Arthur Mizener (New York, 1958).

AT Andrew Turnbull.

CU *The Crack-up*, edited by Edmund Wilson (New Directions, 1945).

FL *The Letters of F. Scott Fitzgerald*, edited by Andrew Turnbull (New York, 1963).

FS *The Stories of F. Scott Fitzgerald*, edited by Malcolm Cowley (New York, 1951).

9, 20 Wordsworth quote: Preface to *Lyrical Ballads* (1800).
15, 14 'Three months before': 'Author's House', AA, p. 184.
18, 12 'I ran away': 'The Death of My Father', *The Princeton University Library Chronicle*, Summer 1951, pp. 188–9.
21, 21 'So the capital', 'That Kind of Party', *The Princeton University Library Chronicle*, Summer 1951, p. 171.
21, 37 'First there was': *The Romantic Egotist*, Chapter I, p. 5.
22, 12 Fitzgerald's early taste in reading: Ledger, pp. 160–63.
22, 24 'enchanting voices in the dusk': Ledger, p. 158.
22, 28 'where he swam': Ledger, p. 161.
23, 1 'he fell madly': Ledger, p. 161.
24, 10 'One afternoon', he recalled: Michael Mok, 'The Other Side of Paradise', *New York Post*, 25 September 1936.
28, 15 'A sunny, light-haired': C. N. B. Wheeler letter to H. Dan Piper.
31, 20 'These sleighrides': *The Romantic Egotist*, Chapter I, pp. 25–6.
32, 15 'The first member': Thoughtbook.
35, 16 'The world will judge': dream which Fitzgerald wrote out for Margaret Eglov.
36, 12 'Never will I': *The Romantic Egotist*, Chapter I, p. 21.
37, 3 'It had a child's': 'The Scandal Detectives': FS, p. 312.
37, 16 'Basil rode over': 'The Scandal Detectives', FS, pp. 312–13.
38, 5 'that though boys': FS, p. 325.
38, 11 'My imagination ran': *The Romantic Egotist*, Chapter I, p. 29.
39, 4 'Beyond the dreary': 'Forging Ahead', AA, p. 34.

40, 38   'It's a good school': Mrs Walter Kennedy (Elizabeth Dean) to AT (interview).

41, 5   'I had a definite philosophy': *The Romantic Egotist*, Chapter I, pp. 32–4.

43, 5   'that if you weren't': 'Author's House', AA, p. 186.

43, 27   'the real matriarch': dream which Fitzgerald wrote out for Margaret Eglov.

45, 26   'a desperate, bent-forward': Cyril Hume to AT (letter).

48, 36   'Only l'Allegro': *This Side of Paradise* (Scribner Library edn, New York, 1960), p. 33.

49, 6   'Yale always seemed': *The Romantic Egotist*, Chapter I, p. 13.

51, 20   'the shoulder pads worn': 'Pasting It Together', CU, p. 84.

52, 2   'where Witherspoon brooded': *This Side of Paradise*, p. 42.

56, 7   'It all depends': 'The Missing All', *The Collected Essays of John Peale Bishop* (New York, 1948), p. 68.

57   Fitzgerald, Ellis, and Campbell: C. Lawton Campbell, unpublished memoir, 'The Fitzgeralds Were My Friends'.

58, 20   'Fitzgerald had': 'The Missing All', *The Collected Essays of John Peale Bishop*, pp. 67–8.

59, 13   'Even as a freshman': Christian Gauss, 'Edmund Wilson, the Campus, and the Nassau Lit', *Princeton University Library Chronicle*, February 1944, p. 50.

61, 9   'The Triangle success': Richard Ziesing to AT (interview).

61, 35   'Dearest Ginevra – Pardon me': Fitzgerald's scrapbook.

62   The passages from Fitzgerald's letters to Ginevra King are quoted in her letters to him, typewritten copies of which have been preserved.

66, 20   'half a dozen men': Fitzgerald squib in *The Tiger* (Fitzgerald's scrapbook).

69, 20   'Oh – is he a poet?': John Bishop's sister, Mrs Allen Myers to AT (interview).

70, 37   'you can stroke': CU, p. 207.

72, 18   'Mr F. Scott Fitzgerald': Fitzgerald's scrapbook.

75, 9   'unaristrocratic groanings': CU, p. 226.

75, 34   'while the moon beat': *The Romantic Egotist*, Chapter I, p. 30.

76, 32   'a year of terrible': Ledger, p. 170.

76, 34   'it seemed on one March': 'Handle with Care', CU, p. 76.

17, 19   'mildly poetic gentlemen': 'Princeton', AA, p. 75.

77, 30   'made me see': FL, p. 88.

78, 33   'poor boys shouldn't think': Ledger, p. 170.

79, 16   'Slowly and inevitably': *This Side of Paradise*, p. 147.

80, 23   'I saw him walking': 'My Lost City', CU, pp. 23–5.

81, 1   'My head ringing': 'Who's Who – And Why', AA, p. 84.

82, 14   'a last burst o fsinging': *This Side of Paradise*, p. 153.

85, 7   'a dazzling golden thing': Fitzgerald review of *The Oppidan* (1922), Album II.

85, 24   'a terrific lot of poetry': FL, p. 317.

88, 7   'smeary pencil pages': 'Who's Who – and Why', AA, p. 85.

94, 29   'There seemed to be': *Save Me the Waltz* (New York, 1932), p. 45.

95, 26   'The prevailing attiude': Alonzo F. Myers, unpublished memoir, 'Lt F. Scott Fitzgerald – U.S. Army'.

97, 32   'As an officer': Alonzo F. Myers, unpublished memoir, 'Lt F. Scott Fitzgerald – U.S. Army'.

99, 2   'New York had': 'My Lost City', CU, p. 25.

99, 15   'I got a raise': Michel Mok, 'The Other Side of Paradise', *New York Post*, 25 September 1936.

100   Fitzgerald at Yale Club: Augustine Healy to AT (letter).

103, 7   'As I hovered': My Lost City', CU, p. 25.

104, 28   'Damn if I know': Richard Washington to AT (interview).

108, 1   'ineffable toploftiness': 'Early Success', CU, p. 86.

110   Fitzgerald's agent: Harold Ober.

111, 24   'shortly before noon': Struthers Burt, *New York Herald Tribune Book Review*, 8 July 1951, p. 2.

112, 16   'greatest, gaudiest': 'Early Success', CU, p. 87.

113, 3   'We were all': Allyn Marsh to AT (interview).

114, 23   'We were there three days': To Marie Hersey.

116, 1   'The first speakeasies': 'My Lost City', CU, p. 28.

116, 9   'our darling': Glenway Westcott, 'The Moral of Scott Fitzgerald', CU, p. 332.

118, 8   'a flower-like quality': Fitzgerald letter to Dr Robert S. Carroll, 19 April 1938 (Psychiatric folder).

122   The Fitzgeralds and Lawton Campbell: C. Lawton Campbell, unpublished memoir, 'The Fitzgeralds Were My Friends'.

122, 28   'riding in a taxi': 'My Lost City', CU, pp. 28–9.

122, 33   'like small children': 'My Lost City', CU, p. 28.

123, 19   'I always felt': Zelda Fitzgerald to H. Dan Piper (interview).

123, 22   'a man divided': FL, p. 32.

123, 26   'The novel goes': To Max Perkins.

124, 1   'a wealthy, happy sun': 'May Day', FS, p. 89.

124, 1   'shyed little golden discs': 'The Offshore Pirate', *Flappers and Philosophers* (New York, 1959), p. 17.

124, 2   'dripped over the house': 'The Ice Palace', FS, p. 61.

124, 26   'No one knows': Perkins to H. Dan Piper (interview).

125, 20   'full of a strange': Wolfe, *You Can't Go Home Again* (New York, 1942), pp. 442–3.

125, 24   'His passion,' said a colleague: John Hall Wheelock. Introduction to *Editor to Author: The Letters of Maxwell E. Perkins* (New York, 1950), p. 7.

126, 27   'Original copy of': Album I.

128   Wilson's criticism of *This Side of Paradise*: 'The Literary Spotlight – VI: F. Scott Fitzgerald', *Bookman*, March 1922.

130   Fitzgerald and the bouncer: C. Lawton Campbell, unpublished memoir, 'The Fitzgeralds Were My Friends', and Mary French to AT (interview).

131, 24   'I don't think': Arthur Mizener, *The Far Side of Paradise* (Boston, 1964), p. 145.

131, 32   'a toy': Shane Leslie to AT (interview).

133, 4   'Oh, Charlie, how wonderful': Mrs C. R. Chambers (letter).

133, 32   'Oh God, goofo': Ledger, p. 176.

134, 32   'Reporting the extreme things': CU, p. 178.

135   Fitzgerald and Hergesheimer: J. Hyatt Downing to AT (letter).

135   The Fizgeralds and Father Barron: J. Hyatt Downing to AT (letter).

139, 34   'we dazzle her exquisite': To Edmund Wilson, 24 January 1924.

140, 2   'a sort of first draft': FL, p. 189.

142, 12   'extremely moveable feasts': Great Neck interview in Zelda Fitzgerald's scrapbook.

142   Fitzgerald and Rebecca West: Mrs Maxwell Perkins to AT (interview).

143, 9   'Visitors are requested': Ernest Boyd, *Portraits: Real and Imaginary* (London, 1924), p. 223.

143   Fitzgerald and Laurette Taylor: Laurence Stallings, 'The Youth in the Abyss', *Esquire,* October 1951, p. 107.

144, 24   'Well, I guess': 'Ring', CU, p. 35.

144, 34   'Readers', said Lardner: Lardner letter to Fitzgerald.

145, 33   'She's the most charming': Zelda Fitzgerald's scrapbook.

146, 7   'at which Fitzgerald': Van Wyck Brooks, *Days of the Phoenix* (New York, 1957), p. 109.

147, 15   'It was,' said Fitzgerald: 'How to Live on $36,000 a Year', AA, pp. 93–4.

148, 16   'to rise from abject': 'How to Live on $36,000 a Year', AA, p. 95.

148, 20   'I really worked': FL, p. 341.

149, 24   'I hate a room': Stanley Dell to AT (interview).

149   The poem 'To Zelda': Zelda Fitzgerald's scrapbook.

149, 26   'The deep Greek': *Save Me the Waltz,* p. 96.

152, 19   'in half an hour': 'How to Live on Practically Nothing a Year', AA, p. 116.

152, 34   'Upon the theme': Ernest Boyd, *Portraits: Real and Imaginary,* pp. 120–21.

153, 18   'to write something *new*': To Max Perkins.

155, 18   'in bigger and grander': 'Auction – Model 1934', CU, p. 58.

155, 25   'a dead land': FL, p. 479.

157, 10   'That was always': Fitzgerald letter to Mrs Harold Ober, 4 March 1938.

157, 15   'the whole idea': To Laura Guthrie Hearne in conversation (quoted in her diary).

157, 13   'something really NEW': FL, p. 182.

159, 31   'a naïf, earnest': *The Papers of Christian Gauss*, eds. Katherine Gauss Jackson and Hiram Haydn (New York, 1957), p. 242.

161, 7   'Mrs Wharton has the grand manner': Mrs Chester Arthur made this remark (Theodore Chanler to AT, interview).

162, 1   Murphy paying the hat tips at Maxim's: Gilbert Seldes to AT (interview): corroborated in Gilbert Seldes letter to AT, 18 August 1962.

163   The Fitzgeralds arriving at the Plage de la Garoupe: John Mosher, *New Yorker*, 17 April 1926, pp. 20–21.

165   Fitzgerald and Wescott: Glenway Wescott, 'The Moral of Scott Fitzgerald', CU, 324–5.

167, 5   'it groups': Hemingway letter to Fitzgerald, 15 December 1925.

168, 20   'passing the winter': To Madeleine Boyd.

169   Fitzgerald and James Rennie: Rennie, 'The Time I Wrote a Play with Scott Fitzgerald', *Players Bulletin, Winter*, 1953–4.

171, 12   'My God, all modern': Mrs Chester Arthur as quoted in Sorbonne thesis by Françoise Féret, *F. Scott Fitzgerald in Paris*, p. 55.

171, 18   'Those Germans are': Stiano Bragiotti to AT (interview).

172   Fitzgerald, MacArthur and the barman: Ben Finncy to AT (interview).

172, 29   'She was very beautiful': Fitzgerald Biography in Sound.

176   Hollywood interview: 'Has the Flapper Changed?', Album III.

176, 31   'a tragic city': FL, 415–16.

177, 36   'Scott, come here!': Carmel Myers, 'Scott and Zelda', *Park East*, May 1951, p. 32.

178, 7   'more glittering': 'Handle wih Care', CU, p. 78.

178, 11   'almost hysterical egotism': 'Magnetism', FS, p. 224.

178, 15   'I had been generally': FL, p. 16.

179, 8   'a woman's idea': Theodore Chanler to AT (interview).

179, 15   'That combination': FL, p. 49.

179   Fitzgerald and Mrs Chanler: Theodore Chanler to AT (interview).

180   The Christmas party: Katherine Ordway to AT (interview).

181, 18   'I wonder how many': Whitney Oates to AT (interview).

182   Fitzgerald and Wilson: T. S. Matthews, *Name and Address* (New York, 1960), p. 195.

184, 19   'Mr Fitzgerald': *New York Tribune*, 2 April 1922.

187, 32   'had wine cheques': Max Perkins to Edmund Wilson, 9 October 1928.

188, 19   'We don't go in': Gerald Murphy to AT (interview).

188   smashing the figurine: Zelda's sister, Mrs Newman Smith, to AT (interview).

189, 6   'I'm afraid I was': FL, p. 492–3.

190, 3   'The restlessness': 'My Lost City', CU, p. 30.

190, 7   'Watching the fading': 'The Swimmers', *Saturday Evening Post*, 19 October 1929, p. 154.

192   Smashing the hat: Notes of Julian Street in Fitzgerald Papers.

193, 10   did not mix liquor with work: To Laura Guthrie Hearne in conversation (quoted in her diary).

193, 28   'Like so many men': Fitzgerald note in the papers of his Ashville secretary, Marie Shank.

193, 32   'I found,' says an alcoholic: 'A New Leaf', *Saturday Evening Post*, 4 July 1931, p. 13.

197, 10   Hemingway speaks of Fitzgerald as patron: Archibald MacLiesh to AT (interview).

198, 24   'Are you under': *Save Me the Waltz*, pp. 168 and 197.

198, 29   'passed each other': *Save Me the Waltz*, p. 210.

198, 36   'with a good ruddy': John Peale Bishop letter to Max Perkins, 27 February 1930.

199   Description of Zelda's illness: Psychiatric folder.

200   Hemingway meets Zelda: Gerald Murphy to AT (interview).

200, 26   'Because the world': Mrs Stephens Wiman to AT (interview).

200, 32   'a country,' he said: 'One Trip Abroad', AA, p. 161.

202, 8   'the necessity of': Pychiatric folder, untitled Fitzgerald memorandum.

202, 19   'Canst thou not': *Macbeth*, Act V, Scene 3.

202, 29   'very few people': Rebecca West to AT (letter).

204   Fitzgerald and Bert Barr: Mrs Louis Goldstein, the former Bert Barr, to AT (interview).

207, 38   'It was like': 'Show Mr and Mrs F. to Number – ', CU, p. 53.

207, 12   The Empire State Building: 'My Lost City', CU, p. 29.

208, 36   story editor: Sam Marx.

210   Remarks by Judge Sayre: Mrs Newman Smith to AT (interview).

210, 36   'the nine months': To Adolph Meyer, 10 April 1933 (Psychiatric folder).

211, 11   The Marine major: Mrs Edward Breslin to AT (interview).

211, 36   'Oh, there's no use': Mrs Edward Breslin to AT (interview).

212, 4   'gotten in some': FL, p. 16.

213, 16   'Unless a story': Zelda's dossier at Phipps Clinic.

213, 28   'Turning up in': Zelda's dossier at Phipps Clinic.

214, 10   'I'm afraid,' he wrote: FL, p. 227.

216, 1   'Vitality,' he wrote Fitzgerald: CU, p. 126.

231, 22   '[borne] him up': 'Echoes of the Jazz Age', CU, p. 13.

231, 24 'It is the custom': Typed notebooks.

232, 30 'Our political and economic': *The American Jitters* (New York, 1932), p. 302.

232, 34 the ghost of Cotton Maher: Bishop letter to Allen Tate, 11 June 1934.

234, 27 'their most utter value': FL, p. 88.

236, 19 'Ernest – until we began': CU, p. 147.

237, 26 'as non-committally': Zelda letter to Max Perkins, October 1932.

237, 33 'less a romance': FL, p. 500.

240, 29 'Stop blaming yourself': Fitzgerald letter to Judge and Mrs Sayre, 1 December 1930 (Psychiatric folder).

243 Fitzgerald and Crisler: Asa Bushnell to AT (interview); Fritz Crisler, 'Old Grads: I like 'Em,' *Saturday Evening Post*, 16 November 1935, p. 30.

247, 9 'If you liked': inscription to Elizabeth Lemmon.

250, 2 'Many writers try': Callaghan letter to Max Perkins, 10 April 1934.

250, 8 'Dear Mr Fitzgerald': Philip Rahv, *Daily Worker*, 5 May 1934, p. 7.

252 calla lily incident: Mrs Don Swann to AT (interview).

253 Young man Fitzgerald sent to Hollywood: Charles Warren.

256, 25 'Couldn't face Ernest': Arnold Gingrich to AT (interview).

257, 28 'I'm keeping my eye': Mrs Leonard Lampert to AT (interview).

258 Meeting with Gertrude Stein: Elizabeth Lemmon and Alice Richardson to AT (interviews).

259, 36 'Can you imagine': Elizabeth Lemmon to AT (interview).

263, 2 a deserted rifle range: 'Handle with Care,' CU, p. 78.

263, 4 'Ye are the salt': 'The Crack-up', CU, p. 74.

263, 10 'Is someone up there': Mrs Julia Lytle to AT (interview).

267, 11 the line Fitzgerald most regretted: Fitzgerald letter to Max Perkins, 13 August 1936.

272 Philip Wylie and Harold Ober: Wylie letter to Mrs Harold Ober.

273, 30 'I had developed': 'Pasting It Together', CU, pp. 80–81.

274, 32 'Scott played hide': Nora Flynn to H. Dan Piper (interview).

275, 3 description of a typical day: 'Afternoon of an Author', AA, pp. 177–82.

278 Zelda dancing at Flynns: Margaret Culkin Banning to AT (interview).

280, 32 *Tender* better in retrospect: Hemingway letter to MP, 8 April 1935.

284, 33 'majestically dipping': CU, p. 186.

285 Fitzgerald and his secretary in the fall of 1936: Marie Shank to AT (interview).

288, 12 'Oh Misseldines': Marie Shank to AT (interview).

288,23 'My wife and I': Struthers Burt, *New York Herald Tribune Book Review*, 8 July 1951, p. 2.

290, 1 the MGM story editor: Edwin Knopf.

293, 4 Fitzgerald and Mann: Edwin Knopf to AT (interview).

293, 20 'personality was worn down': 'Handle with Car', CU, p. 78.

293, 23 'Owen Wister dialogue': Alan Campbell to AT (interview).

298, 12 'not very original': FL, pp. 49–50.

299 Fitzgerald and Dartmouth professors who criticized the script: Otho Lovering to AT (interview).

300, 9 'You know, I used': Budd Schulberg, *New Republic*, 3 March 1941, p. 312.

302, 4 'A writer not writing': FL, p. 548.

302, 18 'I was going': Letter to Mrs Frank Case, May 1939.

304, 10 'I can't write them': undated letter to Dr Robert S. Carroll (Psychiatric folder).

309, 26 'Show me a hero': CU, p. 122.

310, 12 'his peculiar charm': Fitzgerald letter to Kenneth Littauer, 29 September 1939.

310, 15 'inspired the best part': MS draft of Fitzgerald letter to Norma Shearer.

311, 4 'of course they were cut': FL, p. 551.

311, 19 'the thing that lies': FL, p. 96.

311, 27 'I look out at it': Notes for *The Last Tycoon*.

314, 8 Wolfe's 'rich mind': Fitzgerald to Elizabeth Lemmon in conversation.

314, 9 'though a lot': FL, p. 97.

314, 12 'for putting sharp': CU, p. 178.

315, 18 'is quite as nervously': FL, p. 543.

315, 28 'Ernest's *Tale*': Notes for *The Last Tycoon*.

315, 32 'tensity or the freshness': FL, p. 128.

316, 14 'People like Ernest': Notes for *The Last Tycoon*.

318, 21 Wilson's Byronic trait: Alexander McKaig's diary.

320, 38 'almost the same': FL, p. 113.

321, 12 'just in case': Sheilah Graham to AT (interview).

321, 36 'nothing more nor less': Fitzgerald letter to Katharine Fessenden.

322, 3 'a dump . . . A hideous': FL, p. 603.

323, 6 'the voices fainter': Typed notebooks.

323, 26 'It was partly': FL, p. 128.

323, 29 'hard as pulling': FL, p. 129.

323, 33 'digging it out': FL, p. 131.

326, 21 'He was,' wrote Zelda: Zelda letter to Harold Ober.

326, 27 'Maybe he wanted': Zelda letter to John Peale Bishop, 7 January 1941.

326, 32 'save the publishing': Zelda letter to Mrs Bayard Turnbull.

327, 3 'Down here,' she wrote: Zelda letter to Ludlow Fowler.

354

337, 8   'Write that down': Elizabeth Lemmon to AT (interview).

338, 42 Mrs James J. Hill anecdote: James Gray to AT (letter).

340, 29 correspondence with Zelda's psychiatrists: Zelda's dossier at Phipps Clinic.

342, 3   'must avoid Faulkner': Outline plan for *Tender Is the Night*.

342, 5   'Some day when': Notes for *The Last Tycoon*.

343, 9   'I have asked': CU, p. 165.

343, 20 'Ernest,' he presently wrote: Notes for *The Last Tycoon*.

343, 38 'Sure you're romantic': Catherine Drinker Bowen, 'Bernard de Voto,' *Atlantic Monthly*, December 1960, p. 75.

344, 47 Fitzgerald and the producer: Sidney Skolsky, clipping in Fitzgerald's papers dated 8 August 1938.

A Chronology of the main events
in Fitzgerald's life

1896	Sept.	Born in St Paul
1898	April	Family moves to Buffalo
1901	Jan.	Family moves to Syracuse
1901	July	Birth of his sister, Annabel
1903	Sept.	Family moves back to Buffalo
1908	July	Family moves to St Paul
	Sept.	Enters St Paul Academy
1911	Sept.	Enters Newman
1913	Sept.	Enters Princeton
1915	Jan.	Meets Ginevra King
	Dec.	Drops out of Princeton for the rest of the academic year
1917	Sept.	First sale – a poem to *Poet Lore*
	Nov.	Commissioned a Second Lieutenant in the regular army. Reports to Fort Leavenworth, Kansas, for officer's training.
1918	March	Finishes first draft of the *The Romantic Egotist*
	July	Meets Zelda Sayre
1919	Feb.	Discharged from the army and goes to New York
	March	Takes job with the Barron Collier Advertising Agency
	June	Zelda breaks their engagement
	July	Returns to St Paul to rewrite novel
	Sept.	*This Side of Paradise* accepted by Scribners
	Oct.	Sells first story to the *Post* ('Head and Shoulders')
	Nov.	Re-engaged to Zelda
1920	March	*This Side of Paradise* published
1920	April	Marries Zelda
	May	Moves to Westport
	Aug.	*Flappers and Philosophers* published
	Oct.	Moves to apartment near Plaza
1921	May	First trip to Europe
	Aug.	Moves to St Paul
	Oct.	Scottie born
1922	April	*The Beautiful and Damned* published
	Sept.	*Tales of the Jazz Age* published
	Oct.	Moves to Great Neck
1923	Nov.	Failure of *The Vegetable*
1924	May	Moves abroad. Meets Gerald Murphy

1925	April	*The Great Gatsby* published
	May	Meets Ernest Hemingway
1926	Feb.	*All the Sad Young Men* published
	Dec.	Returns to America
1927	Jan.	First trip to Hollywood
	March	Moves to Ellerslie outside Wilmington
1928	April	Goes to Paris for the Summer
	Sept.	Returns to Ellerslie
1929	May	Moves abroad
1930	April	Zelda breaks down
	June	Zelda enters Prangins
1931	Jan.	Visits America to attend his father's funeral
	Sept.	Returns to Montgomery following Zelda's release from Prangins
	Nov.	Second trip to Hollywood
1932	Jan.	Zelda's second breakdown – Phipps
	May	Moves to Baltimore and rents La Paix
1933	Dec.	Moves to 1307 Park Avenue in Baltimore
1934	Jan.	Zelda's third breakdown – Sheppard-Pratt
	April	*Tender Is the Night* published
1935	Feb.	First visit to Tryon
	April	*Taps at Reveille* published
	May	Moves to Asheville
	Sept.	Moves to Cambridge Arms in Baltimore
1936	July	Moves to Asheville
	Sept.	His mother dies
1937	June	Six months' contract with MGM
	July	Moves to the Garden of Allah Hotel in Hollywood. Meets Sheilah Graham
	Dec.	Year's renewal of contract with MGM
1938	April	Moves to Malibu Beach
	Oct.	Moves to Encino
	Dec.	MGM contract not renewed
1939	Feb.	Trip to Dartmouth
	Oct.	Writing first chapter of *The Last Tycoon*
1940	May	Moves to Hollywood, 1403 N. Laurel Ave.
	Nov.	First heart attack
	Dec.	Dies

Index